A JUST RESPONSE

A JUST RESPONSE

The Nation on Terrorism, Democracy, and September 11, 2001

Edited by
Katrina vanden Heuvel

Thunder's Mouth Press/Nation Books
New York

A JUST RESPONSE: The Nation *on Terrorism, Democracy, and September 11, 2001*

Compilation copyright © 2002 by Avalon Publishing Group Incorporated
Introduction © 2002 by Jonathan Schell

Published by
Thunder's Mouth Press/Nation Books
161 William St., 16th Floor
New York, NY 10038

Nation Books is a co-publishing venture of the Nation Institute and Avalon Publishing Group Incorporated.

Library of Congress Cataloging-in-Publication Data is available for this title.

ISBN 1-56025-400-9

9 8 7 6 5 4 3 2 1

Book design: Susan Canavan

Printed in the United States of America
Distributed by Publishers Group West

Table of Contents

Contributors

Eqbal Ahmad was Professor Emeritus of International Relations and Middle Eastern Studies at Hampshire College in Amherst, MA. (p. 325)

Tariq Ali is a Pakistani and British writer, and author of *The Stone Woman.* (p. 132)

Eric Alterman is a columnist for *The Nation*, MSNBC, and a senior fellow of the World Policy Institute. (pp. 153, 170, 182)

Walden Bello is a professor of sociology and public administration at the University of the Philippines. (p. 304)

Praful Bidwai is a South Asian peace activist and columnist with twenty-five Indian newspapers. (p. 122)

Marwan Bishara is a researcher at L'École des Haute Études en Sciences Socials, and a lecturer at the American University of Paris, and the author of *Peace or Apartheid.* (p. 319)

Noam Chomsky is a writer and Institute Professor in the Department of Linguistics and Philosophy at M.I.T. (p. 339)

Alexander Cockburn is *The Nation*'s "Beat the Devil" columnist. (pp. 142, 176)

Stephen F. Cohen is a professor of Russian studies at New York University. His latest book is *Failed Crusade: America and the Tragedy of Post-Communist Russia.* (p. 78)

David Corn is *The Nation*'s Washington, D.C. editor. (pp. 40, 47, 56, 83)

Daphne Eviatar is a staff reporter for *The American Lawyer.* (p. 76)

Richard Falk is Professor Emeritus of International Law at Princeton University and the author of *Religion and Humane Global Governance.* (pp. 210, 246, 266)

Liza Featherstone is a New York journalist. (p. 64)

Lawrence Ferlinghetti is the first Poet Laureate of San Francisco and founder of City Lights Book Store. (p. 298)

Robert Fisk is Middle East correspondent for the *London Independent*. (pp. 42, 105, 335)

Eric Foner, the DeWitt Clinton Professor of History at Columbia University, is the author of *The Story of American Freedom*. (p. 51)

Joshua B. Freeman teaches history at Queens College, and is the author of *Working-Class New York: Life and Labor Since World War II*. (p. 91)

Mark Gevisser is *The Nation*'s Southern Africa correspondent. (p. 120)

William Greider is *The Nation*'s national affairs correspondent. (p. 94)

Dilip Hiro is the author of *Neighbors, Not Friends: Iraq and Iran After the Gulf Wars*. (p. 115)

Christopher Hitchens is a columnist for *The Nation* and *Vanity Fair*. (pp. 147, 156, 161)

Chalmers Johnson is the author of many books on East Asia and political violence, including *Revolutionary Change*. His latest is *Blowback: The Costs and Consequences of American Empire*. (p. 226)

Mary Kaldor is a professor at the London School of Economics. She is the author of *New and Old Wars: Organized Violence in a Global Era*. (p. 277)

Michael Klare is the defense correspondent of *The Nation* and a professor of peace and world security studies at Hampshire College. His latest book is *Resource Wars: The New Landscape of Global Conflict*. (pp. 270, 308)

Naomi Klein is the author of *No Logo: Taking Aim at the Brand Bullies*. (pp. 239)

John le Carré is the author of eighteen novels including his most recent, *The Constant Gardener*. (p. 290)

John R. MacArthur, publisher of *Harper's Magazine*, is the author of *Second Front: Censorship and Propaganda in the Gulf War*. (p. 201)

Michael Massing is a contributing editor at the *Columbia Journalism Review*. (pp. 186, 189, 192, 195, 198, 205)

Bill Moyers is the editor-in-chief of Public Affairs Television. (p. 284)

Victor Navasky is the publisher of *The Nation*. (p. 81)

Steve Negus has worked as a journalist in Egypt since 1993 and is the former editor of the *Cairo Times*. (p. 135)

Katha Pollitt is *The Nation*'s "Subject to Debate" columnist. (pp. 150, 164, 173)

Ahmed Rashid is the author of *Taliban: Militant Islam, Oil and Fundamentalism in Central Asia*. (pp. 110, 125)

Joel Rogers, a *Nation* contributing editor, teaches at the University of Wisconsin. His most recent book (with Ruy Teixeira) is *America's Forgotten Majority: Why the White Working Class Still Matters*. (pp. 101, 300)

Edward W. Said is University Professor of English and Comparative Literature at Columbia University. His most recent book is *Power, Politics and Culture*. (p. 233)

Jonathan Schell, *The Nation*'s peace and disarmament correspondent and the Harold Willens Peace Fellow at the Nation Institute, is the author of among many books *The Fate of the Earth* and most recently *The Unfinished Twentieth Century*. He teaches at Wesleyan University. (pp. xv, 2, 5, 7, 13, 16, 21, 24, 27, 30, 33)

Bruce Shapiro, a *Nation* contributing editor, is co-author of *Legal Lynching: The Death Penalty and America's Future*. (pp. 59, 71, 89)

Wallace Shawn is the author of *The Designated Mourner* and *Four Plays*. (p. 296)

Marc Siegel, a physician and faculty member of New York University, volunteered his services during the September 11 rescue effort. (p. 74)

Calvin Trillin, *The Nation*'s Deadline Poet, is the author of *Message From My Father*, *Travels with Alice*, and his latest book, *Tepper Isn't Going Out*. (p. 349)

Graham Usher is *The Economist*'s Palestine correspondent. (p. 127)

Ana Uzelac is a Moscow-based journalist. (p. 129)

Katrina vanden Heuvel is the editor of *The Nation*. (p. xi, 300)

Patricia J. Williams, a *Nation* columnist, is a Professor of Law at Columbia University. (p. 144, 167, 179)

Ellen Willis directs the cultural reporting and criticism program at New York University. Her latest book is *Don't Think, Smile! Notes on a Decade of Denial*. (p. 216)

Yevgeny Yevtushenko is a Russian poet. (p. 220)

FOREWORD

Katrina vanden Heuvel

"On Tuesday morning, a piece was torn out of our world. A patch of blue sky that should not have been there opened up in the New York skyline. . . . the heavens were raining human beings. Our city was changed forever. Our country was changed forever. Our world was changed forever." So wrote Jonathan Schell in the first issue of *The Nation* following September 11.

At *The Nation*'s office, in the aftermath of the attacks on the World Trade Center Towers, like everyone else in America we watched television—horrified, saddened, angry. People wept, and at the same time took notes and got on the phones. For we had an issue closing the next day. We quickly learned that our communications links to the outer world were severed—our phone lines had run under World Trade Center 7. So, in those first days, we had no incoming calls and the office computer links to the Internet were down. The facts were sketchy and causes of the attack shrouded in a pall of uncertainty thick as the smoke rising from the demolished World Trade Center.

The issue that we assembled and put to bed the next day, Wednesday, September 12, struck a tone and purpose that the magazine has striven to maintain in the weeks since. Paying respect to the human reactions of anger, hurt, and grief, our editorials in that first week, and in the ones that followed, have made the case for an effective and just response to the horrific terrorist acts. We argued that such a response may include discriminate use of military force but that the most promising and effective way to halt terrorism lies in bringing those responsible to justice through non-military actions in cooperation with the global community and within a framework of domestic and international law. As Richard Falk warned in his indispensable "A Just Response," the "justice of the cause" would be "negated by the injustice of improper means and excessive ends."

As the U.S. military response unfolded in the ensuing days, there seemed to be more questions than answers. Who is Osama bin Laden? What is the involvement of the Taliban? What are we doing in Afghanistan anyway? Did U.S. foreign policy create historic resentments and injustices abroad that spawned the terrible attacks? What is the best way for this country to address the root causes of terrorism? What are the aims of the war on it? What are its limits? What is the potential political and human fallout? Who are our allies? What role should the United Nations play? How to limit civilian casualties and provide humanitarian relief? As the autumn in New York merged into Ramadan and Afghanistan's winter, these questions only deepened. It is striking how the essential themes laid out in *The Nation* in those initial weeks, far from being outrun by events, have gained in resonance.

Many of the pieces included in this collection were conceived with those questions in mind. One of my roles as editor has been to figure out the bridge from personal to political. How do you balance individual grief and anger at the attacks with proportionality, justice, and wisdom in response? How do we reconcile legitimate fear of anthrax and future attacks with protection of civil liberties, and carry on a political debate that doesn't ignore concerns of economic and social justice?

To deal with those complex issues, I was fortunate in being able to call on some of the most respected figures on the progressive left. They responded with a series of thoughtful, informed, and provocative essays that appear in these pages. Among them: scholar-philosopher-activist Edward Said demolishing the clash of civilizations argument; Mary Kaldor on the new wars and civil society's role in halting terrorism; Michael Klare on Saudi–U.S. relations and the geopolitics of oil; Ellen Willis on homefront conformity; Chalmers Johnson on blowback and the role of U.S. foreign policy; William Greider on war profiteering; Bill Moyers on Americans' restored faith in government; John le Carré on why this war can't be won. Our regular columnists weighed in with their independent takes. And peace and disarmament editor Jonathan Schell filed a weekly "report from ground zero"—lucid, illuminating, frightening, humane essays that advanced the case for sensible and moral nonmilitary actions. And as a historical ballast to our present-day commentary, the Background section of this collection provides a selection of informative, sometimes prescient articles from past issues and other publications.

The Nation has a long tradition of providing a forum for a broad spectrum of left/progressive views, which sometimes erupt in spirited debates. Christopher Hitchens's column, "Fascism with an Islamic Face," which castigated those on the left who drew a causal relationship between U.S. foreign policy in the Middle East and the terrorist acts, provoked a heated exchange with Noam Chomsky. This exchange ran on our website (www.thenation.com) and drew a raft of comment, with readers almost equally divided. Richard Falk's article "Defining a Just War" also provoked numerous letters pro and con, many of which are published here.

As a fog of national security enveloped official Washington and the war front and the mainstream media enlisted in the Administration's war—flag logos flying—the need for an independent, critical press seemed never more urgent. The speedy passage of the repressive PATRIOT act, with scarcely a murmur of dissent in Congress, the secret detentions of more than one thousand people, and the establishment of military tribunals were troubling signs that a wartime crackdown on civil liberties was under way and called for vigorous opposition. Criticizing government policy in wartime is not a path to popularity. Our independent stand on the war and criticism of what we called "policy profiteering" by conservative Republicans in Congress (who sought to use the war as a pretext to push through their own agenda) drew virulent attacks by the pundits and publications of the right, who questioned our patriotism and trotted out the old chestnut of the left's "anti-Americanism."

Such attacks are nothing new. *The Nation* has always marched to a different drummer, opposing U.S. involvement in the Spanish-American War and World War I and the Vietnam War, while giving all-out support to the U.S. effort in World War II. Former *Nation* editor Ernest Gruening was one of only two senators to vote against the Gulf of Tonkin resolution that led to the Vietnam morass. As Eric Foner writes in this collection, "At times of crisis the most patriotic act of all is the unyielding defense of civil liberties, the right to dissent . . . " Also in times of crisis, the enduring concerns of this magazine and progressives take on new relevance: the dangers of American unilateralism, corrosion of civil liberties, authoritarianism in any nation, dependence on Big Oil, military quagmire, and the urgent necessity of international law and institutions.

This collection is designed to inform honest debate by citizens on key questions that confront us and enable us to ask hard questions of policymakers and the media. And my hope is that this book will guide and enrich the debates that will—and must—come.*

*Issues of the magazine are dated far ahead of when they go to press, so the dates with the articles here are press dates to provide a more realistic timeline. The pressure of another timeline—our book publishing deadline—did not permit us to include some valuable pieces. Readers will find many of these articles on our website (www.thenation.com). A percentage of the royalties from this book will go to the AFL-CIO Union Community Fund's special September 11th Relief Fund.

INTRODUCTION
Jonathan Schell

On September 11, the familiar, known world seemed to disappear, yet without being replaced by any clearly defined alternative. Rather, vast uncertainties opened up on every side. Rarely have the contours of a great crisis been vaguer. The authors of the spectacular attack did not choose even to identify themselves. It was clear from the start that Islamic fundamentalists were responsible, almost certainly in the service of the Al Qaeda terrorist organization, but the magnitude of the force involved remained hazy in the extreme. In the view of some, they amounted to groups numbering at most in the thousands; in the view of others, Samuel Huntington's famous "clash of civilizations" had begun in earnest: the world's one billion Muslims were now arrayed against its Christians. The magnitude of the threat posed by this anonymous, radically indeterminate foe was likewise unknown. It had killed several thousand Americans (even this number kept changing in the weeks since the attack); but could it do far worse? Did it have access to weapons of mass destruction? The arrival in the capital and elsewhere of the letters filled with "weaponized" anthrax suggested that it well might; but investigators were unable to identify the perpetrators, who also had to be placed on the list of unknowns. Did they have nuclear weapons, enabling even a small force to wreak even more terrible destruction on the United States? Government experts doubted it, but Osama bin Laden announced that he did have the bomb, and American officials, including the President, were distressingly noncommittal. Cloudier still were the deeper origins, or "causes" of the attack. Candidates ranged all the way from Bush's belief that the "evildoers" hatred for American democracy was the cause to those who thought that the entire process of economic globalization led by the United States over the last decade was responsible.

Clearly, journalism has had its work cut out to explore the topography—

factual, political and moral—of the new landscape. In the greater part of the news media, however, analysis was confined within certain conspicuous boundaries. One was support for almost any extension of the war on terrorism that the Bush administration might launch. A second was observance of a virtual prohibition against drawing connections between what America had suffered on September 11 and anything America might have done before that date, in the Middle East or elsewhere. The idea that any evils performed by the United States might have something to do with the evil endured by the United States was pretty much ruled out of order. The writers in this collection have by and large ignored both these bans. They have raised fundamental questions about the wisdom of the war, and have reported on reactions to the war from around the world and placed the events in the larger context of the policies of the United States, even of the policies of the Western world as a whole toward Islam over a much longer period.

Some common themes run through these pages: defense of First Amendment rights (Michael Massing and Eric Alterman on the press); defense of civil liberties in general (Bruce Shapiro, Victor Navasky); respect for international law (Richard Falk); advocacy of disarmament (Falk, myself); advocacy of social justice (William Greider); respect for world opinion (the contributors to the Dispatch section); defense of women's rights (Katha Pollitt). Yet permission to oppose current policy has not frozen into new orthodoxy. Some have supported the war, in one form or another; some have thought the occasion wrong to embark on criticism of American policies.

Others have seen early assumptions collapse as events unfolded and been inspired to revise aspects of their earlier views—as I have tried to do in my own Letter from Ground Zero. *The Nation* has of course brought its own rich traditions to bear on the new events yet the freedom that *The Nation* accorded its writers has been just that: freedom.

GROUND ZERO

Letters From Ground Zero: A weekly diary
following the events of September 11, 2001

Jonathan Schell

September 12, 2001
A Hole in the World

On Tuesday morning, a piece was torn out of our world. A patch of blue sky that should not have been there opened up in the New York skyline. In my neighborhood—I live six blocks from the World Trade Center—the heavens were raining human beings. Our city was changed forever. Our country was changed forever. Our world was changed forever.

It will take months merely to know what happened, far longer to feel so much grief, longer still to understand its meaning. It's already clear, however, that one aspect of the catastrophe is of supreme importance for the future: the danger of the use of weapons of mass destruction, and especially the use of nuclear weapons. This danger includes their use by a terrorist group but is by no means restricted to it. It is part of a larger danger that has been for the most part ignored since the end of the cold war.

Among the small number who have been concerned with nuclear arms in recent years—they have pretty much all known one another by their first names—it was commonly heard that the world would not return its attention to this subject until a nuclear weapon was again set off somewhere in the world. *Then*, the tiny club said to itself, the world would awaken to its danger. Many of the ingredients of the catastrophe were obvious. The repeated suicide-homicides of the bombers in Israel made it obvious that there were people so possessed by their cause that, in an exaltation of hatred, they would do anything in its name. Many reports—most recently an article in *The New York Times* on the very morning of the attack—reminded the public that the world was awash in nuclear materials and the wherewithal for other weapons of mass destruction. Russia is bursting at the seams with these materials. The combination of the suicide bombers and the market in nuclear materials was that two-plus-two points toward the proverbial necessary four. But history is a trickster. The fates came up with a horror that was unforeseen. No one had identified the civilian airliner as a weapon of mass destruction, but it occurred to the diabolical imagination of those who conceived Tuesday's attack that it could be one. The invention illumined the nature of terrorism in modern times. These terrorists carried no bombs—only knives, if initial reports are to be believed. In short, they turned the tremendous forces inherent in modern technical society—in this case, Boeing 767s brimming with jet fuel—against itself.

So it is also with the more commonly recognized weapons of mass destruction. Their materials can be built the hard way, from scratch, as Iraq came within an ace of doing until stopped by the Gulf War and as Pakistan and India have done, or they can be diverted from Russian, or for that matter American or English or French or Chinese, stockpiles. In the one case, it is nuclear know-how that is turned against its inventors, in the other it is their hardware. Either way, it is "blowback"—the use of a technical capacity against its creator—and, as such, represents the pronounced suicidal tendencies of modern society.

This suicidal bent—nicely captured in the name of the still current nuclear policy "mutual assured destruction"—of course exists in forms even more devastating than possible terrorist attacks. India and Pakistan, which both possess nuclear weapons and have recently engaged in one of their many hot wars, are the likeliest candidates. Most important—and most forgotten—are the some 30,000 nuclear weapons that remain in the arsenals of Russia and the United States. The Bush Administration has announced its intention of breaking out of the antiballistic missile treaty of 1972, which bans antinuclear defenses, and the Russians have answered that if this treaty is abandoned the whole framework of nuclear arms control built up over thirty years may collapse. There is no quarrel between the United States and Russia that suggests a nuclear exchange between them, but accidents are another matter, and, as Tuesday's attack has shown, the mood and even the structure of the international order can change overnight.

What should be done? Should the terrorists who carried out Tuesday's attacks be brought to justice and punished, as the President wants to do? Of course. Who should be punished if not people who would hurl a cargo of innocent human beings against a fixed target of other innocent human beings? (When weighing the efficiency—as distinct from the satisfaction—

of punishment, however, it is well to remember that the immediate attackers have administered the supposed supreme punishment of death to themselves.) Should further steps be taken to protect the country and the world from terrorism, including nuclear terrorism? They should. And yet even as we do these things, we must hold, as if to life itself, to a fundamental truth that has been known to all thoughtful people since the destruction of Hiroshima: *There is no technical solution to the vulnerability of modern populations to weapons of mass destruction.* After the attack, Secretary of Defense Rumsfeld placed U.S. forces on the highest state of alert and ordered destroyers and aircraft carriers to take up positions up and down the coasts of the United States. But none of these measures can repeal the vulnerability of modern society to its own inventions, revealed by that heart-breaking gap in the New York skyline. This, obviously, holds equally true for that other Maginot line, the proposed system of national missile defense. Thirty billion dollars is being spent on intelligence annually. We can assume that some portion of that was devoted to protecting the World Trade Center after it was first bombed in 1993. There may have been mistakes—maybe we'll find out—but the truth is that no one on earth can demonstrate that the expenditure of even ten times that amount can prevent a terrorist attack on the United States or any other country. The combination of the extraordinary power of modern technology, the universal and instantaneous spread of information in the information age and the mobility inherent in a globalized economy prevents it.

Man, however, is not merely a technical animal. Aristotle pointed out that we are also a political animal, and it is to politics that we must return for the solutions that hold promise. That means returning to the treaties that the United States has recently been discarding like so much old newspaper—the one dealing, for example, with an International Criminal Court (useful for tracking down terrorists and bringing them to justice), with global warming and, above all, of course, with nuclear arms and the other weapons of mass destruction, biological and chemical. The United States and seven other countries now rely for their national security on the retaliatory execution of destruction a millionfold greater than the Tuesday attacks. The exit from this folly, by which we endanger ourselves as much as others, must be found. Rediscovering ourselves as political animals also means understanding the sources of the hatred that the United States has incurred in a decade of neglect and, worse, neglect of international affairs—a task that is highly unwelcome to many in current circumstances but nevertheless is indispensable to the future safety of the United States and the world.

It would be disrespectful of the dead to in any way minimize the catastrophe that has overtaken New York. Yet at the same time we must keep room in our minds for the fact that it could have been worse. To lose two huge buildings and the people in them is one thing; to lose all of Manhattan—or much, much more—is another. The emptiness in the sky can spread. We have been warned. J. S.

September 19, 2001
A Sense of Proportion

The blow against the United States has landed. As we go to press, the counterblow is awaited. Those deciding what it will be face a devilish conundrum. A great injury seems to call for a great response—a "response commensurate to the horror," in the words of Cokie Roberts of ABC News. Unfortunately for the satisfaction of this impulse, a proportional antagonist is not always available. It is a perplexing but inescapable fact of our time that great crimes can be committed by puny forces. The obvious example is assassination—an experience branded in American memory by the assassination of President John Kennedy. The gigantic shock of that event seemed to require a gigantic explanation. The mind recoiled at the idea that a single anonymous person could affect the lives of so many so deeply. Many found their satisfaction in conspiracy theories. The government of the day, however, felt it had to resist these temptations. It was the office of the Warren Commission that had to tidy up the affair, even at the cost of many overlooked suggestive facts, many unpursued leads. During the cold war, the stakes were judged too high to indulge in endless investigations that might undermine the already tense relations of the two hostile superpowers, ready and able to blow each other up in half an hour.

September 11 also presents a maddening disproportion between cause and effect. To be sure, the assault was not the act of an individual; yet at most a few score were directly involved. Behind them—if current speculation is correct—might be a few hundred potential co-conspirators; and behind them, perhaps, some thousands of active supporters. These forces present a dim, vague target. A direct, immediate response against them cannot possibly be "commensurate" with the horror—not only because they are few but because they are dispersed and hidden. That has left the Administration searching for larger targets, and it appears to believe it has found them in its determination to, in George W. Bush's words, "make no distinction between the terrorists who committed these acts and those who harbor them." The deliberate erasure of the distinction between perpetrators and supporters obviously has opened the way to an attack on one or more states—targets that, whatever their level of responsibility, would indeed be commensurate in size with the horror. It was in pursuit of such a target, of course, that the United States in effect dispatched a team of Pakistanis to the Taliban government of Afghanistan to persuade it to yield up its "guest" Osama bin Laden, who is suspected of masterminding the attack.

The Taliban have indeed sheltered bin Laden, and an effort to end that support makes sense. However, a military strike against the Taliban or any other regime is full of perils that—hard as it is to imagine in the wake of the recent tragedy—are far greater than the dangers we already face. Civilian casualties, even in retaliation, stir indignation, as we now know so deeply. Anger is the best recruiter for violent causes, including radical Islam. There is a distinct danger of self-fulfilling prophecy. By striking indiscriminately we can create the "commensurate" antagonist that we now lack. The danger takes many forms. In the first place, moderate Muslims who now dislike U.S. policy toward their countries but who also oppose terror may begin to support it. In the second place, by attacking radical regimes we may undermine other, conservative regimes. One is the repressive, monarchical regime of

Saudi Arabia, possessor of the world's oil supplies. Another is Pakistan. Its leader, Gen. Pervez Musharraf, is a military dictator with a tenuous grip on power. His most powerful opponents are not the democrats he overthrew in his military coup but Islamic militants, who honeycomb his army and could, if angered enough by the humiliation of his regime by demands from the United States, possibly overthrow it. Pakistan, of course, has been a nuclear power since May 1998. Will the United States, in its fury at a terrible attack that was, nevertheless, on the "conventional" scale, create a fresh nuclear danger to itself and the world?

It's rightly said that in the face of the attack, America must be strong. Its military strength is beyond doubt, but strength consists of more than fire-power. The strength now needed is the discipline of restraint. Restraint does not mean inaction; it means patience, discrimination, action in concert with other nations, resolve over the long haul. We live, as we have since 1945, in an age of weapons of mass destruction—nuclear, chemical and biological. During the cold war there was one ladder of escalation that led to oblivion. Now there are many. Now as then, escalation is "unthinkable." It must be avoided at all cost. J.S.

September 26, 2001
The Power of the Powerful

This article is the third in a series of entries in a sort of reflective public diary that will chronicle and comment upon the crisis set in motion by the attacks on the United States on September 11. It will address the issues that are flying in profusion out of this new Pandora's box while seeking to preserve as much as possible the continuity of a single unfolding story.

Of course there can be no such thing as a literal letter from ground zero— neither from the ground zeros of September 11 nor from the potential nuclear ground zero that is the origin of the expression. There are no letters from the beyond. (By now, "zero" has the double meaning of zero distance from the bombardier's assigned coordinates and the nothingness that's left when his work is done.) As it happens, though, I live six blocks from the ruins of the north tower of the World Trade Center, which is about as close as you can be to ground zero without having been silenced. My specific neighborhood was violated, mutilated. As I write these words, the acrid, dank, rancid stink—it is the smell of death—of the still-smoking site is in my nostrils. Not that these things confer any great distinction—they are merely the local embodiment of the circumstance, felt more or less keenly by everyone in the world in the aftermath of the attack, that in our age of weapons of mass destruction every square foot of our globe can become such a ground zero in a twinkling. We have long known this intellectually, but now we know it viscerally, as a nausea in the pit of the stomach that is unlikely to go away. What to do to change this condition, it seems to me, is the most important of the practical tasks that the crisis requires us to perform.

It takes time for the human reality of the losses to sink in. The eye is quick but the heart is slow. I had two experiences this week that helped me along. It occurred to me that I would be a very bad journalist and maybe a worse neighbor if, living just a few blocks from the catastrophe, I did not manage to get through the various checkpoints to visit the site. A press pass was useless; it got me no closer than my own home. A hole in the storm-fence circling the site worked better. I found myself in the midst of a huge peaceable army of helpers in a thousand uniforms—military and civilian. I was somehow unprepared by television for what I saw when I arrived at ground zero. Television had seemed to show mostly a low hillock of rubble from which the famous bucket brigade of rescuers was passing out pieces of debris. This proved to be a keyhole vision of the site. In fact, it was a gigantic, varied, panoramic landscape of destruction, an Alps of concrete, plastic and twisted metal, rising tier upon tier in the smoky distance. Around the perimeter and in the surrounding streets, a cornucopia of food, drinks (thousands of crates of spring water, Gatorade, etc.) and other provisions contributed by well-wishers from around the country was heaped up, as if some main of consumer goods on its way to the Trade Center had burst and disgorged its flood upon the sidewalks. The surrounding buildings, smashed but still standing, looked down eyelessly on their pulverized brethren. The pieces of the facade of the towers that are often shown in photographs—gigantic forks, or bent spatulas—loomed surprisingly high over the scene with dread majesty. Entry into the ruins by the rescue workers was being accomplished by a cage, or gondola, suspended by a crane, as if in some infernal ski resort. When I arrived at the southern rim, the rescuers were all standing silent watching one of these cages being lifted out of the ruins. Shortly, a small pile of something not shaped like a human being but covered by an American flag was brought out in an open buggy. It was the remains, a solemn nurse told me, of one of the firemen who had given his life for the people in the building. And then the slow work began again. Although the site was more terrible even than I had imagined, seeing it was somehow reassuring. Unvisited, the site, so near my home, had preyed on my imagination.

A few days later—one week after the catastrophe—I took my dog for a walk in the evening in Riverside Park, on the upper West Side. Soft orange clouds drifted over the Hudson River and the New Jersey shore. In the dim, cavernous green of the park, normal things were occurring—people were out for walks or jogging, children were playing in a playground. To the south, a slender moon hung in the sky. I found myself experiencing an instant of surprise: So it was still there! It had not dropped out of the sky. That was good. After all, our local southern mountain peaks—the twin towers—had fallen. The world seemed to steady around the surviving moon. "Peace" became more than a word. It was the world of difference between the bottom half of Manhattan and the top. It was the persistence of all the wonderful, ordinary things before my eyes.

Curiously, it was only after this moment of return to confidence in the continuity of life that the shape and size of the change that had been wrought in the world a week before began to come into view. The very immensity of that change—and, what was something different, the news coverage of that change—was itself a prime fact of the new situation. In an instant and without warning on a fine fall morning, the known world had been jerked aside like a mere slide in a projector, and a new world had been rammed into its place. I have before me *The New York Times* of September 11, which went to press, of course, the night before the attack. It is news from Atlantis. "Key Leaders," were talking of "Possible Deals to Revive Economy," a headline said, but who was paying attention now? Were "School Dress Codes" still in a struggle with "A Sea of Bare Flesh"? Yes, but it was hard to give the matter much thought. Was "Morning TV" still a "Hot Market" in "a Nation of Early Risers"? It was, but not for the reasons given in the article. Only one headline—"Nuclear Booty: More Smugglers Use Asia Route"—seemed fit for the day's events.

Has the eye of the world ever shifted more abruptly or completely than it did on September 11? The destruction of Hiroshima of course comes to mind. It, too, was prepared in secrecy and fell like a thunderbolt upon the world. But it came after years of a world war and ended the war, whereas the September 11 attack came in a time of peace and—so our President has said—started a war. The assassination of Archduke Ferdinand on June 28, 1914, starting the First World War, is another candidate. Yet the possibility of war among the great powers had long been discussed, and many previous crises—in the Far East, in the Mediterranean, in the Balkans—had threatened war. It was not the event but the aftermath (we are still living in it)—the war's ferocity and duration and the war-born horrors that sprang out of it to afflict the entire twentieth century—that changed the world. Also, whereas the guns of August touched off a chain of events—the invocation of a web of treaty agreements, the predetermined mobilization schedules of great armies—that statesmanship and diplomacy seemed powerless to prevent, today little seems predetermined, and the latitude of choice, ranging from international police work to multifront major war, seems exceptionally wide.

All the more important, then, is the character and depth of the first public reaction. Today, when it comes to reactions in general, there is a new structural factor of the first importance to keep in mind. This, of course, is the news media, whose very nature it seems to be to magnify stories. These stories can, like coverage of the Gary Condit drama, be trivial and ridiculous or, like the Monica Lewinsky scandal, half serious and half ridiculous, or, like the September 11 attack, wholly serious. There are many hundreds of thousands of journalists in the world today. I think of them—us—as a kind of army, indeed, a very large one, as armies go. It is an army that terrorists almost always seek to recruit. Their deeds seek to influence public opinion, which is to say public will. The terrorist act of September 11, though costing more lives than any other, was no exception. As so many have observed, it was, probably by evil design, a disaster film—even a comic book or video game—brought sickeningly to life: horrific "infotainment" or "reality TV." The use of real life and real lives to enact a plot lifted out of the trashiest entertainments was an element of the peculiar debasement of the event. (The terrorist's use of the disaster genre has of course left Hollywood groping for some new stock-in-trade to amuse us with.)

The media army has thus been faced with an old dilemma on a new scale: If it carried out its responsibility of covering the news, it at the same time risked advancing the agenda of the terrorists. Of course, the terrorists can miscalculate the consequences of recruiting the media army. If the hijackers' hope on the 11th was to weaken the will of the United States to oppose their cause, obviously their plan backfired. American will to defeat them could scarcely be stronger. On the other hand, weakening American will to lash out may not have been their goal. Just the contrary may be the case. If I were a terrorist leader, there is nothing I would be praying for more ardently than an attack by the United States on one or more Islamic countries leading to the death of many innocent Muslims. If this happened, then, having successfully recruited the media army, I would have recruited the armed forces of the United States as well and would be well on my way to creating the war between America and Islamic civilization that at present I could only dream of.

Last week, it looked as if the United States might fall into this trap. Of course it was not media saturation alone that created the possibility. The wish to retaliate on the scale of the injury, an ageless instinct, would have been running powerfully in the country in any case. In his speech before the joint session of Congress, President Bush issued an ultimatum that the Taliban government of Afghanistan was bound to reject (and did reject): It must, among other things, deliver up its "guest" Osama bin Laden and all other terrorists in Afghanistan to American justice, and open its country to full inspection. If the Taliban refused, Bush said, they would "share the fate of the terrorists." Here was a clear declaration, if there ever was one, of an intention to overthrow a government.

By this week, however, there were signs that the effects of the President's high-proof rhetoric, which press and public alike gulped down eagerly, were wearing off, and greater sobriety was setting in. Secretary of Defense Donald Rumsfeld, reported to belong to a hawkish faction in the Administration, eager to topple not only the Taliban but also the regime of President Saddam Hussein of Iraq, was surprisingly asking, "Is it likely that an aircraft carrier or a cruise missile is going to find a person?" He thought not, and suggested instead that "this is going to happen over a sustained period of time because of a broadly based effort where bank accounts are frozen, where pieces of intelligence are provided." As for Afghanistan, it was "not as though there is a front, and that there are good guys and bad guys," he surprisingly opined. In the clearest indication of a reversal of course, President Bush himself said, "We're not into nation-building." Countries that aren't into nation-building are ill advised to get into nation-toppling. However, American forces continued to pour into the Middle East, and the Administration could at any time switch back to a war policy.

Among the public, too, there were signs of cooling fever, if not of lessening resolve. Atlantis—the world of happenings other than those of September 11—began to poke above the waves. Among the recommendations that the Red Cross made for dealing psychologically with national crises was to avoid watching the news all the time. This is sound advice—as good for national policy as for mental well-being. A will to do justice that burns with a steady, low flame will be more useful than one that flares up all at once and then gutters out.

Vaclav Havel once invoked the "power of the powerless," by which he meant the power of the nonviolent weak to defy and defeat totalitarian regimes through unarmed acts of noncooperation and defiance. But the powerful have some power, too. Terrorism is jujitsu, by which the violent weak use the power of the powerful to overthrow them. Nineteen men with plastic knives and box cutters (so far, investigators have been unable to identify a larger network that supported the act) used some of the United States' biggest and most sophisticated aircraft to knock down some of its biggest buildings, all in the apparent hope of enlisting the world's media army to provoke America's real army to commit acts that would rally opinion in the terrorists' part of the world to their own side. But the powerful can refuse to cooperate. Tom Friedman of the *Times* advised that the United States, like the Taliban, should act "a *little bit* crazy." But the Taliban are a poor model. That way lies our undoing. When all is said and done, it is not in the power of America's enemies to defeat us. Only we can do that. We should refrain. J.S.

October 3, 2001
The Phony War

On September 1, 1939, Hitler's armies rolled across the western border of Poland. On September 3, England and France declared war on Germany. But the two great powers, unable to intervene in strength in Poland, did not take action right away. A lull—"prolonged and oppressive," in Churchill's words—followed. The "phony war," as many called it, had begun. (Churchill called it the "twilight war.") England promptly sent bombers over Germany—but only to drop millions of propaganda leaflets. And so the time was also called "the confetti war." Everyone knew, however, that the die had been cast, that real war would come. And it did come, of course, at a cost of some 46 million lives.

On September 20, 2001, war was once again declared—this time by an American President, supported by Congress. But once again there was a lull, a kind of phony war. The President's words before the joint session of Congress were clear enough. Either the Taliban government of Afghanistan must yield up the Islamic extremist Osama bin Laden and other accused terrorists or it would "share in their fate." And yet over the next several days, in perhaps the swiftest climb-down from an ultimatum in American history, this clear commitment appeared to melt away. It was a welcome change to dovish analysts, but vexing to hawks and confusing to all. Did the United States really mean to unseat the Taliban? The President's spokesman, Ari Fleischer, didn't see it that way. When Bush, using much politer language than he had before Congress, suggested that the best way to bring to justice those responsible for the September 11 terrorist attacks was "to ask for the cooperation of citizens within Afghanistan who may be tired of having the Taliban in place," Fleischer rushed out to assure the world that American action "is not designed to replace one regime with another regime." Two days after the attack, Deputy Secretary of Defense Paul Wolfowitz said that U.S. policy should be "ending states who sponsor terrorism," but four days after that Secretary of State Colin Powell said he'd prefer to say that "ending terrorism is where I would like to leave it and let Mr. Wolfowitz speak for himself." At the end of September, Wolfowitz himself said, "I think it can't be stressed enough that everybody who is waiting for military action . . . needs to rethink this thing." It was as if, after their declaration of war on Germany in 1939, France and England had announced the next week that they hadn't exactly meant Germany, maybe hadn't even meant war. Had the President been bluffing? After reflection, was he moving to a more sober policy, without being able to say so?

At the beginning of October, the winds seemed to shift again. Britain's Prime Minister, Tony Blair, declared that the Taliban's choice was "to surrender the terrorists or surrender power," and Bush said that this had been "exactly" his message to Congress. Bush had said that the United States was not "into nation-building," but now an 86-year-old former Afghan monarch, Mohammed Zahir Shah, was rolled forward as the possible leader of a regime to replace the Taliban. Government counsel to the American public was as changeable as policy. Ari Fleischer wanted Americans to get on with a "normal" existence, and President Bush wanted them to "get on board" airplanes again, but Attorney General John Ashcroft warned, "We think that there is a very serious threat of additional problems now," and added, "and, frankly, as the United States responds, that threat may escalate."

The confusion was deeper still. In 1939, England and France did not know when war would come or what form it would take, but they knew without doubt that they were at war, and, what is more important, they knew what a war was. In the phony war of 2001, there was no agreement on either point. Many observers agreed with the *Times*'s Tom Friedman that "the equivalent of World War III" was upon us. But was this true? Are we embarked on a path of horror equivalent to—or greater than—that taken by the world after 1914 and 1939? That was the question that, above all others, has hung terrifyingly in the air in this grief-stricken, nervous, uncertain interval between the injury to the United States and the response, between the attack and the counterattack.

It was not easy to answer. On the one hand, the world of 2001 did not present an array of great hostile powers, ready to wage total war on one another, as the world of 1939 had done. The United States was indeed such a power, but its immediate attackers had been a force of nineteen men armed with box cutters. Years of battle among great alliances of nations was not in the cards. On the other hand, as the attack had shown, the world of 2001 was stocked with technical instruments of destruction that enabled a very few people, or a feeble state, to wreak almost incalculable devastation. It was with good reason that the United States was awakening in shock to the danger of attacks with weapons of mass destruction. In "hot pursuit" (as Bush put it) of the terrorists, the United States had already seriously destabilized one weak yet nuclear-armed power: Pakistan. If Islamist extremists took over that nation, would the United States launch a pre-emptive strike against its nuclear arsenal? If it did, would it succeed, and would the extremist government, or its terrorist allies, find a way to retaliate upon American soil? Would someone else? After September 11, do we still imagine that we are invulnerable?

Some voices were calling for major conventional war. The columnist Charles Krauthammer demanded that the United States overthrow the governments of four countries: Afghanistan, Iraq, Syria and Iran. According to some news reports, there was support in the Administration for such a program. If a campaign on this scale is launched, the prediction that World War III is upon us will become more likely. Is the world of 2001 set on a course that will cost tens of millions of lives, or more? The men with the box cutters cannot by themselves bring it off. But an enraged, blind superpower could manage it. Krauthammer's four wars could do it. They could transform the local catastrophe in New York and Washington into a global one. Yet it remains equally true that a wise, restrained superpower can head off such a fate. Which will it be? The attack of September 11 did not decide. What the United States does now will decide. J.S.

October 10, 2001
Annihilation and the Ways of Peace

One month after September 11, ground zero—six blocks from where I live—remains unquiet. Inextinguishable subterranean fires belch smoke into the neighborhood, as if the ruin were an active volcano, spreading a stench whose source we do not care to think about. The global crisis set in motion by the attack has been active, too. In its fourth week, two major eruptions occurred: the beginning of the Anglo-American war on Afghanistan and the outbreak of anthrax in Florida. The latter could turn out to be the more important of the two. Robert Stevens, a photo editor at *The Sun*, a tabloid paper given to attacking Osama bin Laden in colorful headlines, died of the illness, and a co-worker was exposed. The FBI has made *The Sun* building a crime scene, and experts on anthrax are at a loss to imagine any way that the outbreak can be attributed to natural causes. If the worst fears are borne out—that the terrorists who carried out the September 11 attacks were responsible—then the world will have crossed a dread verge. Weapons of mass destruction—though perhaps used in this instance in sniper fashion to kill only a few—will have been introduced into the conflict. I of course do not wish to suggest that it is unimportant whether these fears are based on fact or not. But everyone knows that the danger that such weapons will be used is the greatest of those inherent in the situation, and the world will make no mistake if it turns out that a false alarm has inspired it to act to protect itself. We might even count ourselves fortunate that we were prompted to respond by an event that was either nonexistent or on a small scale. Action taken under conditions of mass attack is unlikely to be as rational or as carefully considered.

The two events were reflected in the divided mood of the American public. On the one hand, public support for the war was strong. On the other hand, a profound, unmistakable unease was palpable in the land. Fear of weapons of mass destruction was part of it. A sheriff in the small town of Pendleton, Oregon, told a *The New York Times* reporter, "What I realize now for the first time is that we can be big and bad and still be got." But fear was not the only note struck. There were expressions of worry that the Afghans would now suffer what Americans—not used to this sort of thing—had suffered. While the public found the assault in Afghanistan "inescapable and just," the *Washington Post* reported, "the jingoistic call for annihilation was heard less often than the hope that the death of innocents might be kept to a minimum." There were signs that awareness of a common peril had created a feeling of common humanity.

The two currents of reaction have in fact been present since the very first second of the crisis. When the attacks occurred, the thought that flashed spontaneously into millions of minds was that our world had changed forever. But what, exactly, was the change that everyone felt, and why did awareness of it come so quickly? It was, I suggest, an immediate, bone-deep recognition of the utter perishability of all human works and all human beings in the face of human destructive powers. The change was felt immediately because it was the recognition of something already known, if rarely thought about—known since 1945, when Hiroshima was destroyed by an atomic bomb. The twin towers of the World Trade Center were the most massive objects in the City of New York, perhaps in all America. If, without any warning, they could evaporate in the blink of eye, what was safe?

The peril of further terrorist attacks was of course uppermost in people's thoughts, but in the background were the still existing, though strangely missionless, nuclear arsenals currently in the hands of eight nations. These, too, soon obtruded onto the scene. The conceivable overthrow of the military dictatorship in Pakistan by extreme Muslim forces angry that their nation had been coerced by the United States into a supporting role in the attack on Afghanistan raised the specter that Pakistan's nuclear weapons might fall into the hands of a Taliban-like regime. Here in the United States, Billy Graham's son, the Rev. Franklin Graham, called for their use against America's enemies. Defense Secretary Donald Rumsfeld, asked whether the United States was contemplating the use of nuclear weapons, twice declined to rule it out. On the second occasion, he even upped the ante, pointing out that during the cold war the United States had refused to rule out the "first use" of nuclear weapons. That is still U.S. policy, notably in the event of the use of chemical or biological weapons.

The destruction of the twin towers, in short, was a taste of annihilation, a small piece of the end of the world. Recognition of this—let us call it the annihilation model of the shape of the crisis—educated, you might say, the viscera of the public. In the public's conscious mind, on the other hand, another model prevailed, which can be called the war model. In this model, which formed the basis for President George W. Bush's speech before the joint session of Congress, September 11 was Pearl Harbor and the starting gun for a long military conflict—"America's New War," as CNN had it. However, even the Administration soon had to recognize that the war model fit the actual situation imperfectly, at best. The death of 5,000 certainly created moral and legal justification enough for waging war. The right of self-defense is clearly recognized in international law. But not every action that is justifiable is wise. Who, in this picture, was the equivalent of Japan or Nazi Germany? Where were the targets? How were they to be hit? What could be the role of armed forces in fighting against terrorism, in which police forces have traditionally been used? (When the town of Omagh was bombed in 1998, killing twenty-nine people, Britain did not shower Northern Ireland with cruise missiles.) And in fact, in the weeks between the President's warlike speech and the launch of the attacks, the Administration back-pedaled significantly from the war model.

Rumsfeld's definition of U.S. war aims was remarkably modest and vague. It was to "create conditions for sustained antiterrorist action and humanitarian relief." Would ground troops be sent in? Would they occupy Afghanistan? Would the Taliban be overthrown? Would the Northern Alliance be installed to replace them, or perhaps the former King of Afghanistan, Mohammed Zahir Shah? If installed, would either of these seek to "root out" terrorists? Would they succeed? When it was all over, would the number of terrorists be greater or fewer than before? Even if U.S. forces won the war in Afghanistan (no easy task) would it lose the war on terrorism? Military strategy faded into the mist of these unanswered political questions.

If the annihilation model had been the basis for understanding the crisis, policies of a very different character would have been adopted. The dangers of escalation—of heightened fervor in the Islamic world, of tit-for-tat strikes between Islamic forces and American troops—would have been uppermost in official minds. Military restraint then would have been the order of the day from the very beginning of the effort rather than being introduced as an afterthought. War would have been seen as a sort of self-indulgence. Political considerations—the mood and response of the world's 1 billion Muslims, for instance—would now be dominating. The fight against terrorism would take the form of police action, conducted by the international coalition so painstakingly put together by Secretary of State Colin Powell. Military action would play a merely supporting role—in the form, perhaps, of the occasional commando raid to seize or destroy a terrorist cell when its location could be ascertained by intelligence. The model for military action, insofar as it occurred, would not be today's blitzkrieg but a siege.

The distinction between waging war and preventing annihilation is not a new one. The military policies of the entire cold war were based on it. Preventing annihilation was the foremost stated goal of the principal strategy of the age, the doctrine of nuclear deterrence. Policy-makers were keenly aware that actual fighting must be resisted because it could lead to oblivion for all concerned. Now the danger of annihilation has reared its head again, and once again the perils of escalation are before us. The restraint that was slowly learned in the cold war has to be relearned in this new context. This time, however, deterrence can hardly serve. Terrorists have no countries to hold hostage to retaliatory nuclear destruction. They possess only their lives, and these they throw away with their own hands.

New policies to address the new danger of annihilation are needed, and these originate far from the precincts of war. One is a comprehensive global effort to rid the world of weapons of mass destruction—a plan in which a readiness of the great powers to disarm would lay the foundation for unchallengeable policies of nonproliferation, which in turn would lay the basis for the tightest possible international control of these weapons' special materials and technologies. No plan can reduce the danger by 100 percent, but an 80 or 90 percent reduction of risk should be possible. Another, even vaster and more difficult undertaking is a systematic campaign to damp down and then politically resolve the world's festering local conflicts, starting with those in the Middle East. Such steps have always been desirable. Now they have become essential for survival.

Can such sweeping, positive ambitions have any bearing at this hour, which has turned out, for the time being, to be one of war? British Prime Minister Tony Blair, for one, thinks they can. In his speech to the recent Labour Party conference, he proposed a "politics of globalization" to complement the economics of globalization. He called for the international community to address with new resolve the conflicts in Rwanda, in Israel and Palestine, and in Ireland, among others; for action to redress the growing global gap between rich and poor; for measures to remedy global warming and other environmental ills. These were not original ideas, but to set them forth at this moment was original. Blair deserves credit merely for striking this hopeful note at a time of such foreboding. However, Blair located his vision on the far shore of victory in the war on terrorism. The danger is that if the world's response to the growing new threat of annihilation is war, the result will be new acts of annihilation. Blair has won a seat in the war councils with his backing for the United States. Perhaps at some dire turning point in the future, he will use his influence to speak up for restraint. The world is sick. It cannot be cured with America's new war. The ways of peace—adopted not as a distant goal but as a practical necessity in the present—are the only cure. J.S.

October 17, 2001
Seven Million at Risk

The horrors that have been sprung upon the world since September 11 have come with a rapidity that threatens to overwhelm the capacity of the imagination to respond, not to speak of the capacity of governments to frame policies that make sense.

No sooner had the Trade Center fallen and the Pentagon been attacked than the United States was declaring war; no sooner had the United States declared war than it was at war; no sooner was the United States at war than someone was attacking the United States with "weapons-grade" anthrax. The fifth week of the crisis has proceeded likewise. No sooner was anthrax arriving in mailboxes around the nation than still another horror—one that may yet prove the greatest of the entire story—was upon us: the prospect that millions of Afghans could starve to death this winter. On October 12 Mary Robinson, former President of Ireland and now the United Nations commissioner for human rights, sounded a sharp, clear warning. She called for a halt to the bombing of Afghanistan in order to permit humanitarian aid—above all, food—to be sent into Afghanistan before the winter snows cut off access to the population. "It is a very, very urgent situation," she noted. "It is very hard to get convoys of food in when there is a military campaign. . . . You have millions of people, they say up to 7 million, at risk." And she asked, "Are we going to preside over deaths from starvation of hundreds of thousands, maybe millions of people this winter because we did not use the window of opportunity?" Her words, though widely quoted around the world, went almost entirely unreported in the United States. The next day, among the thirty or so newspapers that the Lexis/Nexis database of newspapers calls major, only one—the *San Francisco Chronicle*—saw fit to mention it, and none of the major television networks did. (The day after that, Steven Erlanger briefly mentioned her comments in *The New York Times* in a story about eroding support in Germany for the bombing.) Not until four days later, when an American bomb destroyed a Red Cross warehouse in Kabul and humanitarian groups joined Robinson's call for a bombing halt, did the appeal begin to get attention in this country.

That a catastrophe was developing was not news—or should not have been. The combination of a decade of war by Afghan fighters against the Soviet Union, the civil war that followed the Soviet defeat, the extreme misrule of the victors in that war, the Taliban, and four years of drought have destroyed Afghanistan's ability to feed and care for itself. Humanitarian groups whose aid was already keeping substantial numbers of people alive have been warning of the gathering disaster as it has unfolded. After September 11, foreign aid personnel, advised by the Taliban that it could no longer assure their safety, withdrew from the country. Soon, the nations surrounding Afghanistan closed their borders to refugees. On September 19, Dominic Nutt, the emergency officer for the relief group Christian Aid, told the *Guardian*, "It's as if a mass grave has been dug behind millions of people. We can drag them back from it or push them in." On September 24, two weeks before the military campaign began, the UN warned in a report that "a humanitarian crisis of stunning proportions is unfolding in Afghanistan," and Secretary General Kofi Annan appealed for assistance to head off "the world's worst humanitarian disaster." On October 5 twenty relief organizations again reminded the world that Afghanistan was on the "brink of disaster." "It must be remembered," the statement said, "that these potential refugees are currently trapped inside a closed country." Two days later, the bombing began, and the vast internal migration from the cities to inaccessible rural parts of Afghanistan began. The new element introduced by Robinson's appeal was her delineation of the terrible significance of the bombing campaign in view of the deadline for assistance imposed by approaching winter.

The principal reason for saving the lives of the Afghans must, of course, be those lives themselves. Avenging thousands of innocents in America cannot take precedence over saving millions of innocents in Afghanistan. To say this is to make a moral point, but it is also more than a moral point. The humanitarian crisis of course arrives in the middle of a global military crisis and a political crisis. These last two—and the relationship between them—have dominated public attention and policy in the United States. (I have to admit that this has also been true of this weekly "Letter from Ground Zero.") What, we have been asking, is the outlook for military success in the "war on terrorism"? Will overthrowing the Taliban reduce or increase the terrorist threat? If they are overthrown, who will follow them? Will military success in Afghanistan spell political defeat in Pakistan and/or Saudi Arabia, where brittle, repressive regimes face strong opposition from Muslim extremists? These questions, echoing issues that arose in the Vietnam War, are important, but the answers to every one of them, we can now suddenly see, will depend on whether mass starvation can be headed off in Afghanistan. The spectacle of U.S. special forces roving through a land of the dead and the dying in search of Osama bin Laden is as absurd a prescription for policy as it is offensive to decency.

A reversal of American policy is necessary. At present, political goals have been treated as a footnote to military goals (George W. Bush did not drop his opposition to nation-building in Afghanistan until a week after he ordered the bombing campaign), and humanitarian goals have been treated as a footnote to political goals. (The piteously inadequate food drops from U.S. planes is the embodiment of this footnote.) This policy must be stood precisely on its head. Whatever the operational details, the humanitarian crisis must dominate. The bombing should stop, and a new policy—perhaps one of armed humanitarian intervention on the ground—should be adopted. Such a policy would replace the current iron fist in a humanitarian velvet glove with a helping human hand in a glove of chain mail. Not nation-building but nation-saving—the physical salvation of Afghan lives—must be the controlling consideration. Only if this humanitarian effort is successful can a political policy succeed—whether in Afghanistan itself, in Islamic opinion or in world opinion. And only if these humanitarian and political goals are accomplished will the war on terrorism—whose importance, in our anthrax-menaced world, has become greater than ever—have any chance of going well. J.S.

October 24, 2001
The New Brink

As the conflict that began on September 11 heads into its sixth week, two clouds of danger hang over its two battlefields, the United States and Afghanistan. In the United States the danger is bioterrorism, represented by the attacks on the news media and the federal government by means of anthrax sent in the mail. In Afghanistan it is starvation, which, according to the United Nations and private relief agencies, could claim hundreds of thousands, or even millions, of lives if the flow of international aid, now disrupted both by the war and by interference from the Taliban regime, is not dispatched into the country before the onset of winter. The two dangers exhibit striking similarities. Both raise the stakes of the conflict by an order of magnitude. Both menace civilian populations, not armed forces. Both can, at their worst, cause casualties on a mass scale, yet the extent to which this will occur in either case cannot, for now, be known.

Paradoxically, nothing would do more for the peace of mind of Americans than to discover that an American—some unabomber or right-wing lunatic—was responsible for the anthrax attacks. If that were the case, then the possibility of linkage between those attacks and the war in Afghanistan would disappear, and the reciprocal escalation on the two fronts that is probably the greatest danger the world now faces might be avoided. Hope for such a discovery received a blow, however, when the government, after a two-week delay, disclosed the contents of three of the anthrax-laden letters. All three said, "Death to America. Death to Israel. Allah is great." It didn't sound like the Montana militia.

The precise character of the anthrax was also left vague. When anthrax was found in the office of Senate majority leader Tom Daschle, House minority leader Richard Gephardt declared it to be "weapons-grade," but an unnamed bioterrorism official told the *Washington Post* that the FBI did not yet know whether or not this was true, and *The New York Times* approvingly noted in an editorial that "loose talk" that the material "was weapons-grade has been disavowed by leading senators." This week Gephardt again said that the anthrax was weapons-grade.

The questions that lay behind these conflicting statements were crucial, because they shed light on both the extent of danger and its origin. At issue was whether the United States was in danger of attack by a weapon of mass destruction. If the anthrax has been weaponized, it is suitable for mass attacks and is more likely to have been produced by a technically sophisticated organization, most likely a state. If a state is involved, it might also resort to other weapons of mass destruction, including contagious diseases, such as smallpox, or nuclear weapons. The state most often mentioned is of course Iraq, which is known to have produced anthrax, and very likely still does. However, the possible involvement of Iraq is another matter on which the Administration has given conflicting signals. To determine whether anthrax has been weaponized, three questions must be answered. First, have the spores been "milled" to a small size—"aerosolized"—so they can float in the air, thereby infecting many people; second, have they been selected for virulence; third, have they been engineered to produce immunity to antibiotics? So far, only the third question has been answered—in the negative. Whether the other two go unanswered because the government does not yet know the answers or, as in the case of the letters, has been unwilling to release them, is also unknown.

The dimensions of the threat of starvation in Afghanistan, though also hard to estimate, are clearer than the dangers from anthrax. As mentioned in this column last week, the call by UN Commissioner for Human Rights Mary Robinson for a pause in the bombing so that aid could be increased— a call joined almost immediately by major private relief organizations— went almost entirely unreported in the United States. In England, by contrast, the call was widely reported and a lively debate on the issue is under way. Clare Short, the International Development Secretary, responded that the relief organizations were being "emotional" and that sufficient aid was getting through. The relief organizations held their ground. In testimony solicited by Parliament, Justin Forsyth, Oxfam's policy director, said, "We were not being emotional. We were being practical.

There is not enough food flowing in world food programs." The *Observer* argued in an editorial that the best way to deal with the crisis was to overthrow the Taliban. But Forsyth held that the fall of the Taliban, by creating an "even more chaotic" situation, might worsen the outlook for aid. No comparable hearings—or audible discussion of any kind—of Robinson's call or of the threatened catastrophe occurred here.

If in the weeks ahead the world is luckier than it has been since September 11, neither peril of mass destruction will materialize. The anthrax attacks will trail off, followed by nothing worse. The aid in Afghanistan will somehow get through. However, it is only prudent to ask ourselves now, before any of these things happen, what should be done if the world is not so lucky. If the two disasters occur, they will be linked—perhaps in fact, certainly in people's minds on either side of the conflict. What will America's foes do if Afghans starve by the hundreds of thousands and the U.S. military campaign is held, rightly or wrongly, to be responsible? The terrorists may of course strike at the United States again without any further provocation. But an atmosphere of rage in the Islamic world can only make escalation more likely. What will Americans do if a biological attack then kills equal numbers in this country? On the margins of debate, there have already been discussions of using nuclear weapons—most recently by Representative Peter King, who said that if the only way to stop the use of chemical weapons is nuclear weapons, "obviously we have to use them."

During the cold war, governments and peoples learned that, in our age of weapons of mass destruction, the logic of retaliation led only to annihilation—to "mutual assured destruction." We have arrived at the verge of a new permutation of that outcome—a new brink. We need to back off. A good place to begin would be a full debate in the United States on the consequences of our military actions for the hungry people of Afghanistan, leading to a policy that, in our own interest as well as theirs, places their survival at the center of our concern. J.S.

October 31, 2001
Politics and War

Hawk and dove agree: The war in Afghanistan is not going well. Hawks point to the resilience of the Taliban, which has "surprised" Rear Adm. John Stufflebeem by not collapsing yet. Doves point to the suffering of the civilian population, who face American bombing, Taliban repression and the prospect of mass starvation all at the same time. The problem goes deeper, however, than the unexpected toughness of the foe and stray bombs. It lies in an underlying contradiction in U.S. policy. In a word, the Administration's military policy is at odds with its political policy. And in a war on terrorism—as distinct from a war on a state—it is politics, not military force, that will probably decide the outcome. For it is politics that will determine the size of the terrorist groups' most important asset, namely their pool of available recruits; it is politics that will decide how many countries will actively participate in the international police effort that must be the backbone of any global antiterrorism campaign; and it is politics that will decide how long support for the war will last in public opinion, including opinion on the home fronts.

To understand what is going wrong and why, we must look back at the origins of the war and its declared objectives. They were to uproot the networks of terrorists that sponsored the September 11 attacks, and, more particularly, to capture the alleged leader of those networks, Osama bin Laden. In the weeks leading up to the bombing, let us recall, a debate on strategy was conducted within the Administration and in the press. At issue was the scope of the war. Should it be extended beyond Afghanistan—perhaps to Iraq? The decision was to restrict it to Afghanistan, at least for the time being. Was it necessary to overthrow the Taliban regime—could the terrorist networks be attacked with the Taliban in place? This question was perhaps more extensively debated than any other. One problem was that terrorist groups were located in as many as fifty countries, not in Afghanistan alone. Another problem was that if you overthrew the Taliban, you would have to install another government—an undertaking that would constitute nation-building, which Bush had promised to avoid. Nor had the issue been publicly resolved when the bombing began. As noted in an earlier week on this page, Defense Secretary Donald Rumsfeld's articulation of American goals—to "create conditions for sustained antiterrorist action and humanitarian relief"—was surprisingly unambitious. There was no mention of overthrowing the Taliban, not to speak of any vow to create a substitute regime.

And yet as the bombing proceeded, it gradually became clear that over-throwing the Taliban was, after all, a goal of policy. Rumsfeld went as far as to remark that it might not be possible for the United States to capture bin Laden at all. On the other hand, he noted, overthrowing the Taliban was something that *was* within our power. The United States at that moment seemed to have abandoned what it *wanted* to do in favor of what it *could* do. A twofold strategy emerged. Its first goal was to support the Taliban's ene-mies, the Northern Alliance. Unfortunately, the Alliance members, most of whom belong to Uzbek and Tajik ethnic minorities, had misgoverned the country in the early 1990s. Accordingly, it was thought necessary to foster resistance to the Taliban among the dominant, Pashtun ethnic group in the south. The hope was that the Pashtun southerners—among whom the repres-sive Taliban were widely unpopular—would seize the opportunity of the U.S. bombing to rebel. Then a coalition of anti-Taliban northerners and anti-Tal-iban southerners would ally to create a government friendly to the United States, whose military efforts could then cease.

This hope has been dashed by events. The bombing, far from prompting an anti-Taliban rebellion has, according to all reports, rallied popular sup-port to the previously hated regime. Rarely has the destruction of political opportunity by military action been more clearly displayed. The extent of the reversal was revealed when Pakistan, under U.S. direction, organized a meeting of anti-Taliban Afghan leaders. They promptly issued a call for a halt in the bombing—not, we must suppose, the reaction the United States was looking for. The change in political climate was further illustrated by the case of the Pashtun leader Abdul Haq, who entered the country from Pakistan to launch a rebellion but instead was captured and executed by the

Taliban. There had in any case been something unreal about the expectation that the Taliban—more a social movement than a government—would collapse. "What is a government?" The Foreign Minister of Pakistan, Abdul Sattar, shrewdly inquired. "It has organs, it introduces a certain discipline in a country. But the government has simply ceased to exist in Afghanistan. . . . so it's not a matter of supplanting a state; it's a matter of rebuilding one from scratch." The Taliban was not, he said, "something that can be destroyed right away, because the government doesn't exist, in a way."

In response to these disappointments, many commentators have suggested, in effect, that a political strategy should be dispensed with altogether. Military victory alone will do. In the words of *Washington Post* columnist Charles Krauthammer, the goal of U.S. policy now should be solely "destroying Al Qaeda and the Taliban" with military force. What comes after, he writes, is "an interesting problem. But it comes after." Senator John McCain called for heavier bombing and the introduction of ground troops.

These recommendations have the virtue of being practicable. The United States can unquestionably defeat the Taliban in a ground war and occupy Afghanistan. But politics will not disappear because it has been ignored. The state that is already missing in Afghanistan will still be missing. The Taliban and Al Qaeda will certainly remain as an underground force, exacting a steady price from the occupying armies. The English governed Northern Ireland for a quarter-century without being able to stop the terrorism there. And yet the cost of ending an occupation without creating a new government would be equally high, for there is no reason to suppose that Afghanistan, embittered by military defeat and foreign occupation, would not, once free of the occupier, return to its old ways of tolerating and supporting terrorism. Meanwhile, occupation of a Muslim country by U.S. forces would be an outrage to Muslim opinion and a recruiting poster for terrorist organizations throughout the Middle East, which would almost certainly gain in strength. The United States can win the war in Afghanistan, but only at the cost of losing its war on terrorism. J.S.

November 7, 2001
Niceties

When I began this column after September 11, I chose to name it "Letter From Ground Zero" because it seemed to me that at the heart of the new darkness that had descended upon the world was the peril of annihilation posed by weapons of mass destruction, including, above all, nuclear weapons. The weapon of mass destruction that has actually been used, of course, has been "weaponized" anthrax—delivered, however, only in minuscule amounts. The world awaits the terrorists' decision whether to follow up these retail murders with mass murder.

Meanwhile, the newsmedia in this country, as if in obedience to some secret signal, are suddenly awash in stories dealing with nuclear weapons and nuclear danger. The discussion has developed with stunning rapidity, leading in some quarters to calls for the use of nuclear weapons of a kind not heard since the cold war—if then. The stories come in two categories: warnings of attacks *upon* the United States and warnings of attacks *by* the United States. A raft of stories described the unpreparedness of the Nuclear Regulatory Commission for an attack on American nuclear reactors—attacks that could contaminate thousands of square miles. An article in *The New Yorker* by Seymour Hersh is the most detailed of many that discuss the danger that Pakistan's nuclear arsenal will fall into the hands of Islamic extremists, whether through theft by disaffected elements of the Pakistani nuclear establishment or by the overthrow of the military dictator President Pervez Musharraf. Musharraf, for his part, arrested Bashiruddin Mahmood, a leader for more than thirty years of Pakistan's nuclear weapons program and, more recently, a fervent and active supporter of the Taliban. A story in *The New York Times* offered an unnerving glimpse into the mentality of Islamic nuclear extremism. Mahmood, it reports, is the author of a book distressingly titled *The Mechanics of Doomsday and Life After Death* and also believes that the world's energy crisis can perhaps be solved by tapping the energy of genies—"beings made of fire" described in the Koran. A cover story by Gregg Easterbrook in *The New Republic* called "The Big One" offers an overview of the dangers of nuclear terrorism.

The most alarming stories, however, have been those warning of a direct nuclear attack by Osama bin Laden's organization. His passionate desire to acquire nuclear weapons has long been known, if little noticed. In the trial of those engaged in the 1998 bombing of the U.S. embassies in Kenya and Tanzania, one of his operatives described his failed attempt to buy a cylinder of enriched uranium. In October, UPI's Richard Sale disclosed that according to "a half-dozen serving and former U.S. Government and intelligence officials," the Bush Administration was concerned that "accused terrorist mastermind Osama bin Laden might try to use a small nuclear weapon in a super-spectacular strike to decapitate the U.S. political leadership." The other day, George W. Bush made the concern official: bin Laden, he said, is "seeking chemical, biological and nuclear weapons." Bush notably gave no assurance that bin Laden did not already have nuclear weapons. "If he doesn't have them, we will work hard to make sure he doesn't," he said. "If he does, we'll make sure he doesn't deploy them."

Visions of American cities blown to kingdom come have reminded many of America's own very large arsenal of nuclear weapons. Might it be useful in the circumstances? Some commentators think it will be. We are not condemned merely to be the victims of mass destruction, they point out; we can be the perpetrators of it as well. I was alerted to one of these proposals by an unexpected source—the *New York Post*'s gossip columnist Liz Smith. She wished to commend an article in *Time* magazine by Charles Krauthammer, who, she noted with approval, wanted the United States to wage "total war" against its new enemies. "Have we told Iraq, the Saudis and Pakistan," she asked, that "if there is a nuclear attack . . . by anyone, we will hold them accountable because they have harbored and created these terrorists? We could wipe these countries off the map, and they should be very afraid of that." Krauthammer lived up to Smith's billing. The Bush Administration's policy of trying to avoid civilian casualties might have to go by the board, he thought. In the "total war" he wanted, the distinction was a "nicety" that the United States could no longer afford. Krauthammer had only one country—Iraq—slated for annihilation. In the Gulf War, he claimed, the Administration of Bush Senior had warned President Saddam Hussein that if he used biological or chemical weapons he would be met with weapons that would "wipe Iraq off the face of the earth." Krauthammer wanted to know whether we were still ready to do this in the event of a terrorist use of a nuclear weapon on our soil. "If we are not prepared to wage total war we risk disaster on a scale we have never seen and can barely imagine," he wrote. Another commentator, *The New Republic*'s Easterbrook, had an entire region—the Islamic Middle East—in his sights. At the end of an appearance on *Greenfield at Large* on CNN, he announced that he wanted to leave his audience "with one message." It was that "the search for terrorist atomic weapons would be of great benefit to the Muslim peoples of the world in addition to . . . people of the United States and Western Europe, because if an atomic warhead goes off in Washington—say, in the current environment or anything like it—in the twenty-four hours that followed, a hundred million Muslims would die as U.S. nuclear bombs rained down on every conceivable military target in a dozen Muslim countries."

"Wipe Iraq off the face of the earth," "a hundred million Muslims would die": Listening in shock to these phrases, it occurred to me that wiping a large nation "off the face of the earth"—not to speak of annihilating a dozen nations (and doing so merely because they had "harbored" terrorists)—is something that has never been done. To be fair, Krauthammer and Easterbrook wanted to consider the act only in the context of retaliation, and neither stated unequivocally that he would counsel actually carrying out the threat even then. On the other hand, neither pointed out that the deed they described would, if enacted, be a crime outside all human experience and would blacken the name of the United States in human memory forever. The darkness deepens. Have just two months of "war on terrorism" brought us to this? J.S.

November 21, 2001
In Hindsight

The sudden collapse of the Taliban in most of Afghanistan is one of those events that seem to have been designed by the fates to teach policy-makers and pundits humility. The collapse came, of course, as a surprise; but it was also something more: It arrived in the teeth of almost universal opinion that it was not possible so soon. If there was one thing that the predictors in and out of government—very much including, I regret to say, this Letter—were agreed upon, it was that the campaign to unseat the Taliban (the prelude to attacking Al Qaeda) was going to last a long time—"years, not weeks or months" in the words of Secretary of Defense Donald Rumsfeld, who noted that the formula could mean up to twenty-three months. Hawks and doves in the newsmedia agreed. The hawks said: The bombing isn't working; therefore the United States must send in ground troops. Bombing alone, *The New Republic* editorialized, could not achieve U.S. objectives, even in combination with attacks on the ground by the Northern Alliance, of which the magazine wrote, "Of all the proxies the United States has enlisted over the past half-century, the Northern Alliance may be the least prepared to attain America's battlefield objectives." *The Weekly Standard* agreed. The real problem, the editors believed, was to enlist the Pashtun tribe in the south in the fight—something that would be possible only "if we are not dependent on the Northern Alliance for ground power." Therefore only "a significant deployment (in the tens of thousands) of American ground forces to the country" would serve.

Doves argued: The bombing isn't working, therefore stop the bombing and step up humanitarian aid instead, both for its own sake and because it will head off the increase in terrorism likely to accompany a war in a starving land. Here I can quote my own words against myself. The problem, I wrote in this Letter, was that American military strategy was at odds with its political strategy. In the first days of the war, I noted, the Administration had hoped for an anti-Taliban rebellion in its southern stronghold. The Taliban refused to permit Western journalists to enter Afghanistan, and information was sparse. Yet the capture of one anti-Taliban leader (Abdul Haq) injected from Pakistan and the ejection of another (Ahmed Karzai), among other events, suggested that this policy was failing. But above all, "the bombing, far from prompting an anti-Taliban rebellion, has, according to all reports, rallied popular support to the previously hated regime." History offered many supporting examples of peoples, including the Germans in World War II and the Vietnamese in the Vietnam War, whose will was stiffened rather than broken by bombing. On the basis of this assumption, a host of conclusions seemed to follow: If bombing was solidifying opposition to the United States, the war would last a long time; the humanitarian crisis would worsen; a large ground force probably would be sent in; the age-old Afghan hatred of foreign occupiers would be inflamed, and guerrilla war would ensue; anger at the United States would build around the Islamic world, and terrorism would increase; some Islamic regimes, especially that of nuclear-armed Pakistan, might even fall into extremist hands.

Even the Taliban, it appears, shared in the widespread misconception. Its spokesmen repeatedly threatened that the real war against America would begin only when it invaded on the ground. The fates decided otherwise. If journalists were to devote their columns to correcting their previous mis-judgments, the opinion pages of the papers would be filled with little else; yet nearly universal error does seem to call for at least some reflection by somebody. With the sharper (we can hope) vision of hindsight, it appears that the main mistake was to imagine, on the basis of a few scraps of infor-mation (the capture and execution of Haq, and so forth), that we could know what the temper of the people of Afghanistan was. Even after the fact firm judgments seem risky, yet on the basis of subsequent news reports it appears that many people hated the Taliban far more than they hated the bombing.

The collapse of the Taliban lines outside Kabul was perhaps not sur-prising. The Gulf War had made it clear that troops deployed in fixed posi-tions in open terrain cannot long survive the effectively unlimited violence of American air power. Like the U.S. troops entering Kuwait, the troops of the Northern Alliance faced little resistance when they finally breached Taliban lines. It was what happened next that amazed. The Alliance forces, whose warring factions had turned much of Kabul to rubble just six years before, were nevertheless greeted by many as saviors. Three symbols of liberation were immediately flashed around the world: men shaving unwanted beards; women casting off the tent-like burqas; children flying kites. Meanwhile, it turned out that the Taliban had simply quit the city. Only future investigation will reveal the reasons for their decision, but in the meantime it looks as though they knew that a fight in the streets of Kabul would be doomed with a hostile population at their backs.

A secondary factor seems to have played an important role—the traditional Afghan practice of deciding military confrontations through side-switching in brokered deals. In these deals, the losing side trades in its readiness to cease resistance for leniency or a share in power in the new dispensation. The practice, which permits some of the losers to join the victors, gives exceptional force to the urge to place oneself on the winning side. The Taliban came to power in Afghanistan largely through such deals, and they appear to have lost it in much of the country in the same way.

Of course, the war goes on. Overthrowing the Taliban (still in control of the cities of Kandahar and Kunduz as I write) is one thing; the founding of a new government, another. The same revolving door that ushered the Taliban in could usher in other distasteful characters soon. And American officials are already suggesting that in the "war on terrorism" there may be more wars to fight. But let us leave these questions for another time.

Is there anything to be learned? Use historical analogies sparingly. Reserve judgment when facts are unavailable. Respect the mystery of the will of peoples. Their decisions, can, when made, astonish the world. J.S.

PRESS OF EVENTS

Commentaries and Editorials

September 12, 2001: Editorial
A Great Wound

We have taken a great wound, we Americans, and our first task is to rescue survivors if that is still possible, to grieve and to remain alert until we better understand what happened to us. The time will come soon enough to sort out the causes, who delivered this vicious attack and how we hold them accountable, then to assign official blame at home, if the facts require it. We should also begin deeper arguments about the political meanings, the failures in our own leadership and the role our government has chosen to play in the world. But right now, our minds are swimming in the same ghastly images. Dazed men and women, covered with dust, streaming north on foot from lower Manhattan. A TV videotape replaying the fiendish plot in which commercial airliners are turned into suicide bombs. The smoldering ruins at the Pentagon. The lost skyline in Manhattan. The bolt of fear: Where are my children? Questions spun through our heads, but all the circuits were busy. Terror leaves its sickening residue, the swooning sense of helpless vulnerability. That is the purpose.

One odd privilege of being American is that we have had very little experience with such blindsiding assaults, at least in modern times. Other countries became the battlegrounds, not ours. Other peoples were schooled in stoical expectations, knowing that the worst can happen and sometimes does, but not Americans.

It is essential now to stick to hard facts, not fearsome shadows or injured hubris (or the xenophobic hatreds already in the air). Yet the intelligence agencies that had not a clue what was coming were claiming within hours to have proof of who organized the attack. And figures like Henry Kissinger are already calling for an open-ended war against terrorist organizations—regardless of whether any evidence establishes their culpability.

Civil liberties, already under attack, were immediate targets. Legislators talked of granting the FBI and other agencies broad new powers—this despite the fact that the FBI is already intercepting a record number of calls.

Some called for wholesale closing of U.S. borders. On Tuesday, only Senator Joseph Biden, himself a key supporter of the noxious Anti-Terrorism and Effective Death Penalty bill of 1996, to his credit stood on the Capitol lawn to suggest that any incursions on civil liberties should be resisted.

After the dead are properly mourned, after we have reliably established how this happened and who was responsible, then we Americans must undertake a most difficult conversation among ourselves. Yes, we should speak with one voice expressing our compassion and outrage, but we need a multiplicity of voices, a true national debate about what sane national security means in the twenty-first century. The paradox is that if or when we engage in brutal reprisals, they will serve a cathartic function for the vast majority of justifiably outraged Americans. But let us not delude ourselves; they will inflame rather than deter. In the long run, the only way to deal with international terrorism is to build and support international institutions toward that end.

This is a pivotal moment when we should reconsider our posture toward the world and examine the true burdens and obligations of acting like an empire awesomely more powerful than any others and answerable to no one. To maintain international order, our military occasionally intervenes in what, for us, are meant to be casualty-free wars. Our economic order claims to spread democracy by imposing its own self-interested rules on poorer nations. Yet, as we learned and should have already understood, this great country is vulnerable too, beyond imagination. Whoever planned this vicious attack must have calculated that the United States is at a fragile juncture, its great prosperity sinking and uncertain leaders in power. They probably intended an unraveling, both of financial markets and the national confidence.

It may seem trite to say so, but the calamity does test our character. If we are shrewd about ourselves and truly brave, citizens will not yield to hysteria—or accept draconian new laws that undermine civil liberties—but will force these difficult questions into the political debate.

September 12, 2001
The Dark Smoke
David Corn

In the immediate, before-it-sinks-in aftermath of the September 11 attack, one of the first catch-phrases to take hold—and be widely deployed by TV commentators, politicians and citizen e-mailers—was, "this changes everything." As the media cliché goes, time will tell how much of American life will be altered by the assault. Clearly, politics as we know it will not be the same in the weeks and months, and perhaps years, ahead. As Tim Russert observed, while hellish dust clouds billowed, "Suddenly the Social Security lockbox seems so trivial."

The hideous event will naturally dominate the national conversation. There will be little media space for other matters. The budget battle, the disappeared surplus, the Bush tax cuts, campaign finance reform, patients' bill of rights, trade tussles, global warming—Washington's agenda will be overwhelmed by the attack, to the President's distinct advantage. And the terms of political discussion will dramatically shift—again, mostly to George W. Bush's advantage. Two hours after the first explosion, Representative Curt Weldon, a Republican from Pennsylvania, declared, "The number-one responsibility" of the government is not education or healthcare but the "security of the American people." And national security hawks quickly began to shape the debate to come. The issue for them is not what causes such unimaginable actions. On Day One did you hear *anyone*—in an attempt to understand, not justify, the horror—ask, Why would someone want to commit this evil act? Or note that in this globalized age, U.S. policy—its actions and inactions overseas (justified or not)—can easily lead to consequences at home? No, the national security cadre, out in force, mainly raised questions of how best to bolster the military and intelligence establishment.

Before rescue efforts were up and running, the friends of that establishment were mounting an offensive. Former Secretary of State James Baker blamed the Church Committee, the Senate panel that investigated CIA misdeeds in the 1970s, for what happened: "We went on a real witch hunt with our CIA . . . the Church Committee. We unilaterally disarmed in terms of intelligence." Newt Gingrich assailed rules on intelligence gathering that limit CIA interaction with known terrorists, and he asserted that the intelligence budget (about $30 billion) was "too small." Others decried the prohibition on government-sponsored assassination. Dan Quayle urged that the President be granted "extraordinary powers internationally and domestically" to deal with terrorists. (Asked what he had in mind, Quayle replied, "I'm not going to get too specific.") John McCain, Orrin Hatch and Bob Graham—the last of whom chairs the Senate Intelligence Committee—griped that the United States has concentrated too much on technical intelligence (spy satellites and high-tech eavesdropping) and has been negligent in the ways of "human intelligence"—*humint*, in the parlance of spies. More money would have to be poured into humint, they and others remarked. Hatch also complained that "we've allowed our military to deteriorate" and that the "Russians have a better tactical fighter than we do." Former Secretary of State Lawrence Eagleburger used the moment to claim that "the defense budget is woefully underdone."

Some hawks and others did criticize U.S. intelligence for failing to detect the plot. Kenneth Katzman, a terrorism expert at the Congressional Research Service, said, "How nothing could have been picked up is beyond me—way beyond me. There's a major, major intelligence failure, specially since the [previous] Trade Center bombing produced such an investigation of the networks and so much monitoring." No doubt, there will be official inquiries. But the knee-jerk goal for most of the inquirers will be additional funds for the intelligence community and the Pentagon. The spies will defend their actions and plead, if only our hands were not tied, if only we had more money.

Given the horrors of the attack, these pleas will probably have resonance. But the operating assumptions at work deserve close assessment. Human intelligence against closed societies and secret outfits has long been a difficult, almost impossible, endeavor. Hurling money at it is likely no solution. During the Vietnam War, when resources were unlimited, the CIA failed spectacularly at humint, essentially never penetrating the inner sanctums of the enemy. Its record of infiltrating the Soviet government was unimpressive (and the same goes for China, Cuba and other targets). As for lifting existing restrictions, imagine the dilemmas posed if the CIA actually managed to recruit and pay murderous members of terrorist groups. What would the reaction be, if one of the September 11 conspirators turns out to have had a U.S. intelligence connection?

Do not be surprised if the national security establishment even tries to accelerate its push for Star Wars II before the debris is cleared. The event tragically demonstrated the limits of a national missile defense system. (And consider how much worse the day would have been had the evildoers smuggled a pound of uranium onto any of the hijacked flights.) But the loudest theme in American politics—perhaps the only audible theme—in the time ahead will be the quest for security. With those drums beating, the fans of national missile defense will continue to argue that this remains a dangerous world full of suicidal maniacs wishing the United States harm and that all steps must be taken as fast as possible. Moreover, how many politicians will now question Bush's budget-busting request to raise Pentagon spending by 10 percent? Speaking about Bush, Senator Hillary Clinton said, "We will support him in whatever steps he deems necessary." *Whatever* steps?

As the nation absorbed the shock, leaders and media observers repeated the nostrum that the best way for the country to respond to such a foul crime is to return to normal and signal that the nation's spirit and resolve cannot be undermined. In that vein, one challenge is to not allow the attack to distort the country's political discourse. Unfortunately, extremism begets extremism, and the dark smoke of a dark day will not be easily blown away.

September 12, 2001
Terror in America
Robert Fisk

So it has come to this. The entire modern history of the Middle East—the collapse of the Ottoman Empire, the Balfour declaration, Lawrence of

Arabia's lies, the Arab revolt, the foundation of the state of Israel, four Arab-Israeli wars and the thirty-four years of Israel's brutal occupation of Arab land—all erased within hours as those who claim to represent a crushed, humiliated population struck back with the wickedness and awesome cruelty of a doomed people. Is it fair—is it moral—to write this so soon, without proof, when the last act of barbarism, in Oklahoma, turned out to be the work of home-grown Americans? I fear it is. America is at war and, unless I am mistaken, many thousands more are now scheduled to die in the Middle East, perhaps in America too. Some of us warned of "the explosion to come." But we never dreamt this nightmare.

And yes, Osama bin Laden comes to mind—his money, his theology, his frightening dedication to destroying American power. I have sat in front of bin Laden as he described how his men helped to destroy the Russian Army in Afghanistan and thus the Soviet Union [see Fisk, September 21, 1998]. Their boundless confidence allowed them to declare war on America. But this is not really the war of democracy versus terror that the world will be asked to believe in the coming days. It is also about U.S. missiles smashing into Palestinian homes and U.S. helicopters firing missiles into a Lebanese ambulance in 1996 and American shells crashing into a village called Qana and about a Lebanese militia—paid and uniformed by America's Israeli ally—hacking and raping and murdering their way through refugee camps.

No, there is no doubting the utter, indescribable evil of what has happened in the United States. That Palestinians could celebrate the massacre of thousands of innocent people is not only a symbol of their despair but of their political immaturity, of their failure to grasp what they had always been accusing their Israeli enemies of doing: acting disproportionately. All the years of rhetoric, all the promises to strike at the heart of America, to cut off the head of "the American snake" we took for empty threats. How could a backward, conservative, undemocratic and corrupt group of regimes and small, violent organizations fulfill such preposterous promises? Now we know.

And in the hours that followed the September 11 annihilation, I began to remember those other extraordinary assaults upon the United States and its allies, miniature now by comparison with yesterday's casualties. Did not the suicide bombers who killed 239 American servicemen and 58 French paratroopers in Beirut on October 23, 1983, time their attacks with unthinkable precision?

There were just seven seconds between the Marine bombing and the destruction of the French three miles away. Then there were the attacks on U.S. bases in Saudi Arabia, and last year's attempt—almost successful, it turned out—to sink the USS *Cole* in Aden. And then how easy was our failure to recognize the new weapon of the Middle East, which neither Americans nor any other Westerners could equal: the despair-driven, desperate suicide bomber.

And there will be, inevitably, and quite immorally, an attempt to obscure the historical wrongs and the injustices that lie behind the firestorms. We will be told about "mindless terrorism," the "mindless" bit being essential if we are not to realize how hated America has become in the land of the birth of three great religions.

Ask an Arab how he responds to the thousands of innocent deaths, and he or she will respond as decent people should, that it is an unspeakable crime. But they will ask why we did not use such words about the sanctions that have destroyed the lives of perhaps half a million children in Iraq, why we did not rage about the 17,500 civilians killed in Israel's 1982 invasion of Lebanon. And those basic reasons why the Middle East caught fire last September—the Israeli occupation of Arab land, the dispossession of Palestinians, the bombardments and state-sponsored executions—all these must be obscured lest they provide the smallest fractional reason for the mass savagery on September 11.

No, Israel was not to blame—though we can be sure that Saddam Hussein and the other grotesque dictators will claim so—but the malign influence of history and our share in its burden must surely stand in the dark with the suicide bombers. Our broken promises, perhaps even our destruction of the Ottoman Empire, led inevitably to this tragedy. America has bankrolled Israel's wars for so many years that it believed this would be cost-free. No longer so. But, of course, the United States will want to strike back against "world terror." Indeed, who could ever point the finger at Americans now for using that pejorative and sometimes racist word "terrorism"?

Eight years ago, I helped make a television series that tried to explain why so many Muslims had come to hate the West. Now I remember some of those Muslims in that film, their families burnt by American-made bombs and weapons. They talked about how no one would help them but God. Theology versus technology, the suicide bomber against the nuclear power. Now we have learned what this means.

September 19, 2001: Editorial
Justice, Not Vengeance

The atrocious attacks on the World Trade Center were massive crimes against humanity in both a real-world sense and in a technical legal sense, as Richard Falk reminds us. As such they are appropriately and lawfully the object of concerted U.S. and international efforts to find and punish those responsible. But acknowledging a legitimate right of response is by no means equivalent to an endorsement of unlimited force. Indeed, notes Falk, an overreaction may be what the terrorists were seeking to provoke in order to mobilize popular resentment against the United States on a global scale. We must act effectively, but within a framework of moral and legal restraints.

Americans need to take a deep breath, clear their heads of the political frenzy in Washington and demand much better from their leaders. As we go to press, with combat planes headed for the Persian Gulf and President Bush poised to address the nation, the din of war rhetoric grows louder. But our objective should be justice, not vengeance. We will advance justice, as well as national security, by sticking to the facts and the cooperative procedures of international law and institutions (which means seeking a mandate from the UN Security Council and supporting a special world court to try the perpetrators of terrorism), and by recognizing that a random slaughter of more innocents is immoral and contrary to America's self-interest, as well as to its core beliefs.

At home, the Bush White House is using fears of a recession to advance a partisan and exploitative agenda—repackaging familiar tax cuts for business and capital under a flag of crisis. What would be most effective in staving off recession, however, would be to assist those at the lower end of the economic scale who live from one paycheck to the next. It would also be the right thing to do. The essential reality of American life, long neglected in this era of bubble and boom but revealed again by this tragedy, is our reliance upon the enduring fiber of ordinary workers, from firefighters and police to nurses, flight attendants and janitors. Many of them died and many more will become innocent victims as the recession deepens.

Under the guise of fighting terrorism and in an ominous echo of past ill-conceived wartime measures targeting aliens, the Administration has expanded its powers to detain legal immigrants. It has drafted "antiterrorist" legislation that assumes sweeping powers of deportation but does little to fight terrorists.

The worst consequence of Washington's war talk is how it fogs public thinking, sustaining the nostalgic illusion that the military can somehow conquer this elusive enemy. If the objective is to crush the networks of scattered terrorists—whoever they are—who organized the murderous assault and might strike again, then military force is generally impotent. But the United States and other advanced nations have many effective, nonlethal weapons with which to break up the organizations.

The global financial system is one. A terrorist organization may camp in remote desert caves beyond the reach of strategic bombing or cruise missiles, but its activities depend crucially upon financing. Some of that may be done through informal channels, but some of it is also done through legitimate financial institutions. Governments can stop those money flows. If history is any guide, however—witness the Bush Administration's unwillingness to get tough on money-laundering—they seem unlikely to do so.

We have now entered a new era—one without battlefields and borders, in which old ideas about national security are obsolete. In this new era, Falk tells us, the only viable security is one built on a commitment to "human security" in the form of economic and social well-being for all people. This is the message that must be sent to Washington and the other capitals of the world.

September 19, 2001
The Democrats' Dilemma
David Corn

So long, politics? As George W. Bush mounted Operation Noble Eagle, Republicans and Democrats found little over which to disagree. In the days after the September 11 terror attack, the entire House and Senate—with the exception of one Congresswoman—approved a resolution of war that granted Bush wide latitude. (Congress declared war, but Bush will designate the enemy.) The Senate OK'd by voice vote the controversial nomination of John Negroponte to be UN ambassador. Congress passed $40 billion in emergency funds and ceded Bush great control over their disbursement. The Senate, with little deliberation, endorsed quickly prepared legislation to expand the government's ability to wiretap suspected terrorists and to order the CIA to scuttle rules on the recruitment of informants with violent pasts. A $15 billion bailout of the airline industry nearly sailed through the House. Republican and Democratic Congressional leaders hailed the sublimation of partisan differences. House majority whip Tom DeLay even jettisoned his opposition to paying back dues to the United Nations.

Who can say how long comity will last? The Democrats' agenda has vanished as the party tries to work out the dilemmas of being in opposition during a time of declared (if not actual) war. "We're confused, as you might imagine," says a liberal House Democrat. "My fear is that most members will give Bush everything he wants and try to adjourn as quickly as possible, not have any tough votes, no debates that might get them into trouble. Every Democratic issue is down the drain." For instance, Representative Marty Meehan, a Massachusetts Democrat, suspended his almost-successful attempt at forcing Republican House leaders to bring his campaign finance reform bill up for a vote. "All efforts are on helping New York City and the Pentagon rebuild," a Meehan aide explains. House and Senate Democrats shelved provisions that imposed limits on national missile defense funding. "No one wants to look partisan now," says a Democratic Senate aide. "You can argue SDI money is better spent elsewhere, but no Democrat wants to give Bush and the Republicans the opportunity of pointing a finger and saying, 'There they go.' "

It was Bush, not a Democrat, who publicly noted that Washington must remember that a domestic agenda remains. "Sure," says a Democratic Congressional aide, "education and a patients' bill of rights, on his terms now." As members of Congress returned to Washington, Democrats were hoping the Republicans would not move fast with a proposal for a capital gains tax cut. "If they push this forward under the cover of crisis, it will be very difficult to stop," the aide remarks.

On the Democratic side, Representative Barney Frank has tried to initiate one crafty strategic thrust. The liberal Democrat drafted legislation to rescind the reduction in the top income tax rate that passed as part of Bush's tax cut. That particular cut mainly benefits the top 1 percent, and Frank would devote the billions rescued to Social Security and Medicare. "This would let us spend $100 billion on reconstruction, airport security, military action, the economy, without tapping the Social Security surplus," Frank says. "The Republicans promised not to touch Social Security; this would allow them to keep their promise."

Frank's colleagues applauded when he described the bill at a Democratic caucus meeting. But the GOPers will certainly seek to smother Frank's legislation, and they have the means to do it. Credit Frank with attempting to provide the Democrats an active position of their own. The question is, Do enough of his colleagues want one? "Great idea," says a House Democrat. "I just don't know if we're strong enough to do this."

Another unknown is whether Democrats and Republicans will skirmish over the attack-related matters that will dominate Washington. A dramatic boost in Pentagon spending appears a certainty. Will there be disagreement over how much? (Some GOPers yearn for a 25 percent increase.) The Administration will be pressing assorted law enforcement and security initiatives. Senator Pat Leahy, who chairs the Judiciary Committee, has signaled that he's not eager to rubber-stamp new measures with civil liberties consequences. And Senator Russ Feingold, who chairs a judiciary subcommittee, has declared he feels "a special duty to defend our Constitution against proposals, born of an understandable desire for vengeance and justice, that would undermine the constitutional liberties that make this country what it is." Yet how much of a fight might arise? "The mood is basically to cave," says Julian Epstein, the former minority staff director of the House Judiciary Committee. But Epstein believes a partisan clash could materialize if the Republicans get greedy and push for too much.

"This all will be very frustrating," says a senior House Democratic aide. "Who knows how long a war on terrorism takes?" Noting disappointment with his leader, a Democratic Congressman remarks, "Dick Gephardt said there should be no light and no air between us and the President. But there have to be things worthy of debate. It's not political bickering to deal with the economy and civil liberties. There are debates to be had—even if most people want to run out of town."

September 19, 2001
Barbara Lee's Stand

When Congress voted to authorize the Bush Administration to use military force in response to the September 11 terror attacks on the World Trade Center and the Pentagon, Representative Barbara Lee stood alone in opposition to what she saw as a "rush to judgment." Lee, the California Democrat who holds the Bay Area seat once occupied by antiwar activist Ron Dellums, spoke with John Nichols, The Nation's Washington correspondent, this week.

THE NATION: How did you reach the decision to oppose authorizing the use of force?

LEE: I was at the National Cathedral in Washington. I went to the memorial service on the Friday after the attacks and I prayed. I said to myself, "You've got to figure this one out." I was dealing with all the grief and sorrow and the loss of life, and it was very personal because a member of my staff had lost a cousin in the Pennsylvania crash. I was thinking about my responsibility as a member of Congress to try to insure that this never happens again. I listened to the remarks of the clergy. Many of them made profound statements. But I was struck by what one of them said: "As we act, let us not become the evil that we deplore." That was such a wise statement, and it reflected not only what I was feeling but also my understanding of the threats we continue to face. When I left the cathedral, I was fairly resolved.

THE NATION: Were you also concerned about the constitutional implications of the vote?

LEE: Absolutely. Given the three branches of government, and given that each has a role in the making of monumental decisions such as this, I thought the Congress had a responsibility in this instance especially to step back and say, "Let's not rush to judgment. Let us insist that our democracy works by insuring that the checks and balances work and that the Congress is a part of the decision-making process in terms of when we go to war and with whom. . . . I think we disenfranchised the American people when we took their representatives out of the decision-making on whether to go to war with a specific nation.

THE NATION: Were you surprised that no other members of Congress voted with you?

LEE: It never dawned on me that I would cast the only vote against this resolution. Many members asked me to change my position. They were friends, and they said, "You do not want to be out there alone." I said, "Oh, no, don't worry. There will be others." When there weren't, I said, "Oh my God." I could not believe it. It was an awesome feeling. And a lonely feeling.

THE NATION: You mentioned that other members said, "You don't want to be out there alone." Do you think other members shared your concerns but were unwilling to cast a risky vote with emotions running so high?

LEE: If you read the floor statements, you'll see that there are many members of Congress who share my concerns. I think that, when I cast that vote, I was speaking for other people in Congress and outside Congress who want a more deliberative approach.

THE NATION: At the same time, you have received precisely the sort of criticism that most politicians fear.

LEE: I've been called a traitor, a coward, a communist, all the awful stuff. It's been quite difficult for me. But I still believe that I cast the right vote. My district, I think, understands this vote. . . . I've gotten probably 20,000 e-mails. At first, there were a lot of very harsh messages. But now we are hearing more from people who are saying, "Yes, let's use some restraint. Yes, let's break the cycle of violence if we can." I think the further we get away from that tragic day, the more we will hear those voices of reason.

September 19, 2001
The Most Patriotic Act
Eric Foner

The drumbeat now begins, as it always does in time of war: We must accept limitations on our liberties. The FBI and CIA should be "unleashed" in the name of national security. Patriotism means uncritical support of whatever actions the President deems appropriate. Arab-Americans, followers of Islam, people with Middle Eastern names or ancestors, should be subject to special scrutiny by the government and their fellow citizens. With liberal members of Congress silent and the Administration promising a war on terrorism lasting "years, not days," such sentiments are likely to be with us for some time to come.

Of the many lessons of American history, this is among the most basic. Our civil rights and civil liberties—freedom of expression, the right to criticize the government, equality before the law, restraints on the exercise of police powers—are not gifts from the state that can be rescinded when it desires. They are the inheritance of a long history of struggles: by abolitionists for the ability to hold meetings and publish their views in the face of mob violence; by labor leaders for the power to organize unions, picket and distribute literature without fear of arrest; by feminists for the right to disseminate birth-control information without being charged with violating the obscenity laws; and by all those who braved jail and worse to challenge entrenched systems of racial inequality.

The history of freedom in this country is not, as is often thought, the logical working out of ideas immanent in our founding documents or a straight-line trajectory of continual progress. It is a story of countless disagreements and battles in which victories sometimes prove temporary and retrogression often follows progress.

When critics of the original Constitution complained about the absence of a Bill of Rights, the Constitution's "father," James Madison, replied that no list of liberties could ever anticipate the ways government might act in the future. "Parchment barriers" to the abuse of authority, he wrote, would be least effective when most needed. Thankfully, the Bill of Rights was eventually adopted. But Madison's observation was amply borne out at moments of popular hysteria when freedom of expression was trampled in the name of patriotism and national unity.

Americans have notoriously short historical memories. But it is worth recalling some of those moments to understand how liberty has been endangered in the past. During the "quasi war" with France in 1798, the Alien and Sedition Acts allowed deportation of immigrants deemed dangerous by federal authorities and made it illegal to criticize the federal government. During the Civil War, both sides jailed critics and suppressed opposition newspapers.

In World War I German-Americans, socialists, labor leaders and critics of U.S. involvement were subjected to severe government repression and assault by private vigilante groups. Publications critical of the war were banned from the mails, individuals were jailed for antiwar statements and in the Red Scare that followed the war thousands of radicals were arrested and numerous aliens deported. During World War II, tens of thousands of Japanese-Americans, most of them U.S. citizens, were removed to internment camps. Sanctioned by the Supreme Court, this was the greatest violation of Americans' civil liberties, apart from slavery, in our history.

No one objects to more stringent security at airports. But current restrictions on the FBI and CIA limiting surveillance, wiretapping, infiltration of political groups at home and assassinations abroad do not arise from an irrational desire for liberty at the expense of security. They are the response to real abuses of authority, which should not be forgotten in the zeal to sweep them aside as "handcuffs" on law enforcement.

Before unleashing these agencies, let us recall the FBI's persistent harassment of individuals like Martin Luther King Jr. and its efforts to disrupt the civil rights and antiwar movements, and the CIA's history of cooperation with some of the world's most egregious violators of human rights. The principle that no group of Americans should be stigmatized as disloyal or criminal because of race or national origin is too recent and too fragile an achievement to be abandoned now.

Every war in American history, from the Revolution to the Gulf War, with the exception of World War II, inspired vigorous internal dissent. Self-imposed silence is as debilitating to a democracy as censorship. If questioning an ill-defined, open-ended "war on terrorism" is to be deemed unpatriotic, the same label will have to be applied to Abraham Lincoln at the time of the Mexican War, Jane Addams and Eugene V. Debs during World War I, and Wayne Morse and Ernest Gruening, who had the courage and foresight to vote against the Gulf of Tonkin resolution in 1964.

All of us today share a feeling of grief and outrage over the events of September 11 and a desire that those responsible for mass murder be brought to justice. But at times of crisis the most patriotic act of all is the unyielding defense of civil liberties, the right to dissent and equality before the law for all Americans.

September 26, 2001: Editorial
Rules of Engagement

As this is written, we wait and wonder what the military response will be to the inchoate enemy the President summoned up in his speech to the nation on September 20. Despite the near-unanimous celebration of it by the mainstream media, we were left with troubling questions. The President told the nation it was at war, "a lengthy campaign unlike any we have ever fought," its aim the total "disruption and . . . defeat of the global terror network." But he failed to clearly identify the enemy or specify any limits on the means to be employed, including avoidance of unnecessary civilian casualties. Osama bin Laden was denounced as the prime suspect, but no evidence of his guilt was adduced that night, and the Administration has yet to produce it.

Bush said that this war would bring to bear "every resource at our command"—diplomacy, intelligence, law enforcement, finance. But the military option overshadowed all. And there was no mention of applying international law or working with the United Nations, which could lend international legitimacy to the fight against terrorism, giving political cover to Islamic nations who join it.

The President pledged not to wage war on Islam but then proclaimed, "Every nation in every region now has a decision to make. Either you are with us, or you are with the terrorists." He thus broadened the scope of his war to include, potentially, sanctions or even attacks on nation-states deemed not to be "with us," although state-sponsored terrorism has not been implicated in the World Trade Center attack. Since most of the countries thought to harbor terrorists are Islamic, the possibility of action against them sparking a backlash in the Muslim world remains.

A wider war against Afghanistan will heap more misery on that war-ravaged theocracy without fostering the secularization and democratization it so desperately needs. The threat of war has already unleashed a flood of refugees that could destabilize other shaky states in the region, primarily Pakistan, a nuclear power. Bush's black-and-white worldview could justify eliminating Saddam Hussein, a project pushed by Defense Secretary Donald Rumsfeld and his deputy, Paul Wolfowitz.

We support an all-out but carefully targeted effort to neutralize identified terrorist networks. This may involve a limited military response, like attacks on terrorist bases, but primarily it should rely on such nonmilitary means as exchanges of intelligence among nations, coordinated investigations by law-enforcement agencies in affected countries and pressure on financial institutions and governments to cooperate in cutting off terrorist-group funding.

Beyond this kind of international campaign, the United States should re-examine the role its foreign policy has played in creating the pools of anti-Americanism that breed terrorists. Not that reciting the dismal litany of U.S. interventions and realpolitik "explains" this tragedy; or that America somehow deserved to be attacked on September 11 because of past policies. Rather, such a re-examination should lead to a more humane and truly internationalist foreign policy that recognizes a responsibility to other nations. Chris Patten, European Union external affairs commissioner, called for dealing with such persisting evils as "the whole relationship between poverty, degradation and violence, between drugs and crime and violence, and trade and development and violence." America must moderate the parochial unilateralism that is branded arrogance. It must step up efforts to defuse the festering Israeli-Palestinian dispute and encourage democracy in Saudi Arabia, Egypt, Jordan, Syria and Algeria.

In a sudden—and expedient—conversion to internationalism the Administration pressed Congress to pay long-overdue UN assessments and called on the Senate to ratify two UN conventions dealing specifically with terrorism. That's a start, but more could be done to align U.S. diplomacy with international bodies, including joining the International Criminal Court to help make it an effective tribunal for bringing terrorists to justice; reversing the decision not to sign the biological warfare protocol; ratifying the test ban treaty and curbing nuclear proliferation, thus diminishing terrorists' access to weapons of mass destruction.

On the home front, the newly created Office of Homeland Security should coordinate the overlapping efforts of the two dozen federal departments and agencies that deal with domestic security. The nature of the attack on U.S. soil has blown to bits any possible rationale for national missile defense. That money should go instead to infrastructure and transportation improvements (including railroads) and for training "first responders"—police, fire departments, hospitals, emergency medical services—to deal with the kind of mass disasters terrorists may inflict.

Enhanced homeland defense, constrained by strict protection of civil liberties, could justify a rollback of the U.S. military presence overseas and undercut a rationale for inflated military spending and military interventions. It could also channel the spirit of civilian volunteerism that recently flowered in New York City.

We do not accept the notion that patriotism precludes politics. If waged sensibly, the fight against terrorism will be long, low-level and sustained. Politics can't be suspended during that time. More than a million people have been laid off in this country since July 2000. U.S. trade policies are wiping out industries here and increasing poverty around the world. Millions live without health insurance. The President has called upon us to resume our normal lives. Surely that includes implementing policies to make America better, not suspending vigorous debate and civil liberties for a decades-long fight against terrorism.

September 26, 2001
Is the FBI Up to the Job?
David Corn

In May 2000, Louis Mizell Jr., a terrorism and security expert in Washington, received a call from Jake White, an acquaintance who was a bouncer at a strip club in Omaha. White told Mizell a disturbing story he had heard from a dancer at the club and another bouncer. Several nights earlier, they claimed, the dancer had been asked by two customers who, she believed, were Middle Eastern or Indian to perform privately for them at their home. She agreed and took the other bouncer along for protection. There was almost no furniture in the men's duplex, and on the wall was a picture of a man the dancer and bouncer took to be a religious figure from the Middle East. While in a bedroom with one of the customers, the dancer noticed a shoebox full of cash and items she took to be explosives. The bouncer meanwhile spotted automatic weapons and explosives in the kitchen and watched the other man look at cut-away diagrams of commercial airliners on a computer.

Neither the dancer nor the bouncer wanted to go to the authorities, White says, so he phoned Mizell, a former special agent and intelligence officer for the State Department. Mizell says he "quickly called the FBI and was passed from one agent to another. I then called the FBI in Omaha. They said to call headquarters." Mizell ended up giving the details to the FBI in Omaha, which, according to White, did not contact him, the dancer or the bouncer.

White's version of the tale told by the dancer and bouncer cannot be independently confirmed. A few days after the attack, the dancer appeared to have left town and was unreachable, and the bouncer was demanding to be paid for recounting his story. After September 11, the FBI twice interviewed White. Larry Holmquist, a spokesman for the FBI in Omaha, says the Bureau found no connection between the episode related by the dancer and the bouncer and the World Trade Center and Pentagon assaults. But this is the crucial and troubling point: The FBI apparently did not initially act on the lead provided by Mizell, a credible source of information.

Was the FBI action—or lack thereof—in this matter unusual or representative? This is an important question, for in the aftermath of September 11, many politicians, pundits and national security experts have called for expanding the powers and prerogatives of intelligence and law-enforcement agencies, including the FBI. Attorney General John Ashcroft asked for quick passage of legislation that would expand the ability of federal investigators to conduct secret searches (including wiretaps and the interception of computer communications), to seize assets in nonterrorism cases and to allow for the indefinite detention of noncitizens without judicial review. Members of Congress have urged a boost in the intelligence budget and demanded increased efforts to penetrate terrorist groups.

There is certainly a need to review and strengthen programs and agencies that aim to detect and defuse terrorism. But in order to do so effectively—and without unduly weakening civil liberties—Congress and the federal government ought to examine thoroughly what went wrong in the days, weeks and years preceding September 11. The public record of what may have been missed opportunities (or missed indications) keeps growing. In 1995 U.S. investigators learned that Osama bin Laden's operatives had hatched a plan to bomb eleven U.S. airliners simultaneously and crash another airplane into CIA headquarters. The FBI did nothing after learning that an Islamic extremist suspected of ties to terrorist camps in Afghanistan had been trying to learn how to fly passenger jets. For years law-enforcement officials have known that several people linked to bin Laden attended flight schools in the United States. Assorted warnings and threats against the United States issued this spring and summer were not quickly reviewed by U.S. intelligence, due partly to the lack of analysts and translators. After August 23 the FBI sought two suspected bin Laden associates but failed to find them before they boarded the airliner that was piloted into the Pentagon. The *San Francisco Chronicle* reported that the week before September 11, India's intelligence apparatus intercepted a bin Laden communication referring to the coming assault. According to the *Washington Post*, the FBI has tracked four or five Al Qaeda cells in the United States—none of which have yet been connected to the World Trade Center and Pentagon attacks—but has failed to discern their goals.

Was there a "massive intelligence failure," as Senator Richard Shelby, the ranking Republican on the intelligence committee, declared? (Since the attack, the most prominent critics of the intelligence community have been Republicans.) If Shelby is right, should Congress and the President rush to hand more money and more power to the bureaucracies that messed up? Even if some changes must be implemented quickly in order to locate and punish the mass murderers of September 11 and to discover and thwart immediate threats of terrorism, the mistakes of the past should be carefully raked through before determining how best to improve and reform those agencies charged with protecting Americans. Can it be that a mere phone call to a stripper might have led to the undoing of the September 11 plotters? Probably not. But how sad that it is even a possibility.

October 3, 2001
All in the Name of Security
Bruce Shapiro

"We're likely to experience more restrictions on personal freedom than has ever been the case in our country," Supreme Court Justice Sandra Day O'Connor grimly warned a group of NYU law students after visiting the mangled tomb that was once the World Trade Center. O'Connor's calm acceptance of the proposition that the terrorism crisis means unprecedented incursions on civil liberty—which, given her position on the Court, puts her in a position to be a self-fulfilling prophet—sounds extreme. But it's a prediction firmly grounded in the aspirations of the Bush White House. In contrast to the deliberation that has, so far at least, marked the Administration's military response to the WTC/Pentagon conspiracy, Attorney General John Ashcroft rushed to Capitol Hill with a hodgepodge of legislation to grant the FBI, INS and federal prosecutors powers to spy, jail and interrogate far greater than in any past war or national emergency.

In the days after September 11 it seemed a sure wager that Ashcroft's plan would pass Congress as swiftly as the Pearl Harbor war declaration. G-men would be out with a virtually unlimited license to detain immigrants and round up e-mail. The surprising thing is that for weeks, Congress forcefully resisted the Administration's proposals. By early October Ashcroft was fuming over a House compromise limiting the scope of his most coercive measures. In the Senate, Judiciary Committee chairman Patrick Leahy stood his ground so stubbornly that finally the White House pressured majority leader Tom Daschle into telling Leahy he would bring the bill to the floor without Judiciary approval. Leahy's committee finally voted a compromise bill of its own—in some respects weaker than the House version. By the end of the first week in October both the House and Senate bills were headed for floor votes, though there was still the possibility of some amendments. Why Ashcroft's plan was greeted with such reluctance, and the considerable dangers that still remain, are crucial to understanding what remains a uniquely perilous moment for the Bill of Rights.

Within hours of the Twin Towers' collapse, federal officials were already declaring that the war on terrorism would require new powers. In fact, they were mainly not new powers, but easements the FBI and federal prosecutors have sought for years: cutting judges' review of wiretap orders, opening access to supposedly secret grand jury evidence, detaining undocumented immigrants indefinitely and without appeal. Each year since the Oklahoma City bombing of 1995, Congress has rejected such plans. But the World Trade Center conspiracy seemed, at first, to change the political calculus—a notion with history very much on its side, a series of panics over foreign conspiracy going back to 1798, when whiffs of French revolutionism overwhelmed John Adams's Federalists, who responded by jailing newspaper editors and throwing out immigrants.

For civil libertarians, the political risk was all the greater because this is no imaginary conspiracy. The September 11 attack was murderous, the threat of future violence significant. Civil libertarians cannot casually dismiss the shocked public's hunger for security. Thus the ACLU calls its campaign against Ashcroft's package "Safe and Free," and director Anthony Romero praises Bush Administration plans to require hardened doors in aircraft cockpits; Ralph Neas, president of People For the American Way, calls for "acting appropriately to prevent future such attacks."

But what is "acting appropriately"? Regardless of the final legislation that passes Congress, Attorney General Ashcroft's initial answer—that sweeping law-enforcement wish list covering everything from credit reports to education records—is worth reviewing for what it reveals about the Administration's priorities. Take immigration, for instance. Within days of the World Trade Center and Pentagon attacks, President Bush won plaudits from Muslim-American groups for speaking clearly and loudly against harassment. Bush visited a mosque, and Ashcroft directed the FBI to treat harassment as a hate crime. At the same moment as these symbolic gestures, though, Ashcroft was moving his proposal that would substantively and vastly erode the rights of all immigrants—and, under the current political circumstances, Muslims in particular. After the Oklahoma City bombing, Congress created secret terrorism courts for foreign "terrorist suspects." Ashcroft's new plan goes a step further, skipping the trial altogether: He wants the right to detain foreign "terrorist suspects" indefinitely, with appeal possible only when a suspect faces deportation. "These actions offend the Constitution," says the ACLU's Romero, "and are an affront to millions of law-abiding immigrants in our country as well as millions of other citizens who are the sons and daughters of immigrants."

With wiretapping, the Administration has played a similarly canny game. After September 11 Ashcroft leapt into the breach with a proposal to allow a single wiretap warrant to authorize listening in on all phones and electronic communications of one individual. He described this as a "modest" attempt to bring wiretap law in line with an era of mobile phones. The media played it that way. In fact, as James Dempsey of the Center for Democracy and Technology puts it, this, along with other wiretap provisions proposed by Ashcroft, would "create a more intrusive form of surveillance." Most radical of all, Ashcroft proposed allowing prosecutors to share information from grand jury proceedings with FBI agents in other investigations. This plan, which turns on its head the historic purpose of the grand jury as a protection against prosecutorial excess, still appears likely to pass the House—though perhaps requiring court approval, despite Ashcroft's vociferous objections.

With the country still swept by grief and anger, how did members of Congress find the wherewithal to stand up to Ashcroft? Part of the answer may lie in early leadership from a few senators like Joseph Biden, who on September 11 was already warning of the danger of overreaction. In part it is an accident of history: this year's narrow Democratic control of the Senate, putting the stalwart civil libertarian Leahy instead of Orrin Hatch in charge of the Judiciary Committee. Some in Congress, sources suggest, took it as a personal affront that the Bush Administration was using the crisis to push legislation they had already opposed. Most of all, it's the product of an unusual coalition between liberal civil liberties organizations, computer advocates concerned about Internet privacy and gun-lobby libertarians like Representative Bob Barr, whose sense of government's capacity to abuse its power was heightened by Waco and Ruby Ridge. Barr, a former federal prosecutor, repeatedly warned against gutting the Fourth Amendment.

On Capitol Hill, skepticism of Ashcroft's plan grew as emerging details of the conspiracy began to suggest that none of his proposals would likely have made much difference. To the contrary, the plan appears more and more to be a fig leaf covering significant failures by federal agencies to communicate and act within their current authority. Those deadly box cutters and useless pilot-cabin doors are the result of air security rules more friendly to airlines' bottom lines than passenger safety. Mohammed Atta was on the State Department's terrorist watch list, but no one was watching as—like all the conspirators, apparently—he entered the United States legally and crisscrossed the country by airplane and rental cars under his own name. Word from police in Hamburg, Germany, where Atta and five other hijackers apparently lived, of a plan involving the World Trade Center never made it across the turf boundaries of U.S. law-enforcement agencies.

Even in its compromise House and Senate versions the terrorism bill remains a dangerous package. The wiretap proposal is included nearly intact, except for a two-year limit, after which it must be reauthorized. (Ashcroft, not satisfied, is now lobbying Congress to remove that two-year sunset provision with the argument that terrorism will take more than 24 months to extinguish—as if legislators would not review the bill in a heartbeat. What he really objects to is the Congressional oversight that the two-year review would require.) Immigrants still face up to seven days' detention without charge if they are deemed "terrorist suspects."

The greatest danger in the Ashcroft package—and in the post-September 11 climate generally—has received virtually no attention. It is the question of definition. What is terrorism, and what is a terrorist? With the World Trade Center still smoldering, the answer seems obvious. Yet history teaches that the definition of terrorism is very much a matter of time and place and who is doing the talking. As recently as the 1980s, the FBI spied extensively on the Committee in Solidarity with the People of El Salvador and other dissidents from Central America policy under the terrorism rubric. Nelson Mandela's African National Congress was designated a foreign terrorist organization for decades; Bill Clinton rattled the Foggy Bottom establishment by taking Northern Ireland's Sinn Fein off the terrorism list, allowing Gerry Adams a U.S. visa. There are elderly ladies in Tel Aviv who once built letter-bombs for the Haganah.

The point is simply that terrorism is a term of politics rather than legal precision. But in Ashcroft's vision, it appears to be a label to be applied indiscriminately. Ashcroft's initial bill defined terrorism as any violent crime in which financial gain is not the principal motivation. The House adds more precise language: To qualify, crimes or conspiracies must be "calculated to influence or affect the conduct of government by intimidation or coercion or to retaliate against government conduct." Yet even this definition is big enough to drive a parade wagon through. An unruly blockade of the World Trade Organization could bring down the full force of antiterrorism law as easily as could a bombing.

That is the real point. The antiterrorism debate is not just about the WTC/Pentagon attacks, and it involves far more than the language of Ashcroft's package. It is also an attempt to "normalize" entirely new surveillance, intelligence-gathering and arrest powers—measures already employed with increasing vigor against corporate-globalization protesters. It is about a culture of civil liberties, not just law; about what it means, for instance, when the White House spokesman warns *Politically Incorrect*'s Bill Maher and others to "watch what they say" when criticizing U.S. military policy.

The real and elusive threat of future Al Qaeda atrocities is unquestionably a challenge in an open society. It's clear that government needs to utilize all its constitutional powers in realistic protection of the public. But what the Bush Administration is pushing through Congress—though not without resistance—is something different, first named in the 1970s by civil liberties scholar Frank Donner: surveillance "as a mode of governance," rather than as a limited and accountable tool of criminal investigation.

Whatever particulars of the Ashcroft plan pass, we will likely be living under that mode of governance for some time.

October 3, 2001
A Peaceful Justice?
Liza Featherstone

"We need to make it very clear," said one veteran activist at a recent meeting of a nascent New York City antiwar coalition, "that we want to punish the criminals." She meant, of course, any living accomplices in the September 11 World Trade Center massacre. That night, activists were unable to come to any kind of agreement on the need to bring the murderers to justice, and their confusion and division mirrored that of antiwar demonstrators around the nation. During the last weekend in September, antiwar protests in the nation's capital underscored the movement's difficulty in articulating a message that might make sense to a broader public. That difficulty was amplified by the happy fact that, as one demonstrator put it, "it's hard to protest a war that's not happening." While things may yet get brutal, George Bush is not presently proposing to take any military action against innocent Afghan civilians, and the Administration is now seriously considering schemes that, when suggested by peace activists a week ago, sounded absurdly whimsical—like "bombing" Afghanistan with food.

Originally, more than 10,000 foot soldiers of the global economic justice movement, from the controversial hooded Anti-Capitalist Convergence (or "Black Bloc") to the AFL-CIO, had planned to show up to protest September 30's IMF/World Bank meeting. That meeting was canceled. Most protest groups canceled their actions too, and not only because there were no meetings to oppose. At a moment of sorrow and panic, demonstrators risked being ignored—or worse, reviled as unpatriotic or insensitive to the memories of the dead. In a statement explaining their withdrawal from the protests, United Students Against Sweatshops declared September in the capital "neither the time nor the place to gather in opposition."

Not everyone felt that way. The Anti-Capitalist Convergence decided to hold an antiwar demonstration Saturday morning, using, according to David Graeber of New York City's Direct Action Network, who works closely with the ACC, "less controversial tactics. None of these," he laughed, pointing to a brick in the middle of the sidewalk. The Black Bloc anarchists, known for illegal actions, refrained from any destruction of property, and the weekend ended with only eleven arrests. The ACC march drew about 1,000 (organizers claimed 2,000–3,000). Some—being anarchists—rejected any action that the state might take, even against terrorism, and rejected any international tribunal as a tool of the state.

The second, and best-publicized, march was organized by an antiwar front group assembled by the International Action Center (IAC), in turn a front for (if you're still following) the Workers World Party, which is justly reviled for supporting Slobodan Milosevic, among other gruesome dictators. Still, a few thousand people, from high school students to graying peaceniks, eventually joined by the ACC, showed up. IAC organizers subjected these demonstrators to three hours of speeches, none of which mentioned bringing the killers to justice, before the all-too-brief march from Freedom Plaza to the Capitol began. Bland sloganeering and predictable references to eclectic causes (Free Mumia!) had the effect of reducing the peril of World War III to the trivial status of another pet left crusade. There was no doubt about the sincerity of the demonstrators, who carried signs like ANOTHER ALASKAN FOR PEACE, but the IAC's involvement gave the event—which drew maybe 7,000 at its peak, though organizers claimed 20,000—the flavor of a kind of generic McProtest.

The third march, held on Sunday and organized by the Washington Peace Center and other groups, was smaller than the IAC event but achieved an appropriately serious tone. Some of Saturday's demonstrators (from the well-behaved Black Bloc to the Bread and Puppet Theater) turned up, along with many locals—a crowd of some 3,000. Speakers, many of them clergy, quoted venerable sources: the Bible, the Koran, the Talmud, Martin Luther King Jr. and Gandhi. Signs often bore scriptural messages, and one playfully queried GEORGE BUSH, WWJD? Speakers read letters from family members of September 11 victims who did not want war in the name of their loved ones. Others stressed the need for reflection and the challenges of turning our grief into a cry for global peace. The event also suggested some practical alternatives to war, emphasizing justice and law over military force. Alan Mattlage, an organizer of the Washington Peace Center event and a member of the Maryland Green Party, echoed many of his fellow protesters in saying that the World Trade Center attacks should be treated not "as an act of war but as a criminal matter. [Those accused] should be tried before an international tribunal."

All three antiwar marches attracted activists who had planned to protest the IMF. Students showed up in large numbers (a nationwide network of more than 150 student antiwar groups, some calling themselves Students for a Peaceful Justice, has been holding campus vigils, protests and teach-ins). Labor organizations, by contrast, from the AFL-CIO to Jobs with Justice, were conspicuously absent. That makes some sense, given that many of their constituents may support military responses to the September 11 attacks. One of countless reasons to hope for peace is that a prolonged war—and antiwar activism—could test the warm solidarity developed in recent years between labor and other progressives, especially students. On the other hand, it's encouraging to see how quickly the global economic justice movement has embraced peace and security issues—and that peace organizations seem ready to tackle the economic roots of violence and to connect U.S. militarism to global economic inequality.

Activists were united on a few points: There will be no peace without economic justice, and U.S. civilians will not be safe until our government stops waging—and funding—war on other innocents. Some offered hope that our nation's suffering could open our eyes to the rest of the world's pain. At an interfaith service on peace and justice at St. Aloysius Church Saturday night, Njoki Njoroge Njehu of the 50 Years Is Enough Network advised Americans to "hold that vulnerability, to understand how people around the world live with U.S. violence. And let us finally understand the obscenity of the phrase 'collateral damage.' Will it ever have the same casual reference again?"

October 10, 2001: Editorial
The Limits of War

The war in Afghanistan, coming after the atrocities of September 11, provokes a welter of contradictory emotions. On the one side, a desire for justice and a yearning for security. And on the other side, dread of a war unrestrained by national boundaries, time frame or definable goals.

We believe that America has a right to act in self-defense, including military action, in response to a vicious, deadly attack on U.S. soil by a terrorist network identified with Osama bin Laden. There is a real threat of further attacks, so, as Richard Falk argues, action designed to hunt down members of the terrorist network and those in the Taliban government who collaborate with it is appropriate.

But acknowledging a right of response is by no means an endorsement of unlimited force. We must act effectively but within a framework of moral and legal restraint. Our concern is that airstrikes and other military actions may not accomplish the ends we endorse and may exacerbate the situation, kindling unrest in other countries and leading to a wider war. They have already triggered bloody riots in Pakistan and Indonesia and on the West Bank, where the cease-fire is in shreds.

This effort ideally should have been carried out under the aegis of the United Nations Security Council and bin Laden and his associates brought to justice for their crimes by an international court. The United States should still seek a mandate from the Security Council for its military actions. This would give the campaign the international legitimacy it needs to avoid playing into the hands of those charging an American war against Islam, and it would offer some protection against the calamity of a wider and uncontrolled war. It would also help strengthen the UN's policing and peacekeeping capacity.

If limited military action in self-defense against bin Laden and his backers and cohorts is justified, an open-ended "crusade" against pariah nations to stamp out ill-defined evil is not. There are already ominous rumblings in the

Pentagon that such interventions are contemplated. The Administration has notified the Security Council that it might pursue terrorists in other nations. This may be more of a threat than a promise, especially as it pertains to the Philippines and Indonesia. But it is no secret that hard-liners hanker to expand the war to include strikes against Iraq, Iran, Syria and other hard cases.

Military actions inside Afghanistan must be circumscribed by limited political objectives and carried out with a minimum of civilian casualties. The report of the killing of four Afghan UN employees (engaged in clearing the deadly harvest of mines sowed by two decades of war in that nation) in the second day's bombing underscores the potential costs when vast firepower is unleashed against a poor nation with comparatively few military targets. As civilian casualties mount and more refugees are driven from their homes, international support for the U.S. effort will dwindle.

The U.S. air war has already magnified humanitarian problems that call for urgent attention. In addition to 7.5 million Afghans facing famine before the war, which has interrupted overland shipments of food, half a million refugees have fled the bombing. American cargo planes dropping 37,000 box lunches cannot mitigate this problem, so U.S. contributions to international agencies giving food and medical aid must be stepped up. With fleeing Afghans massing at border chokepoints, the Pakistani government should be pressured to allow aid to go through. The UN, with U.S. assistance, must expand the number of camps that will take in the uprooted.

Also looming in Afghanistan is the prospect of the Taliban government falling and leaving a power vacuum, into which rush the furies of anarchy and civil war. The UN should immediately convene a coalition of opposition groups (including those representing Afghan women) in an attempt to ease the transition to a new government that is broadly representative of the Afghan people.

Here in America, responsible members of Congress should demand clarification of the Administration's goals in this war and oppose the President's attempts to curtail Congressional oversight of the conflict. In this regard, we hope that the courageous statement of Representative Jim McDermott that the Administration lacked a "fully developed and comprehensive strategic plan" will hearten more of his fellow Democrats to engage in similar scrutiny. And let us also praise Senator Russell Feingold for at least slowing down an antiterrorism package that the Senate leadership was trying to rush through Congress by severe limiting amendments or debate.

As the fog of national security closes in Washington, the press must resume its appropriate watchdog role. Civil liberties groups should stay on high alert, flashing early warnings against unconstitutional laws and violations of civil rights—especially those of innocent aliens apprehended in early antiterrorist sweeps.

As we have said before, military means are only one weapon in the fight against terrorism—and a very limited one. Of greater importance are diplomatic, law enforcement and intelligence efforts. Beyond those, instead of more U.S. military attacks we need a multinational coalition dedicated to attacking the conditions breeding terrorism—the endless Israel-Palestine conflict, the corruption of U.S.-supported Arab regimes, the world inequality and poverty spawned by globalization. And on another front, as Jonathan Schell warns, the question of weapons of mass destruction has acquired a new salience as a result of the recent events. Nuclear disarmament, a test ban and stronger nonproliferation measures are sorely needed. We should not let the military action overshadow these greater challenges.

As Schell writes, "The world is sick. It cannot be cured with America's new war. The ways of peace—adopted not as a distant goal but as a practical necessity in the present—are the only cure."

October 17, 2001: Editorial
Call in the UN

This year the Nobel Peace Prize committee got it stunningly right when it honored the United Nations and Secretary General Kofi Annan. For all its bureaucratic and political timidity, the UN has kept alive and vital the idea of collective action for peace by the nations of the world that was central to its founding—an idea of particular importance right now as the world struggles to find a way to deal with terrorism. Despite being handicapped by U.S. indifference, if not hostility, it has made a major contribution in places like East Timor and Cambodia and has galvanized international action on problems like small arms and AIDS.

Central to the UN's renewed credibility on the world stage has been the leadership of Kofi Annan, which has elevated morale within the organization and won the trust of its 189 fractious members. Annan has exhibited a talent for soothing the tender egos of potentates and chieftains jealous of their sovereignty—including the U.S. Congress, whose members he charmed into paying up a portion of America's back dues.

Of course, much of what the UN has accomplished in recent years has been in spite of the United States, which has used it to advance parochial interests or dumped it whenever it wanted to act unilaterally. This do-it-our-way-or-we're-picking-up-our-marbles relationship is unworthy of the UN's importance. It is also contrary to America's national interest.

U.S. foreign policy would be better served if Washington let the UN be a moral as well as a practical guide to American diplomacy. As Washington has discovered, the battle against terrorism is also a battle for the political soul of millions in the Arab and Islamic worlds. Conferences like the recent one in Durban, on racism, tell us just how out of touch America is with the sentiments of many people around the globe.

Now with the bombing in Afghanistan sparking upheavals in the Muslim world and threatening to create a humanitarian crisis, the need for Washington to work with and through the UN has never been more compelling. The allies need a large blue UN umbrella to counter Muslim charges of a U.S. holy war against Islam. Significantly, Iran, a theocracy at odds with America, endorsed the concept of a UN-led fight against terrorism and offered assistance in rescuing downed U.S. fliers. UN participation is essential to preserving a broad coalition against terrorism, and even George W. Bush admits that the UN has a role to play in planning for reconstruction in Afghanistan. Washington should throw full support behind Annan's seasoned special representative for Afghanistan, Lakhdar Brahimi. But the real test of Washington's newfound appreciation of the UN is whether America will provide the resources the UN needs to carry out its mission.

Even more urgent is action on the humanitarian front, as Afghans flee their homes and food supplies dwindle. Here the call by UN human rights commissioner Mary Robinson for a pause in the bombing to permit a massive international relief effort before the imminent arrival of winter makes great sense. The U.S. should heed Robinson's call, simultaneously advancing a political vision for Afghanistan in which the UN plays the leading role. Preventing widespread starvation should be a major concern of the United States and its allies. If it is not, all the claimed moral and legal justifications for military action vanish.

October 17, 2001
Anthrax Anxiety
Bruce Shapiro

Jitters are not among the clinical symptoms of anthrax. The spore-borne illness that has so far killed tabloid photo editor Robert Stevens and contaminated dozens of people in media and government is usually treatable with antibiotics and perhaps a follow-up vaccine. But the arrival of those spores threatens to unbalance an already anxious nation. As I write, the story changes hourly. On Tuesday, the anthrax is described as potent—laboratory-grade; on Wednesday it's declared "naturally occurring." Spores are reported in Congressional ventilation ducts; then the report is declared false. The House closes for a five-day sweep, while Tom Daschle—thirty-one of whose staff members are found to have spores in their nasal passages—says the Senate will remain open. Governor Pataki's New York City office tests positive for spores; an infant who visited ABC News contracted the infection. The scale is nothing like the September 11 attacks; but just as the box-cutters made it clear that mass destruction requires neither nuclear weapons nor even machine guns, so the spread of anthrax through envelopes turns upside down James Bond images of nerve gas and death rays.

The people sending those envelopes know what they're doing: infecting first the media, the retinal nerve of democratic perception, before turning to the pols. A nervous press means a nervous public. What is striking about the initial round of white-powder letters is the sophisticated consideration of media dynamics and demographics: the ultratabloid *Sun*, the ultra-respectable *New York Times*; old-media Tom Brokaw, dot-com Microsoft. (Some militia-watchers theorize that the anthrax is coming from McVeigh type scaremongers piggybacking the current crisis. But the circumstantial evidence—particularly the fact that one of the first letters went to the *Times*'s Middle East and terrorism specialist, Judith Miller—does suggest Al Qaeda adherents, as does the apparent purity of the strain.)

A few things about the anthrax scare need to be said. First, at its current scale—with doctors nationwide now on the lookout for anthrax symp-toms—it is indeed a scare rather than a medical nightmare. Second, should the number of cases or the distribution of spores grow more widespread, the greatest danger comes not from the easily treatable disease but from the long degradation of the nation's public-health infrastructure. For the past twenty years, Republicans and Democrats alike have regarded public health, and any excess capacity in the healthcare system, as an insult to the free market. In large cities, public hospitals have been closed and privatized and community clinics converted to bottom-line-driven HMOs. Under-staffed and underfunded city and state health departments track illness with out-of-date computer software; 10 percent of local health departments don't even have e-mail. Last year, the federal government spent less than $50 million on improving state and local public health infrastructure—a piddling amount when spread among fifty states.

It's a problem not just of funding but of management philosophy—one that has left the public less protected from epidemics and terrorism than a decade ago. "One of the responses to financial pressures has been to cut out excess capacity," Tara O'Toole, MD, of the Johns Hopkins Center for Civil-ian Biodefense Studies testified in July before the Senate's internal security subcommittee. "The entire hospital in virtually every town in this country, whether it's the Johns Hopkins Medical Center or a small rural hospital, is basically now functioning on 'just in time' models. The number of nurses that are going to be working at Hopkins tomorrow is based upon the number of patients in the hospital today, likewise for supplies, for antibiotics, for what have you. . . . Few, if any, hospitals in America today could handle a hundred patients suddenly demanding care." Simply put, today's public health system has no surge capacity. After a devastating fire in a high-rise building, the Maryland secretary of health conducted a study of hospitals' preparation for a large number of people needing ventilators, a likely scenario in a biological attack. Though Maryland is home to a major city, sprawling suburbs and two major medical centers, officials found only about 100 ventilators statewide.

The political culture has left public health so far behind that official Washington seems to have taken little notice of the near-complete absence of the nation's top medical officials from the media as the anthrax cases spread. Remember Surgeon General David Satcher? A quick Nexis search reveals only two mentions of Satcher in the scare's first five days. Remember the Centers for Disease Control? Doctors nationwide are complaining that the CDC and its director, Dr. Jeffrey Koplan, are offering only scant information about the detection and treatment protocols for anthrax. For days, the public's only information came from Attorney General John Ashcroft and HHS Secretary Tommy Thompson—and from Thompson it was often misinformation that infuriated medical professionals. The Bush Administration seems to be applying the same extreme strictures on medical information that it's enforcing at the Pentagon. Researchers say off the record that everyone at CDC is terrified of talking. Johns Hopkins's Tara O'Toole puts it this way: "It is normal in a criminal investigation to withhold information. But this is not a normal situation. The public is panicking. People need information desperately. If there is anything we have learned from past disasters, it is that people do better with more information, even if it is disturbing information."

Biological warfare is not a new threat here. As historian Elizabeth Fenn recounts in her new book *Pox Americana*, George Washington worried that the British would wound his soldiers with arrowheads dipped in smallpox-infected sores, and in 1763 British General Jeffery Amherst approved distribution of smallpox-infected blankets to Indians. *Jane's Intelligence Review* reports 110 alleged cases of biological agents in warfare in this century. What makes today's anthrax cases distinctly threatening is not the sadism and criminality of the attacks. It is the speed with which panic can spread through a mass medium that is itself the center of attack—amid a political culture that for twenty years has refused to regard public health as a bottom-line indicator of national security.

October 17, 2001
Profits of Fear
Marc Siegel

Every closet in my medical office is suddenly filled with samples of Ciprofloxacin, an ordinary antibiotic intended primarily for use with bladder infections. This week, every patient phone call I receive and almost every patient visit to my office includes a request for this antibiotic. Physicians as well as patients are stockpiling the drug. One of my patients returns home to his wife, and she relays to me that instead of reassuring her with news of his normal test results, he instead brags, "I've got it. I've got it," brandishing his hoard of Cipro samples that he must have smuggled from my closet. Another patient calls me from Philadelphia to ask whether she can take Cipro to prevent anthrax. "Not unless you live by a certain building in Boca Raton," I reply. Five minutes later she calls me back frantic—her neighbor is returning from Boca wheeling her possibly contaminated luggage down the hall. "No," I groan. "No Cipro."

Bayer, the Cipro manufacturer, is stoking this frenzy and playing into public hysteria by promoting the drug. The drug reps drop off hundreds of sample cartons at my office without saying what for, though I can see them frowning when they hear me say, "I am not prescribing Cipro for anthrax."

Why Cipro? What the drug company is not telling either patient or doctor is that Cipro was originally tested as an alternative treatment for anthrax only for penicillin-allergic patients. Antibiotics have never been properly tested for prophylaxis, so Cipro's usefulness for prevention is speculative, though there is clearly some rationale for prophylaxing patients with close exposure. But doxycycline, a generic, is just as effective and costs one-tenth of what Cipro costs. A month's supply of Cipro costs more than $300; the equivalent amount of doxy is $32. In fact, there are multiple antibiotics available with similar efficacy, many of which are cheaper.

Which is not to say that any of these antibiotics should be prescribed. Prolonged use of Cipro, for example, without a real treatment target or reasonable endpoint, could cause significant side effects—including diarrhea, rash, colitis, gastrointestinal bleeding and insomnia—in a large population. Insomnia affects 5 percent of Cipro users, a fact that may be of interest to the drug rep for Ambien who follows the Cipro rep into my office to encourage me to prescribe more sleeping pills.

Another problem is drug resistance. Cipro, a milestone drug when it first appeared, has already lost some effectiveness because of excess use over the years and has largely been replaced by other drugs in its class, such as levofloxacin. I worry that continued unnecessary use will further cripple Cipro until people who really need it, for conditions ranging from the most minor kidney infection all the way to life-threatening cystic fibrosis, could find it useless.

Plus, if all the antibiotics stores are used up by a panicking though healthy public, people who really need the drugs for life-threatening conditions may find that they are out of luck. If antibiotic prophylaxis on a small scale does become necessary, then doxycycline or other relatively inexpensive antibiotics will represent a more cost-effective approach.

Most of all, I am concerned about a perpetuation of unsavory sales practices. In contrast to the altruism and heroism that rescue and healthcare workers have shown in the wake of the disaster of September 11, many of them working through the night without sleep or food, a drug company is attaching itself to the exact fear that is crippling us. The well-dressed Cipro rep whose territory includes my office and who plies me with "free lunches" is justifying the fear by pretending that there is a treatment for it. With the drug industry returning to what it knows best, parasitism, we find our dread exploited by a monolith that can't resist an opportunity to make more money.

October 17, 2001
Mugging the ICC
Daphne Eviatar

While the United States has spent the past few weeks imploring other countries to cooperate with our war on terrorism, behind the scenes it's apparently retaining an isolationist agenda. In a particularly ill-timed maneuver, the Administration on September 25 pledged to support the deceptively titled American Servicemembers Protection Act (ASPA), sponsored by Republicans Jesse Helms, Henry Hyde and Tom DeLay.

Although it has largely eluded public attention, ASPA is a slap in the face to the many allies that have spent years struggling to construct a legitimate vehicle for combating the most vicious war crimes, crimes against humanity and genocide. For ASPA not only prohibits all U.S. cooperation with the International Criminal Court (ICC), it suspends military assistance to any non-NATO member (except certain allies like Israel, Japan and Egypt) that joins the court, rejects participation in any UN peacekeeping operations unless the Security Council exempts American soldiers from prosecution by the court and authorizes the President to use "all means necessary" to liberate Americans or allies held by the international tribunal (hence its European nickname, "The Hague Invasion Act").

Until now, the bill might have been dismissed as meaningless venting by a handful of extremists. But the Administration's support gives it a far more sober—and sinister—tone. The Administration signed on after negotiating changes that eliminate some of the original bill's thornier constitutional problems. (The President could now provide military assistance to a country that participates in the ICC if he deems it in the national interest, for example.) But those changes and Bush's support also make it far more likely that this public proclamation opposing an international effort to bring per- petrators of terrorism and genocide to justice will become law.

This obstruction is particularly ironic now, when the United States is insisting on world collaboration against terrorism. But it's also distressing because our government is a signatory to the 1998 Rome treaty that created the court. Although Clinton expressed reservations when he signed it, he at least committed the United States to work toward creating an international court it could support. Even if this Administration won't ratify the treaty in its current form, supporting a bill that undermines a treaty we've already signed and threatening the treaty's supporters is a remarkably underhanded maneuver, given the mask of international cooperation we're now strutting out on the world stage.

Sure, Jesse Helms labels it a "kangaroo court," but keep in mind what the International Criminal Court will be. Hammered out over more than five years by hundreds of international lawyers, scholars and diplomats, including many Americans, the court—which is expected to receive the nec- essary sixty ratifications by next summer—will be a permanent institution based in The Hague equipped to try, in addition to genocide and strictly defined war crimes, just the sort of crime against humanity we saw on Sep- tember 11. Setting aside whether military action is justified to seize the per- petrators, if the court existed today it's possible we could have avoided the issue altogether. An international court holds a legitimacy in the eyes of the international community that a United States court cannot. Even a govern- ment like the Taliban might have a harder time refusing to turn over sus- pected terrorists to an international tribunal than to what it views as suspect U.S. authorities.

Opponents claim the court would place American soldiers and officials at risk of frivolous political prosecutions. That ignores the many elaborate constraints written into the Rome statute. Moreover, the court will be con- trolled by our allies. Right now, we're aligned with countries like Iraq that oppose it. But all NATO members (except Turkey) have signed and most have ratified the treaty, as have most of the nations in the EU, which has announced its intent to ratify, calling it "an essential means of promoting respect for international humanitarian law and human rights." Recently, Great Britain—now our closest ally in the war against terrorism—became the forty-second country to ratify. (Switzerland is the latest to follow suit.)

Republicans have whipped up fears that the ICC is a rogue court that would prosecute Americans and deny them due process. But the treaty provides virtually all rights guaranteed by the U.S. Constitution except a jury trial. Notably, the American Bar Association—always sensitive to such concerns and hardly a body of radicals—is a strong ICC supporter.

Given all the statute's safeguards, the only people truly threatened by the International Criminal Court are those who commit genocide, intentional large-scale war crimes or "widespread or systematic" crimes against humanity. The Administration's support for ASPA suggests it wants to raise American officials above international law. This is a bad time to be pressing that point, both on our allies and before our enemies. For if part of what sparks hostility toward the United States is our arrogance, then actively undermining this landmark step toward worldwide enforcement of the rule of law will only fuel it.

October 17, 2001
Second Chance With Russia
Stephen F. Cohen

The monstrous events of September 11 have given the United States a second historic chance, after the squandered opportunity of the 1990s, to establish a truly cooperative relationship with post-Communist Russia. Such a relationship is essential for coping with today's real security dangers, which exceed those of the cold war and make the United States so vulnerable that even it can no longer meaningfully be considered a "superpower." Indeed, both the decay of Russia's nuclear infrastructure since 1992 and the "low-tech, high-concept" attacks on America in September may be omens of an unprecedented dark age of international insecurity. None of its dangers can be dealt with effectively without Russia, the world's only other fully nuclearized country and its largest crossroad of civilizations.

President Vladimir Putin's agreement to cooperate with Washington's military campaign against terrorism, specifically in neighboring Afghanistan, opens the way to such a relationship, but it will require major revisions in U.S. policies that existed before September 11. Those unwise steps had led to a Russia seething with anti-American sentiment and a cold peace between the former cold war rivals. They included the Clinton Administration's policies of virtually imposing shock-therapy economic measures, along with crushing foreign debt, on Moscow in the name of "reform"; violating a U.S. promise to the Kremlin in 1990–91 not to expand NATO eastward; and bombing Serbia, Russia's fellow Slav nation.

During its first eight months in office, the Bush Administration also based its policy on the prevailing myopic notion that "Russia no longer matters." Disdaining serious negotiations with Moscow, it declared its intention to push NATO all the way to Russia's borders by including the former Soviet republics of Lithuania, Latvia and Estonia, and to unilaterally abrogate the 1972 Anti–Ballistic Missile Treaty, which Moscow considers vital to its nuclear security.

Despite grudging applause for Putin's decision to participate in the U.S. antiterrorism campaign, there is no sign of any American official or media rethinking of these policies. (It does not seem to matter, for instance, that since September 11 Russia has become more important to U.S. objectives than are most NATO members.) There are instead reaffirmations of those policies and dire editorial warnings against making any substantial concessions in return for Moscow's participation, particularly in regard to the Kremlin's brutal war in Chechnya.

But it is unlikely that Putin can stay the American course against terrorism without significant U.S. concessions, if only because he is surrounded by political elites deeply distrustful of Washington and unhappy with his decision. They are already reminding him of the despised "Gorbachev-Yeltsin syndrome"—a pattern of far-reaching Russian concessions in the

1980s and 1990s that were met only by broken Western promises and aggrandizement. They are warning, for example, that the Bush Administration will transform permission to use bases in Uzbekistan into a permanent U.S. military presence in former Soviet Central Asia; exploit Russian assistance in Afghanistan to install a pro-American regime in Kabul; and use the "coalition" to settle accounts with Iraq, a move long opposed by Moscow.

Nor is a softening of U.S. opposition to the Chechen war, which has always been mostly rhetorical, high on Putin's list of needed concessions. Of much greater importance are NATO expansion (few people on either side take seriously the talk of Russian membership), the ABM treaty and Moscow's inability to invest in its ravaged economy and impoverished people while servicing its foreign debt of some $165 billion.

U.S. policy changes on all three issues are both necessary and desirable. Can we really expect Moscow to support NATO's war against terrorism while that same cold war alliance is creeping toward Russia? Can we expect Moscow, whose defense budget is only some 15 percent of Washington's, to bear the costs of military cooperation in Afghanistan and possibly elsewhere without debt relief? And can the White House ask the Kremlin to trust its intentions after the United States no longer needs Russian help while continuing to refuse to negotiate on missile defense and the ABM Treaty?

Still more, all of these "concessions" would be in America's long-term national interest. A Russia whose Western borders are menaced by NATO, whose nuclear security is undermined by U.S. strategic unilateralism and whose economy is in bondage to Western debt will eventually respond by doing what the United States should hope it will not do—by seeking reliable allies in the East, by further overloading its decrepit nuclear infrastructures with more weapons and by selling more arms to states Washington has accused of sponsoring terrorism.

Thus the events of September 11 confront George W. Bush with not one but two historic challenges—to defend America from unprecedented dangers and to develop an unprecedented relationship with Russia. Properly understood, they are inseparable.

October 17, 2001
Profiles in Cowardice
Victor Navasky

My three favorite media stories in recent weeks were how Bill "Politically Incorrect" Maher kept his job at ABC-TV, how Ann Coulter got herself fired from *National Review* and how all the networks simultaneously agreed to the Bush Administration's request that they suppress any future Osama bin Laden tapes.

I also got a kick out of the Dan Rather interview on a cable channel in which he answered questions about whether it's OK for a network in the interests of objectivity to ban anchors from wearing American flags on their lapels, while a simulated American flag flew in the logo on the lower left-hand corner of the screen. (Rather himself prefers not to wear a flag but said nothing about appearing with a flag logo in the lower left-hand corner.)

Bill Maher got into trouble on *Politically Incorrect* when he correctly observed in the aftermath of September 11 that it's wrong to call the suicide bombers "cowards" and impolitically added, "We have been the cowards, lobbing cruise missiles from 2,000 miles away: That's cowardly. Staying in the airplane when it hits the building, say what you want about it, it's not cowardly."

Two advertisers, Sears and Federal Express, pulled their ads, seventeen stations canceled his program and Maher apologized for being, well, politically incorrect. Or rather for being misinterpreted ("I offer my apologies for anyone who took it wrong," he said), although why he should apologize to people who misinterpreted him he never explained. The defecting advertisers claimed patriotism, but in fact they were the cowards for withdrawing ads from fear of the controversy Maher's remarks might spark.

So what do we learn from this first profile in cowardice? Maher demonstrated that at best he is only incorrect within permissible limits. The advertisers should come back, the seventeen stations should reinstall the show (if they haven't already) and Maher should resign, not for what he said but for flying under false colors. You can't have a show called *Politically Incorrect* and then abjectly apologize for not being PC.

Next case. Ann Coulter, rudely dismissed by the *Boston Globe*'s Alex Beam as "a right-wing telebimbo" for her colorful but intemperate attacks on the Clintons, was fired by *National Review* after she wrote in *National Review Online* that "we should invade their countries, kill their leaders and convert them to Christianity." My question is, In which order?

Technically, they didn't give her the boot until she wrote a follow-up about requiring passports from "suspicious-looking swarthy males." Now there are two possibilities here: One is that *National Review* fired her because they didn't like what she said. The other is that *National Review* fired her because by saying what too many *National Review* readers believe, she embarrassed the home team. Solution: After Maher apologizes for apologizing and resigns, *Politically Incorrect* should hire the truly politically incorrect Coulter.

Finally, on the networks, I don't understand why Condoleezza Rice didn't include Al Jazeera in the request to suppress the bin Laden tapes. It's true that Washington doesn't control the Qatar network, but it doesn't control the major U.S. networks either, and surely Al Jazeera has a higher quotient of terrorist viewers. Originally, I thought the Administration's request had to do with not showing enemy propaganda, and I wondered whether this meant that the networks' much-vaunted claims of political neutrality—giving equal time to both sides in a dispute—stopped at the water's edge. But the Administration said the issue had to do less with propaganda than with national security, claiming that bin Laden might be using the occasion to send a message by secret code.

Since potential terrorists can still get bin Laden's message via Al Jazeera and via the Internet, I am baffled as to the networks' true motives, unless, like Maher, his advertisers and *National Review*, they are also in the controversy-avoidance business.

What this incident does show is that you don't need media concentration to have homogenization of the news. The simultaneous capitulation of all the major TV networks proves that concentration or no concentration, they are perfectly capable of marching in lockstep on their own.

October 17, 2001
The Secret War to Come
David Corn

What if they waged a war, and there was nothing to see?

When the first missiles of President Bush's war on terrorism were launched, television screens displayed night-green fuzz occasionally interrupted by white bursts. Little could be discerned, but still, it was something to watch. Bush and his aides repeatedly say that much of the new war will be mounted in secrecy. In other words, no pictures, no words. After the present campaign in Afghanistan ends—or, conceivably, while it continues—military and paramilitary action presumably will occur there and elsewhere without the knowledge of American citizens. This could be the start of a yearslong effort in which the government will attempt to keep significant aspects of war out of sight and unacknowledged. Though past administrations have engaged in clandestine warfare, Bush is leading the country into new turf. This will present the President, the press and especially other politicians with assorted challenges.

How will Bush demonstrate that he is waging his war successfully? He will hail diplomatic initiatives, humanitarian efforts, bureaucratic reorganizations, improvements in border security and moves that freeze the funds of terrorists. There might occasionally be arrests to announce. But White House briefings are unlikely to cover operations mounted by intelligence agencies and the special forces, the highly secretive military units, numbering 40,000 or so troops, that are expected to play a leading role in the new war. If a Navy SEAL team manages to sneak into a Manila apartment building and kill the leader of an Al Qaeda cell (and, say, a neighbor or two), that is not a victory that will be celebrated in a White House press release. To keep voters behind him, Bush may have to tell part of the secret story at some point (assuming there's success to cite). In the meantime, the Bush crowd will try to maintain a tight lid on information, an act that—coincidence or not—will enable it to better control the public image of the war.

A state of war will intensify the Bush crew's stronger-than-average penchant for information management. This Administration is a direct descendant of the White House that in 1991 strove mightily to curtail media coverage of the Gulf War. Before bombs fell on Afghanistan, Secretary of State Colin Powell indicated that the Administration would release unclassified material to present the case against Osama bin Laden, but the White House shot down that idea. (British Prime Minister Tony Blair then issued such a white paper.) Days later, Bush ordered senior Administration officials to limit classified briefings on Capitol Hill to eight senior lawmakers. After senators and representatives threw a fit, the White House defended the decision by accusing legislators of leaking, but then backed off. Nevertheless, the White House noted that members of relevant committees would hear only about past operations or those happening at the moment, not actions scheduled to occur.

Although legislators howled about Bush's attempt to shut them out, their desire to audit this war closely is open to question. In years past, Congressional oversight of covert actions has not been assiduous. "A lot of oversight is informal," notes Loch Johnson, a former aide to a House intelligence subcommittee. "If you have ten overseers [on a committee], maybe you will have two or three who are go-getters. And it's difficult for them to know what questions to ask." Previous administrations have given the intelligence committees the slip. In 1985, for instance, the CIA was involved—in a wink-and-nod way—with Saudi intelligence in an assassination plot against a prominent terrorist supporter in Lebanon. A car bomb exploded in a Beirut suburb, killing eighty people but not the target. CIA chief William Casey did not report this to the intelligence committees.

Under existing law, when the President orders covert action he must give Congress (the intelligence committees or a smaller group of lawmakers) a written "finding," which outlines the operation in a "timely" fashion. Legislators cannot veto the mission. They can merely argue against it. Over the years, disputes have occurred over what constitutes "timely," and findings can be broad, leaving out significant particulars. It is possible—experts disagree on this point—that Bush, acting as Commander in Chief in wartime, might have authority to wage covert military actions without informing Congress.

Applying checks on Bush's secret war will be tough for Congress. Consider this scenario: During a classified briefing, a lawmaker is provided information leading him or her to conclude that the President has lied to the public about the war. "It puts the member in a very difficult spot," notes Lee Hamilton, a former chairman of the House Intelligence Committee. "I wrestled with situations like that several times. Under Congressional rules, you're not allowed to reveal classified information." A member is permitted to say anything on the House or Senate floor, free of penalty, yet that's a step rarely taken. "I tried to work it out in a behind-the-scenes way," Hamilton says. "Any President will use his power of information for his own purposes. And during a war, all the cards are with the executive branch. Congress cannot stop covert actions. In the long run, it can limit funds. In the short term, the President can do basically what he wants."

If Bush wishes to maintain public support for an unseen war, it will be in his interest to keep the large egos of Congress somewhat in the know and on his side. But in the past, secret warriors in the White House have maneuvered to remain unburdened by Congressional busybodies. The overseers of Congress ought to bear in mind that the Bush White House hired Elliott Abrams for a senior National Security Council post, showing little concern that he pleaded guilty to misleading Congress during the Iran/contra scandal. And the Administration has contemplated handing an NSC post to Duane "Dewey" Clarridge, a former CIA counterterrorism official indicted for lying to Iran/contra Congressional investigators. Both Clarridge and Abrams were pardoned by Bush I.

Few precedents suggest that Congress can effectively monitor an extensive secret war. No legislators are speaking in public yet about how to supervise such an endeavor. "We've mainly been reacting to events and not looking too far ahead," says an aide to one prominent liberal Democratic senator. Another such aide remarks, "My guy is concerned but hasn't thought about what to do. There's a fine line between what's appropriate to be kept secret and what's not." One intelligence committee aide notes, "Congress is just beginning to wonder about how to oversee a secret war." There is one certainty: It will be awfully difficult for any lawmaker to confront the White House regarding its handling of such a war. The don't-rock-the-boat tradition in Congress—particularly the Senate—is most powerful regarding classified matters.

Despite the Administration briefings, most members may not be informed enough to challenge the White House, since legislators who don't serve on key committees—a majority of Congress—will likely be shut out of the information flow. "After Afghanistan, we may never know what's going on," says a House Democrat who does not serve on the relevant committees. "Some of us are trying to figure out how to make clear that we want information. We don't know yet how to do it. Dick Gephardt is not laying out a Democratic strategy or thinking about how to be a loyal opposition. When the war started I was in my district and people said to me, 'Don't they need you back in Washington?' It was embarrassing to say, 'No, I don't know anything, and I'm not needed there.'"

Left-in-the-dark lawmakers won't be able to turn to the media for help, because a secret war serves up problems for the news business too. If there is another reality, separate from the White House version, will the press be able to discover it? Like Congress, the media do not boast a strong track record in keeping tabs on White House secret wars—like the preparations for the 1961 Bay of Pigs invasion, the secret war in Laos in that same decade and the Reagan Administration's covert war against Nicaragua. On the other hand, cable networks crave One Big Story these days and have ratings incentives to pursue details of the secret war. The Internet makes it harder for media organizations to sit on information they might be queasy about publishing. Still, major news outfits will probably have trouble establishing a fix on this planetwide war and regularly penetrating the world of clandestine conflict.

As Bush's war on terrorism proceeds, how can the public be confident that what is being done in its name, with its tax dollars, is reasonable? Can it depend upon Congress to monitor the war thoroughly and to withhold funds if the secret war goes awry? Probably not. Can it rely on journalists to unearth the full truth of this war? That may be asking too much. The public will probably not be supplied the information necessary to evaluate the war's conduct. That will be one more uncertainty of life post-9/11. As Bush said recently, "All of us are going to have to adjust."

October 24, 2001: Editorial
Big Pharma's Payoff

Talk about good times for Washington's mercenary culture. Even as officials scrambled to explain why they had not acted more quickly to protect postal workers from anthrax contamination—or to deal with the public's fears regarding the disease—they were showing solicitous concern for Bayer, the maker of the anthrax-fighting antibiotic Cipro.

Faced with the choice of protecting public health or protecting a corporation's intellectual property, Health and Human Services Secretary Tommy Thompson instinctively chose to stand by Bayer, whose Cipro patent doesn't expire until late 2003. Never mind that it could take Bayer twenty months, working nonstop, to meet the government's target of a sixty-day supply for 12 million people, while generic drug companies say they could jointly reach that goal in three months. Initially, Thompson said he had no authority to override Bayer's patent, and it was only after public and Congressional criticism that he used his leverage to force Bayer to reduce its price for Cipro. Of course, if Thompson were to invoke federal law allowing the compulsory licensing of Bayer's Cipro patent to meet the current emergency (paying the company a fair royalty), he would be hard-pressed to keep arguing against similar measures to address the AIDS epidemic in the developing world.

The highly profitable pharmaceutical industry has invested heavily—doubling its campaign contributions between 1996 and 2000 to more than $26 million—to insure that it gets a Congress and Administration friendly to its interests. And it has paid off. In July the House soundly defeated an amendment sponsored by Bernie Sanders that would have allowed U.S. wholesalers and pharmacies to import FDA-approved U.S.-made drugs sold overseas. Given the price differential, such a change could have saved Americans $30 billion or more a year. According to Public Campaign, members who voted to protect Big Pharma from competition received, on average, $9,000 in campaign contributions from that lobby in 1999–2000, compared with $2,800 to members who voted the other way.

Nor are the drug companies alone in enjoying a special level of concern in Washington. Emboldened by Congress's hasty and over-generous bailout of the airlines, leaders of the insurance industry threatened to take the economy down with them if they too weren't promised a multibillion-dollar rescue package. Hollywood wants a tax break to keep it from moving studios abroad. Restaurants and hotels want taxpayers to subsidize 100 percent of the cost of their customers' three-martini lunches and golf junkets. Travel agents, car rental agencies and amusement parks want to give everybody a $500 tax credit to bolster their businesses. And every money-making corporation that ever got caught trying to avoid paying its fair share of taxes now hopes that this is the moment to kill off the alternative minimum tax. Meanwhile, the hundreds of thousands of workers who are out of a job since September 11, or barely hanging on, can't get Congress to extend their unemployment benefits or to help them keep their healthcare.

The lesson for an anxious public wondering whether the government can protect them—from sickness, from joblessness, from being treated as second-class citizens—is that it's time to throw the money-changers out of the temple. While battling terrorism abroad, we must also fight corporate greed here at home.

October 24, 2001
Information Lockdown
Bruce Shapiro

Viewers of the old spy spoof *Get Smart* will remember the Cone of Silence—that giant plastic hair-salon dryer that descended over Maxwell Smart and Control when they held a sensitive conversation. Today, a Cone of Silence has descended over all of Washington: From four-star generals to lowly webmasters, the town is in information lockdown. Never in the nation's history has the flow of information from government to press and public been shut off so comprehensively and quickly as in the weeks following September 11. Much of the shutdown seems to have little to do with preventing future terrorism and everything to do with the Administration's laying down a new across-the-board standard for centralized control of the public's right to know.

The most alarming evidence of the new climate emanates from the Justice Department. Investigators still hold in custody 150 of the 800 people rounded up in the aftermath of the attacks. (One detainee died in custody in New Jersey.) No charges have been filed, no hearings convened. The names of nearly all those still held remain classified, as do the reasons for their incarceration. Lawyers for some of the hundreds cleared and released have told reporters of questionable treatment of their clients—food withheld, attorneys blocked from access. Of the 150 who remain detained, only four presumed Al Qaeda suspects have been publicly named. FBI agents frustrated at the lack of progress in their interrogations of those four now mutter in the *Washington Post* about using sodium pentothal, or turning the suspects over to a country where beatings or other torture is used. The government's stranglehold on information about other arrests makes it impossible to know just how far agents have already gone down that road, or whether the dragnet was mainly a public-relations exercise.

Just as damaging as these detentions is an October 12 memo from Attorney General John Ashcroft reversing longstanding Freedom of Information

Act policies. In 1993 then–Attorney General Janet Reno directed agencies to disclose any government information upon request unless it was "reasonably foreseeable that disclosure would be harmful." Ashcroft reverses this presumption, instead calling on agencies to withhold information whenever the law permits: "You can be assured that the Department of Justice will defend your decisions," he writes. Ashcroft is in effect creating a "born secret" standard; in the words of the Federation of American Scientists, the order "appears to exploit the current circumstances" to turn FOIA into an Official Secrets Act.

One after another, federal agencies are removing public data from their websites or restricting access to their public reading rooms. Caution is understandable, but OMB Watch and Investigative Reporters and Editors have both documented egregious examples that seem at best tangentially related to terrorism and more likely designed as butt-coverage for mid-level bureaucrats. The Energy Department has removed information from its web-posted Occurrence Reporting Program, which provides news of events that could adversely affect public health or worker safety. The EPA removed information from its site about the dangers of chemical accidents and how to prevent them, information the FBI says carries no threat of terrorism. More relevant than Al Qaeda, it appears, was hard lobbying by the chemical industry, which found the site an annoyance. The FAA pulled the plug on long-available lists of its security sanctions against airports around the country—depriving reporters of their only tool for evaluating the agency's considerable failures to enforce its own public safety findings. At the Pentagon, news has been reduced to a trickle far more constricted than anything during Kosovo, which in turn was more restrictive than during the Gulf War. So comprehensive is the shutdown that on October 13, presidents of twenty major journalists' organizations declared in a joint statement that "these restrictions pose dangers to American democracy and prevent American citizens from obtaining the information they need."

In the short run, the Cone of Silence did most damage at the Centers for Disease Control. Could the two (at this writing) Washington, D.C., postal workers who died of inhalation anthrax have been protected by earlier treatment? Did any of the CDC's doctors or scientists recommend a course of antibiotics for postal workers along the trajectory of anthrax-laden letters? Who knows? With the CDC's staff muzzled, the public and postal workers alike were left with politicians as the conduits for contradictory and inadequate information about the risk.

The uncertain dimensions of the Al Qaeda threat make equally uncertain which information the government publishes might contribute to another attack and what to do about it. But it should be noted that the World Trade Center and Pentagon attacks apparently involved data no more confidential than an airline schedule. The Administration's response has been to treat all information and press access as suspect—an approach that will subvert public confidence and undercut legitimate media scrutiny more than it will damage Al Qaeda. During Vietnam, the famous credibility gap resided at the Pentagon, with briefings and Congressional testimony at odds with battlefield evidence. Just weeks into this war, the Bush Administration is risking a new credibility gap roughly the size of the District of Columbia.

October 24, 2001
Working-Class Heroes
Joshua B. Freeman

The September 11 attack on the World Trade Center led journalists and image-makers to rediscover New York's working class. In an extraordinary essay in *Business Week* titled "Real Masters of the Universe," Bruce Nussbaum noted that during the rescue effort, "big, beefy working-class guys became heroes once again, replacing the telegenic financial analysts and techno-billionaires who once had held the nation in thrall." Nussbaum fulsomely praised "men and women making 40 grand a year . . . risking their own lives—to save investment bankers and traders making 10 times that amount." In *The New York Times Magazine*, Verlyn Klinkenborg, describing the construction workers who formed the second wave of rescuers, wrote,

"A city of unsoiled and unroughened hands has learned to love a class of laborers it once tried hard not to notice."

Until September 11, working-class New Yorkers had disappeared from public portrayals and mental maps of Gotham. This contrasted sharply with the more distant past. When World War II ended, New York was palpably a working-class city. Within easy walking distance of what we now call ground zero were myriad sites of blue-collar labor, from a cigarette factory on Water Street to hundreds of small printing firms, to docks where long-shoremen unloaded products from around the world, to commodity markets where the ownership of goods like coffee was not only exchanged, but the products themselves were stored and processed.

Much of what made post-World War II New York great came from the influence of its working class. Workers and their families helped pattern the fabric of the city with their culture, style and worldview. Through political and ethnic organizations, tenant and neighborhood associations and, above all, unions they helped create a social-democratic polity unique in the country in its ambition and achievements. New York City became a laboratory for a social urbanism committed to an expansive welfare state, racial equality and popular access to culture and education.

Over time, though, the influence and social presence of working-class New Yorkers faded, as manufacturing jobs disappeared, suburbanization dispersed city residents and anti-Communism made the language of class unacceptable. Then came the fiscal crisis of the 1970s, which saw a rapid shift of power to the corporate and banking elite. When the city recovered, with an economy and culture ever more skewed toward a narrow but enormously profitable financial sector, working-class New York seemed bleached out by the white light of new money.

The September 11 attack and the response to it have once again made working-class New Yorkers visible and appreciated. Not only were the rescuers working class, but so were most of the victims. They were part of a working class that has changed since 1945, becoming more diverse in occupation, race and ethnicity. Killed that day, along with the fire, police and emergency medical workers, were accountants, clerks, secretaries, restaurant employees, janitors, security guards and electricians. Many financial firm victims, far from being mega-rich, were young traders and technicians, the grunts of the world capital markets.

The newfound appreciation of working-class New York creates an opening for insisting that decisions about rebuilding the city involve all social sectors. Whatever else it was, the World Trade Center was not a complex that grew out of a democratic city-planning process. We need to do better this time. Labor and community groups must be full partners in deciding what should be built and where, how precious public funds are allocated and what kinds of jobs—and job standards—are promoted. Some already have begun pushing for inclusion; others should begin doing so now.

In the coming weeks and months, we need to rethink the economic development strategies of the past half-century, which benefited many New Yorkers but did not serve others well. Might some of the recovery money be better spent on infrastructure support for local manufacturing, rather than on new office towers in lower Manhattan? And perhaps some should go to human capital investment, in schools, public health and much-needed housing, creating a work force and environment that would attract and sustain a variety of economic enterprises.

Winning even a modest voice for working-class New Yorkers in the reconstruction process won't be easy. Already, political and business leaders have called for appointing a rebuilding authority, empowered to circumvent zoning and environmental regulations and normal controls over public spending. The effect would be to deny ordinary citizens any role in shaping the city of the future. As the shameful airline bailout—which allocated no money to laid-off workers—so clearly demonstrated, inside operators with money and connections have the advantage in moments of confusion and urgency.

But altered perceptions of New York may change the usual calculus. On September 11, working-class New Yorkers were the heroes and the victims, giving them a strong moral claim on planning the future. Rightfully, they had that claim on September 10, too, even if few in power acknowledged it. It ought not require mass death to remind us who forms the majority of the city's population and who keeps it functioning, day after day after day.

October 24, 2001
Pro Patria, Pro Mundo
William Greider

A recent *New York Times* headline asked an insinuating question: "After the Attacks, Which Side Is the Left On?" The *Times* should find the nerve to put the same question to the major players of business and finance. Which side is Citigroup on? Or General Electric and Boeing? Where does loyalty reside for those American corporations that have rebranded themselves as "global firms"? Our resurgence of deeply felt patriotism, with official assurances that Americans are all-in-this-together, raises the same question. At a deeper level, the patriotic sense of unity collides with familiar assumptions advanced by the architects and cheerleaders of corporate globalization. The nation-state has been eclipsed, they explain, and no longer has the power to determine its own destiny. The national interest, they assert, now lies in making the world safe for globalizing commerce and capital.

In these threatening times, such claims sound suddenly unpersuasive. Frightened citizens turn naturally to their government for security—the original purpose of the nation-state—and business enterprises do the same. The global corporation, however, intends to have it both ways: American first when that serves its interest, but otherwise aloof from mere nationality. Since these companies are busy waving the flag at the moment, one needs to recall how they described themselves during the past decade, as they dispersed production worldwide and planted their logos in many distant lands. "The United States does not have an automatic call on our resources," a Colgate-Palmolive executive once explained. "There is no mindset that puts this country first."

The much-admired CEO of General Electric, Jack Welch, portrayed GE as a "borderless company," and he brutally enforced the logic. When GE wanted additional cost savings on turbines, jet engines and appliances, it told its U.S. suppliers to pick up and leave, or else—that is, move the jobs to Mexico or other locales where the labor is much cheaper, or GE would find different suppliers. A GE executive in Taiwan once remarked, "The U.S. trade deficit is not the most important thing in my life . . . running an effective business is."

An aerospace executive who supervised McDonnell Douglas's production in China told the *New York Times*: "We're in the business of making money for our shareholders. If we have to put jobs and technology in other countries, then we go ahead and do it." A few years later, McDonnell was swallowed by Boeing, which likewise subscribes to an unsentimental view of national identity. Boeing's on-site manager at the Xian Aircraft Company in China, where $60-a-month machinists make tail sections for the 737, told me, "We've got suppliers that we've dealt with for fifty years, and we're asking all of them to offload production to China." In addition to the low wages, American firms trade U.S. jobs and technology for access to such burgeoning markets. The U.S. government looks the other way or sometimes even facilitates the transactions.

Then there is Citibank, a pioneer in global banking and now part of the mammoth financial conglomerate called Citigroup. John Reed, Citibank's former CEO, used to complain regularly about the stultifying bank regulations imposed by the United States, and he often threatened to relocate Citibank's headquarters to a more banker-friendly nation. "The United States is the wrong country for an international bank to be based," Reed asserted (though the U.S. government more than once bailed out his bank when it was on the brink of failure). Citibank, it happens, is also a notorious channel for wealthy autocrats trying to spirit ill-gotten fortunes (including drug money) out of their home country ($80–100 million for Raul Salinas, the corrupt brother of Mexico's corrupt former president). Citigroup has lobbied to weaken the new regulatory rules required to halt the flows of terrorist money in the global financial system.

Which side are you on? In the aftermath of September 11, the question was swiftly resolved by the multinational lobbyists who mobbed Washington for handouts. Boeing, the second-largest military contractor, expects to be a big winner from the crisis (never mind the 30,000 workers it is laying off) because Boeing agents, in and out of Congress, are pushing for huge new orders of modified jetliners and cargo transports for the Air Force and Navy. IBM, though the majority of its work force is now non-American, has lined up at the trough with Silicon Valley's high-tech firms to lobby for new government subsidies. American International Group, the world's biggest insurer and a leading apostle of unfettered global markets, is out front promoting a new federal safety net for the insurance companies—a bailout that will compel U.S. taxpayers to share in the industry's risks. GE, Citigroup, AIG and other financial-services firms persuaded House Republicans that the U.S. economy should be stimulated by giving them a $21 billion tax break for their overseas operations. When the going gets tough, these guys turn out to be real, red-blooded Americans.

Other Americans will be rightly infuriated as they see the urgent need for national unity exploited for private gain. Activists associated with the Seattle movement might devote some energy to educating other citizens who don't yet grasp the contradiction. But this new crisis exposes much more fundamental issues than corporate hypocrisy. It upends the fictitious premises used to sell the supposed inevitability of corporate-led globalization. Nation-states, at least the largest and strongest ones, have not lost any of their powers to tax and regulate capital and commerce, to control international capital flows and other globalizing practices. In the face of market pressures, major nations simply retreated from exerting those powers. The United States, as principal promoter and defender, led the way. Other advanced economies gradually followed, often reluctantly. Poorer nations, of course, did not have much choice but to go along if they wished to attract investment capital from the wealthy economies.

Now, crisis requires leading governments, especially that of the United States, to do an abrupt about-face and begin to employ their neglected sovereign powers, that is, to intrude purposefully in the marketplace and impose some rules in behalf of society. The most compelling example is the need for new regulatory controls on capital flows in the global financial system in order to smash the terrorists' critical support base—the secretive, cross-border access to money. The global bankers, led by Citigroup, resisted, claiming it's too complicated to trace movements of illicit money. Complexities do exist, but the plain truth is that the United States, joined by a handful of wealthy nations (Germany, Japan, France, Britain and a few others), has the power to shut down any subsidiary banking system in the world that refuses to cooperate—simply by rejecting all money transfers from that country.

Citigroup and other major banks want weak enforcement not because they are soft on terrorism but because they recognize that policing terrorist money can lead to tougher enforcement aimed at their own activities—their profitable role serving wealthy clients in money laundering and the massive tax evasion that occurs through offshore banking. The evasion of national laws is a principal hallmark of the laissez-faire global system, one that governments have lacked the will to confront. The Bush Administration's sincerity will be tested on this issue since it must choose between defending the privileges of international banking and protecting the security of American citizens.

Imposing new forms of accountability on global finance leads ultimately to a much larger question—how to exert moderating controls (and taxation) on the destabilizing surges of capital that have ignited recurring financial crises (and led to massive bailouts by unwitting taxpayers). Only nations have the power to solve this problem. "At some point, we have to ask whether utterly free capital is a benefit to everyone," a financial economist with a leading hedge fund once told me. "Free capital is certainly a benefit to people who own the capital. But they couldn't exist if these governments did not exist to protect them. No one wants to locate the Chicago Board of Trade in Bangkok or Jakarta."

The logic of globalization has led, in fact, to a redefinition of national interest, at least for the United States, in which government policy assumes that advancing the well-being of shareholders and global firms—as opposed to the general population, workers and communities—provides the highest overall benefit. This preferential order is never frankly acknowledged, of course, but it has been embraced by both Democratic and Republican

Presidents. The contradictions for the nation have long been visible, but they were explained away with propagandistic economic claims (much the way authorities ignored obvious contradictions in the stock-market bubble). Over the past twenty-five years, for instance, the wage levels of ordinary working people have been stagnant in real terms as the prime manufacturing jobs moved offshore. Partly in consequence, the United States became a debtor nation—buying more from abroad than it sells and borrowing the money to do so—with accumulated indebtedness that has surpassed 20 percent of GDP. The multinationals claim U.S. trade deficits don't matter—for them, they don't. For the rest of us, this condition has led to a deepening dependence on foreign investors and the potential for an eventual breakdown of the global system itself, when the proud leader and principal consumer in global trade someday taps out.

My point is this: The patriotic tensions generated by war and recession can spawn a rare clarifying moment—the political opportunity to educate and agitate Americans on these deeper contradictions in power between the nation-state and the global system. Inattentive citizens are no longer so passive, but suddenly paying attention to world news. The Seattle movement, as Kevin Danaher of Global Exchange observed, has a potential to connect with a much broader audience, now ready to listen and learn. The teach-in curriculum should begin closer to home, not for narrow nationalistic purposes or to stop globalization but to build support for fundamental change in how globalization proceeds. If the global system is to be reformed—made more humane and democratic, more equitable and respectful of each society's values—the power to achieve those goals belongs only to national governments, not to remote international institutions. For obvious reasons, that power resides especially in the politics of Washington, D.C.

An important first step is to re-establish the nation's sovereign prerogative to legislate its own standards of decency as governing values in global trade. The exercise of national legislative initiatives is not as remote as it may sound. Bipartisan legislation is pending, for instance, to close U.S. markets to goods exported by Burma until that notorious regime halts its forced labor practices (American-in-name-only companies like Unocal are complicit). The measure's leading sponsors are ideological opposites—Senators Jesse Helms and Tom Harkin—who share outrage over the trading system's laissez-faire tolerance of gross human abuses. Their measure, on its face, seems to violate World Trade Organization rules; in fact, the advocates actually hope it will provoke the Burmese generals into filing a formal complaint with the WTO. If the WTO upholds the U.S. law, it would open the way for broader measures of social reform. If the WTO rules against the United States, the indifference to brutality will further discredit the WTO.

Another, similar measure is "right to know" legislation that would require multinationals based in the United States to report the location and conditions of their overseas factories—everything from toxic pollution to health and safety standards to the status of labor rights. The bill does not attempt to set standards of behavior for foreign countries but requires U.S. companies to report the facts to local workers and communities as well as to the U.S. government—information that can stimulate grassroots agitation for change. The measure would establish an important principle: Congress cannot impose American values on others, but it does have the right to impose them on multinationals that call themselves American.

A more ambitious project would be to confront U.S. multinationals on the ambivalent nature of their own patriotism. Air the facts and name the names. If the companies are truly global and without responsibility to this particular nation, then why are U.S. taxpayers expected to subsidize their success and bail them out of failure? The legislative vehicle for forcing a debate on these questions would be recurring amendments to cut off the firms unwilling to accept explicit obligations to nation and citizens. One might describe these measures as "homeland security."

Critical questions about global corporations are no longer abstract propositions. As is already clear from recent actions in Washington, some Americans are regarded as special in crisis—and awarded billions of dollars in protection from malign market forces. Other Americans are told to keep a stiff upper lip. This malformed definition of national unity is ripe for attack by the true patriots.

October 31, 2001: Editorial
War Measured

If September 11 was this generation's Pearl Harbor, the Bush Administration's war on terrorism is still in early 1942, when the news from the front was bad, and the home front was panicky and confused. Now the instant-gratification warriors of the press are rushing in to turn things around. Columnists William Kristol and Charles Krauthammer grumble that the Administration is operating under too many constraints. Impatience with the air campaign has sparked calls by the Sunday morning punditocracy to send in substantial ground troops beyond the small contingent already there. Senator John McCain calls for B-52 carpet-bombing. Polls show a rising number of Americans doubt the war on terrorism will succeed.

Our concern is less about fine points of military strategy than about the possibility that the human and political costs of the war might outweigh any gains in national security and undermine America's moral credibility in the fight against the perpetrators of September 11. The bombing campaign may or may not be militarily effective—who knows, since our only information comes from the Pentagon and Al Jazeera—but civilian casualties are eroding support among coalition allies. TV pictures of devastated neighborhoods and wounded civilians fuel anger against America throughout the Arab and Muslim world and provide rallying cries for extremists, who could destabilize fragile governments in Pakistan, Indonesia and elsewhere. Sketchy reports from inside Afghanistan suggest that the bombing is turning people's loyalty back to the Taliban—making more difficult any covert operations aimed at capturing the "Evil One." It has sent waves of humanity to huddle on Pakistan's closed borders. As winter sets in, as many as 5 million face dire food shortages.

At home, Congress passes a counterterrorism bill "without deliberation and debate," according to Senator Russ Feingold, the lone senator who cast a historic vote against the ill-named PATRIOT Act. The act grants the Feds sweeping powers that break down the firewall between intelligence-gathering and criminal justice. Nothing in the bill would have prevented the disaster of September 11. And yet Bush and House GOP leaders still balk at passing the one measure that could have: federalizing airport security. Meanwhile, the Justice Department continues to resist legitimate requests for information about the 1,107 people it has detained in connection with the September 11 attacks. Civil liberties organizations and others, including this magazine, have filed a Freedom of Information Act request for information about those detained, warning that the government's "official silence prevents any democratic oversight of [its] response to the attacks." The government should comply.

Ultimately, the antiterrorism campaign could have disastrous consequences if America alienates its allies abroad and its people at home. The United States must reassure—by words and deeds—the majority of Muslims who oppose the terrorist attacks that the purpose of U.S. military action is not to punish Afghans for the actions of Osama bin Laden. To this end, it should work more closely with the United Nations by curtailing military actions that hamper relief activities and by supporting UN efforts to build a coalition government that represents all parties in Afghanistan.

Polls show that an overwhelming majority of Americans favor a multilateral effort against terrorists, including working through the UN. Add to this stepped-up international policing efforts that must be the backbone of any global antiterrorism campaign and financial countermeasures that target identifiable terrorist groups. As Jonathan Schell writes, "In a war on terrorism—as distinct from a war on a state—it is politics, not military force, that will probably decide the outcome."

September 17, 2001
The End of Innocence
Joel Rogers

Given my filing deadline, I'm writing this column last Friday morning—

seventy-two hours after the historic, heart-stopping and thoroughly nauseating terrorist attacks on the United States. Like you last Friday, I don't yet know the precise death or injury count, much less what the United States proposes to do in response, or to whom and with what rationale or justice. And like most Americans, I'm still in something of a state of shock—saddened, angry, worried about friends from whom I still haven't heard, worried more about what my country may be about to do to itself and others—if also oddly calmed and focused by what seems clearly the beginning of a long war.

So much has already been said about the events of September 11 that saying more risks saying nothing. And pretending to say something when really nothing can be said can actually obscure the truth, which here is that we now stand before a chasm of political uncertainty the likes of which none of us has even seen before, much less crossed. Tuesday's events clearly change our world, and mostly in bad ways, but having led reason to that precipice they abruptly turn away as guides. Speculating on what comes next is only speculation, at once empty and somehow inappropriate to this moment's sorrow. Nor can it be more than speculation, or should it be, since what comes next should be a political decision made only after a thorough national, and international, debate that has not yet even started.

Despite this, an establishment consensus has already formed on the task at hand. That is to destroy, by root and branch, the terrorist infrastructure that platformed this attack. The "enemy" is not just some group of vengeful maniacs. It also is those governments that support or even tolerate them. Here the current list is long—Iraq, Libya, Sudan, and Syria, as well as Afghanistan, with combined civilian populations of better than 160 million—and may always be extended.

September 11, we are told, did not just remind us of our vulnerability. It also ended the innocence, even wrongness, of living the purposeless peace we briefly did after the end of the cold war. In fact, peace, like freedom, is a constant struggle, which requires an enemy to struggle against. And today the enemy must be named as terrorism, or more broadly as any who might disrupt the spread of "open societies"—characterized by procedural liberty and the free movement of investment, people and goods. To those who would we must now say, in John McCain's latest soundbite, "May God have mercy on you, because we will not."

But it seems to me that all this begs a prior question, which is whether we should accept this definition of our national purpose in the first place—or if not, what other we are prepared to offer in its place. Answering that question requires an extended conversation with ourselves, not just a leap to "get even."

I believe we should insist on that conversation, and insist as well on the relevance of at least two observations not included in the establishment consensus. Both are entered here, I emphasize, without any intended diminution of all the good the United States has done in the world, or any diminution of the inexcusable terror of what has just been done to us.

The first is that our own government, through much of the past fifty years, has been the world's leading "rogue state." Merely listing the plainly illegal or unauthorized uses of force the U.S. was responsible for during the long period of cold war, and continued during the past decade of "purposeless peace"—assassinations, engineered coups, terrorizing police forces, military invasions, "force without war," direct bombings, etc.—would literally take volumes. And behind that list reside the bodies of literally hundreds of thousands, if not millions, of innocents, most of them children, whose lives we have taken without any pretense to justice.

As Amnesty International summarized in the mid-nineties: "Throughout the world, on any given day, a man, woman, or child is likely to be displaced, tortured, killed, or 'disappeared,' at the hands of governments or armed political groups. More often than not, the United States shares the blame."

And as Auden wrote in "September 1, 1939," as World War II commenced:

> I and the public know
> What all schoolchildren learn.
> Those to whom evil is done
> Do evil in return.

That—if only in the tiniest of measures—the immediate relatives and descendants of our own terror now comprise or tolerate a group of maniacs intent upon a similar destruction of innocents in the United States should be mourned, and must enrage, but it cannot shock. And simply doing more now of what we have done in the past cannot be thought a solution to our security problems, much less a guardian of our souls.

The second observation is that any real security depends on the active generation of peace and public safety, not just their protection. It requires institutions more nurturing than the military or police, and arrangements more respectful of human life than the barren rules of an "open society." But for more than a generation now, we have sought public safety in the U.S. more through force than reason, and incarceration more than economic opportunity. And we have sought it abroad through a mindless confidence that "free" markets are the best guarantors of human happiness.

Today we see the fruits of this. At home a prison population that has swollen in that time from a few hundred thousand to better than 2 million, once great cities whose centers have largely rotted out, a society where inequality and privilege stand on their highest peaks in history. Abroad: a community of nations, indeed more procedurally democratic than before, but with less real ability to control their destiny before the amoral workings of profit-seeking capital.

This path too cannot be indefinitely continued if the United States is to be free of the threat of terrorizing violence—whether dressed up as a moral or political crusade or not, whether emanating from abroad or, as more commonly the case so far, from within our own population. The implications of this point apply much more broadly than to airline safety, though they might start even there—where ill-trained and poverty-wage workers now improbably stand as our first line of defense against hijacking, and a deregulated industry operates without enforcement of engine safety standards, with pilots and flight crews often paid little more.

Along with more bodies, I hope that in Tuesday's rubble we also find the ability, as a people, to speak candidly of these things among ourselves. And I do not believe that this hope is irrational. Often, just after the crash of spectacular violence, there is a moment in which there's a collective intake of breath, and quiet interrupts the noise. This is one of those moments. And as awful as what produced it is, we must also make sure that it continues uninterrupted—for however long it takes us as a nation to have that conversation.

(Originally published in *The Capital Times*.)

October 3, 2001
Just Who Are Our Allies in Afghanistan?
Robert Fisk

"America's New War," is what they call it on CNN. And of course, as usual, they've got it wrong. Because in our desire to "bring to justice"—let's remember those words in the coming days—the vicious men who planned the crimes against humanity in New York and Washington last month, we're hiring some well-known rapists and murderers to work for us.

Yes, it's an old war, a dreary routine that we've seen employed around the world for the past three decades. In Vietnam, the Americans wanted to avoid further casualties; so they re-armed and re-trained the South Vietnamese army to be their foot-soldiers. In southern Lebanon, the Israelis used their Lebanese militia thugs to combat the Palestinians and the Hizbollah. The Phalange and the so-called "South Lebanon Army" were supposed to be Israel's foot-soldiers. They failed, but that is in the nature of wars-by-proxy. In Kosovo, we kept our well-armed Nato troops safely out of harm's way while the KLA acted as our foot-soldiers.

And now, without a blush or a swallow of embarrassment, we're about to sign up the so-called "Northern Alliance" in Afghanistan. America's newspapers are saying—without a hint of irony—that they, too, will be our "foot-soldiers" in our war to hunt down/bring to justice/smoke out/eradicate/liquidate Osama bin Laden and the Taliban. U.S. officials—who know full well the whole bloody, rapacious track record of the killers in the "Alliance"—are suggesting in good faith that these are the men who will help us bring democracy to Afghanistan and drive the Taliban and the terrorists out of the country. In fact, we're ready to hire one gang of terrorists—our terrorists—to rid ourselves of another gang of terrorists. What, I wonder, would the dead of New York and Washington think of this?

But first, let's keep the record straight. The atrocities of 11 September were a crime against humanity. The evil men who planned this mass-murder should (repeat: should) be brought to justice. And if that means the end of the Taliban—with their limb-chopping and execution of women and their repressive, obscurantist Saudi-style "justice"—fair enough. The Northern Alliance, the confederacy of warlords, patriots, rapists and torturers who control a northern sliver of Afghanistan, have very definitely not (repeat: not) massacred more than 7,000 innocent civilians in the United States. No, the murderers among them have done their massacres on home turf, in Afghanistan. Just like the Taliban.

Even as the World Trade Centre collapsed in blood and dust, the world mourned the assassination of Ahmed Shah Masood, the courageous and patriotic Lion of Panjshir whose leadership of the Northern Alliance remained the one obstacle to overall Taliban power. Perhaps he was murdered in advance of the slaughter in America, to emasculate America's potential allies in advance of U.S. retaliation. Either way, his proconsulship allowed us to forget the gangs he led.

It permitted us, for example, to ignore Abdul Rashid Dustum, one of the most powerful Alliance gangsters, whose men looted and raped their way through the suburbs of Kabul in the Nineties. They chose girls for forced marriages, murdered their families, all under the eyes of Masood. Dustum had a habit of changing sides, joining the Taliban for bribes and indulging in massacres alongside the Wahhabi gangsters who formed the government of Afghanistan, then returning to the Alliance weeks later.

Then there's Rasoul Sayaf, a Pashtun who originally ran the "Islamic Union for the Freedom of Afghanistan," but whose gunmen tortured Shia families and used their women as sex slaves in a series of human rights abuses between 1992 and 1996. Sure, he's just one of 15 leaders in the

Alliance, but the terrified people of Kabul are chilled to the bone at the thought that these criminals are to be among America's new foot-soldiers.

Urged on by the Americans, the Alliance boys have been meeting with the elderly and sick ex-King Mohamed Zahir Shah, whose claim to have no interest in the monarchy is almost certainly honourable—but whose ambitious grandson may have other plans for Afghanistan. A "loya jerga," we are told, will bring together all tribal groups to elect a transitional government after the formation of a "Supreme Council for the National Unity of Afghanistan." And the old king will be freighted in as a symbol of national unity, a reminder of the good old days before democracy collapsed and communism destroyed the country. And we'll have to forget that King Zahir Shah—though personally likeable, and a saint compared to the Taliban—was no great democrat.

What Afghanistan needs is an international force—not a bunch of ethnic gangs steeped in blood—to re-establish some kind of order. It doesn't have to be a UN force, but it could have Western troops and should be supported by surrounding Muslim nations—though, please God, not the Saudis—and able to restore roads, food supplies and telecommunications. There are still well-educated academics and civil servants in Afghanistan who could help to re-establish the infrastructure of government. In this context, the old king might just be a temporary symbol of unity before a genuinely inter-ethnic government could be created.

But that's not what we're planning. More than 7,000 innocents have been murdered in the USA, and the two million Afghans who have been killed since 1980 don't amount to a hill of beans beside that. Whether or not we send in humanitarian aid, we're pouring more weapons into this starving land, to arm a bunch of gangsters in the hope they'll destroy the Taliban and let us grab bin Laden cost-free.

I have a dark premonition about all this. The "Northern Alliance" will work for us. They'll die for us. And, while they're doing that, we'll try to split the Taliban and cut a deal with their less murderous cronies, offering them a seat in a future government alongside their Alliance enemies. The other Taliban—the guys who won't take the Queen's shilling or Mr. Bush's dollar—will snipe at our men from the mountainside and shoot at our jets and threaten more attacks on the West, with or without bin Laden.

And at some point—always supposing we've installed a puppet government to our liking in Kabul—the Alliance will fall apart and turn against its ethnic enemies or, if we should still be around, against us. Because the Alliance knows that we're not giving them money and guns because we love Afghanistan, or because we want to bring peace to the land, or because we are particularly interested in establishing democracy in south-west Asia. The West is demonstrating its largesse because it wants to destroy America's enemies.

Just remember what happened in 1980 when we backed the brave, ruthless, cruel mujahedin against the Soviet Union. We gave them money and weapons and promised them political support once the Russians left. There was much talk, I recall, of "loya jergas," and even a proposal that the then less elderly king might be trucked back to Afghanistan. And now this is exactly what we are offering once again.

And, dare I ask, how many bin Ladens are serving now among our new and willing foot-soldiers?

America's "new war," indeed.

(Originally published in the *London Independent.*)

DISPATCHES

Articles from around the world on the events
of September 11, 2001

September 19, 2001

Pakistan, the Taliban and the U.S.

Ahmed Rashid

LAHORE

Pakistan's military ruler, Pervez Musharraf, has pledged full cooperation with the United States against terrorism, but Pakistan will need to carry out a U-turn in its policy of support for the Taliban if it is to regain the West's confidence and end its present diplomatic isolation. The stark policy choices the military faces may also require a complete turnaround from twenty years of clandestine support to *jihadi* parties and the growth of a *jihadi* culture, which has sustained its policies in Kashmir and Central Asia.

After having spent the past seven years providing every conceivable form of military, political and financial support to the Taliban, Pakistan is now essentially being asked by Washington to help the U.S. bomb the Taliban leadership, along with their guest Osama bin Laden, and topple the Taliban regime.

In an immediate follow-up to Musharraf's rhetorical pledge to assist the United States in countering international terrorism, President George W. Bush and Secretary of State Colin Powell asked Pakistan to take concrete measures to prove its sincerity. "We thought as we gathered information and as we look at possible sources of the attack it would be useful to point out to the Pakistani leadership at every level that we are looking for and expecting their fullest cooperation," Powell said at a news conference on September 12. A day later, after mentioning Musharraf's message of support, Bush said, "Now we'll just find out what that means, won't we? We will give the Pakistani government a chance to cooperate and to participate as we hunt down those people."

The United States has given the military regime a list of demands in order to facilitate Washington's expected attack on bin Laden. They are believed to include permission for the use of Pakistani airspace for the bombing of bin Laden's camps, an immediate end to Pakistan's supply of fuel and other goods to the Taliban, closure of Pakistan's borders with Afghanistan in order to prevent the escape of Arab militants to Pakistan and the sharing of intelligence with the United States about bin Laden and the Taliban.

The list is clearly only the first step in testing Pakistan's resolve. More demands are almost certain to follow, among them U.S. use of military bases, airports and harbors for the expected military offensive. Washington has asked for a comprehensive report from Pakistan's Inter-Services Intelligence (ISI) about every detail it has on bin Laden, including his contacts with Pakistani extremists, his use of Pakistani militants to carry messages around the world and his hiding places in Afghanistan.

At the same time, Washington has given the ISI a little time—"no more than a week or so," according to Western diplomats—to see if it can persuade the Taliban to hand over bin Laden and dismantle the multinational network of extremists belonging to his Al Qaeda (the Base) organization. Within days of the World Trade Center/Pentagon attacks, senior ISI officers were in Kandahar holding intensive talks with Taliban leader Mullah Mohammed Omar in a bid to convince him that if he does not hand over bin Laden, U.S. strikes will also target the Taliban leadership. The chances of success are bleak, because of the close relationship between Omar and bin Laden. The Taliban have sounded alternately defiant and conciliatory, but on September 15, Omar issued a bellicose statement against the United States, saying the Taliban were ready to defend bin Laden and die. There does appear to be panic in the movement; several ministers in Kabul and commanders in the field have sent their families to Peshawar and Quetta in Pakistan—indicating that they themselves are ready to flee.

Washington is thus for the moment adopting a two-track policy, pressuring Pakistan but at the same time giving it space to absolve itself of its past support for the Taliban and deliver bin Laden, something the ISI has refused to do over the past five years. Since September 11, Musharraf has been huddled with his top generals, giving no public statement of his intentions; in his two brief television appearances he has looked exhausted. After meeting with all his generals, his Cabinet and his National Security Council, the government has only said, without giving details, that it will stand by the United States.

Clearly, Musharraf has every reason to be worried. Pakistan has a 1,560-mile-long border with Afghanistan, and the United States would need Islamabad's full military and intelligence cooperation if it were to launch an attack. But for the past seven years Pakistan has been the main provider of military supplies, fuel and food to the Taliban army, and Pakistani officers have advised the Taliban on their military campaigns. Over the same period, up to 60,000 Pakistani Islamic students, three-quarters of whom were educated in Pakistani *madrassahs*, or religious schools, have fought in Afghanistan for the Taliban. One year ago, when the Taliban captured Taloqan in northeastern Afghanistan, then headquarters of the anti-Taliban United Front, more than sixty Pakistani military officers and a small unit of the Special Services Group—Pakistani commandos—were supporting and advising the Taliban force of 12,000 troops, which included some 4,000 non-Afghan militants.

At present, 3,000–4,000 Pakistani Islamic militants are fighting with the Taliban in their offensive against the anti-Taliban alliance. Thousands of Pakistani and Kashmiri militants also train in Afghanistan for the war in Kashmir. Pakistan's knowledge of the Taliban's military machine, storage facilities, supply lines and leadership hierarchy is total. Pakistan also has the most comprehensive information about the role of foreign militants, their bases and their numbers. The United States is now asking the ISI to turn over all this information to the CIA.

If the army decides to commit fully to Washington, Musharraf will have to do even more. He will have to evacuate Pakistani military advisers from Afghanistan, withdraw Pakistan's recognition of the Taliban regime as the legitimate government of Afghanistan, condemn the Taliban and force them to expel thousands of Pakistani fighters, in addition to a cutoff of fuel and other supplies, at the very moment when they will be preparing to resist a U.S. invasion.

Musharraf will also have to crack down hard on Pakistan's Islamic extremists, who provide bin Laden's Al Qaeda with logistics, communications and other support. He may also be obliged to ban those Pakistani groups, like Harakat ul-Ansar (Volunteers Movement) and Jaish-e-Mohammed (Army of

Mohammed), that are listed by Washington as terrorist organizations and could pose a threat to U.S. forces. The largest Pakistani party fighting in Kashmir, Lashkar-e-Taiba (Army of the Pure), is on the U.S. terrorist watch list. All these groups have received tacit state support in the past; stopping their activities will be a major problem for Musharraf.

If Musharraf decides to fall in line with U.S. policy, he will receive widespread support from the majority of Pakistanis—especially the urban, educated middle class—who are tired of the country's dire economic crisis and the chronic lawlessness largely caused by Islamic extremists, and who are concerned about the rapid "Talibanization" of Pakistani society. In early September neo-Taliban Pakistani groups in the Northwest Frontier Province prevented UNICEF from carrying out a polio immunization campaign for children because they considered it un-Islamic. The same groups have smashed TV sets and forced women to stay at home, as the Taliban have done in Afghanistan.

At the same time, Pakistan could negotiate major concessions from the United States for its support—the lifting of U.S. sanctions against Pakistan imposed in response to Islamabad's 1998 nuclear tests, a partial write-off of the country's $38 billion international debt, more loans from the IMF and the World Bank, greater U.S. pressure on India to settle the Kashmir dispute on terms acceptable to Pakistan, and the re-establishment of a close military and intelligence relationship with the United States to counter Washington's growing military and economic links with New Delhi. However, many Pakistanis fear that the United States may just use Pakistan, as it did in the 1980s against the Soviet Union, and then walk away once the U.S. mission is over, establishing a closer military alliance with India and leaving Pakistan in chaos. That fear is not only expressed by Islamic groups but also by Pakistani liberals.

What the military is most concerned about is a backlash from Islamic parties and conservative Islamicists within the officer corps, who will accuse Musharraf of kowtowing to the Americans. Maulana Samiul Haq, who heads a string of *madrassahs* that many Taliban leaders attended in the early

1990s and that are now attended by Central Asian Islamic militants, has warned Musharraf that there will be a huge public backlash if Pakistan bends to U.S. demands. "I am sure the Pakistani Army will not allow this to happen, and Musharraf will be mindful of the sentiments of his under-command. There will be a strong public backlash also," Haq said on September 14. Haq's provocative comments reflect moves by Islamic fundamentalists to increase pressure on Musharraf from within the army. Several senior generals and former ISI chiefs known for their hard-line Islamic views have been even more provocative, claiming that the attacks in the United States were carried out as part of an Israeli-Jewish conspiracy in league with the CIA in order to give Israel a free hand to crush the Palestinians and defame Muslims.

Musharraf is deeply concerned about U.S. intentions toward the Taliban, and the Pashtun ethnic group in particular, from whom the Taliban are drawn and who straddle the border between Pakistan and Afghanistan, and what the future state of Afghanistan will look like. The United States is likely to target the Taliban leadership and its military formations and encourage an anti-Taliban uprising in the Pashtun belt in the south and east of Afghanistan, which is the Taliban heartland.

There is already growing U.S. and international support for the Loya Jirga (tribal council) peace process in Afghanistan, headed by former King Zahir Shah, now in exile in Rome. The LJ process is almost certain to become the main political alternative for Afghanistan and will probably be backed in coming months by the United States and NATO. Pakistan does not support the LJ and would insist to the United States that Islamabad continue to have a major say in the formation of any future government in Kabul. If Pakistan is fully on board with Washington, Islamabad will be able to influence the outcome of the U.S. attack and may retain influence in determining the future Afghan government. If it balks, Washington is unlikely to listen to Pakistani demands.

Musharraf is between a rock and a hard place, and the way he goes could determine the future viability of the Pakistani state. This is a moment of reckoning for Pakistan. It has to decide whether it wants to be part of the international community or go it alone, at the risk of turning into a pariah nation and possibly even state collapse.

September 19, 2001
Bush and bin Laden
Dilip Hiro

London

With 7,000 employees of the Federal Bureau of Investigation working round the clock and European intelligence agencies actively cooperating with their U.S. counterparts, it is a matter of time before the Bush Administration apprehends the perpetrators of the terrorist atrocities in New York and Washington on September 11.

The U.S. record in such investigations is impressive. The culprits of the explosion in the World Trade Center in February 1993, which killed six, were tracked down and punished. The same fate befell four of those responsible for bombing the U.S. embassies in Kenya and Tanzania in 1998, who were found guilty and given life sentences in New York in July. They were members of Al Qaeda (the Base), an organization headed by Osama bin Laden, the 44-year-old Saudi fugitive hiding in the mountain fastness of Afghanistan, a country administered by the Taliban Islamic movement according to puritanical interpretations of the Sharia (Islamic law) that most Muslims outside Afghanistan find repulsive.

While the Bush Administration pursues its official policy of arresting and trying bin Laden in a U.S. court, however, it must also re-examine its policies in the Middle East: on the Israel-Palestine conflict, on economic sanctions against Iraq, on isolating Iran and on its stationing of U.S. troops and military hardware on the Arabian Peninsula. That is the only sure way to prevent a recurrence of the September 11 tragedy.

In American eyes bin Laden is the epitome of evil. But, sadly and frustratingly, many Afghans and Pakistanis revere him as a veteran of the 1980s anti-

Soviet *jihad* in Afghanistan, which resulted in the expulsion of Soviet troops. He led the Arab section of foreign Muslims—the mujahedeen, based in Pakistan, who numbered 30,000 throughout the decade—in that campaign.

Working closely with the CIA—which embraced the mujahedeen to further its own cold war geopolitical aims—bin Laden collected funds for the *jihad* from affluent Saudi citizens, using hard cash in briefcases instead of banks, because of the poor financial infrastructure of Pakistan. These contacts remained useful to him after he was expelled from Saudi Arabia in 1994.

After most of his and his front companies' cash assets were frozen in the wake of the 1998 bombing of the U.S. embassies in Kenya and Tanzania—in which he was a prime suspect—bin Laden is known to have raised funds by trafficking in heroin and smuggling durable consumer goods from the Persian Gulf port of Dubai into Pakistan, Central Asia and Iran. Instead of using conventional methods of raising and transferring funds through banks, bin Laden and his associates have adopted the informal "hundi" system in vogue in South Asia. A Pakistani or Indian expatriate working in the Gulf hands over his money to a local moneylender, who has agents in Pakistani or Indian towns and villages and who communicates with them through handwritten notes or faxes in coded messages. Last year, for every $27 remitted home by Pakistani workers in the Gulf through the normal banking system, an estimated $100 was transmitted through the hundi system, for a total of $3.7 billion. The hundi system has since been extended to Pakistani immigrants in North America and Britain, thus providing Al Qaeda with greater resources to tap.

The terrorist carnage in New York and Washington gave the hunt for bin Laden greater urgency, but it was already under way. Since the 1998 embassy bombings, he has been at the center of the most thorough intelligence campaign against any individual in recent years. This campaign consists of closely monitoring Afghanistan with U.S. satellites, deploying the most sophisticated eavesdropping equipment to record bin Laden's conversations and using supercomputers to track his bank dealings around the world.

When approached by the Clinton Administration in August 1998 to extradite bin Laden to the United States, Mullah Mohammed Omar, the Taliban regime's chief, said: Pass on the evidence against him to us, and we will prosecute him according to Islamic law; we cannot hand over a pious Muslim to a non-Muslim regime for trial. When the United States failed to do so, the Taliban's supreme judge declared bin Laden innocent. It is the same story now. Bin Laden denies any involvement in the September 11 attacks, and the Taliban regime has made repeated claims that, sitting in Afghanistan, he could not have masterminded a highly complex operation in the United States.

Capturing bin Laden without the cooperation of the Taliban will be no easy task. Let us assume, however, the best-case scenario for the Bush Administration: It captures him, prosecutes him successfully and wins the death penalty from the court. Will that be the end of Al Qaeda, which has an estimated 5,000 members organized in cells in thirty-four countries, from the Philippines to North America—including South Asia, East Africa, the Middle East and North Africa? Not likely.

"I am ready to die for Islam," bin Laden wrote in a letter delivered by hand to Hameed Mir, editor of the Peshawar-based *Ausaf* daily, after the bombings in New York and Washington. "If I am killed there will be 100 bin Ladens." In other words, bin Laden represents a sociopolitical phenomenon rather than a one-man mission. For bin Laden and Al Qaeda, attacking American targets is a means, not an end, which is to bring about the overthrow of the corrupt, pro-Washington regimes in Saudi Arabia, Egypt and Jordan through popular uprisings.

Were the Bush Administration to overreact and perpetrate a slaughter in Afghanistan or another Muslim country, it would likely aggravate the grievances that many Muslims throughout the world nurse against America: its close alliance with Israel against the Palestinians and its immunity to the suffering of Iraqis caused by United Nations sanctions, which have claimed an estimated 500,000 lives in eleven years (the Iraqi authorities put the figure at over 1 million). It might raise the temperature to the point of explosion in some Arab capitals, and thus inadvertently play into the hands of bin Laden and Al Qaeda.

Bin Laden's dispute with the status quo in the Middle East started with his native Saudi Arabia. When Iraqi President Saddam Hussein invaded Kuwait in August 1990 and menaced Saudi Arabia, bin Laden proposed a defense plan, based on popular mobilization, to Saudi King Fahd. It was dismissed outright. Instead, the Saudi monarch invited U.S. troops into the country, despite the argument of bin Laden and others that under Islamic law it was forbidden for foreign, infidel forces to be based in Saudi Arabia under their own flag. They referred to the Prophet Mohammed's words on his deathbed: "Let there be no two religions in Arabia." Their discontent rose when, having liberated Kuwait in March 1991, the Pentagon failed to carry out full withdrawal of its 550,000 troops from the kingdom while the Saudi authorities kept mum on the subject.

Following a truck bombing in June 1996 near the Dhahran air base in Saudi Arabia, which killed nineteen U.S. servicemen, the Saudi authorities grudgingly acknowledged the presence of 5,000 American troops on their soil. This figure is widely believed to be only a quarter to a third of the actual total.

That is when bin Laden, then based in Afghanistan, issued his call for a *jihad* against the Americans in Saudi Arabia. "The presence of the American Crusader forces in Muslim Gulf states . . . is the greatest danger and [poses] the most serious harm, threatening the world's largest oil reserves," he said.

"The ordinary Saudi knows that his country is the largest oil producer in the world, yet at the same time he is suffering from taxes and bad services," he added. "Our country has become a colony of America. The Saudis now know their real enemy is America." Then, taking advantage of the series of crises between Baghdad and Washington on the question of UN weapons inspectors in Iraq, bin Laden widened his political canvas.

"Despite the great devastation inflicted on the Iraqi people by the Crusader-Zionist alliance . . . the Americans are once again trying to repeat the horrific massacres," he said as the leader of the International Islamic Front, consisting of militant organizations from Egypt, Pakistan and Bangladesh, in February 1998. "The Americans' objectives behind these wars are religious and economic; their aim is also to serve the Jews' state, and divert attention away from its occupation of Jerusalem and murder of Muslims there." The eruption of the Palestinian *intifada* in September 2000 gave further fillip to bin Laden's rhetoric.

In July an Al Qaeda recruiting videotape, released in the Middle East, intercut gory images of Israeli soldiers shooting unarmed Palestinian protesters with Al Qaeda volunteers undergoing military training in Afghanistan.

To counter such propaganda effectively, the United States would need to address certain specific issues urgently. One is the Israeli-Palestinian conflict. Interestingly, the Bush Administration dropped its insistence on "total quiet" for one week by the Palestinians as a precondition for the peace talks to resume. But Israeli Prime Minister Ariel Sharon rebuffed a personal appeal by President Bush and vetoed Shimon Peres's scheduled meeting with Yasir Arafat on September 16. In response, the least Bush can do is to publicly ban the use of U.S.-made and -supplied F-16s and Apache attack helicopters against the Palestinians. This would make Sharon sit up and take notice. And it would go some way toward pacifying popular opinion in the Muslim world.

Second, there is the question of the presence of American troops on the Arabian Peninsula. Is it absolutely essential to station 170 U.S. fighters, bombers and tank-killers on the soils of Saudi Arabia and Kuwait? Those who say yes, and argue that they are needed to enforce the no-fly zone in southern Iraq, must remember that these planes complement the ones parked on U.S. aircraft carriers in the Persian Gulf. There is no military reason why the Pentagon cannot shift the responsibility for monitoring the no-fly zone exclusively to these carriers, and thus deprive bin Laden and company of an effective propaganda tool.

Most fundamentally, the United States must sensitize itself to the feelings and perceptions of Muslims everywhere. President Bush's use of the word "crusade"—a highly loaded and negative term from the Muslim viewpoint, referring to the Christian crusades into Muslim lands, and mirroring bin Laden's labeling of Americans as crusaders—illustrates the enormous gap that exists between the White House and the Islamic world. One way for Bush to counter the rising popular animosity toward the United States in the Islamic world would be to appoint a Muslim American to a high-profile Administration post.

Those who argue that now is not the time for Washington to review its Middle Eastern policies for fear of appearing to appease the terrorists miss the fundamental point: Cause precedes effect. To remove the symptom you must tackle the root cause—and the sooner the better.

September 26, 2001

Mark Gevisser

Johannesburg

Makhaola Ndebele, a 30-year-old writer on an AIDS educational TV drama, says his first response to the attacks in the United States was disbelief. But then, he says, "this turned to excitement at the enormity of the event. 'America's being hit!' Later, when I saw how many lives were lost, reality set in, but my excitement was, 'It's finally happening to them, whereas they thought they were invincible.' " Ndebele says almost everyone he knows feels that "America got its comeuppance."

Ndebele is not alone. Although the South African government's official line is one of unconditional support for the United States, just after the bombing a provincial premier, Makhenkhesi Stofile, said U.S. citizens "had to look into themselves" to find out why the attack happened, and even questioned the use of the word "terrorist" to describe the hijackers.

According to Zweli Silangwe, 25, when he and other students in an international relations class at the University of the Witwatersrand discussed whether the United States should attack Afghanistan, the vast majority of the whites in the class supported such retaliation, while the vast majority of blacks opposed it. This echoes a survey of 500 South Africans, in which 52 percent of the whites polled felt that South Africa should participate in the United States' declared war against terrorism, as opposed to only 30 percent of the blacks. But John Kuhn, 23, the deputy-president of the Wits Students' Representative Council, says he has noticed—even among those who are deeply upset about the attacks—"a deep-seated anti-Americanism among almost all students here, whatever their color or background."

The perception is that young postapartheid South Africans are politically apathetic. South African university-goers are major consumers of U.S. popular culture and commodities, and they have identities that are often more global than national. Where, then, does the anti-Americanism come from?

In students, at least, it stems in part from the anti-privatization campaigns that have racked South African universities over the past two years, bringing the issue of globalization, and the role that the United States plays in the global economy, onto campus. Among black students it is also an identification with the Palestinians, and with the struggle for freedom against an imperial power, as well as perceived indifference by the West to African genocides such as in Rwanda. The U.S. withdrawal from the UN's recent World Conference Against Racism in Durban was severely criticized at the time; now the attack and its consequences are being read through the politics of race. Says Silangwe, who is the branch chairman of the SA Students Congress, which is aligned with the African National Congress, "Most white South Africans are still not comfortable with a government ruled by black people—and this makes them aggressive in their approach. The United States is perceived as a white state, something they identify with, and they need to support it against attacks by 'black' people. On the other hand, most blacks respond that anything coming from the United States is racist—and so they oppose it."

Perhaps ironically, television appears to be most to blame for the groundswell of antipathy toward the United States at a time when, one might imagine, it should expect the most sympathy. The result of America's dominance of global media means that the tragedy and its aftermath are being broadcast into our homes as if we were Americans ourselves: We are called upon not just to grieve and mourn, but to summon up anger and outrage as if we were personally attacked. And we hear, incessantly, one dominant voice: the baying for blood. If South Africans—and other people of the South—thought the United States was arrogant before, this was only confirmed in the aftermath of the attacks. "We have been wronged," the message went, "so the whole world must go to war." The distasteful consequence is, among many South Africans, a lack of empathy for a deeply wounded nation, an admiration for unjustifiable terror tactics and a limited understanding of the attack's global consequences.

Watching television with friends on the night of the attacks, Makhaola Ndebele says, one of them made the analogy between U.S. officials' calls for heightened security and the way crime-obsessed middle-class South Africans barricade themselves behind high walls and electric fences. "But more security won't help," Ndebele's friend said. "You still have the hungry world outside the big house." The point being, of course, that if you want to stop violence—be it crime or world terror—you must change the global inequities that cause it in the first place.

September 26, 2001

Praful Bidwai

New Delhi

As the United States puts together a broad alliance to avenge the September 11 atrocities, two major candidate-members of the coalition in the region south of Afghanistan are dangerously intensifying their mutual rivalry. Barely two months after their Agra summit, India and Pakistan have again locked horns in ways characteristic of their bitter rivalry during the cold war. Today, in an ironic twist of history, once-nonaligned India and former U.S. ally Pakistan are clashing, although they are on the same side—with the United States.

Military action by the U.S.-led coalition in Afghanistan threatens serious domestic trouble in India, besides plunging South Asia into new uncertainties. If President Bush thinks the coalition offers "an opportunity to refashion the thinking between Pakistan and India" to promote reconciliation, he is likely to be proven wrong. Responses in New Delhi and Islamabad to his September 22 lifting of sanctions imposed after the 1998 nuclear tests have been divergent. Indian policy-makers see this as long expected but "asymmetrical," and as an ill-deserved reward to Pakistan for belatedly breaking with the Taliban. The Pakistanis call it inadequate. They want removal of sanctions imposed after the 1999 Musharraf coup and a further "correction" of the recent pro-India tilt in U.S. policy.

Since September 11, India and Pakistan have been vying to become America's "frontline" partners in Afghanistan—for parochial reasons. India offered full military cooperation to the United States even *before* there was significant evidence on responsibility for the attacks. Indian policy-makers and -shapers could barely hide their glee at this "historic" chance for an Indian-U.S. "strategic partnership." The United States had finally come around to understanding India's suffering under "cross-border terrorism"— that is, Pakistan's support for Kashmiri-secessionist militants—a rather facile explanation of the Kashmir crisis, which is rooted more in New Delhi's policies and popular alienation than in Pakistan's proxy war.

India's unsolicited offer of support was buttressed by Prime Minster Atal Behari Vajpayee, who echoed Bush's insistence on obliterating the distinction between terrorism and states that support it. Vajpayee demanded that "we must strike at [the terrorists'] organizations, at those who condition, finance, train, equip and protect them . . . and thus compel the states that nurture and support them." This brazen alignment with Washington disturbed and astonished Indian public opinion. New Delhi was so preoccupied with its self-serving stand on Kashmir that it offered to join forces with Washington without demanding the multilateral approach it is traditionally known for. India has conventionally opposed unilateral action by states or groupings like NATO and insisted that any use of military force be properly authorized by the UN's Security Council under Chapter VII of its charter. India's failure to ask for such a mandate today is largely explained by its Kashmir preoccupation and urge to isolate Pakistan.

For its part, Pakistan made a momentous choice on September 19: It will dump the Taliban and join the U.S.-led coalition, thereby overcoming global opprobrium for supporting *jihadi* militants. It cashed in on its obvious locational and logistical advantage and its leverage over the Taliban. This produced resentment within New Delhi's ruling establishment. Each establishment is abusing and maligning the other, and parodying its intentions and plans. Musharraf didn't help matters when he announced the decision: Three of the four reasons he cited for it pertain directly or indirectly to India. Two of them, Kashmir and "safeguarding" nuclear weapons, have direct implications for India-Pakistan strategic hostility. Musharraf told India to "lay off" and attacked its "grand game plan" to "win over America to its side" while harming Pakistan's vital interests.

This drew an immediate rebuke from New Delhi. India accused Musharraf of conducting "an anti-India tirade . . . instead of focusing on terrorism, which is responsible for the present situation," and it held Pakistan responsible for the Taliban's "birth, growth and nurturing." The mutual resentment is likely to grow as Pakistan and the United States "neutralize" and work with Afghanistan's rebel Northern Alliance, which India recognizes as that country's legitimate government and in which it has invested significantly over the years.

Rivalry with Pakistan has blinded New Delhi to the dislocations and implosions the current situation could produce if Islamicist opposition grows in Pakistan. It has been equally insensitive to the domestic need to defend pluralism and secularism as these come under increasing pressure from militant Hindu chauvinists, who see September 11 as an opportunity to malign Islam, paint all Muslims with the *jihadi*-terrorist brush and present them as a threat to "civilized" countries. Such elements are most strongly represented in Vajpayee's own Bharatiya Janata Party, which heads India's twenty-seven-party ruling coalition. The BJP claims to speak for 80 percent of Indians, who are Hindu, but it holds less than a quarter of the national vote. The coming confrontation in Afghanistan is likely to further disturb Hindu-Muslim relations and aggravate sectarian trends in India. It has already spurred demands for a "tough" line on Kashmir and for draconian antiterrorism laws, which would severely curtail civil liberties.

However, there is rising opposition to this policy not just from political parties—including some within the ruling coalition—but from civil society and India's growing peace movement. This movement questions New Delhi's unconditional and uncritical support of Bush's "you're with the United States, or you're with the terrorists" line (which Indian ministers have described as "brilliant"); demands a proper UN mandate for action against the September 11 culprits; and opposes excessive use of force and "collateral damage" (highly likely in Afghanistan's conditions). India has witnessed small but spirited demonstrations against any unilateral U.S. (or coalition) action. And there is a vigorous public debate over the wisdom of using force, as well as over the U.S. record of military intervention in the Third World, including Iraq.

Above all, there is serious concern about the nuclear dimension of any instability that the imminent confrontation might produce in South Asia— with grim global consequences. The United States, ironically, will have contributed in no small measure to this through its own addiction to nuclear weapons, coupled with its flawed nonproliferation, as distinct from disarmament-based, approach to arms control.

September 26, 2001

Ahmed Rashid

Lahore

President Pervez Musharraf is walking a knife edge at home as he tries to keep a deeply polarized country from tearing itself apart, now that his military regime has pledged full support to the United States in its war against terrorism.

The first test for the regime came on September 21, when thirty-five religious parties called for a nationwide strike and demonstrations after Friday prayers to oppose the government's decision to join the U.S.-led alliance. However, the demonstrations were small by Pakistani standards and largely involved mullahs and teenagers from the thousands of *madrassahs*, or religious schools, from which the Taliban draw many of their recruits. Most people stayed at home. Although the low turnout made it clear that the vast majority of the population is presently unwilling to support the Islamic parties' antigovernment campaign, the mood could change once U.S. forces are based in Pakistan and military action begins.

Polls vary widely on the question of how much opposition there is to the government's decision to go along with the Americans; the most reliable estimates put it at around 25 percent. Musharraf has appealed to people not to react emotionally, but to put Pakistan's interests first. He said that Islamabad could not afford to be alienated from the international community by trying to defend the Taliban. He has also bluntly told the nation that if Pakistan had not committed bases and other facilities to U.S. troops, India would have done so, which would have posed a severe threat to Pakistan's nuclear program and stance on the disputed territory of Kashmir.

Musharraf's problem is that he is head of a military rather than a political regime, and he has made little attempt to broaden the political base of his government or win over the silent majority, who support his stance. His political skills are severely limited. He has appeared only once on national TV since the September 11 attacks, has given no interviews and has remained largely closeted with his generals. "Pakistan's Islamic groups thrive when the only measure of public support is demonstrations in the streets, and their importance diminishes at times of elections," says Hussain Haqqani, a political analyst and former adviser to Prime Ministers Nawaz Sharif and Benazir Bhutto. "Musharraf is probably now regretting that he marginalized the mainstream political parties, leaving the Islamists as the only show on the streets," Haqqani added. "Now he has to demonstrate some political skills and limit the Islamists' capacity for violence."

The real threat to instability and Musharraf is the economy. Pakistan was in its fourth year of severe recession when the terrorists struck. Foreign investment in the recently ended fiscal year (July 2000–June 2001) was the worst in a decade, and GDP growth was only 2.6 percent, compared with last year's 4.8 percent. The crisis has led to a further crash in business and economic confidence. Pakistan's three stock exchanges were shut down after suffering massive losses in the three days following the attacks in the United States. Now the Bush Administration has announced that it is waiving sanctions and putting together an aid package, which means Washington has recognized the crisis.

Economists say Pakistan is asking for an immediate debt forgiveness of several billion of its $38 billion total foreign debt, resumption of U.S. military aid and quick disbursement of loans from the United States and the World Bank to restore business confidence. On September 21 Japan announced a $40 million emergency loan, and the United States and the European Union are expected to follow. If Pakistan can garner international economic aid, Musharraf can point out the benefits of allying himself with the West.

American military operations against bin Laden and the Taliban are expected to be largely covert. Forces have already been sent to several Arab Gulf regimes and, according to Central Asian diplomats and wire reports, to Uzbekistan and Tajikistan as well, where authoritarian and highly controlled regimes can keep the U.S. presence secret and completely out of the public eye. In Pakistan, which is expected to host the largest U.S. military force because of its proximity to Afghanistan, such a feat will not be possible. That's when the Musharraf regime's alliance with the United States will be truly tested.

September 26, 2001

Graham Usher

Jerusalem

In Israel and the occupied territories, the attacks in the United States have produced an eerie sense of déjà vu. In Israel, hospitals are on high alert and people are stocking up on gas masks, a precaution fueled by news stories—some of them Israeli-inspired—that Iraq too is on America's hit list and so Israeli cities may again be targeted by Saddam Hussein's Scud missiles.

In the 1991 Gulf War, Palestinians were placed under a six-week curfew. Today their 700 towns, villages and refugee camps are blockaded by earth ramparts and army checkpoints that are manned, occasionally, by tanks. Back then, they danced on the roofs when missiles rained on Tel Aviv. Now they are trying to live down media images of a handful of their people celebrating the carnage in America.

What links the two wars and two peoples is pessimism. After a year of the latest, bloodiest and most desperate conflict, all expect that things can only be worse this time around. And both nations have already tasted the future: Palestinians via a ferocious Israeli assault on their communities; Israelis via unusually tough arm-twisting by their chief ally, the United States. In the week after two airliners plowed into the World Trade Center, the Israeli army killed twenty-eight Palestinians (most of them civilians) and invaded Jenin and Jericho, two West Bank cities under the full control of the Palestinian Authority. Israeli leader Ariel Sharon apparently assumed the world would buy his comparison that Yasir Arafat is "our bin Laden" and grant license to bring him to heel. It wasn't granted. Under European and U.S. pressure—and criticism from Sharon's increasingly dissident Foreign Minister, Shimon Peres—the offensive was curbed, aided by Palestinian moves that for once wrested the initiative out of Israel's hands.

Convinced that Israel would use the attacks on America to destroy his authority—personal and institutional—Arafat urged a campaign replacing the stereotype of gleeful Palestinians with images of Palestinians praying, lighting candles and donating blood. He also ordered a cease-fire "on all fronts," expressing his people's "readiness to be part of the international alliance for ending terrorism against unarmed innocent civilians." Palestinians, mostly, endorsed the call. Washington nodded to Israel to reciprocate. With extreme reluctance, Sharon did so. On September 18 he authorized his army to cease all "initiated actions" (incursions and assassinations) in the Palestinian areas and withdraw tanks from Jericho and Jenin. His only rider was that there be "forty-eight hours of quiet" in the occupied territories prior to any meeting between Peres and Arafat.

But this was a condition that could not be met—at least in the armed garrison that is the West Bank and Gaza. On September 26—again due to U.S. prodding—Sharon allowed Peres to meet with Arafat in Gaza, where they announced a cease-fire, despite a bomb blast at an Israeli army base and a clash erupting at a Palestinian refugee camp a mere three miles from where the meeting was held. These two interruptions of "quiet" left a Palestinian teenager dead and a dozen wounded, including three Israeli soldiers.

Palestinians—including the Islamist movements of Hamas and Islamic Jihad—have broadly accepted Arafat's cease-fire as meaning an end to attacks on civilians inside Israel and firing on Jewish settlements from PA areas. But they will not give up armed resistance against soldiers and settlers in those areas in the West Bank and Gaza where Palestinians live under direct Israeli occupation. "The cease-fire is not an order. We are not an army and this is not a classical war. It is a process. What the Palestinians are saying is the more Israel lifts the restrictions on our lives the more the cease-fire can take hold," says Palestinian analyst Ghassan Khatib. "What Arafat is signaling is he is ready to trade the *intifada* for anew political process with greater U.S. involvement," he adds. After an uprising that has cost them much and brought them little, many Palestinians would accept the trade, even if certain of their factions would not. But the transaction doesn't depend on them only.

It also depends on whether, in exchange for "a cessation of hostilities," real international pressure will be brought to bear on Israel to first lift the siege and then end the longest military occupation in recent history. The Palestinian fear is that the United States is only pressing for a cease-fire now so that the "coalition against terror" can include Muslim and Arab states without snagging on "local disputes" like Israel versus Palestine, and that the occupied territories will remain unlit by hope.

If that fear is confirmed, one thing is certain. Whatever comes from America's imminent strike on the Taliban and Osama bin Laden, the fallout will not be confined to Afghanistan. The hatred for all things American will reverberate much wider than that.

September 26, 2001

Ana Uzelac

Moscow

It was an obvious thing to do in London, Paris or Amsterdam. But for the vast majority of Muscovites, laying flowers along the walls of the U.S. Embassy, fastening the Stars and Stripes to its fence and weeping in grief for

Russia's former cold war enemy was something they could hardly have imagined doing before September 11. And yet, the enormity of the tragedy that hit New York and Washington seems to have dwarfed the differences that have strained relations between the two countries for the past couple of years.

In the hours after the attack, Russia emerged as the first country to offer its sympathy and a promise to fight terrorism shoulder to shoulder with the United States. Two weeks later, Russian President Vladimir Putin presented a concrete list of how the Kremlin will help the U.S.-led international coalition if it targets Afghanistan. The list includes sharing intelligence, opening air corridors for aid shipments, supplying the Afghan opposition with weapons and participating in search-and-rescue operations there. But possibly most important was Putin's decision not to prevent the former Soviet republics of Central Asia from giving the United States the right to use their airports—a move that could make the crucial difference in the looming war.

Putin seems to be the very embodiment of Russian public opinion, which—just two years after the U.S. Embassy was pelted with eggs because of the NATO airstrikes in Yugoslavia—is ready to grant the United States the right to conduct some kind of military operation. A poll conducted by the All-Russian Center for Public Opinion Research (VTsIOM) just days after the attack shows that 32 percent of Muscovites would "understand" if the United States attacked terrorists' training camps, and 29 percent would even "approve." The number of people who would "disapprove" of such action is 26 percent. Still, this is no carte blanche. Sixty-eight percent would condemn attacks on countries that harbor terrorists; only 5 percent would approve them. And 72 percent would like America to make sure it knows who is responsible for the attacks and only then take action.

But Russia's engagement is not a risk-free venture, and there are voices calling for caution. "Russia should participate in the American actions proceeding exclusively from its national interest," said Mikhail Leontyev, an influential TV anchor on the public channel ORT, summing up the prevailing political climate. As long as the Taliban are the target, interests will coincide.

The movement was proclaimed one of Russia's biggest security threats last year, and the Kremlin said it was already providing Washington with intelligence on them. Veterans of the Soviet Union's decade-long Afghan war have valuable firsthand knowledge of the terrain and the people; many have already warned the United States that it is heading for a protracted and bloody conflict. The Kremlin has also been gathering intelligence on radical Islamic groups operating in Central Asia, and it maintains links with the anti-Taliban opposition in Afghanistan.

But the focus of Russia's worries is Central Asia, the place where the new U.S. partnership will be most seriously tested. The most fragile of all countries there are Tajikistan and Uzbekistan, which emerged from Soviet rule as corrupt secular autocracies with strong ties to Moscow. Both border Afghanistan and both have experienced Islamic insurgencies in recent years. Both countries are ideally placed to serve as bases for clandestine U.S. operations into Afghanistan. Pakistan's former Foreign Secretary Niaz Naik recently told the BBC that plans for such actions existed even before September 11. But there are voices warning that a U.S. military presence in Central Asia could trigger new uprisings and destabilize the region. Igor Rotar, a Central Asia expert writing for the daily *Nezavisimaya Gazeta*, warned that these impoverished countries are already "too tempting a prey for the champions of the new *jihad*." But it's a risk they seem increasingly ready to take, as one Central Asian nation after another offers help to the United States—from Turkmenistan's readiness to open air space to Kazakhstan's offer of the use of its military bases.

Putin's political will and the potential benefits of ridding the region of the Taliban have managed to overcome the Russian military's fears that a U.S. presence could end the days of unquestioned Russian dominance in Central Asia. But the Kremlin's long deliberations fueled speculation that it was seeking possible trade-offs for its willingness to cooperate—suspension or slowing down of NATO's eastward expansion, easing Russia's access to the World Trade Organization and extending large-scale debt relief.

Independently of this, Russia is already enjoying the first benefits of the new political climate: Despite the White House's assurances that the human rights situation in Chechnya will not slip off its radar, there is little chance that Washington will now criticize the Kremlin's brutal ways of fighting the insurgency there. Moscow has branded the rebels "terrorists" and accused them of links to Osama bin Laden. This is now more than enough to muffle the already ignored complaints of Chechnya's battered civilians. Taking this opportunity, Putin offered Chechen rebels seventy-two hours to sever their links with "international terrorists," approach his representatives in the region and start negotiating the technicalities of their surrender. He didn't say what would happen after the deadline had passed. He didn't really need to.

The September 11 attacks may have given the Kremlin more grounds to argue against U.S. plans for a national missile defense system. "The shield would never have protected the United States from this attack," said Dmitry Rogozin, head of the Russian parliamentary committee on foreign affairs, the very next day. "The whole idea should be reconsidered." At least the Kremlin has been given more time to think about how to continue negotiating once the talks on NMD resume. Earlier, Washington warned that if the deal was not reached by November, it would unilaterally abrogate the Anti-Ballistic Missile Treaty. Now it looks as if it will have other things on its mind.

September 17, 2001
A Political Solution is Required
Tariq Ali

London

On a trip to Pakistan a few years ago I was talking to a former general about the militant Islamist groups in the region. I asked him why these people, who had happily accepted funds and weapons from the United States throughout the cold war, had become violently anti-American overnight. He explained that they were not alone. Many Pakistani officers who had served the United States loyally from 1951 onward felt humiliated by Washington's indifference.

"Pakistan was the condom the Americans needed to enter Afghanistan," he said. "We've served our purpose and they think we can be just flushed down the toilet."

The old condom is being fished out for use once again, but will it work? The new "coalition against terrorism" needs the services of the Pakistani Army, but General Pervez Musharraf will have to be extremely cautious.

An overcommitment to Washington could lead to a civil war in Pakistan and split the armed forces. A great deal has changed over the past two decades, but the ironies of history continue to multiply. In Pakistan itself, Islamism derived its strength from state patronage rather than popular support. The ascendancy of religious fundamentalism is the legacy of a previous military dictator, General Mohammed Zia ul-Haq, who received solid backing from Washington and London throughout his eleven years as dictator. It was during his rule (1977–88) that a network of *madrassahs* (religious boarding schools), funded by the Saudi regime, were created.

The children, who were later sent to fight as mujahedeen in Afghanistan, were taught to banish all doubt. The only truth was divine truth. Anyone who rebelled against the imam rebelled against Allah. The *madrassahs* had only one aim: the production of deracinated fanatics in the name of a bleak Islamic cosmopolitanism. The primers taught that the Urdu letter *jeem* stood for *jihad*; *tay* for *tope* (cannon), *kaaf* for *Kalashnikov* and *khay* for *khoon* (blood); 2500 *madrassahs* produced a crop of 225,000 fanatics ready to kill and die for their faith when asked to do so by their religious leaders. Dispatched across the border by the Pakistani Army, they were hurled into battle against other Muslims they were told were not true Muslims. The Taliban creed is an ultra-sectarian strain, inspired by the Wahhabi sect that rules Saudi Arabia. The severity of the Afghan mullahs has been denounced by Sunni clerics at al-Azhar in Cairo and Shiite theologians in Qom as a disgrace to the Prophet.

The Taliban could not, however, have captured Kabul on their own via an excess of religious zeal. They were armed and commanded by "volunteers" from the Pakistani Army. If Islamabad decided to pull the plug, the Taliban could be dislodged, but not without serious problems. The victory in Kabul counts as the Pakistani Army's only triumph. To this day, former U.S. Secretary of State Zbigniew Brzezinski remains recalcitrant. "What was more important in the world view of history?" he asks with more than a touch of irritation. "The Taliban or the fall of the Soviet Empire? A few stirred-up Muslims or the liberation of Central Europe and the end of the cold war?"

If Hollywood rules necessitate a short, sharp war against the new enemy, the American Caesar would be best advised not to insist on Pakistani legions. The consequences could be dire: a brutal and vicious civil war creating more bitterness and encouraging more acts of individual terrorism. Islamabad will do everything to prevent a military expedition to Afghanistan. For one thing, there are Pakistani soldiers, pilots and officers present in Kabul, Bagram and other bases. What will be their orders this time, and will they obey them? Much more likely is that Osama bin Laden will be sacrificed in the interests of the greater cause, and his body dead or alive will be handed over to his former employers in Washington. But will that be enough?

The only real solution is a political one. It requires removing the causes that create the discontent. It is despair that feeds fanaticism, and that is a result of Washington's policies in the Middle East and elsewhere. The orthodox casuistry among loyal factotums, columnists and courtiers of the Washington regime is symbolized by Tony Blair's personal assistant for foreign affairs, ex-diplomat Robert Cooper, who writes quite openly, "We need to get used to the idea of double standards." The underlying maxim of this cynicism is, We will punish the crimes of our enemies and reward the crimes of our friends. Isn't that at least preferable to universal impunity?

To this the answer is simple: "Punishment" along these lines does not reduce criminality but breeds it, by those who wield it. The Gulf and Balkan Wars were copybook examples of the moral blank check of a selective vigilantism. Israel can defy UN resolutions with impunity, India can tyrannize Kashmir, Russia can destroy Grozny, but it is Iraq that has to be punished and it is the Palestinians who continue to suffer. Cooper continues: "Advice to postmodern states: accept that intervention in the premodern is going to be a fact of life. Such interventions may not solve problems, but they may salve the conscience. And they are not necessarily the worse for that." Try explaining that to the survivors in New York and Washington. The United States is whipping itself into a frenzy. Its ideologues talk of this as an attack on "civilization," but what kind of civilization is it that thinks in terms of blood revenge?

For the past sixty years and more the United States has toppled democratic leaders, bombed countries in three continents and used nuclear weapons against Japanese civilians, but it never knew what it felt like to have its own cities under attack. Now they know. To the victims of the attack and their relatives one can offer our deep sympathy, as one does to people whom the U.S. government has victimized. But to accept that somehow an American life is worth more than that of a Rwandan, a Yugoslav, a Vietnamese, a Korean, a Japanese, a Palestinian . . . that is unacceptable.

(From *The Nation* website.)

October 31, 2001

Steve Negus

Cairo

Eleven years ago, the last time the United States fought a major war in the Muslim world, I was doing a year abroad at the American University in Cairo. President Hosni Mubarak sent Egyptian troops to fight alongside the Americans, for which the government received a $14 billion debt write-off from the United States and Saudi Arabia as an explicit quid pro quo. I remember a fair amount of antiwar sentiment on our campus, while at the less privileged but more politicized Cairo University across the Nile, students marched out onto the streets in defiance of martial law. Several were killed by police gunfire.

Going about the city, however, I was surprised to see how eager many Cairenes were to see Egyptian troops get to grips with the Iraqis. I was treated to endless rousing speeches about how Egypt and the United States together would beat Saddam. Palestinians, perceived as Iraqi sympathizers, were harassed and sometimes assaulted. Back then, the state media still had a monopoly on the airwaves, and they used it to cast Hussein as an untrustworthy tyrant ready to wreak havoc throughout the Middle East—admittedly not a difficult assignment.

Today, however, Egypt's political agenda is increasingly set by the wide-ranging viewpoints aired over Arab satellite media, in particular the Qatari-owned Al Jazeera. There's clearly much less enthusiasm here for America's new war than there was for the old. I have yet to hear anyone repeat the official Egyptian government line: that Osama bin Laden is to blame for the September 11 attacks and the United States has the right to retaliate against him. It's never easy to sample public opinion here, as people tend to be reticent in front of those who look like they might be connected with officialdom, and independent pollsters tend to get arrested. However, the recently released results of a survey by Cairo University's mass communications department conducted prior to the U.S. bombing campaign (only 10 percent of respondents believed bin Laden had masterminded September 11, and 96 percent opposed an international military coalition against Afghanistan) seem to correlate pretty well with the opinions of my neighbors around downtown Cairo's Kasr Al Aini Street. "America creates its own terrorism," declares grocer Marwan Abdel Gawar. "It doesn't do anything about Israeli terrorism, but complains when it is hit by terrorists." He adds, "Anyway, where is the evidence?"

Jazeera, which went on the air only five years ago, claims some 35 million viewers worldwide. It is now almost certainly Egypt's most-watched satellite channel in prime time. Satellite penetration in Egypt is only 8 percent, but a few more points could be added for people who watch at friends' or relatives' homes and in coffee shops. The numbers understate Jazeera's influence, however, as journalists and other opinion-makers are almost sure to subscribe. Moreover, during the current crisis Jazeera has been providing other stations with much of their material. "They really feed the Arab world with the news," says American University mass communications professor Hussein Amin. "They are the main player."

Columnist Salama Ahmed Salama has termed Jazeera "a stone in the stagnant waters of the official and traditional media." A typical news broadcast from state-TV several years ago might have involved interminable shots of Arab leaders sipping coffee with one another while the presenter read from a state wire-service dispatch. Today, Jazeera camera teams go into the middle of whatever action zone they can find. A typical state TV talk show might feature a government-approved academic explaining that the problem of development has social, economic and political dimensions. Jazeera puts Egypt's feminist iconoclast Nawal Al Saadawi and the ultraconservative Sheik Yousef Al Badri on the same program and lets them go at each other.

Some critics say Jazeera's talk shows contain more shouting than substance. The hosts sometimes jump into the debate and harangue their guests; other times they stage rather silly stunts, like an infamous phone/Internet poll on whether Zionism is worse than Nazism (result: 84.6 percent say Zionism is worse). Jazeera journalists, however, boast that they don't close the doors to any opinion. If you want to watch a frank debate on polygamy, or hear what an Israeli sounds like, or a radical Islamist (or a moderate Islamist, for that matter), there aren't too many other places you can go.

Jazeera's 500-odd staff is drawn from a reasonable cross-section of Arab political opinion, although given that the station hires people who have chosen not to work in the state media, there's certainly an anti-establishment overtone. The critics point out that Qatar, which subsidizes the station, gets let off the hook; so, to a lesser extent, does the emirate's powerful and temperamental neighbor, Saudi Arabia. Other Arab regimes, however, do not. As of last year, the Qatari foreign ministry had logged 400 official complaints about Jazeera's content.

Cairo gets particularly touchy when Jazeera challenges its claims regarding Israel and the protection of Arab rights, as when the channel highlighted how Egypt had blocked meaningful sanctions on Israel at the Arab summit last October or when it subsequently broadcast Palestinian demonstrators bearing an effigy of Egyptian President Mubarak as a donkey. The state press declared that Jazeera was a Mossad front whose goal was to run down Egypt's reputation, while the minister of information threatened to shut down a Jazeera studio outside Cairo. In the end, the Egyptian state limply expressed its discontent by kicking the brother of a Jazeera presenter out of the country.

Despite Jazeera's novelty, its ratings a few years ago still came in behind Lebanese satellite stations known mainly for their mix of dance videos and classic movies. That all changed with the outbreak of the Al Aqsa *intifada*. Egyptian viewers experienced what the United States first did in the 1960s: a war brought into their living rooms. Regular Jazeera viewer Cherine Hussein describes the content: "Little kids getting beaten up by Israeli soldiers and throwing rocks, and their mothers crying about the children that died. . . . It's really emotional, and if you watch it long enough you get really pissed off."

In this atmosphere, Jazeera's videotaped speech of Osama bin Laden saying "America and those who live in America cannot dream of security before it becomes reality in Palestine" was pitched well to an audience that, night after night, has been watching Palestinians being brutalized on TV. Egypt's own bloody internecine conflict in the 1990s has soured the population on radical Islam, but analysts here say bin Laden's address resonates because he downplays the radicals' ideological battle with "infidel" Arab regimes and sticks to an area where the Arab world shares a consensus: U.S. Middle East policy. Bin Laden is probably not a hero to most, or even many, but he's certainly a hero to a few.

I watched a clip of a Jazeera presenter arguing with a young student at a demonstration outside Cairo University. Bin Laden was no terrorist, the student insisted. But didn't he kill civilians? the presenter countered. No, she said, "they" killed civilians first.

Jazeera journalists bristle at the suggestion that they served bin Laden's agenda by airing his tape on the first day of the U.S. bombing campaign. No journalist would refuse such a *cadeau* (gift), says Cairo bureau chief Hussein Abdel Ghani. Jazeera has also not refused *cadeaux* from a growing list of Western policy-makers who've apparently taken *The New York Times* up on its suggestion to "shower Al Jazeera with offers of interviews" to woo

Arab public opinion. This hasn't mollified critics. The British press has said that Jazeera showed its bias during the current crisis when interviewer Sami Haddad asked Prime Minister Tony Blair "harsh" questions about Iraq, Palestine and his own enthusiasm for war. Haddad countered that he just wanted to raise Arab viewers' concerns. As for more general accusations of bias, Jazeera's talk-show hosts are an opinionated lot, and its field reporters make little effort to spare viewers footage of *intifada* deaths or civilian casualties in Afghanistan. Whether that's bias or merely par for the course in TV journalism is open to debate.

Whatever effect Jazeera may have on public opinion, it is certainly no threat to Mubarak's government, at least in the short run. Egypt's fifty-year-old military regime is good at nothing if not staying in power. However, the state has lost one of its clear assets—the ability to rally citizens around the flag. Jazeera has seriously undercut Egypt's ability to pose as the protector of Palestinian and Arab rights; it has also rammed home to audiences the constraints of their current political system. For years, Egypt's regime could take potentially unpopular positions for the sake of its alliance with the United States; it may not be able to in the future.

THE COLUMNISTS

Eric Alterman, Alexander Cockburn, Christopher Hitchens, Katha Pollitt, and Patricia J. Williams

September 12, 2001
Faceless Cowards?
Alexander Cockburn

"Faceless cowards." This was mini-President Bush in the first of his abysmal statements on the assault. Faceless maybe, but cowards? Were the Japanese aviators who surprised Pearl Harbor on December 7, 1941, cowards? I don't think so, and they at least had the hope of returning to their aircraft carriers. The onslaughts on the World Trade Center and the Pentagon are being likened to Pearl Harbor, and the comparison is just. From the point of view of the assailants the attacks were near miracles of logistical calculation, timing, audacity in execution and devastation inflicted upon the targets. And the commando units captured four aircraft, armed only with penknives. Was there ever better proof of Napoleon's dictum that in war the moral is to the material as three is to one?

Beyond the installation of another national trauma, there may be further similarity to Pearl Harbor. The possibility of a Japanese attack in early December of 1941 was known to U.S. Naval Intelligence. The day after the September 11 attack, a friend told me that a relative working at the U.S. Army's Picatinny Arsenal in New Jersey said that six weeks earlier the arsenal had been placed on top-security alert. In late August Osama bin Laden, a prime suspect, said in an interview with Abdel-Bari Atwan, the editor in chief of the London-based *al-Quds al-Arabi* newspaper, that he planned "very, very big attacks against American interests." On the evening of September 11, Senator John Kerry said he had recently been told by Director of Central Intelligence George Tenet that the agency had successfully preempted earlier attacks by bin Laden's people. Maybe the intelligence agencies didn't reckon with the possibility of assaults in rapid succession.

The lust for retaliation traditionally outstrips precision in identifying the actual assailant. The targets abroad will be all the usual suspects. The target at home will be the Bill of Rights. Less than a week ago the FBI raided InfoCom, the Texas-based web host for Muslim groups such as the Islamic

Society of North America, the Islamic Association for Palestine and the Holy Land Foundation. Declan McCullagh, political reporter for *Wired*, has described how within hours of the blast FBI agents began showing up at Internet service providers demanding that they install the government's "Carnivore" e-mail tracking software on their systems.

The explosions were not an hour old before terror pundits like Anthony Cordesman, Wesley Clark, Robert Gates and Lawrence Eagleburger were saying that these attacks had been possible "because America is a democracy," adding that now some democratic perquisites might have to be abandoned. What might this mean? Increased domestic snooping by U.S. law enforcement and intelligence agencies, ethnic profiling, another drive for a national ID card system.

That dark Tuesday did not offer a flattering exhibition of America's leaders. For most of the day the only Bush who looked composed and controlled was Laura, who happened to be waiting to testify on Capitol Hill. Her husband gave a timid and stilted initial reaction in Sarasota, Florida, then disappeared for an hour before resurfacing at an Air Force base near Shreveport, Louisiana, where he gave another flaccid address. He then ran to ground in a deep shelter in Nebraska, before someone finally had the wit to suggest that the best place for an American President at a time of national emergency is the Oval Office.

Absent national political leadership, the burden of rallying the nation fell as usual upon the TV anchors, most of whom seem to have resolved early on, commendably so, to lower the emotional temper and eschew racist incitement. One of the more ironic sights of Tuesday evening was Dan Rather talking about retaliation against bin Laden. It was Rather, wrapped in a burnoose, who voyaged to the Hindu Kush in the early 1980s to send back paeans to the *mujahedeen* being trained and supplied by the CIA in its largest-ever covert operation, which ushered onto the world stage such well-trained cadres as those now deployed against America.

Tuesday's eyewitness reports of the collapse of the two Trade Center buildings were not inspired, at least for those who have heard the famous eyewitness radio reportage of the crash of the Hindenburg zeppelin in Lakehurst, New

Jersey, in 1937. Radio and TV reporters these days seem incapable of narrating an ongoing event with any sense of vivid language or dramatic emotive power.

The commentators were similarly incapable of explaining with any depth the likely context of the attacks. It was possible to watch the cream of the nation's political analysts and commentating classes, hour after hour, without ever hearing the word "Israel," unless in the context of a salutary teacher in how to deal with Muslims. One could watch endlessly without hearing any intimation that these attacks might be the consequence of the recent Israeli rampages in the occupied territories, which have included assassinations of Palestinian leaders and the slaughter of Palestinian civilians with the use of American arms and aircraft; that these attacks might also stem from the sanctions against Iraq, which have killed more than half a million children; that these attacks might in part be a response to U.S. cruise missile destruction of the Sudanese factories that were falsely fingered by U.S. intelligence as connected to bin Laden.

The possibility of a deep plunge in the world economy was barely dealt with in the initial commentary. Yet before the attacks the situation was extremely precarious, with the chance of catastrophic deflation as the 1990s bubble burst, and the stresses of world overcapacity and lack of purchasing power taking an ever greater toll. George Bush will have no trouble in raiding the famous lockbox, using Social Security trust funds to give more money to the Defense Department. That about sums it up. Three planes are successfully steered into three of America's most conspicuous buildings, and the U.S. response will be to put more money into missile defense as a way of bolstering the economy.

September 12, 2001
Pax Americana
Patricia J. Williams

Where were you when it happened? Over and over one hears this, the question always asked when time stands still.

I was sitting at my computer pondering an inquiry posed by a friend regarding the conference that had just ended in Durban, South Africa, "How did a meeting on racism end up so side-tracked by the Middle East?" Everyone was using that word, "sidetracked." Anyway, a moment later, the world had turned upside-down, and I was on the phone with another friend who was asking, "Who on earth would do this?"

The first of these questions was easier to answer than the second. Few newspapers devoted space to the full title, but it was, after all, the World Conference Against Racism, Racial Discrimination, Xenophobia and Related Intolerance. It had been titled broadly for the explicit purpose of being as inclusive as possible—an ambitious agenda, and therefore perhaps something of a lightning rod for all the world's wars and discontents. But both questions are swirling in my mind right now, linked because of horrible happenstance, and I suppose that anything I write will be wrong, skewed by fear, drenched with terrible foreboding in a moment of pure chaos. But given chaos, my mind draws a line between the only two dots I have been able to retain: the point before and the point just after. And so I connect the degree to which Americans dismissed the world conference and the degree to which the newscasters to whom I am listening seem almost surreally naïve about resentment of American policies in various places around the globe.

Just last week in the old world, in the other time zone, thousands of delegates were engaged in an unprecedented struggle to communicate across a dizzying array of cultures, laws, linguistic divides and histories of hostility. The American press dismissed the meeting as a Tower of Babel. "Doomed to irrelevance," is how a front-page story in the *International Herald Tribune* described it. In the margin, I had written with what now rings with grimmer and greater irony than I could have anticipated: "Not doomed to irrelevance—rather invisibility. And invisibility dooms us all."

As I write this, a terrified voice on the radio I have kept on for hours now asks, "Why now, when the world is basically at peace?" Perhaps it is because I follow world news more obsessively than most, but I find that sort of statement deeply unnerving. The last several weeks have been marked by a war in Macedonia, a fight for land in Zimbabwe, and Protestants' lobbing

missiles at small Catholic schoolgirls in Northern Ireland. A Palestinian suicide bomber blew himself up in front of a French lycée in Jerusalem, his
head landing in the playground as children arrived for classes. In Congo,
old-fashioned mercenaries, reborn as global corporate armies-for-hire like
Executive Outcomes, used high-tech weaponry to obliterate angry, destitute
villagers so as to protect the interests of mineral and metal merchants. In
Israel, leaders defended a policy of "surgical" assassination. And in Fiji, tensions continued between its indigenous and its ethnic Indian populations.

At the World Conference itself, there was so much more than what was
reported in the general American media: the Dalit protested the caste system in India, Japanese untouchables did the same and Roma peoples presented claims of human rights violations. North, Central and South
Americans expressed concern about the socially destructive and racially
divisive consequences of police profiling and the drug war. The Maori of
New Zealand, the Inuit of Canada, the Twa of Rwanda, Han ethnics from
China, and Tibetan exiles—all these and more sent representatives and concerns to the World Conference.

Back home in the United States, in weird counterpoint to this roiling
competition for land, resources and respect, the Bush Administration spoke
of the virtues of a new, global U.S. dominance, or world American empire.
While media within the United States celebrated this as though it were a cultural inevitability rather than a stated political plan—the appeal of Hollywood movies, the delights of McDonald's burgers and the liberating
influence of L'il Kim were often cited—much of the world beyond decried it
as a breathtaking and untimely proclamation of executive hubris.

That all seems very distant now. "We will make no distinction between
the terrorists who committed these acts and those who harbored them,"
says the President as I write. He means Afghanistan, explains a commentator. But someone else mentions Pakistan, and someone else, a suspicious
Korean jet that has been forced to land near Seattle. A little while later, the
announcer says that some of the hijacking suspects may have been harbored
in Broward County, Florida, of all places. Someone else points to Canada,
or Maine, or Boston. Two of the suspects, according to officials, rented a

car with a New Jersey driver's license. Although there is not yet any clear person or place against whom to retaliate, 90 percent of the American people want revenge, according to call-in polls (for not even in so great a tragedy as this can we seem to dispense with call-in polls). There are reports of bombs exploding in Kabul, although the State Department denies any involvement, and some Arab-Americans fear becoming targets.

On the ground there are rumors of hundreds dead at the Pentagon and anywhere from 5,000 to 50,000 unaccounted for in New York, but no authority has provided an official estimate. Who knows? Who knows anything anymore? As during the Gulf War, I sense that we're facing a great paralyzing white wall of not knowing.

There is an eerie absurdity to the landscape in this moment, as I sit writing and waiting to hear the fate of friends who work downtown. It is as though someone planned not just to terrorize America but to do so by scripting a scenario straight out of Hollywood's own lexicon of scary movies. In slow motion reversal of all those scripts of guts and glory, the Emmys have been canceled, the Latin Grammys have been canceled, baseball and Jay Leno have been canceled, and throughout the tri-state area, cosmetic surgeries have been rescheduled to free hospital workers for the victims of an altogether different kind of fantasy made real.

September 19, 2001
Against Rationalization
Christopher Hitchens

It was in Peshawar, on the Pakistan-Afghanistan frontier, as the Red Army was falling apart and falling back. I badly needed a guide to get me to the Khyber Pass, and I decided that what I required was the most farouche-looking guy with the best command of English and the toughest modern automobile. Such a combination was obtainable, for a price. My new friend rather wolfishly offered me a tour of the nearby British military cemetery (a well-filled site from the Victorian era) before we began. Then he slammed a cassette into the dashboard. I braced myself for the ululations of some mullah but received instead a dose of "So Far Away." From under the turban and behind the beard came the gruff observation, "I thought you might like Dire Straits."

This was my induction into the now-familiar symbiosis of tribal piety and high-tech; a symbiosis consummated on September 11 with the conversion of the southern tip of the capital of the modern world into a charred and suppurating mass grave. Not that it necessarily has to be a symbol of modernism and innovation that is targeted for immolation. As recently as this year, the same ideology employed heavy artillery to destroy the Buddha statues at Bamiyan, and the co-thinkers of bin Laden in Egypt have been heard to express the view that the Pyramids and the Sphinx should be turned into shards as punishment for their profanely un-Islamic character.

Since my moment in Peshawar I have met this faction again. In one form or another, the people who leveled the World Trade Center are the same people who threw acid in the faces of unveiled women in Kabul and Karachi, who maimed and eviscerated two of the translators of *The Satanic Verses* and who machine-gunned architectural tourists at Luxor. Even as we worry what they may intend for our society, we can see very plainly what they have in mind for their own: a bleak and sterile theocracy enforced by advanced techniques. Just a few months ago Bosnia surrendered to the international court at The Hague the only accused war criminals detained on Muslim-Croat federation territory. The butchers had almost all been unwanted "volunteers" from the Chechen, Afghan and Kashmiri fronts; it is as an unapologetic defender of the Muslims of Bosnia (whose cause was generally unstained by the sort of atrocity committed by Catholic and Orthodox Christians) that one can and must say that bin Ladenism poisons everything that it touches.

I was apprehensive from the first moment about the sort of masochistic e-mail traffic that might start circulating from the Chomsky-Zinn-Finkelstein quarter, and I was not to be disappointed. With all due thanks to these worthy comrades, I know already that the people of Palestine and Iraq are victims of a depraved and callous Western statecraft. And I think I can claim to have been among the first to point out that Clinton's rocketing of Khartoum—supported by most liberals—was a gross war crime, which would certainly have entitled the Sudanese government to mount reprisals under international law. (Indeed, the sight of Clintonoids on TV, applauding the "bounce in the polls" achieved by their man that day, was even more repulsive than the sight of destitute refugee children making a wretched holiday over the nightmare on Chambers Street.) But there is no sense in which the events of September 11 can be held to constitute such a reprisal, either legally or morally.

It is worse than idle to propose the very trade-offs that may have been lodged somewhere in the closed-off minds of the mass murderers. The people of Gaza live under curfew and humiliation and expropriation. This is notorious. Very well: Does anyone suppose that an Israeli withdrawal from Gaza would have forestalled the slaughter in Manhattan? It would take a moral cretin to suggest anything of the sort; the cadres of the new *jihad* make it very apparent that their quarrel is with Judaism and secularism on principle, not with (or not just with) Zionism. They regard the Saudi regime not as the extreme authoritarian theocracy that it is, but as something too soft and lenient. The Taliban forces viciously persecute the Shiite minority in Afghanistan. The Muslim fanatics in Indonesia try to extirpate the infidel minorities there; civil society in Algeria is barely breathing after the fundamentalist assault.

Now is as good a time as ever to revisit the history of the Crusades, or the sorry history of partition in Kashmir, or the woes of the Chechens and Kosovars. But the bombers of Manhattan represent fascism with an Islamic face, and there's no point in any euphemism about it. What they abominate about "the West," to put it in a phrase, is not what Western liberals don't like and can't defend about their own system, but what they *do* like about it and *must* defend: its emancipated women, its scientific inquiry, its separation of religion from the state. Loose talk about chickens coming home to roost is the moral equivalent of the hateful garbage emitted by Falwell and Robertson, and exhibits about the same intellectual content. Indiscriminate murder is not a judgment, even obliquely, on the victims or their way of life, or ours. Any decent and concerned reader of this magazine could have been on one of those planes, or in one of those buildings—yes, even in the Pentagon.

The new talk is all of "human intelligence": the very faculty in which our ruling class is most deficient. A few months ago, the Bush Administration handed the Taliban a subsidy of $43 million in abject gratitude for the assistance of fundamentalism in the "war on drugs." Next up is the renewed "missile defense" fantasy recently endorsed by even more craven Democrats who seek to occupy the void "behind the President." There is sure to be further opportunity to emphasize the failings of our supposed leaders, whose costly mantra is "national security" and who could not protect us. And yes indeed, my guide in Peshawar was a shadow thrown by William Casey's CIA, which first connected the unstoppable Stinger missile to the infallible Koran. But that's only one way of stating the obvious, which is that this is an enemy for life, as well as an enemy of life.

September 19, 2001
Put Out No Flags
Katha Pollitt

My daughter, who goes to Stuyvesant High School only blocks from the World Trade Center, thinks we should fly an American flag out our window. Definitely not, I say: The flag stands for jingoism and vengeance and war. She tells me I'm wrong—the flag means standing together and honoring the dead and saying no to terrorism. In a way we're both right: The Stars and Stripes is the only available symbol right now. In New York City, it decorates taxicabs driven by Indians and Pakistanis, the impromptu memorials of candles and flowers that have sprung up in front of every firehouse, the chi-chi art galleries and boutiques of SoHo. It has to bear a wide range of meanings, from simple, dignified sorrow to the violent anti-Arab and anti-Muslim bigotry that has already resulted in murder, vandalism and arson around the country and harassment on New York City streets and campuses. It seems impossible to explain to a 13-year-old, for whom the war in Vietnam might as well be the War of Jenkins's Ear, the connection between waving the flag and bombing ordinary people half a world away back to the proverbial stone age. I tell her she can buy a flag with her own money and fly it out her bedroom window, because that's hers, but the living room is off-limits.

There are no symbolic representations right now for the things the world really needs—equality and justice and humanity and solidarity and intelligence. The red flag is too bloodied by history; the peace sign is a retro fashion accessory. In much of the world, including parts of this country, the cross and crescent and Star of David are logos for nationalistic and sectarian hatred. Ann Coulter, fulminating in her syndicated column, called for carpet-bombing of any country where people "smiled" at news of the disaster: "We should invade their countries, kill their leaders, and convert them to Christianity." What is this, the Crusades? The Rev. Jerry Falwell issued a belated mealy-mouthed apology for his astonishing remarks immediately after the attacks, but does anyone doubt that he meant them? The disaster was God's judgment on secular America, he observed, as famously secular New Yorkers were rushing to volunteer to dig out survivors, to give blood, food, money, anything—it was all the fault of "the pagans, and the abortionists, and the feminists, and the gays and the lesbians . . . the ACLU, People for the American Way." That's what the Taliban think too.

As I write, the war talk revolves around Afghanistan, home of the vicious Taliban and hideaway of Osama bin Laden. I've never been one to blame the United States for every bad thing that happens in the Third World, but it is a fact that our government supported militant Islamic fundamentalism in Afghanistan after the Soviet invasion in 1979. The mujahedeen were freedom fighters against Communism, backed by more than $3 billion in U.S. aid—more money and expertise than for any other cause in CIA history—and hailed as heroes by tag-along journalists from Dan Rather to William T. Vollmann, who saw these lawless fanatics as manly primitives untainted by the West. (There's a story in here about the attraction Afghan hypermasculinity holds for desk-bound modern men. How lovely not to pay lip service to women's equality! It's cowboys and Indians, with harems thrown in.) And if, with the Soviets gone, the vying warlords turned against one another, raped and pillaged and murdered the civilian population and destroyed what still remained of normal Afghan life, who could have predicted that? These people! The Taliban, who rose out of this period of devastation, were boys, many of them orphans, from the wretched refugee camps of Pakistan, raised in the unnatural womanless hothouses of fundamentalist boarding schools. Even leaving aside their ignorance and provincialism and lack of modern skills, they could no more be expected to lead Afghanistan back to normalcy than an army made up of kids raised from birth in Romanian orphanages.

Feminists and human-rights groups have been sounding the alarm about the Taliban since they took over Afghanistan in 1996. That's why interested Americans know that Afghan women are forced to wear the total shroud of the burqa and are banned from work and from leaving their homes unless accompanied by a male relative; that girls are barred from school; and that the Taliban—far from being their nation's saviors, enforcing civic peace with their terrible swift Kalashnikovs—are just the latest oppressors of the miserable population. What has been the response of the West to this news? Unless you count the absurd infatuation of European intellectuals with the anti-Taliban Northern Alliance of fundamentalist warlords (here we go again!), not much.

What would happen if the West took seriously the forces in the Muslim world who call for education, social justice, women's rights, democracy, civil liberties and secularism? Why does our foreign policy underwrite the clerical fascist government of Saudi Arabia—and a host of nondemocratic regimes besides? What is the point of the continuing sanctions on Iraq, which have brought untold misery to ordinary people and awakened the most backward tendencies of Iraqi society while doing nothing to undermine Saddam Hussein? And why on earth are fundamentalist Jews from Brooklyn and Philadelphia allowed to turn Palestinians out of their homes on the West Bank? Because God gave them the land? Does any sane person really believe that?

Bombing Afghanistan to "fight terrorism" is to punish not the Taliban but the victims of the Taliban, the people we should be supporting. At the same time, war would reinforce the worst elements in our own society—the flag-wavers and bigots and militarists. It's heartening that there have been peace vigils and rallies in many cities, and antiwar actions are planned in Washington, D.C., for September 29–30, but look what even the threat of war has already done to Congress, where only a single representative, Barbara Lee, Democrat from California, voted against giving the President virtual carte blanche.

A friend has taken to wearing her rusty old women's Pentagon Action buttons—at least they have a picture of the globe on them. The globe, not the flag, is the symbol that's wanted now.

September 19, 2001
The Uses of Adversity
Eric Alterman

> Sweet are the uses of adversity,
> Which, like the toad, ugly and venomous,
> Wears yet a precious jewel in his head;
> And this our life, exempt from public haunt,
> Finds tongues in trees, books in the running brooks,
> Sermons in stones, and good in everything.
>
> —As You Like It, II. i. 12

On the ground in downtown Manhattan, I see the best of our collective selves. Firemen and rescue workers risking their lives to save others; anonymous individuals pitching in to help strangers. Nobody whines about their losses, the inconvenience or even the inevitable screw-ups. It's a city I never knew existed. I go for walks and come back all choked up.

But then I get home, check in with my television and computer to see the latest screeds that pass for analysis in our benighted punditocracy, and my inner cynic is rekindled. "Nothing will ever be the same in America ever again," we are instructed. Well, yes and no. For many pundits, this tragedy is just one more excuse to explain how right they were in the first place. The discourse is dominated by a center-right argument, expressed most cogently by ex-Secretary of State Lawrence Eagleburger, advising his successors, "We've got to be somewhat irrational in our response. Blow their capital from under them." (Not to put too fine a point on things, but terrorism has no capital. Remember, that's the problem.)

Sometimes it takes the near-destruction of a village to discover just how crazy some of these erstwhile respectable conservatives can be. George W. Bush did backflips and handflips during the Republican primary season to win the endorsements of Jerry Falwell and Pat Robertson, who concur that we got "what we deserve," adding that the ACLU has "got to take a lot of blame for this." Just in case anyone misunderstood, Falwell clarified their position: "I really believe that the pagans, and the abortionists, and the feminists, and the gays and the lesbians who are actively trying to make an alternative lifestyle, the ACLU, People for the American Way—all of them who have tried to secularize America—I point the finger in their face and say, 'You helped this happen.' " (Robertson and Falwell apologized, but did not really retract.)

These crazies are not exactly alone on the Republican right. Over at *National Review Online*, Ann Coulter published an ostensible tribute to Solicitor General Ted Olson's wife, Barbara Olson, who died in the Pentagon crash, in which she first noted that Olson "praised one of my recent columns and told me I had really found my niche. Ted, she said, had taken to reading my columns aloud to her over breakfast." Finally came the red meat: "We know who the homicidal maniacs are. They are the ones cheering and dancing right now. We should invade their countries, kill their leaders and convert them to Christianity." This column, quite amazingly, also appeared on the website of a right-wing outfit, *Jewish World Review*, until the geniuses there figured out that by Coulter's theology they were next, and dumped it. Another confused NRO/*JWR writer*, Iran-contra adventurer Michael Ledeen, believes Olson "was killed by a fraudulent and arrogant establishment."

In another not quite shocking development Marty Peretz explained that the crime was the fault of insufficient hatred of Arabs. "I do not understand why so many people are so surprised by the radical evil emanating from the

Muslim world," Peretz writes. To be fair, I suppose those of us who witnessed the terrorism of Meir Kahane, Baruch Goldstein and Menachem Begin have only ourselves to blame if we are surprised by the radical evil emanating from the Jewish world.

Over at *The Wall Street Journal* editorial pages, the editors discovered in this self-consciously low-tech attack yet another argument for space-based missile defense. Why? "Hijacking a jet and flying it into a target is now yesterday's threat." Now they tell us. Even the discredited "terrorist expert" Steven Emerson, who once upon a time tried to blame the Arabs for Oklahoma City, has seen his fortunes revived as a talking head: a perfect metaphor for a medium without a memory.

The right has been without a rallying point since the end of the Soviet Union. Now they have one again. By fortunate happenstance it coincides exactly with the desire of many of them to make Israel a vassal state of a global American empire. Note that among the commentators who seek to blame Yasir Arafat in some way for the atrocities and even mention the Palestinian Authority on a possible list of targets—a group that includes Seth Lipsky, Michael Kelly, Mark Helprin and George Will—not one even bothers to argue that Arafat had anything to do with the attacks. Rather, this horrific tragedy looks to be just one more excuse to try to get the U.S. military to do Israel's dirty work rather than pursue the more difficult but constructive business of resuming the search for a workable peace.

To achieve the ends they have always sought, these conservatives demean considered analyses of our predicament with the epithet "appeasement." Andrew Sullivan—the author of a book on friendship—has already accused his friend Robert Wright of exactly this crime in response to the latter's thoughtful musings about some of the difficulties of retaliation. As if possessed by the spirit of an A. Mitchell Palmer or J. Edgar Hoover, the famed "gay-catholictory" has taken to listing the names of those he considers to be appeasers. And if that's not enough, Sullivan also warned that "the great red zone that voted for Bush is clearly ready for war. The decadent left in its enclaves on the coasts is not dead—and may well mount a fifth column." Yes, you read that right.

The grave risk in allowing these self-serving arguments to hijack the public discourse is that we will embark on a self-destructive cycle of retribution that does little more than indulge our wholly understandable desire for vengeance as it simultaneously exacerbates the problem we attempt to address. No, I don't have a better idea right now, but what's the rush? We are a great nation. We can afford to take our time.

September 24, 2001
Of Sin, the Left & Islamic Fascism
Christopher Hitchens

Not all readers liked my attack on the liberal/left tendency to "rationalize" the aggression of September 11, or my use of the term "fascism with an Islamic face," and I'll select a representative example of the sort of "thinking" that I continue to receive on my screen, even now. This jewel comes from Sam Husseini, who runs the Institute for Public Accuracy in Washington, D.C.:

> The fascists like Bid-Laden could not get volunteers to stuff envelopes if Israel had withdrawn from Jerusalem like it was supposed to—and the U.S. stopped the sanctions and the bombing on Iraq.

You've heard this "thought" expressed in one way or another, dear reader, have you not? I don't think I took enough time in my last column to point out just what is so utterly rotten at the very core of it. So, just to clean up a corner or two: (1) If Husseini knows what was in the minds of the murderers, it is his solemn responsibility to inform us of the source of his information, and also to share it with the authorities. (2) If he does not know what was in their minds—as seems enormously more probable—then why does he rush to appoint himself the ventriloquist's dummy for such a faction? Who volunteers for such a task at such a time?

Not only is it indecent to act as self-appointed interpreter for the killers, but it is rash in the highest degree. The death squads have not favored us with a posthumous manifesto of their grievances, or a statement of claim about Palestine or Iraq, but we are nonetheless able to surmise or deduce or induct a fair amount about the ideological or theological "root" of their act (Husseini doesn't seem to demand "proof" of bin Laden's involvement any more than the Bush Administration is willing to supply it) and if we are correct in this, then we have considerable knowledge of two things: their ideas and their actions.

First the actions. The central plan was to maximize civilian casualties in a very dense area of downtown Manhattan. We know that the killers had studied the physics and ecology of the buildings and the neighborhood, and we know that they were limited only by the flight schedules and bookings of civil aviation. They must therefore have been quite prepared to convert fully loaded planes into missiles, instead of the mercifully unpopulated aircraft that were actually commandeered, and they could have hoped by a combination of luck and tactics to have at least doubled the kill-rate on the ground. They spent some time in the company of the families they had kidnapped for the purpose of mass homicide. It was clearly meant to be much, much worse than it was. And it was designed and incubated long before the mutual-masturbation of the Clinton-Arafat-Barak "process." The Talibanis have in any case not distinguished themselves very much by an interest in the Palestinian plight. They have been busier trying to bring their own societies under the reign of the most inflexible and pitiless declension of shari'a law. This is known to anyone with the least acquaintance with the subject.

The ancillary plan was to hit the Department of Defense and (on the best evidence we have available) either the Capitol Dome or the White House. The Pentagon, for all its symbolism, is actually more the civil-service bit of the American "war-machine," and is set in a crowded Virginia neighborhood. You could certainly call it a military target if you were that way inclined, though the bin Ladenists did not attempt anything against a guarded airbase or a nuclear power station in Pennsylvania (and even if they had, we would now doubtless be reading that the glow from Three Mile Island was a revenge for globalization). The Capitol is where the voters send their elected representatives—poor things, to be sure, but our own. The White House is where the elected President and his family and staff are to be found. It survived the attempt of British imperialism to burn it down, and the attempt of the Confederacy to take Washington, D.C., and this has hallowed even its most mediocre occupants. I might, from where I am sitting, be a short walk from a gutted Capitol or a shattered White House. I am quite certain that in such a case Husseini and his rabble of sympathizers would still be telling me that my chickens were coming home to roost. (The image of bin Laden's men "stuffing envelopes" is the perfected essence of such brainless verbiage.) Only the stoicism of men like Jeremy Glick and Thomas Burnett prevented some such outcome; only those who chose who die fighting rather than allow such a profanity, and such a further toll in lives, stood between us and the fourth death squad. One iota of such innate fortitude is worth all the writings of Noam Chomsky, who coldly compared the plan of September 11 to a stupid and cruel and cynical raid by Bill Clinton on Khartoum in August 1998.

I speak with some feeling about that latter event, because I wrote three *Nation* columns about it at the time, pointing out (with evidence that goes unrebutted to this day) that it was a war crime, and a war crime opposed by the majority of the military and intelligence establishment. The crime was directly and sordidly linked to the effort by a crooked President to avoid impeachment (a conclusion sedulously avoided by the Chomskys and Husseinis of the time). The Al-Shifa pharmaceutical plant was well-known to be a civilian target, and its "selection" was opposed by most of the Joint Chiefs and many CIA personnel for just this reason. (See, for additional corroboration, Seymour Hersh's *New Yorker* essay "The Missiles of August"). To mention this banana-republic degradation of the United States in the same breath as a plan, deliberated for months, to inflict maximum horror upon the innocent is to abandon every standard that makes intellectual and moral discrimination possible. To put it at its very lowest, and most elementary, at least the missiles launched by Clinton were not full of passengers. (How are you doing, Sam? Noam, wazzup?)

So much for what the methods and targets tell us about the true anti-human and anti-democratic motivation. By their deeds shall we know them. What about the animating ideas? There were perhaps seven hundred observant followers of the Prophet Muhammed burned alive in New York on September 11. Nobody who had studied the target zone could have been in any doubt that some such figure was at the very least a likely one. And, since Islam makes no discrimination between the color and shade of its adherents, there was good reason to think that any planeload of civilians might include some Muslims as well. I don't myself make this point with any more emphasis than I would give to the several hundred of my fellow Englishmen (some of them doubtless Muslims also) who perished. I stress it only because it makes my point about fascism. To the Wahhabi-indoctrinated sectarians of Al Qaeda, only the purest and most fanatical are worthy of consideration. The teachings and published proclamations of this cult have initiated us to the idea that the tolerant, the open-minded, the apostate or the followers of different branches of The Faith are fit only for slaughter and contempt. And that's before Christians and Jews, let alone atheists and secularists, have even been factored in. As before, the deed announces and exposes its "root cause." The grievance and animosity predate even the Balfour Declaration, let alone the occupation of the West Bank. They predate the creation of Iraq as a state. The gates of Vienna would have had to fall to the Ottoman *jihad* before any balm could begin to be applied to these psychic wounds. And this is precisely, now, our problem. The Taliban and its surrogates are not content to immiserate their own societies in beggary and serfdom. They are condemned, and they deludedly believe that they are commanded, to spread the contagion and to visit hell upon the unrighteous. The very first step that we must take, therefore, is the acquisition of enough self-respect and self-confidence to say that we have met an enemy and that he is not us, but someone else. Someone with whom coexistence is, fortunately I think, not possible. (I say "fortunately" because I am also convinced that such coexistence is not desirable).

But straight away, we meet people who complain at once that this enemy is us, really. Did we not aid the grisly Taliban to achieve and hold power? Yes indeed "we" did. Well, does this not double or triple our responsibility to remove them from power? A sudden sheep-like silence, broken by a bleat. Would that not be "over-reaction"? All I want to say for now is that the under-reaction to the Taliban by three successive United States administrations is one of the great resounding disgraces of our time. There is good reason to think that a Taliban defeat would fill the streets of Kabul with joy. But for the moment, the Bush Administration seems a hostage to the Pakistani and Saudi clients who are the sponsors and "harborers" the President claims publicly to be looking for! Yet the mainstream left, ever shuffling its feet, fears only the discomfort that might result from repudiating such an indefensible and humiliating posture. Very well then, comrades. Do not pretend that you wish to make up for America's past crimes in the region. Here is one such crime that can be admitted and undone—the sponsorship of the Taliban could be redeemed by the demolition of its regime and the liberation of its victims. But I detect no stomach for any such project. Better, then—more decent and reticent—not to affect such concern for "our" past offenses. This is not an article about grand strategy, but it seems to me to go without saying that a sincere commitment to the secular or reformist elements in the Muslim world would automatically shift the balance of America's up-to-now very questionable engagement. Every day, the wretched Arafat is told by Washington, as a favor to the Israelis, that he must police and repress the forces of Hamas and Islamic Jihad. When did Washington last demand that Saudi Arabia cease its heavy financing of these primitive and unscrupulous organizations? We let the Algerians fight the Islamic-fascist wave without saying a word or lending a hand. And this is an effort in which civic and social organizations can become involved without official permission. We should be building such internationalism whether it serves the short-term needs of the current Administration or not: I signed an anti-Taliban statement several months ago and was appalled by the eerie silence with which the initiative was greeted in Washington. (It ought to go without saying that the demand for Palestinian self-determination is, as before, a good cause in its own right. Not now more than ever, but now as ever. There are millions of Palestinians who do not want the future that the pious of all three monotheisms have in store for them.)

Ultimately, this is another but uniquely toxic version of an old story, whereby former clients like Noriega and Saddam Hussein and Slobodan Milosevic and the Taliban cease to be our monsters and become monstrous in their own right. At such a point, a moral and political crisis occurs. Do "our" past crimes and sins make it impossible to expiate the offense by determined action? Those of us who were not consulted about, and are not bound by, the previous covert compromises have a special responsibility to say a decisive "no" to this. The figure of six and a half thousand murders in New York is almost the exact equivalent to the total uncovered in the death-pits of Srebrenica. (Even at Srebrenica, the demented General Ratko Mladic agreed to release all the women, all the children, all the old people and all the males above and below military age before ordering his squads to fall to work.) On that occasion, U.S. satellites flew serenely overhead recording the scene, and Milosevic earned himself an invitation to Dayton, Ohio. But in the end, after appalling false starts and delays, it was found that Mr. Milosevic was too much. He wasn't just too nasty. He was also too irrational and dangerous. He didn't even save himself by lyingly claiming, as he several times did, that Osama bin Laden was hiding in Bosnia. It must be said that by this, and by other lies and numberless other atrocities, Milosevic distinguished himself as an enemy of Islam. His national-socialist regime took the line on the towelheads that the Bush Administration is only accused, by fools and knaves, of taking. Yet when a stand was eventually mounted against Milosevic, it was Noam Chomsky and Sam Husseini, among many others, who described the whole business as a bullying persecution of—the Serbs! I have no hesitation in describing this mentality, carefully and without heat, as soft on crime and soft on fascism. No political coalition is possible with such people and, I'm thankful to say, no political coalition with them is now necessary. It no longer matters what they think.

October 3, 2001
Blaming bin Laden First
Christopher Hitchens

Just once more, and then we'll really have to get on with more pressing business. I could subscribe myself at any time to any of the following statements:

- An Arab child born in Nablus should have no fewer rights in his or her homeland than a Jewish child born in Flatbush.
- The United States of America has been the patron of predatory regimes on five continents.
- The United States of America exports violence by means of arms sales and evil clients.

You can probably fill in a few extras for yourself. However, none of the above statements means the same thing if prefaced with the words: "As Osama bin Laden and his devout followers have recently reminded us . . . " They wouldn't mean the same thing politically, that is to say, and they wouldn't mean the same thing morally. It's disgraceful that so many people on the periphery of this magazine should need what Noam Chomsky would otherwise term instruction in the elementary.

Here are two brief thought experiments that I hope and trust will put this degrading argument to rest. Both of them, as it happens, involve the date September 11.

I have long kept September 11 as a day of mourning, because it was on that date in 1973 that Salvador Allende was murdered and Chilean democracy assassinated along with him. We know all the details now, from the way the giant corporations subsidized subversion to the way that U.S. politicians commissioned "hit jobs" and sabotage. It took the Chilean opposition many years of patient struggle to regain their country and their democracy, and the small help I was able to offer them is one of the few things in my life of which I can be proud. There was one spirited attempt to kill Augusto Pinochet himself during this period, with which I had some sneaking sympathy, but on the whole the weaponry of terror (death squads, car bombs, the training of special killers) was in the department of horror employed by Chilean and U.S. officials working for, or with, the dictatorship. And now Chilean dignity has been restored, and Pinochet himself is a discredited and indicted figure, spared the rigor of law only for humanitarian reasons. We may even live to see justice done to some of his backers in Washington, though the holding of breath would be inadvisable.

I don't know any Chilean participant in this great historic struggle who would not rather have died—you'll have to excuse the expression—than commit an outrage against humanity that was even remotely comparable to the atrocities in New York, Washington and Pennsylvania. And I think I'll leave it at that, since those who don't see my point by now are never going to do so.

There are others who mourn September 11 because it was on that day in 1683 that the hitherto unstoppable armies of Islam were defeated by a Polish general outside the gates of Vienna. The date marks the closest that proselytizing Islam ever came to making itself a superpower by military conquest. From then on, the Muslim civilization, which once had so much to teach the Christian West, went into a protracted eclipse. I cannot of course be certain, but I think it is highly probable that this is the date that certain antimodernist forces want us to remember as painfully as they do. And if I am right, then it's not even facile or superficial to connect the recent aggression against American civil society with any current "human rights issue."

Why not pay attention to what the cassettes and incantations of Al Qaeda actually demand: a holy war in which there are no civilians on the other side, only infidels, and a society of total aridity in which any concept of culture or the future has been eradicated?

One ought to be clear about this: The Ottomans who besieged Vienna were not of that primeval mentality. But the Wahabbi fanatics of the present century are. Glance again at the trite statements I made at the beginning of this column. Could Osama bin Laden actually utter any of them? Certainly not. He doesn't only oppose the entire Jewish presence in Palestine; he opposes the Jewish presence in *America*. He is the spoiled-brat son of one of our preferred despotisms and the proud beneficiary of the export of violence. Why, then, do so many fools consider him as the interpreter of their "concerns," let alone seek to appoint their ignorant selves as the medium for his?

Thanks to all those who demand that I tell them what is to be done. As the situation develops, they may even ask themselves this question as if it really demanded a serious answer. We certainly owe a duty to Afghanistan's people, whose lives were rendered impossible by the Taliban long before we felt any pain. We might even remember that the only part of Iraq where people are neither starving nor repressed is in the Kurdish area, now under international protection as a result of public pressure on Bush Senior's vaunted "coalition." (See especially David Hirst's two engrossing reports from northern Iraq in the London *Guardian* of August 1 and 2: Hirst himself is probably the most consistently anti-imperialist journalist in the region.) But wait! That might mean that one could actually *do* something. Surely we are too guilt-stained for that.

Thanks also to all those who thought it was original to attack me for writing from an "armchair." (Why is it always an armchair?) As it happens, I work in a swivel chair, in an apartment on the top floor of one of Washington's tallest buildings. In the fall of 1993 the State Department's Office of Counterterrorism urgently advised me to change this address because of "credible" threats received after my wife and daughter and I had sheltered Salman Rushdie as a guest, and had arranged for him to be received at the cowering Clinton White House. I thought, then as now, that the government was doing no more than covering its own behind by giving half-alarmist and half-reassuring advice. In other words, I have a quarrel with theocratic fascism even when the Administration does not, and I hope at least some of my friendly correspondents are prepared to say the same.

October 3, 2001
Where Are the Women?
Katha Pollitt

Are there any people on earth more wretched than the women of Afghanistan? As if poverty, hunger, disease, drought, ruined cities and a huge refugee crisis weren't bad enough, under Taliban rule they can't work, they can't go to school, they have virtually no healthcare, they can't leave their houses without a male escort, they are beaten in the streets if they lift the mandatory burqa even to relieve a coughing fit. The Taliban's crazier requirements have some of the obsessive particularity of the Nazis' statutes against the Jews: no high heels (that lust-inducing click-click!), no white socks (white is the color of the flag), windows must be painted over so that no male passerby can see the dreaded female form lurking in the house. (This particular stricture, combined with the burqa, has led to an outbreak of osteomalacia, a bone disease caused by malnutrition and lack of sunlight.)

Until September 11, this situation received only modest attention in the West—much less than the destruction of the giant Buddha statues of Bamiyan. The "left" is often accused of "moral relativism" and a "postmodern" unwillingness to judge, but the notion that the plight of Afghan women is a matter of culture and tradition, and not for Westerners to judge, was widespread across the political spectrum.

Now, finally, the world is paying attention to the Taliban, whose days may indeed be numbered now that their foreign supporters—Saudi Arabia, the United Arab Emirates, Pakistan—are backing off. The connections between religious fanaticism and the suppression of women are plain to see (and not just applicable to Islam—show me a major religion in which the inferiority of women, and God's wish to place them and their dangerous polluting sexuality under male control, is not a central original theme). So is the connection of both with terrorism, war and atrocity. It's no accident that so many of the young men who are foot soldiers of Islamic fundamentalism are reared in womanless religious schools, or that Osama bin Laden's recruiting video features bikinied Western women as symbols of the enemy.

But if fundamentalism requires the suppression of women, offering desperate, futureless men the psychological and practical satisfaction of instant superiority to half the human race, the emancipation of women could be the key to overcoming it. Where women have education, healthcare and personal rights, where they have social and political and economic power—where they can choose what to wear, whom to marry, how to live—there's a powerful constituency for secularism, democracy and human rights: What educated mother engaged in public life would want her daughter to be an illiterate baby machine confined to the four walls of her husband's house with no one to talk to but his other wives?

Women's rights are crucial for everything the West supposedly cares about: infant mortality (one in four Afghan children dies before age 5), political democracy, personal freedom, equality under the law—not to mention its own security. But where are the women in the discussion of Afghanistan, the Middle East, the rest of the Muslim world? We don't hear much about how policy decisions will affect women, or what they want. Men have the guns and the governments. Who asks the women of Saudi Arabia, our ally, how they feel about the Taliban-like restrictions on *their* freedom? In the case of Afghanistan, the Northern Alliance presents itself now to the West as women's friend. A story in *The New York Times* marveled at the very limited permission given to women in NA-held territory to study and work and wear a less restrictive covering than the burqa. Brushed aside was the fact that many warlords of the Northern Alliance are themselves religious fighters who not only restricted women considerably when they held power from 1992 to '96 but plunged the country into civil war, compiling a record of ethnically motivated mass murder, rape and other atrocities and leaving the population so exhausted that the Taliban's promise of law and order came as a relief. It's all documented on the Human Rights Watch website (www.hrw.org).

Now more than ever, the Revolutionary Association of the Women of Afghanistan (RAWA), which opposes both the Taliban and the Northern Alliance as violent, lawless, misogynistic, and antidemocratic, deserves attention and support. "What Afghanistan needs is not more war," Tahmeena Faryel, a RAWA representative currently visiting the United States, told me, but massive amounts of humanitarian aid and the disarming of both the Taliban and the Northern Alliance, followed by democratic elections. "We don't need another religious government," she said. "We've had that!" The women of RAWA are a different model of heroism than a warlord with a Kalashnikov: In Afghanistan, they risk their lives by running secret schools for girls, delivering medical aid, documenting and filming Taliban atrocities. In Pakistan, they demonstrate against fundamentalism in the "Talibanized" cities of Peshawar and Quetta. Much as the victims of the WTC attack need our support, so too do Afghans who are trying to bring reason and peace to their miserable country. To make a donation to RAWA, see www.rawa.org.

I got more negative comment on my last column, in which I described a discussion with my daughter about whether to fly an American flag in the wake of the WTC attack, than on anything I've ever written. Many people pitied my commonsensical, public-spirited child for being raised by an antisocial naysayer like me. And if *The Weekly Standard* has its way—it's urging readers to send young "Miss Pollitt" flags c/o *The Nation*—she will soon have enough flags to redecorate her entire bedroom in red, white and blue, without having to forgo a single Green Day CD to buy one for herself. (See this issue's Letters column for some of the mail on the flag question.)

Fortunately, for those who want to hang something a bit more global out their window, there are alternatives. The peace flag (www.peaceflags.org) reshapes Old Glory's stars into the peace sign; the Earth flag (www.earth-flag.net) displays the Apollo photo of the Earth on a blue background.

October 10, 2001
New World Order
Patricia J. Williams

As I write, the world is filled with fear. I am having one of those reactions that psychologists describe as a stress response. I suppose I'm not alone, though. A friend calls and says, "You hung a flag yet? Anyone who's been to Cuba, you better hang a flag." "Cuba?" I ask, startled. "You don't mean that weeklong human rights trip seventeen years ago?"

"You poor naïve child. I'm sending you a big one. Hang it on your porch."

In the newspaper, I read of Muslims who are shaving their beards and removing their veils. I read of blacks who are embracing suspect profiling. There's an unsubstantiated rumor on the Internet of Barney Frank hugging Strom Thurmond just before he fainted.

"It's that list they'll be drawing up in the Office of Homeland Security," explains a fellow paranoid as we shop for bottled water. "Nobody wants to be on that." Then she points out the physical resemblance between Tom

Ridge and J. Edgar Hoover. She believes in reincarnation. I do not, but . . .
it really is uncanny.

Another friend calls to say she's been reading the *Washington Post*.
"Sally Quinn's got gas masks for everyone in her family. Her doctor gave
her a stock of antibiotics, enough for her and all the servants." The word
"triage" begins to rise uncomfortably in my mind. Who gets to stockpile
antibiotics in this new world order? If I went to a doctor for a little "extra"
medication, he'd turn me in for drug dealing. If minorities suffer from
unequal access to medical treatment now, what happens when panicked
hordes make a run on hospitals for limited supplies of anthrax vaccine?

Not that any of this will do any good anyway, I suppose. My mother
reminds me of the bomb shelters that sprang up during the 1950s. "I worried too," she said. "But you can't control this sort of thing on an individual level. Will you never go to the beach for fear of being too far from the
shelter? Will you never take off the gas mask for fear of smelling the roses?"
A friend of mine who's a psychologist says that it is precisely the terrifying
lack of control that is sending so many people over the edge. She says that
lots of fragile sorts have been showing up at Bellevue to apologize for having driven a plane into the World Trade Center. The less fragile ones have
been busy actually hijacking Greyhound buses and rushing into cockpits in
states of extreme agitation.

On the news, crusty old senators disclose that they have participated in
various government war games, in which they role-played all sides of the
conflict in the event of hypothetical disasters. The crusty old senators worry
me; they move stiffly and are so relentlessly formal that they refer to themselves in the third person, like Bob Dole. I suspect them of playing these
games in the groves of the Bohemian Club, with the expectation that whatever happens they will retire to the bar for whisky sours afterward. All this
is a too glib way of saying that I simply don't see them coming up with quite
the same strategies and outcomes that Al Qaeda might.

I think that if the Pentagon really wants to role-play doomsday scenar-
ios here at home, they need to lock Jerry Falwell in a small room with Elián
González's Miami relatives, G. Gordon Liddy, Louis Farrakhan, Jack

Kevorkian, Charlton Heston, Al Sharpton, Kenneth Starr and a horde of neglected, riot-prone, inner-city kids who under the circumstances feel as though they have nothing left to lose. We get O.J. Simpson to keep a body count and Larry King to report what's happening. We give them $43 million worth of weaponry (the sum George Bush, as recently as August, thought would be a nice amount to send to the Taliban), an airdropped bundle of peanut butter sandwiches and ten minutes to reproduce Afghanistan's religiopolitical structure. Does anyone seriously doubt that this much of an experiment would end up destabilizing all of human history?

"People are screaming through the cracks," says a colleague. I had never heard that expression before. She says it means that people are too scared to say what they mean when you ask them to speak on the record. "But if you ride the buses, talk to truck drivers, go to church, hang out with teenagers in the pool hall, they're terrified of this war. No one knows why all this is happening."

It is true that everyone has a different conspiracy theory of this war. When I first heard of the bombing, I thought it was retribution for Timothy McVeigh's execution and that "the terrorists" had chosen New York because it's a city of miscegenated minorities. A Jewish friend was equally certain that New York was chosen because "it's a Jewish city." A stockbroker friend finds it obvious that "they" were out to destroy world trade and global economics. Pat Robertson blames Bill Clinton. A Christian evangelical friend says that it's all about "the rapture," which is apparently that moment just short of end-time when the sanctified will be transported directly to heaven and the rest of us will perish. Maureen Dowd, Washington's favorite material girl, flips mournfully through the Neiman Marcus Christmas catalogue and concludes that it's because foreign agents don't want us to enjoy our "stuff." The White House blames "not all Muslims." And Ari Fleischer blames Bill Maher.

There's a brilliant trilogy by children's author Philip Pullman titled *His Dark Materials*. The tale features armored bears enlisted in the fight between good and evil—great clanking white bears who smash through enemy armies, clumsy but immense in their power. In my mind, I keep seeing those big armored bears as American warplanes bombing away, strong and accurate and deadly. But I am also visited by images of "the network" that they're fighting as more of a global spider web, very thin, fine lines of connection—tough, resilient and almost invisible. I keep worrying that armored bears aren't much use against a foe like that. The bears are entirely capable of wreaking havoc in a given spot, but the spider web is small, silent, hard to see—drawing strength from structure, not from size; from belief, not from force. And as long as we do not come to terms with the more subtle nature of that kind of adversary, I will not be able to visualize any good end in sight.

October 10, 2001
Patriot Games
Eric Alterman

Patriotism requires no apologies. Like anti-Communism and anti-Fascism, it is an admirable and thoroughly sensible a priori assumption from which to begin making more nuanced judgments. Nor does patriotism need to be exclusionary. I am an American patriot, a Jewish patriot and a New York chauvinist pig. My patriotism is not about governments and armies; it's about unions, civil rights marches and the '69 Mets. It's not Kate Smith singing "God Bless America"; it's Bruce Springsteen singing "This Land Is Your Land."

Of course, not everyone on the left concurs. While many nonpatriots share an idealistic belief in a kind of cosmopolitan, humanist internationalism, some—like Jerry Falwell and Pat Robertson on the right—really do hate this country. These leftists find nothing to admire in its magnificent Constitution; its fitful history of struggle toward greater freedom for women, minorities and other historically oppressed groups; and its values, however imperfectly or hypocritically manifested in everyday life. This became obvious in a few of the immediate reactions we heard in the wake of September 11. How could anyone say with certainty why we were attacked when we couldn't be sure who attacked us? All they could know, really, is why they thought we deserved it.

This "Hate America" left must be rejected for reasons of honor and pragmatism. It is difficult enough to "talk sense to the American people" in wartime without having to defend positions for which we have no intellectual or emotional sympathy. Many on the right are hoping to exploit a pregnant political moment to advance a host of antidemocratic policies. Principled dissent is never more necessary than when it is least welcome. American history is replete with examples of red scares, racist hysteria, political censorship and the indefensible curtailment of civil liberties that derive, in part, from excessive and abusive forms of superpatriotism. We are already seeing the beginnings of a concerted attack on civil liberties, freedom of expression and freedom of the press. Given the importance most Americans place on patriotism as a bedrock personal value, it is folly to try to enjoin them in a battle that fails to embrace their most basic beliefs.

Moreover, the refusal to draw this line invites the kind of McCarthyite thuggishness we see on display in the writings of pundits like Andrew Sullivan and Michael Kelly, and in the pages of (predictably) *National Review* and (sadly) *The New Republic*, tarring anyone with a wartime question or criticism as a pro-terrorist "Fifth Column" (Sullivan's term). Casting as wide a net as possible for their poisonous attacks, they choose examples so tiny as to be virtually nonexistent. In defense of his slander of the people of New York as well as virtually everyone else who voted against George Bush in the "red" areas of the nation, Sullivan pointed to an obscure website based in Denmark run by something called United Peoples. To smear opponents of unfettered free trade and globalization, *TNR* editor Peter Beinart seized on a bunch of anonymous postings to another, no less obscure, website whose name I cannot even remember. Kelly has now devoted two *Washington Post* columns to attacking all pacifists as "evil," "objectively pro-terrorist" and "Liars. Frauds. Hypocrites." But in neither column could he find the space—or the courage—to name a single one.

Because none of these writers have yet developed the reputation for malevolent hysteria enjoyed by, say, Marty Peretz on Israel or David

Horowitz and Ann Coulter on everything, there is a serious chance that the larger mass media, never good at making distinctions on the left in the best of times, will swallow and repeat their reprehensible assertions. The net result will be the exclusion of all progressives, America-hating or no, from the spectrum of "responsible" debate where decisions are made and the nation's future is determined.

The potential for politically motivated official censorship—beyond that which is genuinely necessary to protect the safety and security of our troops—is never far away in wartime. Politicians and generals quite understandably find the temptation to abuse this power irresistible. We saw countless such examples during the Gulf War, and we can discern hints of future threats from the lips of presidential press secretary Ari Fleischer, who endorsed the attempts of a few Madison Avenue mullahs to withdraw advertising from ABC's moronic talk show *Politically Incorrect* when host Bill Maher used the word "cowards" regarding the U.S. military's use of cruise missiles. "There are reminders to all Americans that they need to watch what they say, watch what they do, and this is not a time for remarks like that; there never is." (Speaking of cowardice, the White House edited Fleischer's remarks in its official transcript of the exchange.)

Yet another wartime peril to democracy derives from hyper-caution and self-censorship on the part of the media themselves. Why are newspapers like *Newsday* and the *Daily News* censoring comics who raise even the gentlest questions about George Bush? Exactly whom does the communications conglomerate Clear Channel imagine it is defending when it instructs its deejays not to play "Bridge Over Troubled Water" or "Ticket to Ride" on the radio? Why do newspaper publishers in Grants Pass, Oregon, and Galveston County, Texas, feel the need to fire writers and editors who wondered why the President "skedaddled" into a "Nebraska hole" on the day of the attack? Most disturbing of all, why has the consortium of national news organizations decided to postpone, apparently indefinitely, the news of who really won the Florida election last winter? The estimated publication date for the collective effort, overseen by the University of Chicago's National Opinion Research Center and costing more than $1 million, had been September 17.

But *The New York Times* political reporter Richard Berke wrote that the now "utterly irrelevant" report "might have stoked the partisan tensions."

In other words, the threat of "partisan tensions" arising from a potentially stolen election is more dangerous than continuing to live the lie. How wise of our media minders to decide that America needs to be protected—not from terrorists, but from truth.

October 17, 2001
War and Peace
Katha Pollitt

How depressing was the October 13 peace rally in Washington Square? Well, the Bread and Puppet Theater performed—that should give you an idea. "It's the sixties all over again," murmured the portly graybeard standing next to me as the funereal drum thudded and the players, holding their papier mâché body masks, paraded glumly through the crowd of perhaps 500 people—most, by the look of them, veterans of either the peace and justice or sectarian left. Look on the bright side, I thought: At least we don't have to sing "Down by the Riverside," as happened at the peace rally in Union Square on October 7, a few hours after bombs started falling on Afghanistan.

I don't like to criticize the activists who put together what little resistance to the bombing there is. But the 2000s aren't the 1960s, and whatever else Afghanistan is, it isn't Vietnam, any more than international terrorism or Islamic extremism is the new communism. Essential to the movement against the war in Vietnam was the pointlessness of our involvement: What had Ho Chi Minh ever done to us? The Vietcong never blew up American office buildings and murdered 5,000 ordinary American working people. You didn't have to be a pacifist or an opponent of all intervention everywhere to favor getting out of Vietnam—there were dozens of reasons, principled, pragmatic, humanitarian, self-serving, to be against the war. This time, our own country has been attacked, and the enemies are deranged fanatics. No amount of military force short of nuclear weapons would have defeated the North Vietnamese and Vietcong, who really did swim like fish in the sea of the people and had plenty of help from the Soviet Union besides; the Taliban, by contrast, are widely, although not universally, hated in Afghanistan, and Osama bin Laden's men, known as the Arab-Afghans, are viewed there by many as a hostile foreign presence.

Faced with a popular air war conducted, at least on paper, in such a way as to minimize civilian casualties, the peace movement falls back on boilerplate: All war everywhere is wrong, no matter what evils pertain; any use of force merely perpetuates the "cycle of violence"; the war is "racist," whatever that means; it's a corporate plot. The most rousing and focused speech at Washington Square was physicist Michio Kaku's denunciation of Star Wars—but no one I heard (I missed the noted foreign policy experts Al Sharpton and Patti Smith) grappled with the central question: If not war, what? Realistically, some of the alternatives that have been proposed would also involve military action. Osama bin Laden is not likely to mail himself to the International Criminal Court to be tried for crimes against humanity; the disarming of both the Taliban and the Northern Alliance by United Nations peacekeepers, followed by free and democratic elections—the course favored by the Revolutionary Association of the Women of Afghanistan—is not likely to happen peacefully either.

The attack on the World Trade Center, an unspeakable and unjustifiable crime, created a sense of urgency and feelings of fear and anger that do not easily accord with calls for a deeper understanding of America's role in the Muslim world. It's hard to care that the U.S. government armed and bankrolled the fundamentalist mujahedeen in Afghanistan to fight the Soviets, or that it supports clerical-fascist Islamic governments like the one in Saudi Arabia, when you're afraid to fly in an airplane or open your mail. Say for the sake of argument that the "chickens" of American foreign policy "are coming home to roost": You can see why many would answer, Well, so what? Why not just kill the chickens and be done with it? That may prove much more difficult than today's pro-war pundits acknowledge—what if one only hatches more chickens?—but it's not totally off the wall, like Alice Walker's embarrassing and oft-cited proposal that bin Laden be showered with love and "reminded of all the good, nonviolent things he has done."

Right now, the argument that the war will have unforeseen and disastrous consequences may sound like handwringing, but it is doubtless true. Given the millions who are starving in Afghanistan, the 37,500 mini-meals that have fallen from the sky are a cruel joke. And even if the Al Qaeda network is destroyed and the Taliban overthrown, the circumstances that created them will remain. This is the case whether one sees the attack on the WTC as inspired by religiously motivated hatred of modernity and Enlightenment values, like Christopher Hitchens, or as a response to particular American policies in Israel, Iraq and Saudi Arabia, as Noam Chomsky argues. Experts can debate the precise amount of motivation this or that factor contributes to terrorism—but unless the Muslim world is transformed on many levels, it is hard to see how the bombing of Afghanistan will keep Americans safe or prevent new Al Qaedas and Talibans from forming. For that, we would have to be able to look down the road ten years and see a peaceful, well-governed, rebuilt Afghanistan; a Pakistan in which the best chance for a poor boy or girl is public school, not a *madrassah* for him and nothing for her; a Saudi Arabia with a democratic, secular government; an Egypt without millions living in abject poverty and a hugely frustrated middle class. This is all the more true if militant Islam is relatively independent of concrete grievances like Israel and Iraq.

Unfortunately, anyone who tries to talk about the WTC attack in this way—as Susan Sontag did in her entirely reasonable but now infamous *New Yorker* piece—is likely to find themselves labeled a traitor, a coward, anti-American or worse. (I found this out myself when I made the mistake of going on the radio with mad Andrew Sullivan, who has said the "decadent left . . . may well mount a fifth column," and who accused me of objectively supporting the Taliban and likened me to someone who refuses to help a rape victim and blames her for wearing a short skirt.) But a war can be "just" in the sense that it is a response to aggression—as Vietnam was not—and also be the wrong way to solve a problem.

October 24, 2001
The Left and the Just War
Alexander Cockburn

The left is getting itself tied up in knots about the Just War and the propriety of bombing Afghanistan. I suspect some are intimidated by laptop bombardiers and kindred bully boys handing out white feathers and snarling about "collaborators" and being "soft on fascism." A recent issue of *The Nation* carried earnest efforts by Richard Falk and an editorial writer to mark out "the relevant frameworks of moral, legal, and religious restraint" to be applied to the lethal business of attacking Afghans.

I felt sorry for Falk as he clambered through his moral obstacle course. This business of trying to define a just war against Afghanistan is what C. Wright Mills used to call crackpot realism. War, as the United States has been fighting it in Iraq and Yugoslavia, consists mostly of bombing, intended to terrify the population and destroy the fabric of tolerable social existence.

Remember too that bombs mostly miss their targets. Colonel John Warden, who planned the air campaign in Iraq, said afterwards that dropping dumb bombs "is like shooting skeet; 499 out of 500 pellets may miss the target, but that's irrelevant." There will always be shattered hospitals and wrecked old folks' homes, just as there will always be Defense Department flacks saying that the destruction "cannot be independently verified" or that the hospitals or old folks' homes were actually sanctuaries for enemy forces or for "command and control."

How many bombing campaigns do we have to go through in a decade to recognize all the usual landmarks? What's unusual about the latest onslaught is that it is being leveled at a country where, on numerous estimates from reputable organizations, around 7.5 million people were, before September 11, at risk of starving to death. On September 16 *The New York Times* Islamabad correspondent John Burns reported that the United States "demanded elimination of truck convoys that provide much of the food and other supplies to Afghanistan's civilian population."

In early October the UN's World Food Program was able to resume shipments at a lower level, then the bombing began and everything stopped once more, amid fierce outcry from relief agencies that the United States was placing millions at risk, with winter just around the corner. On October 15 UN special rapporteur Jean Ziegler said the food airdrops by the same military force dropping bombs undermined the credibility of humanitarian aid. "As special rapporteur I must condemn with the last ounce of energy this operation called snowdropping [the air drops of food packages]; it is totally catastrophic for humanitarian aid." Oxfam reckons that before September 11, 400,000 were on the edge of starvation, 5.5 million "extremely vulnerable" and the balance of the overall 7.5 million at great risk. Once it starts snowing, 540,000 will be cut off from the food convoys that should have been getting them provisions for the winter.

So, by the time Falk was inscribing the protocols of what a just war might be, the United States was already engineering civilian deaths on an immense scale. Not, to be sure, the ghastly instant entombment of September 11, what Noam Chomsky has called "the most devastating instant human toll of any crime in history, outside of war," but death on the installment plan: malnutrition, infant mortality, disease, premature death for the old and so on. The numbers will climb and climb, and there won't be any "independent verification" such as the Pentagon demands.

Let's not be pettifogging and dwell on the point that nothing resembling proof of bin Laden's responsibility for the September 11 attack has yet been put forward either by the United States or its subordinate in Downing Street. Let's accept that the supreme strategist of the September 11 terror is Osama bin Laden. He's the Enemy. So what have been the Enemy's objectives? He desires the widest possible war: to kill Americans on American soil, to destroy the symbols of U.S. military power, to engage the United States in a holy war.

The first two objectives the Enemy could accomplish by itself; the third required the cooperation of the United States. Bush fell into the trap, and Falk, *The Nation* and some on the left have jumped in after him.

There can be no "limited war with limited objectives" when the bombing sets match atop tinder from Pakistan and Kashmir to Ramallah, Bethlehem, Jerusalem. "Limited war" is a far less realistic prospect than to regard September 11 as a crime, to pursue its perpetrators to justice in an international court, using all relevant police and intelligence agencies here and abroad.

The left should be for peace, which in no way means ignoring the demands of either side. Bin Laden calls for: an end to sanctions on Iraq; U.S. troops out of Saudi Arabia; justice for Palestinians. The left says aye to those, though we want a two-state solution whereas bin Laden wants to drive Jews along with secular and Christian Palestinians into the sea. The U.S. government calls for a dismantling of the Terror Network, and the left says aye to that too. Of course we oppose networks of people who wage war on civilians, as Seth Bardacke remarked to his dad after September 11. What the American people should have learned from September 11 is that bombing civilians is wrong. As Doug Lummis then wrote in Japan: "Fully grasping the total criminality and horror of those attacks can be used to grasp the equal criminality and horror of similar acts in the past. This understanding can provide a solid ground for opposing all similar acts (including state terrorism) in the future."

So we're pretty close to supporting demands on both sides, but we know these demands are not going to be achieved by war. What is this war about? On Bush's side it's about the defense of the American Empire; on the other, an attempt to challenge that in the name of theocratic fundamentalist Islam. On that issue the left is against both sides. We don't want anyone to kill or die in the name of the American Empire, for the "war on terror" to be cashed in blood in Colombia or anywhere else, or for anyone to kill or die in the name of Islamic fundamentalism. Go to the UN, proceed on the basis that September 11 was a crime. Bring the perpetrators to justice by legal means.

October 24, 2001

Homeland Insecurity

Patricia J. Williams

It is hard to write a column like this under the present circumstances. It is hard to comment on what is happening in the world if the military regulates everything. And yet it is impossible not to write about this moment when civil rights and liberties seem under attack from both within and without. "Civil libertarians should not become Luddites," says Alan Dershowitz, who spent most of the past decade railing against identity politics. These days, he's suggesting that we loosen up and get national identity cards. Sure it's been used by repressive regimes the world over, he admits, but "the reasons for not having them don't really apply here."

The gently centered Quaker part of me is trying hard to calm the Help!-Flee!-We're-Going-to-Hell-in-a-Handbasket! part of me. I do that by settling down to the task of stringing random notes together, a scattered kind of witness.

First, we are at war. Although no one but the Pentagon admits to knowing what is happening, one sign is the dark whumpa-whumpa sound of the quiet, low-flying surveillance planes. Last night, when my son had finished practicing "Three Blind Mice" on his trombone, my ears were filled with a dull reverberation somewhat greater than that which ordinarily troubles the air in the wake of his prodigious renditions. We looked out the window and saw three large lights on a dark aircraft that was floating along only a little way above the treetops. It looked as though aliens were landing—it slid quietly overhead like something out of *The Empire Strikes Back*. "They're on the watch for submarines," said a friend whose father is in the military. So I know we are at war.

Even my son has been recruited. He came home from school and looked for ways to earn a dollar. "I need money to send to George Bush," he explained. "Come wha . . . ?" I asked. It turned out he was answering the President's call for every child in America to donate a dollar to help feed refugee children. "I think this money is probably for UNICEF," I said. "No," insisted my son, who has heard a little about a lot. "George Bush is going to use it to give Afghan children some social security."

Second, our public health system is imploding. You can tell how panicked officials are by their bizarre yet perky incoherence in the face of emergency. "No cause for worry," they keep saying while trotting out the law of averages, like a schoolboy by the ear, to show how much more dangerous it is to drive a car. "Since 1975 there has been only one case . . . uh, make that two . . . uh, three . . . oops, a fourth . . . uh, maybe a fifth . . ." They spent the last week proclaiming that even though they had closed down Congress and the Capitol building, "no one should worry"—that phrase again—because there was no way that the bacterium "would present itself outside a sealed envelope."

They had to revise that assessment, of course, after four people at the Brentwood Postal Facility in Washington, DC, came down with the inhaled form. Since then, the government says it's going to set things right by mailing nearly every U.S. household a postcard with reassuring words and information listing the characteristics of missives worthy of suspicion. They will be mailing this bit of reassurance, presumably, from a large central postal facility. I wake up in the middle of the night imagining spores hitching rides on the coattails of mailmen as they fan out from our nation's capital and spread across the homeland. I know that this is an irrational thought, but still—it wakes me up. A former student tells me that he was sitting around at his cigar club (doesn't it just beg for parody? But . . . another time) and everyone was puffing away and asking each other how many units of Cipro they had "scored." "It's the new Ecstasy," he marvels. I see it as more like the new Agony.

Third, the word "homeland" has burrowed its way into ordinary conversation and multiplied with astonishing rapidity. It is not just the curious name of an office merging police and intelligence functions. It is a lowercase reference to purple mountains' majesty and all those fruited plains. Suddenly, "America the Beautiful" has become some sort of bad translation from the German. Like "Fatherland" or "empire," labels channel unspoken allegiances. I wonder about the line-drawing such an odd term was calculated to evoke—it sounds at once intimate and abstract—like the good-guy quadrant in some strategic computer game? Like the Bush team's attempt to sound epic? Like some effort to denationalize and fuse enemy status with that of domestic criminality—as in home-wreckers, home invaders, domestic abusers? "Homeland Security" is the new office of what they keep calling "psy-ops," after all. There's gotta be an angle.

The thing that worries me most about this time is how hard it is to talk about anything but fear. The fight has been framed as a war with "terror," a battle against an unruly if deadly emotionalism, rather than a war against specific bodies, specific land, specific resources. A war against terrorism is the inverse of a war "for" courage. It is a war of the mind, so broadly defined that the enemy becomes anybody who makes you afraid.

National Public Radio broadcast a conversation with Dr. Jerrold Post, a professor of something called "political psychology." Dr. Post discussed passages from an Al Qaeda training handbook in which operatives are advised to "blend in," to stay clean-shaven, not to talk too much over coffee and to pay their parking tickets in a timely fashion. The conversation was a classic bind in which the implied message is to trust no one, just tell the authorities every move your suspiciously average neighbors make.

It seduces, this corrosive distrust. Call me a Luddite, but I think this is a formula for panic. There are, of course, perfectly rational reasons to be afraid just now, but our unalloyed ideology of efficiency combined with a traumatic amount of actual bureaucratic bumbling has left us poised at the gateway of an even more fearsome world in which the "comfort" and convenience of high-tech totalitarianism gleam temptingly, yet in which our American-ness endures only with hands up! so that our fingerprints can be scanned, and our nationalized identity scrutinized for militarily defined signs of abnormal normativity.

October 24, 2001
'Blowback,' the Prequel
Eric Alterman

The story of what historians call the second cold war often begins with the Soviet invasion of Afghanistan in December 1979, which shocked Americans into their own overreaction in Central America and Africa, as well as into arming the mujahedeen resistance. Today, it is a truth universally acknowledged in the punditocracy that while the United States may have played an indirect role in the creation of the Taliban and perhaps even the bin Laden terrorist network through our support for the radical Islamic guerrillas in Afghanistan, we did so only in response to that act of Soviet aggression. As Tim Russert explained on *Meet the Press*, "We had little choice." Speaking on CNN, former U.S. Ambassador to Afghanistan Peter Tomsen speaks of our "successful policy with the ordnance we sent to the mujahedeen to defeat the Soviets." Writing on "The 'Blowback' Myth" in *The Weekly Standard*, one Thomas Henriksen of the Hoover Institution rehearses the Soviet invasion and then notes, "First President Carter, then, more decisively, Ronald Reagan moved to support the Afghan resistance."

The truth is that the United States began a program of covert aid to the Afghan guerrillas six months *before* the Soviets invaded.

First revealed by former Director of Central Intelligence Robert Gates in his 1996 memoir *From the Shadows*, the $500 million in nonlethal aid was designed to counter the billions the Soviets were pouring into the puppet regime they had installed in Kabul. Some on the American side were willing—perhaps even eager—to lure the Soviets into a Vietnam-like entanglement. Others viewed the program as a way of destabilizing the puppet government and countering the Soviets, whose undeniable aggression in the area was helping to reheat the cold war to a dangerous boil.

According to Gates's recounting, a key meeting took place on March 30, 1979. Under Secretary of Defense Walter Slocumbe wondered aloud whether "there was value in keeping the Afghan insurgency going, 'sucking the Soviets into a Vietnamese quagmire.' " Arnold Horelick, CIA Soviet expert, warned that this was just what we could expect. In a 1998 conversation with *Le Nouvel Observateur*, former National Security Adviser Zbigniew Brzezinski admitted, "We didn't push the Russians to intervene, but we knowingly increased the probability that they would."

Yet Carter, who signed the finding authorizing the covert program on July 3, 1979, today explains that it was definitely "not my intention" to inspire a Soviet invasion. Cyrus Vance, who was then Secretary of State, is not well enough to be interviewed, but his close aide Marshall Shulman insists that the State Department worked hard to dissuade the Soviets from invading and would never have undertaken a program to encourage it, though he says he was unaware of the covert program at the time. Indeed, Vance hardly seems to be represented at all in Gates's recounting, although Brzezinski doubts that Carter would have approved the aid unless Vance "approved, however unenthusiastically."

No one I interviewed—those who did not mind the idea of a Soviet invasion, and those who sought to avoid it—argues that Carter himself wished to provoke one. Gates, who was then an aide to Brzezinski, says the President did not think "strategically" in that fashion. "He was simply reacting to everything the Soviets were doing in that part of the world and felt it required some kind of response. This was it." Brzezinski, similarly, says he did not sell the plan to Carter on these terms. The President understood, he explained on the phone, that "the Soviets had engineered a Communist coup and they were providing direct assistance in Kabul. We were facing a serious crisis in Iran, and the entire Persian Gulf was at stake. In that context, giving some money to the mujahedeen seemed justified." Why Carter actually approved the aid remains unclear, however. Carter, it should be added, does not seem to remember much about the initial finding. Otherwise, he would not have asked his aide to fax me the pages from his memoir *Keeping Faith*, which ignores it entirely, and like the rest of the pre-Gates memoirs of the period, professes great shock and horror regarding the onset of the Soviet tanks.

The news of the covert program has provoked considerable confusion among those who seek to blame the United States for the September 11 massacre. Proponents of an overly schematic "blowback" scenario, including at least one vocal supporter of the Soviet "rape" of Afghanistan, have seized Brzezinski's comments to claim that Osama bin Laden is merely one of America's "chickens coming home to roost." This is both simplistic and obscene. Blowback exists in absolutely every aspect of life, because nothing comes without unintended consequences. Does it make sense to blame the destruction of the World Trade Center on a $500 million nonlethal aid program that took place more than twenty years ago? We cannot even know for certain why the Soviets decided on their invasion.

Nor can we ever know for certain whether the U.S. officials wished to inspire one. Memories deceive, records get destroyed and even original documents can be written to be deliberately misleading, as were the period's official memoirs—save, ironically, that of Gates, the former spymaster. The covert action was undoubtedly approved by those involved for a host of reasons, some of which may be contradictory. Helping the Afghans resist Soviet domination was not exactly a controversial policy in 1979, though no one at the time could even dream that it might lead to the evil empire's eventual disintegration.

Brzezinski argues that even given the 20/20 hindsight after September 11, the covert aid remains justified. He shares the common view that America's most significant mistake was to abandon the nation to its unhappy fate following the Soviet withdrawal. Our terrorist problem, he insists, would be much worse with the Soviets still around to support their terrorist minions among the Palestinians, the Syrians, the Libyans, the Iraqis, etc.

Certainly this is much too kind to the Reagan-era military aid to Taliban-like elements. But a more accurate historical record can only lead to more intelligent debate about the future.

PRESS WATCH

September 26, 2001
Press Watch
Michael Massing

A few minutes into ABC's *World News Tonight* on September 21—the night after George W. Bush's speech to Congress—Peter Jennings somberly noted that it was "time for all Americans to begin learning more about Afghanistan." I immediately perked up. Since the calamitous events of September 11, the networks had focused heavily on the human and physical toll of the attacks and on the nation's fitful efforts to come to terms with them. And they performed admirably in those initial days, consoling and comforting the public even as they were informing it. But as the days passed, and as the government prepared to strike at Osama bin Laden and his Afghan hosts, the need for some sharp political analysis became urgent, and here, on cue, was Jennings, promising a mini-tutorial.

Leaning forward, I looked expectantly at my TV screen—only to find it filled with the pale, bespectacled face of Tony Cordesman. Cordesman, of course, was a ubiquitous talking head during the Gulf War, and now he was back, holding forth in the same nasal monotone. He dutifully recited some basic facts about Afghanistan—the small size of the Taliban army, the limited number of tanks and aircraft at its disposal, the scarcity of bombing targets on the ground. "The job is extraordinarily difficult if not impossible if you set deadlines and demand instant success," Cordesman burbled. Then he was gone, and the program was back to its ongoing coverage of victims, heroes and terrorists. We learned nothing about the level of support for the Taliban, about the strength of the opposition, about America's long history of involvement in the region.

The segment was typical. As the nation prepares to go to war, the coverage on TV—the primary source of news for most Americans—has been appallingly superficial. Constantly clicking my remote in search of insight, I was stunned at the narrowness of the views offered, at the Soviet-style reliance on official and semiofficial sources. On *Meet the Press*, for instance,

Tim Russert's guests were Colin Powell and (as he proudly announced) the "four leaders of the United States Congress"—Dennis Hastert, Richard Gephardt, Trent Lott and Tom Daschle. "How did the events of September 11 change you?" the normally feisty Russert tremulously asked each. Seeking wisdom on the question of Why They Hate Us, Barbara Walters turned to former Bush communications director, now senior White House counselor, Karen Hughes. "They hate the fact that we elect our leaders," Hughes vacuously replied. On NBC, Brian Williams leaned heavily on failed-drug-czar-turned-TV-consultant Barry McCaffrey ("Americans are natural fighters," McCaffrey fatuously informed us), while on *The Capital Gang* Mark Shields asked former Middle East diplomat Edward Walker, "Can the antiterrorism coalition really count this time on Saudi Arabia?"

To a degree, such deference reflects TV's customary rallying around the flag in times of national crisis. Such a stance is understandable; in light of the enormity of the attack, even atheists are singing "God Bless America." But the jingoistic displays on TV over the past two weeks—the repeated references to "we" and "us," the ostentatious sprouting of lapel flags, Dan Rather's startling declaration that "George Bush is the President, he makes the decisions and, you know, as just one American, he wants me to line up, just tell me where"—have violated every canon of good journalism. They have also snuffed out any whiff of debate and dissent; the discussion taking place within the Bush Administration is no doubt more vigorous than that presented on TV.

But there's more than simple patriotism at work here. The thinness of the coverage and the shallowness of the analysis seem a direct outgrowth of the networks' steady disengagement from the world in recent years. Since the end of the cold war, overseas bureaus have been closed, foreign correspondents recalled and the time allocated to international news sharply pared. Having thus plucked out their eyes, the networks—suddenly faced with a global crisis—are lunging about in the dark, trying desperately to find their footing.

No outlet has seemed more blinkered than CNN. The network that once emulated the BBC has instead become another MSNBC, and while it can still count on Christiane Amanpour to parachute into the world's hot zones, and on the game efforts of such on-the-ground assets as Nic Robertson in Kabul, the network has seemed thoroughly flummoxed by the complex political forces set in motion by the events of September 11. Consider, for instance, that famous brief clip showing a clutch of Palestinians celebrating the attack on the World Trade Center. Within days, word began circulating on the Internet that the footage had actually been shot during the Gulf War. The furor became so great that CNN eventually had to issue a statement describing where it got the tape (from a Reuters cameraman in East Jerusalem who insisted that he had not encouraged the celebration, as some claimed).

The real scandal, though, is that CNN repeatedly showed the clip without commentary, without attempting to place it in the broader context of reactions from the Islamic world. What were people in Gaza and the West Bank actually saying? Where were the interviews with clerics in Cairo, editorial writers in Amman, shopkeepers in Jakarta and schoolteachers in Kuala Lumpur? It was certainly not hard to obtain such views—witness Ian Fisher's sparkling dispatch from Gaza in *The New York Times* ("In the Gaza Strip, Anger at the U.S. Still Smolders") and Peter Waldman and Hugh Pope's excellent front-page roundup in *The Wall Street Journal*: "Some Muslims Fear War on Terrorism Is Really a War on Them; West Undercuts Islam, They Say, by Backing Israel, Autocratic Mideast Rule."

Not all was bland on CNN. Jeff Greenfield, for one, made some genuine efforts to probe the Islamic world's complex love-hate relationship with the United States. On September 20, for instance, he had a spirited discussion with Afghanistan hands Barnett Rubin of New York University and Shibley Telhami of the University of Maryland, along with Farid Esack, a Muslim scholar at Auburn Theological Seminary. Far more representative, though, was "What Do We Know About Islam?" an exceedingly brief Sunday segment in which a Christian minister and a Muslim cleric offered very vague observations about relations between Christianity and Islam. It was followed by an interview with a Muslim-American who assured us that "Islam means peace." Shot in Boston and New York, the segment drove home how CNN has lost that precious journalistic ability to work the streets of the world and discover what's really taking place there. Given CNN's critical part in keeping the world informed, one can only hope that it will soon regain its bearings.

October 3, 2001

Michael Massing

Of all the programs I've seen on Afghanistan, not one was more chilling than *Beneath the Veil*, an hourlong documentary that has appeared frequently on CNN. Its narrator, Saira Shah, a British woman of Afghan descent, spent five days in the country to see what life there was really like. Shah managed to penetrate places few Westerners get to see, including a secret classroom for girls and a village that suffered Taliban atrocities. She also visited a Kabul soccer stadium that, she said, had served as a public execution ground. To back up her point, the documentary featured a clip of a man putting a rifle to the head of a woman clad in a burqa and blowing her brains out. In an interview with the Taliban foreign minister, Shah asked what he thought the international donors who gave money for the stadium would say if they knew it was being used for executions rather than for sports. Well, the minister said, if they didn't like it, they should give money to build a separate arena for executions.

Shah's report captures just how horrendous life in Afghanistan has become. The Taliban's police-state tactics, together with its harboring of terrorists, has fed a groundswell of support for its ouster. That, in turn, has focused new attention on the Taliban's main opponents, the United Front, or, as it's more familiarly known, the Northern Alliance. Eager to report on it, U.S. journalists have swarmed into the sliver of territory the alliance controls in northeastern Afghanistan, where they're cordially taken on tours by rebel commanders.

"We're with the troops of the Northern Alliance," MSNBC's Tom Aspell reported on September 27. The alliance, he said, was eager to act as a guide for American forces entering Afghanistan. CNN's Chris Burns, gesturing toward a mountain ridge, said, "Thirty miles beyond that, is where Kabul is. And they say if they had help from the Americans, they could take that city." Meanwhile, a procession of alliance spokesmen have appeared on TV to plead for U.S. assistance.

The print media have been no less accommodating. "Front-line Taliban Foes Eager to Help U.S.," *The New York Times* declared on its front page. Reporter David Rohde described how a Northern Alliance general "swaggered across the top floor" of a demolished airfield control tower and pointed southward. " 'On the other side of those mountains,' he said, his voice filled with yearning, 'is Kabul.' " While the alliance did not pose an immediate military threat to the city, Rohde noted, it did have "encyclopedic knowledge of the Taliban and its bombing targets, units and tactics." The *Washington Post* has run a series of glowing reports about the alliance and its grit, savvy and "discipline." That discipline, correspondent Peter Baker noted in one dispatch, has survived the September 9 assassination of Ahmed Shah Massoud, the guerrilla leader who "by sheer force of personality had managed to hold together this eclectic group of warriors."

In death, Massoud has been lionized by the U.S. press—literally. "The legendary 'Lion of the Panjshir,' " the *Los Angeles Times* called him. "A Lion's Death," *The New Yorker* declared in a headline atop a one-page eulogy by Jon Lee Anderson. In 1992, Anderson reported, Massoud's "moderately conservative group" defeated the brutish regime backed by the Soviets, and he served as defense minister and vice president until 1996, when the Taliban gained control of most of the country.

What neither Anderson nor the rest of the press has reported is that during their time in power, Massoud and his fellow warlords ruthlessly fought one another, reducing much of Kabul to rubble and killing tens of thousands of people, most of them civilians. According to a meticulously documented report by Human Rights Watch (*Afghanistan: Crisis of Impunity*, available at www.hrw.org), the front "amassed a deplorable record of attacks on civilians" between 1992 and 1996. It was the lawlessness and brutality that prevailed under these warlords that paved the way for the Taliban. Since then,

Human Rights Watch reports, both the Taliban and the United Front "have repeatedly committed serious violations of international humanitarian law, including killings of detainees, aerial bombardment and shelling, direct attacks on civilians, rape, torture, persecution on the basis of religion, and the use of antipersonnel landmines."

In one of the few departures from the pack, Patricia Gossman noted in a *Washington Post* Op-Ed that Afghans have been fleeing Kabul "not only out of fear of U.S. airstrikes but out of panic that the [Northern Alliance] might take power there again." Gossman, a writer whose research has been funded by the U.S. Institute of Peace, wrote that when she was in Kabul last year, "I was told time and again that the only thing people there feared more than the Taliban was that the warlords of the Northern Alliance might return to power."

Michael Sullivan, in a fine piece for NPR, pointed out that the Northern Alliance is made up of Afghanistan's ethnic Tajik and Uzbek minorities, "with only token representation from the country's ethnic Pashtun majority, who've dominated Afghanistan's political landscape for most of the country's history." Without involving the Pashtuns, a Pakistani security analyst told him, having a stable government in Afghanistan "would be simply impossible." (The Taliban is made up mostly of Pashtuns.)

What accounts for the media blackout on the United Front's true colors? As Ken Silverstein observed in an astute piece for *Salon*, the front's many abuses "can't be a surprise" to reporters. Since September 11, he notes, several thousand people, "presumably many of them journalists," have requested the Human Rights Watch report on Afghanistan, but "most reporters and pundits seem to be patriotically turning a blind eye to our new partner's shortcomings."

The press may at last be opening its eyes. *Time*, in its October 8 edition, offered a balanced piece on the United Front, referring to its "fractious makeup" and "disappointingly thin" intelligence. And David Rohde, in another front-page piece in the *Times* on the Northern Alliance, used the w-word—warlords—and described their recruitment of fighters as young as 12.

According to the *Times*, the Bush Administration has decided to provide covert aid to several groups opposed to the Taliban, the United Front included. In light of the urgent need to root out war criminals like Osama bin Laden, it can be argued that Washington needs every bit of help it can get. But at the very least, the American public needs to know whom we are embracing. After all, it was just a few years ago that the CIA—eager to confront the Soviets—backed the mujahedeen, including many of the same Taliban fighters we are now seeking to overthrow.

October 10, 2001

Michael Massing

The press conference that Defense Secretary Donald Rumsfeld held shortly after the United States began bombing Afghanistan on October 7 was painful to behold. The questions posed by reporters tended to be either trivial—Did the B-2s involved in the mission depart from the United States?—or thoughtless. Since September 11 Rumsfeld had repeatedly said that he would not divulge any information that might endanger ongoing operations, but that did not stop reporters from trying to elicit it. CNN's Jamie McIntyre, for instance, kept demanding to know whether the United States planned to send ground troops into Afghanistan. Rumsfeld did his best to ignore him, but, as McIntyre persisted, the Secretary finally fixed him with an icy stare and said, "We don't discuss operational details."

The briefing reminded me of the famous *Saturday Night Live* sketch aired during the Persian Gulf War, in which reporters—despite being warned not to ask about matters that could aid the enemy—posed questions like, "What date are we going to start the ground attack?" and "Where are our forces most vulnerable to attack?" The sketch captured the public's disdain for the media's mindless aggressiveness and reinforced the first Bush Administration's inclination to restrict the flow of information about the war.

Now, with a new conflict upon us, the second Bush Administration seems intent on imposing similar controls. "Although the administration says it is not engaged in censorship," Elisabeth Bumiller reported in *The New York Times*, "officials throughout the government readily say they have been ordered to be circumspect about their remarks." This is certainly troubling. Without access to battle sites and timely information, the press—whatever its faults—will have a hard time assessing the success of U.S. actions. Accordingly, U.S. news organizations have been pushing the Pentagon to be more open.

That seems unlikely to happen, however. As during the Gulf War, the public seems to support the Administration's approach. Rather than sit around and grumble, though, reporters and editors should rededicate themselves to the real task at hand, which is providing the fullest possible coverage of the complicated new era we have entered. That, in turn, requires journalists to show such qualities as independence, enterprise and, yes, courage. Regardless of how much information the government provides, the press must pose uncomfortable questions, challenge broadly held assumptions and solicit opinion from a wide range of sources.

There are some hopeful signs. During the Gulf War, the press uncritically accepted Pentagon assertions about the accuracy of its missiles. Postwar studies showed those claims to be vastly exaggerated, and many journalists felt burned. A month into the current conflict, some journalists have shown their determination to avoid a repeat. Thus, after the Rumsfeld briefing, Richard Hawley, a former U.S. general turned ABC news consultant, told Peter Jennings that in bombing Afghanistan, the United States was using precision-guided weapons so as to avoid "collateral damage." Jennings immediately pounced. During the Gulf War, he observed, generals "repeatedly talked about precision-guided weapons, and they turned out to be anything but precise. How much better is it now?" Hawley said that U.S. missiles now have GPS-aided navigational devices that make for "far fewer stray rounds." Whether that's so remains to be seen, of course, but the exchange shows how some journalists, at least, have learned from that past conflict.

The current one, however, offers a host of new challenges, especially in covering the political dimensions of the conflict. And here the press could do much better. To cite one example, the Pentagon revealed on October 7 that in addition to dropping bombs on Afghanistan, it was dropping humanitarian food packages. In all, it said, it was delivering about 37,000 packages. Most news organizations accepted at face value the Pentagon's explanation that this showed America's concern for the well-being of the Afghan people. In all, though, millions of Afghans face starvation, and the next day NPR reported that Doctors Without Borders had condemned the U.S. food drop as "propaganda" and, further, that the bombing had caused the UN World Food Program in Pakistan to suspend its daily shipments of 700 tons of food into Afghanistan. In reporting this, NPR did not rely on handouts from the Pentagon; rather, it went into the field and developed its own sources of information. (In fairness, Washington says it plans to increase greatly the size of its food drops once it is safe to do so.)

Another, more serious example of the press's credulity has been its coverage of the U.S. intelligence services. In light of the failures to predict the September 11 attacks, the press has almost unanimously concluded that the United States needs to beef up its spying abroad and to "unleash" the CIA to fight terrorism. In a piece for *The New Yorker*, for instance, Seymour Hersh, relying heavily on sources within the U.S. intelligence community, lambasted the CIA for turning away from the rough-and-tumble methods it used during the cold war. "Look," one agent told Hersh, "we recruited assholes. I handled bad guys. But we don't recruit people from the Little Sisters of the Poor—they don't *know* anything." A piece in *The New York Times*'s Week in Review section echoed Hersh. "The CIA's spies are ill-equipped to fight a dirty war in the world's back alleys," lamented Tim Weiner, who went on to cite the need for American intelligence to rebuild its capacity for "old-fashioned espionage" and satisfy the "urge for covert action to combat an invisible foe."

These articles offered no independent assessments as to how much impact such a buildup could actually have in combating terrorism. Even more troubling, they showed no awareness of the serious costs of past U.S. covert operations, from the Congo to Cambodia to Latin America. This omission seemed especially dismaying in the case of Hersh, who over the years has broken so many stories about clandestine mischief abroad.

Clearly, the United States needs to improve its ability to confront invidious groups like Al Qaeda. We are indeed fighting a new kind of war, and it requires new types of responses. Yet the unthinking acceptance of premises like the need to "unleash" the CIA does not advance the discussion. More than ever, U.S. journalists must avoid the temptation to engage in groupthink and—without seeming reflexively adversarial—must ask sharp questions. In the end, the danger they face is not just censorship, but self-censorship.

October 17, 2001

Michael Massing

Since September 11, Thomas Friedman has been in fine form. In his *New York Times* column, he has composed a letter for George W. Bush to send to Osama bin Laden, urged Vladimir Putin to enlist the Russian mafia to rub him out and berated those who would use the Trade Center and Pentagon attacks to raise questions about U.S. foreign policy. In an October 5 column headlined, "Yes, but What?" Friedman wrote, "One can only be amazed at the ease with which some people abroad and at campus teach-ins now tell us what motivated the terrorists. Guess what? The terrorists didn't leave an explanatory note. Because their deed was their note: We want to destroy America, starting with its military and financial centers." Friedman reserved special scorn for those seeking to use the attacks to renew the Israeli-Palestinian peace process: "Have you ever seen Osama bin Laden say, 'I just want to see a smaller Israel in its pre-1967 borders,' or 'I have no problem with America, it just needs to have a lower cultural and military profile in the Muslim world'? These terrorists aren't out for a new kind of coexistence with us. They are out for our nonexistence. None of this seems to have seeped into the 'Yes, but . . .' crowd, whose most prominent 'Yes, but' states: This terrorist act would never have happened if America hadn't been so supportive of Israel."

Friedman is hardly alone in pushing this line. In *Newsweek*, for instance, Jonathan Alter blasted "Blame America Firsters" who have "repeatedly breached" the line "between explaining terrorism and rationalizing it." Jim Hoagland, in the *Washington Post*, warned that the United States should not be inhibited from using "coercive power" in the Middle East by "excessive fear of reaction in the so-called 'Arab street.' " *The New Republic* has repeatedly inveighed against what it sees as the capitulationism of the Yes, but-ers, and Christopher Hitchens in these pages kicked up a storm by arguing against "rationalization" of terror. "Does anyone suppose that an Israeli withdrawal from Gaza would have forestalled the slaughter in Manhattan?" he asked.

Against this backdrop, I was fascinated to read "Why Do They Hate Us?" Fareed Zakaria's cover story in the October 15 *Newsweek*. Zakaria is a blue-chip member of the foreign policy establishment. A native of India who earned a BA from Yale and a PhD from Harvard, he served from 1993 to 2000 as managing editor of *Foreign Affairs*. A sort of junior Kissinger, Zakaria has never hidden his disdain for those naïve souls who do not share his hardheaded balance-of-power worldview. I recall attending a discussion group several years ago, when the Clinton Administration was still debating whether to intervene in Bosnia; Zakaria expressed world-weary impatience with those who argued for humanitarian intervention and nation-building.

I was thus surprised by his 7,000-word take on the current crisis. Zakaria devotes the first part of his article to an astute dissection of the failures of the Arab world. Today, he observed, almost every Arab country "is less free than it was 30 years ago." Analyzing the causes of that decline, Zakaria described how young Arab men, often better educated than their parents, leave their villages in search of work and "arrive in noisy, crowded cities like Cairo, Beirut and Damascus." Here, "they see great disparities of wealth and the disorienting effects of modernity; most unsettlingly, they see women, unveiled and in public places, taking buses, eating in cafes and working alongside them." Surrounded by the shiny products of globalization but unable to consume them, and denied all outlets for venting their frustrations, these alienated young men have fed a resurgence of Islam.

That, in turn, has sparked a wave of what he calls "raw anti-Americanism." In exploring the roots of this, Zakaria harshly scrutinizes U.S. policies in the region. As recently as the 1960s, he writes, America was widely admired in the Arab world. Since then, however, "the daily exposure to Israel's iron-fisted rule over the occupied territories has turned this into the great cause of the Arab—and indeed the broader Islamic—world. Elsewhere, they look at American policy in the region as cynically geared to America's oil interests, supporting thugs and tyrants without any hesitation. Finally, the bombing and isolation of Iraq have become fodder for daily attacks on the United States." Zakaria especially faults the United States for its "sins of omission," including its failure to press Arab regimes to open up. In response to the current crisis, he goes on, the United States should adopt a long-term strategy on three fronts—a military effort, aimed at the "total destruction of Al Qaeda"; a political effort, stressing multilateralism, cooperation with the United Nations and a solution to the Israeli-Palestinian conflict; and a cultural strategy seeking to help Islam "enter the modern world," in part by pressing Muslim nations to reform.

This seems a far cry from Henry Kissinger. And, toward the end of his piece, Zakaria acknowledges his changing views: "I have myself been skeptical of nation-building in places where our interests were unclear and it seemed unlikely that we would stay the course." In the current instance, he added, "stable political development is the key to reducing our single greatest security threat. We have no option but to get back into the nation-building business."

Zakaria's interest in nation-building and a peace settlement in the Middle East does not mean he's rationalizing terrorism. On the contrary, he fully supports the current campaign against Al Qaeda and the Taliban. His position shows that re-examining the U.S. role in the region does not preclude taking a tough stand on terrorism. In fact, it can be argued that adjusting U.S. policies in the Middle East—for instance, by resolving the Palestinian problem—could further the campaign against bin Laden by making it easier for Washington to keep its coalition together.

At least one other conservative has made an about-face similar to Zakaria's. George Bush's recent endorsement of nation-building in Afghanistan and his expressions of support for a Palestinian state show that he readily accepts the need to reassess U.S. policies in the Islamic world. To the extent that there is a "Yes, but . . ." crowd, the President seems to be its leading member.

October 24, 2001
Seven Days in October
Michael Massing

A month ago, when thirty-seven neoconservatives, led by William Kristol, William Bennett and Jeane Kirkpatrick, signed an open letter warning George Bush that failure to attack Iraq would "constitute an early and perhaps decisive surrender in the war on international terrorism," they were widely dismissed as extremists. But in one short week, the extreme became the mainstream, thanks largely to the anthrax scare and to the media's role in fanning it.

On Tuesday, October 16, Senator Tom Daschle announced that the anthrax discovered in a letter sent to his office was of a "very potent" form. On Wednesday, the headlines blared. "Sign of Escalating Threat," *The New York Times* declared atop a story by Stephen Engelberg and Judith Miller. This "high grade" anthrax, they wrote, "finely milled so that it would float a considerable distance on the smallest of air currents," suggested that "for the first time in history a sophisticated form of anthrax has been developed and used as a weapon in warfare or bioterrorism." It also suggested that "somewhere, someone has access to the sort of germ weapons capable of inflicting huge casualties." A prime suspect, Engelberg and Miller noted, was Iraq. But, they cautioned, it was too early to say for sure whether Iraq was responsible.

On the next day's Op-Ed pages, even that caveat was missing. In the *Times*, Richard Butler, a former UN weapons inspector in Iraq, wrote that, based on his visits to Iraq from 1997 to 1999, he had concluded that "biological weapons are closest to President Hussein's heart because it was in this area that his resistance to our work reached its height." Noting reports that hijacker Mohamed Atta had met with an Iraqi intelligence agent in Prague last year, Butler observed that this "may have been an occasion on which anthrax was provided" to him.

In the same day's *Wall Street Journal*, former Director of Central Intelligence R. James Woolsey held forth about "The Iraq Connection," as the headline put it. The "professionally prepared and precisely sized anthrax spores" that closed down the Capitol, he wrote, made it essential to determine with whom we are "at war." Offering various bits of circumstantial evidence against Saddam Hussein, including that Mohamed Atta meeting in Prague, Woolsey urged the Bush Administration to move against Baghdad.

Meanwhile, in the *Washington Post*, Richard Cohen, in a column headlined "Public Enemy No. 2," noted that while it was not yet clear whether Saddam was responsible for the anthrax in Daschle's office, it didn't really matter. "Neither the United States nor the rest of the world should countenance any state—especially a rogue one—developing weapons of mass destruction," Cohen wrote. "Saddam and his bloody bugs have to go."

The next day, Tom Ridge, the director of the Office of Homeland Security, announced that further testing showed that the strain of anthrax in Daschle's mail was indistinguishable from that found in the offices of NBC in Manhattan and the *National Enquirer* in Florida, and, moreover, that the tests "have shown that these strains have not been, quote, unquote, weaponized."

Then, on Saturday, the *Times*, in a story filed by John Tagliabue from Prague, reported that Czech officials, upon investigation, had concluded that Atta had *not* met with an Iraqi intelligence official during his stop in Prague.

Buried on page B6, the *Times* story received little attention. One person who noticed it, however, was George Stephanopoulos, and he brought it up in an exchange with George Will on ABC's *This Week* on Sunday morning. "Iraq's fingerprints were all over the '93 bombing of the World Trade Center," said Will, one of the most vocal proponents of going after Saddam Hussein. "We know that Mohamed Atta met in Prague with Iraqi agents——"

"We actually don't know that," Stephanopoulos interrupted. "The

Prague intelligence services have said they can't confirm that. They're still working on it."

"As Rumsfeld says, 'The absence of evidence is not the evidence of absence,' " Will sniffed. "The fact is, there's lots of reports of contacts in Sudan and Afghanistan and in Prague that suggest that Iraq is involved. And there is a large constituency in this town desperate not to see that because it then does dictate action." In other words, Will seemed to say, Don't bother me with the facts.

Will's was not the only voice raised against Iraq on the Sunday morning talk shows. On NBC's *Meet the Press*, Senators John McCain and Joe Lieberman urged the Administration to attack Saddam. On CBS's *Face the Nation*, Dr. Richard Spertzel, a former UN biochemical weapons inspector in Iraq, said that he did in fact believe the anthrax found in Daschle's office was weapons grade and that "most likely" it came "from some other country." Spertzel was followed by Jim Hoagland, a *Washington Post* columnist who has also vigorously advocated attacking Iraq. While we don't yet have the evidence that Iraq was involved in the anthrax incidents, Hoagland said, they "should bring home to us the danger of having a regime in place" that has the motivation.

Taking in all this, I was struck by how monolithic and unquestioning coverage had become. Because anthrax had been discovered in New York and Washington, the political and journalistic establishment suddenly seems united in wanting to attack Iraq. Here and there I found a few notes of skepticism. In the London *Guardian*, for instance, in a piece headlined, "Don't Blame Saddam for This One," Scott Ritter, another former weapons inspector in Iraq, observed that Iraq's main biological weapons facility was destroyed as part of the inspection process and that all the tests before the inspectors were kicked out had produced "no evidence of anthrax or any other biological agent." And Sharon Begley, in a fine article in *Newsweek*, noted that "thousands of scientists around the world have learned how to turn anthrax into a weapon" and that the equipment needed to do so is "not hard to acquire."

None of this, of course, rules out the possibility that Iraq does indeed have a bioterrorism capability. For the most part, though, the press seems uninterested in reporting on this or other key questions. What is the evidence of Iraq's ties to Al Qaeda? What did the UN inspectors find in Iraq, and what has been taking place there since they stopped visiting? If Iraq is shown to have ties to the anthrax attacks, or to September 11, what practically could the United States do about it? If, as the hawks seem to want, we did invade Iraq, what would the consequences be? Clearly, it's time for more facts and less opinion.

October 31, 2001
Unleash the Press
John R. MacArthur

For the straight-faced Pentagon press corps—assured by so many commentators that irony ended on September 11—Defense Secretary Donald Rumsfeld's pointedly ironic remarks on October 18 about war news must have come as a great surprise. "Let's hear it for the essential daily briefing, however hollow and empty it might be," Rumsfeld gibed, in open mockery of the beat reporters' request for regular updates from the Afghanistan front. "We'll do it. Five days a week, not seven." The straight men, converted to court jesters, laughed heartily at the Secretary's joke.

Thus do we witness the death throes of independent war coverage by a free press, a once-popular notion that reached its apogee in the latter stages of the war in Vietnam. Rumsfeld is old enough to remember the infamous "Five O'Clock Follies" in Saigon—dubbed as such by a skeptical media—at which U.S. military spokesmen spouted all manner of upbeat nonsense to bored reporters. But in those days most of the media knew that the briefings were shot through with lies—they made fun of the briefers, not the other way around. Today the government is prosecuting its military campaign in near-complete secrecy, confident that journalists will salute without the slightest irony.

How we got to Rumsfeld's joke is not, of course, very funny. The military establishment, particularly within the Army, was deeply wounded, not only by losing the actual war in Vietnam but also by losing the image of morality and innocence that accompanied U.S. soldiers into battle in World War II and Korea. The smartest among them decided to promote the absurd idea that the press "lost" Vietnam by demoralizing the American people with inaccurate, sensational reporting born of too much access to the battlefield. The public relations war planners were ably assisted by journalists like Peter Braestrup, who argued, for example, that the Tet offensive, while clearly a public relations defeat for the United States, was in reality a decisive military defeat for the Vietcong. Hence, protested the revisionists, the television images of besieged American GIs in Hue unfairly portrayed a losing cause, when victory was still within our grasp. We could have won the war!

Attached to this theory was the equally specious suggestion that U.S. reporters were fundamentally unpatriotic and cynically scoop-hungry, happy to reveal military secrets that would get American soldiers killed. In truth they were overly patriotic in the early years of Vietnam. And as for fatal security breaches, they never occurred—not once—though that hasn't stopped the government propagandists from establishing ground rules for coverage worthy of *Catch-22*: "We would much rather have open reporting," purrs Pentagon spokesperson Victoria Clarke, as long as it doesn't endanger the troops. But it always turns out that "open reporting" compromises "operational security."

Successive administrations and the Pentagon, impressed by British media control of the Falklands/Malvinas war, refined their wartime PR strategy with each post-Vietnam operation: During the Grenada invasion they simply kept quiet and left the press behind; in Panama they formed combat "pools" (small, closely supervised and noncompetitive groups of reporters required to share information) that departed Washington well after the first wave of troops had landed and then were confined to a military base until most of the action was over; in the Gulf War the pools were enlarged, but their military minders made sure that they never arrived in time to see any killing. Not only were pictures of corpses banned during the Gulf War but pictures of coffins were banned as well. The first Bush Administration was distressed by split-screen TV images showing rows of pine boxes from the Panama invasion at Dover Air Force Base, while the adjacent President glorified the sacrifice of U.S. troops in Operation Just Cause.

During the bombing of Belgrade, in a weird turn of political correctness, the Clinton PR apparatus even forbade reporters from revealing the last names of bomber pilots for fear their families might receive hate mail. The Clintonites had learned their lesson about information management the hard way in Somalia in October 1993, during the so-called UN peacekeeping mission. There, U.S. reporters were run out of the capital by Somali violence against journalists and by dire warnings from the U.S. military. Fortunately, a courageous Canadian reporter, Paul Watson of the *Toronto Star*, stayed on to witness the bloody disaster that ensued when U.S. Army Rangers helicoptered in to try to seize the warlord Mohammed Farah Aidid. Watson's photograph of the half-naked corpse of an American soldier being dragged through the streets of Mogadishu shocked the nation, and Clinton pulled out the troops, minus Aidid.

The current Bush public relations team fears a Somalia scenario even more than pictures of dead Afghan civilians. Jubilant Taliban soldiers stomping on mutilated Americans might chill the hot-blooded majority, gulled since Grenada into thinking wars can be fought cleanly, surgically and casualty free. Consequently, the Pentagon hasn't even bothered to form the national media pools promised ten years ago in its last round of negotiations with the Washington bureau chiefs of the major newspapers and TV networks. It hardly matters whether the Defense Department invokes official censorship, since getting to the scene of combat will be next to impossible. As with the Kosovo campaign, in which Serbian state television provided the best pictures, the land of the free will essentially be left with the Al Jazeera network for its war coverage. The Taliban hates war correspondents even more than Colin Powell does.

The White House news policy is unremarkable, given that all governments lie in wartime and all governments try to stem the flow of bad news. What *is* remarkable is the passivity of the U.S. media. Evidently afflicted with a guilt complex after Vietnam, the owners of the major newspapers and networks long ago ceased to protest Pentagon manipulation, and now they feel justified by simple-minded polls that show reflexive support for "military security." Ted Turner was the last media baron to stand up to the government—over its objection to Peter Arnett's presence in Baghdad during the Gulf War—but he no longer owns CNN and Arnett doesn't work there anymore.

The most revealing statement about the supine state of the media comes from *Washington Post* ombudsman Michael Getler: "There's got to be a forceful advocate at a high place in the administration who also understands that the press's ability to carry out its mission is important." Why not his chairman of the board, Donald Graham, or Arthur Sulzberger Jr. of *The New York Times*?

Does anyone care about the principle of informed consent, implied though not specified in the Constitution? Does anyone think the people need to know what the military is doing in their name? Or, put another way, does anyone think that citizens have a right to change their minds, based on accurate, corroborated information about the war? What about soldiers led by incompetent commanders; don't they need witnesses too?

The Nation, along with other small publications and Agence France-Presse, sued unsuccessfully to break up the media pool racket in 1991. The lawsuit was mooted by the end of the Gulf War, but the judge wrote a favorable dismissal, so perhaps a new legal challenge is in order. Meanwhile, we can watch Al Jazeera, based in freedom-loving Qatar, and hope for the reappearance of Paul Watson.

November 14, 2001
Uncle Ben Goes to War
Michael Massing

Finally, the Bush Administration is getting serious about the fight for public opinion in the war on terrorism. To combat the Taliban's daily denunciations of the U.S. bombing campaign in Afghanistan, the White House has set up a twenty-four-hour news bureau in Pakistan to issue a "message of the day." Top officials, after attempting to pressure Al Jazeera to tone down its anti-American programming, are now making themselves available to the news channel. Karl Rove, a senior political adviser to George W. Bush, has met with Hollywood executives to discuss how they can promote the U.S. war effort. And most significant of all, the White House has hired Charlotte Beers, a former advertising executive who in the past helped market Uncle Ben's rice, to craft a multipronged PR campaign that, Administration officials feel confident, will help win the hearts and minds of the Islamic world.

Right.

The Administration's belated recognition of the importance of public opinion in its war effort is certainly commendable. Yet its new campaign seems likely to fall short. For in selling a product, the packaging can get you only so far; ultimately, it's the quality of the product that counts. And in this case the product, U.S. policy, seems defective in several key respects.

For a sense of them, one need only consult the daily fare on Al Jazeera. First, the channel features much criticism of Washington's role in the Middle East, especially its support for repressive governments. Then there's the nightly footage of the U.S. bombing raids over Afghanistan, with frequent images of civilians who've been injured or killed in them. Finally, there's the ongoing coverage of Israeli military operations in the West Bank and Gaza, full of clips of Palestinian civilians—including many children—shot by Israeli soldiers.

The impact of the Palestinian issue, in particular, cannot be emphasized enough. Earlier this year, Shibley Telhami, a professor at the University of

Maryland, commissioned a survey of public opinion in Egypt, Saudi Arabia, the United Arab Emirates, Kuwait and Lebanon. Most of those polled ranked the Palestinian issue as the most important one for them personally. Of course, some argue that to take up that issue would be to reward terrorism, but that's not a reason to avoid what we should have been doing anyway.

If the White House really wants to make headway in its battle for public opinion, it would appoint not Charlotte Beers but a new special envoy to the Middle East whose main task would be to press the two sides to resume negotiations. To fully capitalize, the Administration would assign a camera crew to shadow the envoy on his trips to the region, and it would make the resulting footage immediately available to Al Jazeera and other Arab outlets. To help out, Bush would make frequent statements about the need for both sides in the conflict to put aside their differences and work toward an agreement. And, while he was at it, the President would make clear America's determination to develop a plan to help the nations of the Middle East overcome the political stultification and economic backwardness that have made life so wretched for so many.

Bush actually had a prime opportunity to do that on November 10, when he addressed the United Nations General Assembly. With dozens of world leaders present, the President spent most of his twenty-two-minute speech reiterating his familiar message about the evils of terrorism and the urgent need to fight it. Only briefly did he refer to the Israeli-Palestinian conflict, and while he committed his Administration to "working toward the day when two states—Israel and Palestine—live peacefully together within secure and recognized borders," he also warned against those "trying to pick and choose . . . terrorist friends"—a clear reference, as Karen DeYoung noted in the *Washington Post*, to "his calls for a Palestinian rejection of anti-Israel militants."

As DeYoung further reported, some delegates questioned Bush's decision to focus almost entirely on the fight against terrorism, "largely ignoring the issues of poverty and underdevelopment that are their biggest concern." While all the other leaders who addressed the assembly condemned the

September 11 attacks, most "spent major portions of their speeches calling for action on other world problems." Several times during the President's speech, DeYoung added, he appeared to pause for a reaction, but there was none; only when he finished did the delegates applaud, and then only "politely."

Isn't it comforting to know that Charlotte Beers is hard at work on the case?

ESSAYS AND OBSERVATIONS

September 19, 2001
A Just Response
Richard Falk

America and Americans on September 11 experienced the full horror of what must surely be the greatest display of grotesque cunning in human history. Its essence consisted in transforming the benign, everyday technology of commercial jet aircraft into weapons of mass destruction. There has been much talk about Americans discovering the vulnerability of their heartland in a manner that far exceeds the collective trauma associated with the attack on Pearl Harbor. But the new vulnerability is radically different and far more threatening. It involves the comprehensive vulnerability of technology closely tied to our global dominance, pervading every aspect of our existence. To protect ourselves against the range of threats that could be mounted by those of fanatical persuasion is a mission impossible. The very attempt would quickly turn the United States into a prison-state.

And yet who can blame the government for doing what it can in the coming months to reassure a frightened citizenry? Likely steps seem designed to make it more difficult to repeat the operations that produced the WTC/Pentagon tragedy, but it seems highly unlikely that a terrorist machine intelligent enough to pull off this gruesome operation would suddenly become so stupid as to attempt the same thing soon.

The atrocity of September 11 must be understood as the work of dark genius, a penetrating tactical insight that endangers our future in fundamental respects that we are only beginning to apprehend. This breakthrough in terrorist tactics occurred in three mutually reinforcing dimensions: (1) the shift from extremely violent acts designed to shock more than to kill, to onslaughts designed to make the enemy's society into a bloody battlefield, in this instance symbolically (capitalism and militarism) and substantively (massive human carnage and economic dislocation); (2) the use of primitive capabilities by the perpetrators to appropriate technology that can be transformed into weaponry of mass destruction through the mere act of seizure and destruction; (3) the availability of competent militants willing to carry out such crimes against humanity at the certain cost of their own lives. Such a lethal, and essentially novel, combination of elements poses an unprecedented challenge to civic order and democratic liberties. It is truly a declaration of war from the lower depths.

It is important to appreciate this transformative shift in the nature of the terrorist challenge both conceptually and tactically. Without comprehending these shifts, it will not be possible to fashion a response that is either effective or legitimate, and we need both. It remains obscure on the terrorist side whether a strategic goal accompanies this tactical escalation. At present it appears that the tactical brilliance of the operation will soon be widely regarded as a strategic blunder of colossal proportions. It would seem that the main beneficiaries of the attack in the near future are also the principal enemies of the perpetrators. Both the United States globally and Israel regionally emerge from this disaster with greatly strengthened geopolitical hands. Did the sense of hatred and fanaticism of the tactical masterminds induce this seeming strategic blindness? There is no indication that the forces behind the attack were acting on any basis beyond their extraordinary destructive intent.

And so we are led to the pivotal questions: What kind of war? What kind of response? It is, above all, a war without military solutions. Indeed it is a war in which the pursuit of the traditional military goal of "victory" is almost certain to intensify the challenge and spread the violence. Such an assessment does not question the propriety of the effort to identify and punish the perpetrators and to cut their links to government power. In our criticism of the current war fever being nurtured by an unholy alliance of government and media we should not forget that the attacks were massive crimes against humanity in a technical legal sense, and those involved in carrying them out should be punished to the fullest extent. Acknowledging this legitimate right of response is by no means equivalent to an endorsement of unlimited force. Indeed, an overreaction may be what the terrorists were seeking to provoke so as to mobilize popular resentment against the United States on a global scale. We need to act effectively, but within a framework of moral and legal restraints.

First of all, there should be the elementary due process of convincingly identifying the perpetrators and their backers. Second, maximum effort should be made to obtain authorization for any use of force in a specific form through the procedures of the United Nations Security Council. Unlike the Gulf War model, the collective character of the undertaking should be integral at the operational level, and not serve merely as window dressing for unilateralism. Third, any use of force should be consistent with international law and with the "just war" tradition governing the use of force—that is, it should discriminate between military and civilian targets, be proportionate to the challenge and be necessary to achieve a military objective, avoiding superfluous suffering. If retaliatory action fails to abide by these guidelines, with due allowance for flexibility depending on the circumstances, then it will be seen by most as replicating the fundamental evil of terrorism. It will be seen as violence directed against those who are innocent and against civilian society. And fourth, the political and moral justifications for the use of force should be accompanied by the concerted and energetic protection of those who share an ethnic or religious identity with the targets of retaliatory violence.

Counseling such guidelines does not overcome a dilemma that is likely to grow more obvious as the days go by: Something must be done, but there is nothing to do. What should be done if no targets can be found that are consistent with the guidelines of law and morality? We must assume that the terrorist network anticipated retaliation even before the attack, and has taken whatever steps it can to "disappear" from the planet, to render itself invisible. The test, then, is whether our leaders have the forbearance to refrain from uses of forces that are directed toward those who are innocent in these circumstances, and whether our citizenry has the patience to indulge and accept such forbearance. It cannot be stressed too much that the only way to win this "war" (if war it is) against terrorism is by manifesting a respect for the innocence of civilian life and by reinforcing that respect with a credible commitment to the global promotion of social justice.

The Bush Administration came to Washington with a resolve to conduct a more unilateralist foreign policy that abandoned the sort of humanitarian pretense that led to significant American-led involvements in sub-Saharan Africa and the Balkans during the 1990s. The main idea seemed to be to move away from liberal geopolitics and to downsize the international U.S. role by limiting overseas military action to the domain of strategic interests, and to uphold such interests by a primary reliance on America's independent capabilities. Behind such thinking was the view that the United States does not need the kind of help that it required during the cold war, and at the same time that it should not shoulder the humanitarian burdens of concern for matters that are remote from its direct interests. Combined with the Administration's enthusiasm for missile defense and weapons in space, such a repositioning of foreign policy was supposed to be an adjustment to the new realities of the post-cold war world. Contrary to many commentaries, such a repositioning was not an embrace of isolationism, but was a revised version of internationalism based on a blend of unilateralism and militarism. In the early months of the Bush presidency this altered foreign policy was mainly expressed by repudiating a series of important, widely supported multilateral treaty frameworks, including the Kyoto Protocol dealing with global warming, the ABM treaty dealing with the militarization of space and the Biological Weapons Convention dealing with implementing the prohibition on developing biological weaponry. Allies of the United States were stunned by such actions, which seemed to reject the need for international cooperation to address global problems of a deeply threatening nature.

And then came September 11, and an immediate realization in Washington that the overwhelming priority of its foreign policy now rests upon soliciting precisely the sort of cooperative international framework it worked so hard to throw into the nearest garbage bin. Only time will tell whether such a realization goes deeper than a mobilization of support for global war. Unlike the Gulf War and the Kosovo War, which were rapidly carried to their completion by military means, a struggle against global terrorism even in its narrowest sense would require the most intense forms of intergovernmental cooperation ever experienced in the history of international relations. The diplomacy needed to receive this cooperation might set some useful restraints on the current U.S. impulse to use force excessively and irresponsibly.

A root question underlying the U.S. response is the manner in which it deals with the United Nations. There is reportedly a debate within the Bush

Administration between those hardliners who believe that the United States should claim control over the response by invoking the international-law doctrine of "the inherent right of self-defense" and those more diplomatically inclined, who favor seeking a mandate from the Security Council to act in collective self-defense. Among the initiatives being discussed in the search for meaningful responses is the establishment through UN authority of a special tribunal entrusted with the prosecution of those indicted for the crime of international terrorism, possibly commencing with the apprehension and trial of Osama bin Laden. Such reliance on the rule of law would be a major step in seeking to make the struggle against terrorism enjoy the genuine support of the entire organized international community.

It must be understood that the huge challenge posed by the attacks can be met effectively only by establishing the greatest possible distance between the perpetrators and those who are acting on behalf of their victims. And what is the content of this distance? An unconditional respect for the sacredness of life and the dignity of the individual. One of the undoubted difficulties in the weeks and months ahead will be to assuage the bloodthirst that has accompanied the mobilization for war while satisfying the rest of the world that the United States is acting in a manner that displays respect for civilian innocence and human solidarity. A slightly related challenge, but with deeper implications, is the need to avoid seeming to exempt state violence from moral and legal limitations, while insisting that such limitations apply to the violence of the terrorists. Such a double standard will damage the indispensable effort to draw a credible distinction between the criminality of the attack and the legitimacy of the retaliation.

There are contradictory ways to address the atrocities of September 11. The prevailing mood is to invoke the metaphor of cancer and to preach military surgery of a complex and globe-girdling character that must be elevated to the status of a world war, and that bears comparison with World Wars I and II; the alternative, which I believe is far more accurate as diagnosis and cure, is to rely on the metaphor of an iceberg. The attack on America was the tip of an iceberg, the submerged portions being the mass of humanity that is not sharing in the fruits of modernity, but finds itself under the heel of U.S. economic, military, cultural and diplomatic power. To eliminate the visible tip of the iceberg of discontent and resentment may bring us a momentary catharsis, but it will at best create an illusion of victory. What must be done is to extend a commitment to the sacredness of life to the entire human family—in effect, joining in a collective effort to achieve what might be called "humane globalization."

The Israel/Palestine conflict, its concreteness and persistence, is part of this new global reality. All sides acknowledge its relevance, but the contradictory narratives deform our understanding in serious respects. Israel itself has seized the occasion to drop any pretense of sensitivity to international criticism or calls for restraint in its occupation of the Palestinian territories. Israeli spokespersons have been active in spreading the word that now America and the world should appreciate the adversaries Israel has faced for decades, and should learn from Israel's efforts to control and destroy its terrorist enemies. In contrast, those supporting Palestinian rights argue that the kinds of violence generated by Israeli oppression and Israel's refusal to uphold international law and human rights give rise to a politics of desperation that includes savage attacks on Israeli civilian society. They argue that giving a suppressed people the choice between terrorism and surrender is abusive, as well as dangerous.

On the deepest level, the high-tech dominance achieved by U.S. power, so vividly expressed in the pride associated with "zero casualties" in the 1999 NATO war over Kosovo, is giving to the peoples of the world a similar kind of choice between poverty and subjugation, on the one hand, and vindictive violence, on the other.

Is our civil society robust enough to deliver a just response in some effective form? We cannot know, but we must try, especially if we value the benefits of discussion and debate as integral to the health of democracy. Such an imperative seems particularly urgent because of the vacuum at the top. There has been, in these terrible days of grieving for what has been lost, no indication of the sort of political, moral and spiritual imagination that might begin to help us better cope with this catastrophe. We should not fool ourselves by blaming George W. Bush or Republicans. The Democratic Party and its leaders have shown no willingness or capacity to think any differently about what has occurred and what to do about it. Mainstream TV has apparently seen its role as a war-mobilizing and patrioteering mechanism, with no interest in including alternative voices and interpretations. The same tired icons of the establishment have been awakened once more to do the journeyman work of constructing a national consensus in favor of all-out war, a recipe for spreading chaos around the world and bringing discredit to ourselves.

We are poised on the brink of a global, intercivilizational war without battlefields and borders, a war seemingly declared against the enigmatic and elusive, solitary figure of Osama bin Laden, stalking remote mountainous Afghanistan while masterminding a holy war against a mighty superpower. To the extent that this portrayal is accurate it underscores the collapse of a world order based on relations among sovereign territorial states. But it also suggests that the idea of national security in a world of states is obsolete, and that the only viable security is what is being called these days "human security." Yet the news has not reached Washington, or for that matter the other capitals of the world. Instead there is the conviction that missile defense shields, space weaponry and grand antiterrorist coalitions can keep the barbarians at bay. In fact, this conviction has turned into a frenzy in the aftermath of the attacks, giving us reason to fear the response almost as much as the initial, traumatizing provocations. As the sun sets on a world of states, its militarism appears ready to burn more brightly than ever.

September 26, 2001
Dreaming of War
Ellen Willis

You don't have to be Sigmund Freud to surmise that war has a perverse appeal for the human race, nor is the attraction limited to religious fanatics committing mass murder and suicide for the greater glory of God. Among the so-called civilized it takes many insidious and sublimated forms. In the week after September 11, one of the more disturbing themes to surface in the press was the suggestion that as devastating as this attack has been, something good may come of it: an improvement in the American character or, at any rate, a salutary blow to our purported complacency and self-indulgence.

An editorial in *The New York Times* opined, "There has been a sense that whatever comes next must naturally be diminished. That need not be true. . . . Americans desperately want to commit to something greater than themselves. That was the secret of what we admired in the World War II era, and it is what this new war against terrorism will require as well. The awful week of death and destruction that has just ended might be the invitation to create a great new generation and a finer United States." The *Financial Times* gave us Francis "End of History" Fukuyama: "As with individuals, adversity can have many positive effects. Enduring national character is shaped by shared trauma . . . . Peace and prosperity, by contrast, encourage preoccupation with one's own petty affairs." Americans have been allowed to "wallow in such self-indulgent behaviour as political scandal or identity politics." (Of course, a terrorist attack by Islamic militants *is* identity politics carried to its logical extreme, but never mind.)

And then there was *The New York Times* Op-Ed columnist Frank Rich, who concluded that any event with the power to force shark attacks off *People's* cover can't be all bad: "Not all of what's gone may be a cause for mourning. . . . This week's nightmare, it's now clear, has awakened us from a frivolous if not decadent decadelong dream . . . that we could have it all without having to pay any price, and that national suffering of almost any kind could be domesticated into an experience of virtual terror akin to a theme park ride." Gary Condit, Lizzie Grubman, overblown fears of school shootings, Elián González, the California blackout that wasn't, *Survivor*, a Hollywood-sanitized Pearl Harbor—all are breathlessly invoked as horrible examples of ersatz catastrophe now swept away by the real cleansing thing. President Bush, Rich declares, must prepare us for sacrifice, "something many living Americans, him included, have never had to muster"—as though that gap in experience were self-evidently to be deplored.

Have we come to this? Purification of our national soul through war? It has a ring to it, all right; an unnervingly familiar ring at that. The authors of these commentaries cannot be accused of war fever, exactly. They are not, after all, among the ranters venting their anger by demanding that we wipe most of the Middle East off the map. They merely hope to use a lemon to make lemonade, as it were. But if that hope resonates with enough people—if Americans are seduced into going for the secret erotic payoff of sacrifice, discipline and submergence in the collective will—the effect will be more repressive than a crude crackdown on civil liberties could ever be.

To begin with, the premise that this country ("That fat, daydreaming America," in Rich's words) has been corrupted by prosperity is a lie. The "prosperity" of the past decade has mainly consisted of the dramatic concentration of wealth among 20 percent of the population. Most people have continued to struggle economically; their daydreams, if any, were about the riches they were told they were supposed to have, but that had somehow eluded them. In any case the boom was already over, without any help from terrorists.

It's true, as Fukuyama argues, that in recent years "many Americans lost interest in public affairs, and in the larger world . . . others expressed growing contempt for government." True too, as the *Times* suggests, that most Americans have been disinclined to commit themselves to any larger cause. But this is not because we are too well fed. Rather, a triumphalist corporate capitalism, free at last of the specter of Communism, has mobilized its economic power to relentlessly marginalize all nonmarket values; to subordinate every aspect of American life to corporate "efficiency" and the bottom line; to demonize not only government but the very idea of public service and public goods.

Will putting the country on a war footing do anything to change this, other than getting the free marketeers to tone down their antistatist rhetoric? On the contrary, things have just gotten infinitely more difficult for the nascent rebellion against "globalization," which is to say world domination by transnational capital. The mass demonstration that was to have taken place in Washington September 29–30 has been canceled. Few would have had the stomach for it anyway. And though some smaller groups are still going, how can the public possibly hear them the way they wish to be heard? A serious effort to put public affairs back on the American agenda, to revive people's sense that they have a stake in the way our society is run, would require a national debate on privatization, deregulation, income redistribution, the rights of workers, the share of our national wealth that should be devoted to subsidizing healthcare, childcare, education, support for the aged. Implementing such an agenda would require massive infusions of public funds. Does anyone believe this crisis will stimulate such a debate or encourage public spending for anything other than the military, law enforcement, the national security infrastructure, relief for the airlines and other stressed industries? Will Congress, in the interest of national solidarity, rush to repeal Bush's tax cut for the rich?

As for the obsession with violence and scandal that so exercises Frank Rich, its source is not an excess of contentment but chronic anxiety, at times blossoming into full-blown panic. The day the frame froze, it was on a culture that had become ambivalent to the point of schizophrenia: caught between the still-potent hype of the boom and the reality, for most, of a stagnant and increasingly insecure standard of living; enmeshed in our ongoing, seemingly intractable tensions between the impulse to freedom and the fear of it; between desire and guilt, secular modernity and religious moralism (here too this latter conflict breeds violent fundamentalists). The boundaries of political debate had steadily narrowed, not because we were fat and happy but because it was taboo to challenge in any serious way the myth that we were fat and happy. The notion that there might be any need for, or possibility of, profound changes in the institutions that shape American life—work, family, technology, the primacy of the car and the single-family house—is foreign to the mainstream media that define our common sense. And so conflicts that cannot be addressed politically have expressed themselves by other means. From public psychodramas like the O.J. Simpson trial, the Lewinsky scandal and Columbine to disaster movies, talk shows and "reality TV," popular culture carries the burden of our emotions about race, feminism, sexual morality, youth culture, wealth, competition, exclusion, a physical and social environment that feels out of control.

Will this confrontation with real terror kill our taste for the vicarious kind? Perhaps; but it does not follow that we will be less susceptible to illusion. As many have pointed out, if this is war it is a mutant variation: a war in which the enemy is protean and elusive, and how to strike back effectively is far from clear. Yet for a decade Americans have been steeped in the rhetoric of "zero tolerance" and the faith that virtually all problems from drug addiction to lousy teaching can be solved by pouring on the punishment. Even without a Commander in Chief who pledges to rid the world of evildoers, smoke them out of their holes and the like, we would be vulnerable to the temptation to brush aside frustrating complexities and relieve intolerable fear (at least for the moment) by settling on one or more scapegoats to crush. To imagine that trauma casts out fantasy is a dangerous mistake.

Similarly, while the need to focus on our national crisis will no doubt supplant the excruciating triviality of our usual political conversation, it will if anything reinforce the denial of our deeper social problems. In emergencies—and war is the ultimate emergency—such long-range concerns are suspended. This may be unavoidable, but it is never desirable, except to tyrants. I'm not a pacifist—I believe that war is sometimes necessary—but I agree with pacifists that there's nothing ennobling about it. I accept that in this emergency, national defense must be our overriding concern. But let's not compound our losses with deluded bombast about what we have to gain.

September 26, 2001
Babi Yar in Manhattan
Yevgeny Yevtushenko

Tatyana Samoilova is running up the staircase, wrapped in smoke from the fire following a German bombing, jumping over the pulsating hoses. A fireman with a blackened face, looking like a coal miner, tries to stop her, but she slips from his hands and pushes open the door of the apartment, where she had left her parents. . .

The floor has vanished. After the threshold, an abyss—only a half-burned lampshade is swaying, and from the ticking ancient wall clock, a small mechanical bird is sounding a farewell "cuckoo." Only a week before the terrorist attacks in New York and Washington, my young students in Oklahoma, at the University of Tulsa, were watching this bombing of Russia on the screen as I showed them the famous 1957 Russian film *The Cranes Are Flying*. (This film symbolized "the thaw" in Russia and won many international prizes.) The students were watching, holding their breath, some of them with tears in their eyes.

I was shocked when one girl wrote in her paper that she was glad my course helped her discover so much kindness in the Russian people "despite the fact that Russia during WWII fought together with the Germans against America." To be honest, I was no less bitterly surprised in my homeland when some Russian teenagers answered in a questionnaire that they didn't know who Yuri Gagarin was. Sometimes in teaching cinema and poetry, it seems that I also teach history.

I was glad that *The Cranes Are Flying*, together with the beloved Italian film *The Bicycle Thief*, was so highly appreciated by my American students. But one wrote that it was very bad, even for a completely desperate unemployed man, to steal a bicycle in the presence of his little son. "Why didn't the father of the boy, instead of stealing, buy a new bicycle?" the student asked. How happy they are, I thought. They have always been able to buy new bicycles, and they have never seen a war on their land, only in the cinema.

But now war has come to their land. Empires with borders on the map are less dangerous than ones without geographical and moral borders. A new Air Empire of global terrorism unexpectedly turned the sharp noses of American planes against American skyscrapers. The scriptwriters and producers of this war created it in full Hollywood style, like a grandiose world show with visual and sound effects, and they didn't need to direct tens of thousands of involuntary "extras" to show horror in their eyes. But these scriptwriters miscalculated something. They didn't understand that non-ketchup blood in their real-life thriller could not make enthusiastic fans, except among the brainwashed. This tragedy in the United States happened, to the month, on the sixtieth anniversary of the Nazi massacre at Babi Yar—the ravine near the city of Kiev where they killed tens of thousands of Jews, together with some Russians and Ukrainians. (It is also the fortieth anniversary of my poem "Babi Yar" and nearly that of Shostakovich's Symphony No. 13, based on my poetry.) But even in my worst nightmare, I did not imagine a new Babi Yar in the heart of Manhattan. Today, Russia is crying together with America—I haven't seen anything like it since President John Kennedy was killed. I hope that these common tears can wash away everything that still divides us.

Planes stuffed with innocent victims, including children, ripped through more than skyscrapers. They ripped through the greatest books: the Bible, the Koran, Dante, Shakespeare, Goethe, Hugo, Dostoyevsky, Whitman. Many of the world's museums, dedicated to World War II, warn us of the potential catastrophe of culture by exhibiting books pierced by bullets. But where could we show skyscrapers pierced by planes? These planes were exploded inside us, and their fragments forever will wander under our skin. For a very long time, in our dreams we will see people jumping from inflamed floors to the asphalt. One of them, falling down, with his own body killed a would-be savior. For a very long time in our delirium, we will listen for signals of cellular phones under the ruins, even after all the debris has been trucked away. Something inside us has become ruined forever.

Thank God if it is only the ruins of our superiority over others. Thank God if it is only the ruins of our self-confidence, our boasting, our criminal carelessness. But God save us if it is to be the ruins of our kindness, on which we'll dance savagely with an evil vindictiveness that is always blind and always punishes those who are not really guilty.

To defend civilization we can act only in a civilized way. Otherwise we will look like those morally uncivilized, cruelly unreasonable fellow earthlings, transformed into aliens by fanaticism and desperation, who instead of sharing the grief of so many American mothers, triumphantly showed, with their fingers, before the TV cameras, the letter "V." Poor creatures, they don't understand that the cursed sunny morning of that Black Tuesday was also the darkest day for themselves.

The slogan "Terror Against Terror" is dangerous, because our wish to catch criminals as soon as possible, to point our finger at the first suspect, could lead to unforgivable mistakes. Using more and more terror as our only response, we'll have less and less pity, compassion and kindness inside us. I am *not* talking about pity toward the terrorists—they don't deserve it. It would be stupid to consider the walls of our houses hospitably inviting cheeks out of a mistaken Christian impulse—"If they strike one wall, turn to them the other." But, it will be terrible if instead of burning down terror we burn down our souls with our white-hot hatred, and become indistinguishable from those we fight against.

Today, terrorists invented a way to transform passenger planes into giant gas bombs. What if tomorrow, terrorists are equipped with atomic mini-bombs, or chemical or biological weapons, and other countries become the next targets? World evil has quick legs, but the legs of goodness are tired. New kamikazes—for whom will be reserved, their criminal teachers promise, the best virgins in the other world—will be ready, even tomorrow, thinking that they are messengers of the highest justice, to rip through the Eiffel Tower, the Kremlin, the Sistine Chapel, the Cathedral of Cologne, Big Ben. Aggressive fundamentalism begins with the explosion of the main foundations of humanity.

I grew up during Stalin's terror against our own people. Marxist fundamentalism justified that terror. But if Marx could have seen the nightmare of our concentration camps—the gulag archipelago—he would himself have become an anti-Marxist. Nazi fundamentalism shaped the idea of the gulag into the gas chambers of the Holocaust. Marxist fundamentalism used the explosion of churches, afterward transformed into potato stores or horse stables, to explode the Christian morality and spiritual testament of Dostoyevsky: that no ideals are worth one tear of an innocent, tortured child. (Despite their confrontation, Marxist fundamentalism was very close to Western right-wing fundamentalism in shamelessly cynical politics.) Marxist fundamentalism, crushing with tanks the spring of Prague, switched the idealist Dubcek for the opportunist Husak, and Western right-wing fundamentalism switched liberal-socialist Allende for dictator Pinochet, by the common principle "Yes, he is a bastard, but he is our bastard." Maoist fundamentalism tried to cross out all Western culture, trapping the best translators of literature in foreign languages into so-called camps of improvement. The Russian Orthodox Church's fundamentalism, a hundred years ago, cursed Leo Tolstoy with anathema, and until recent days our humanist patriarch hadn't found time to cancel it. The official Soviet fundamentalist writers expelled Pasternak from the Writers' Union, in what became his civic death. Iranian fundamentalism simply condemned Salman Rushdie to death with no need of adjectives. Fundamentalism is the transformation of earthlings into aliens.

If we want to finish terrorism, we must not become terrorists to all others who are simply different. We must not stoop down to the level of complete suspicion of other political views and religious beliefs. Tough policy toward terrorism must not become a police conglomerate of the richest countries against the Third or Fourth World of pariahs. As long as there is hunger and poverty on our planet, there will also be desperation and terrorism. If you hide a bomb in a pocket with many holes, there are many chances that it will slip out.

Are the professional politicians of the world ready to solve such problems? Don't some of them waste too much time on election rallies? Don't they, too quickly after being elected, immediately begin to prepare for the next election or for a comfortable retirement? Don't they pay too much attention to their own security at the expense of the security of those who elected them?

A 23-year-old student of mine in Tulsa, Christopher Fitzwater, wrote: "Our 'cold wars' turn into wars against people instead of an ideology. People are basically all the same: our similarities far outweigh our differences. It takes politics, money and other intangible things to tear us apart. It is a pity that they do it so well." And another student, 24-year-old Ahmad Al-Kaabi, from United Arab Emirates, counsels that when it comes to aggression, we learn from nature: "In a world where humans stupidly fight to kill millions, cranes fly together in harmony and look for better choices."

We can be sure of the future if it belongs to such young people. Unfortunately, in too many countries, the young and talented squeamishly avoid politics, thinking it an unwashable, dirty kitchen, and they dive into business, into technology, into university teaching, sarcastically criticizing their governments. But politics, like all the rest of nature, won't tolerate a vacuum. As a result, those with negative energy and skill in its use are able to jump into politics and rule those more intelligent and honest than they. Now is a prime time to change this greasy deck of political cards. We need a wide movement of young, unstained people into politics, otherwise we will never untie or cut the Gordian knot of so many problems, one of which is the problem of mutual creation of aliens from each other. Israelis make aliens from Palestinians; Palestinians, from Israelis. Serbs from Albanians; Albanians from Serbs. Basques from Spaniards; Spaniards from Basques. Irishmen from Irishmen, simply because some are Protestants and others are Catholics. And we Russians, having made so many aliens from other Russians, killed them in the past and continue to kill them now.

Imagine two young Russian soldiers from the same village, bunked together fearfully in a cold tent somewhere in the mountains of Chechnya. (Chechens, to these Russian soldiers, have been made aliens.) One of the soldiers leaves the tent, not going far—just to the first little bush. The second soldier wakes up, looks for his friend and, finding him gone, crawls outside. He stands in horror, seeing near his boots the bloody head of his childhood friend, cut off by a Chechen dagger. This soldier is not a coward, and he has a machine gun in his hand. What is he going to do? He runs to find the killers, outraged by madness after his loss. Then he shoots at two uncertain figures that suddenly sway before him, speaking Chechen in the milky fog. Immediately he is seized by a Russian patrol, for he has blindly killed two peaceful peasants. But how do you understand who is peaceful and who is not in such fog . . . ?

Only twenty-five miles from the city of Grozny, which is full of debris after ground battles and bombings, is the Cossack village of Starogladovskay, where there stands only one undestroyed monument to a Russian—to Leo Tolstoy, who was here in the military service many years ago. The museum of the great writer is guarded by a Chechen family, who have only one old hunter's rifle to do their job. Can you imagine that nobody has touched, even with a finger, this village or this museum? "War couldn't be there, where Tolstoy is," says the head of the family. Probably more than anything else, mankind needs now a people with such compassion and dignity, who could paralyze with their words the mutual hatred, like the words of Tolstoy.

Over our wounded mother Earth are flying not only terrorist planes. Cranes still fly, too. . .

(Translated by the author with Marcia Farrell and Irene and Frank Letcher.)

September 26, 2001
Blowback
Chalmers Johnson

For Americans who can bear to think about it, those tragic pictures from New York of women holding up photos of their husbands, sons and daughters and asking if anyone knows anything about them look familiar. They are similar to scenes we have seen from Buenos Aires and Santiago. There, too, starting in the 1970s, women held up photos of their loved ones, asking for information. Since it was far too dangerous then to say aloud what they thought had happened to them—that they had been tortured and murdered by U.S.-backed military juntas—the women coined a new word for them, *los desaparecidos*—"the disappeareds." Our government has never been honest about its own role in the 1973 overthrow of the elected government of Salvador Allende in Chile or its backing, through "Operation Condor," of what the State Department has recently called "extrajudicial killings" in Argentina, Paraguay, Brazil and elsewhere in Latin America. But we now have several thousand of our own disappeareds, and we are badly mistaken if we think that we in the United States are entirely blameless for what happened to them.

The suicidal assassins of September 11, 2001, did not "attack America," as our political leaders and the news media like to maintain; they attacked American foreign policy. Employing the strategy of the weak, they killed innocent bystanders who then became enemies only because they had already become victims. Terrorism by definition strikes at the innocent in order to draw attention to the sins of the invulnerable. The United States deploys such overwhelming military force globally that for its militarized opponents only an "asymmetric strategy," in the jargon of the Pentagon, has any chance of success. When it does succeed, as it did spectacularly on September 11, it renders our massive military machine worthless: The terrorists offer it no targets. On the day of the disaster, President George W. Bush told the American people that we were attacked because we are "a beacon for freedom" and because the attackers were "evil." In his address to Congress on September 20, he said, "This is civilization's fight." This attempt to define difficult-to-grasp events as only a conflict over abstract values—as a "clash of civilizations," in current post-cold war American jargon—is not only disingenuous but also a way of evading responsibility for the "blowback" that America's imperial projects have generated.

"Blowback" is a CIA term first used in March 1954 in a recently declassified report on the 1953 operation to overthrow the government of Mohammed Mossadegh in Iran. It is a metaphor for the unintended consequences of the U.S. government's international activities that have been kept secret from the American people. The CIA's fears that there might ultimately be some blowback from its egregious interference in the affairs of Iran were well founded. Installing the Shah in power brought twenty-five years of tyranny and repression to the Iranian people and elicited the Ayatollah Khomeini's revolution. The staff of the American embassy in Teheran was held hostage for more than a year. This misguided "covert operation" of the U.S. government helped convince many capable people throughout the Islamic world that the United States was an implacable enemy.

The pattern has become all too familiar. Osama bin Laden, the leading suspect as mastermind behind the carnage of September 11, is no more (or less) "evil" than his fellow creations of our CIA: Manuel Noriega, former commander of the Panama Defense Forces until George Bush *père* in late 1989 invaded his country and kidnapped him, or Iraq's Saddam Hussein, whom we armed and backed so long as he was at war with Khomeini's Iran and whose people we have bombed and starved for a decade in an incompetent effort to get rid of him. These men were once listed as "assets" of our clandestine services organization.

Osama bin Laden joined our call for resistance to the Soviet Union's 1979 invasion of Afghanistan and accepted our military training and equipment along with countless other mujahedeen "freedom fighters." It was only after the Russians bombed Afghanistan back into the stone age and suffered a Vietnam-like defeat, and we turned our backs on the death and destruction we had helped cause, that he turned against us. The last straw as far as bin Laden was concerned was that, after the Gulf War, we based "infidel" American troops in Saudi Arabia to prop up its decadent, fiercely authoritarian regime. Ever since, bin Laden has been attempting to bring the things the CIA taught him home to the teachers. On September 11, he appears to have returned to his deadly project with a vengeance.

There are today, ten years after the demise of the Soviet Union, some 800 Defense Department installations located in other countries. The people of the United States make up perhaps 4 percent of the world's population but consume 40 percent of its resources. They exercise hegemony over the world directly through overwhelming military might and indirectly through secretive organizations like the World Bank, the International Monetary Fund and the World Trade Organization. Though largely dominated by the U.S. government, these are formally international organizations and therefore beyond Congressional oversight.

As the American-inspired process of "globalization" inexorably enlarges the gap between the rich and the poor, a popular movement against it has gained strength, advancing from its first demonstrations in Seattle in 1999 through protests in Washington, DC; Melbourne; Prague; Seoul; Nice; Barcelona; Quebec City; Güteborg; and on to its violent confrontations in Genoa earlier this year. Ironically, though American leaders are deaf to the desires of the protesters, the Defense Department has actually adopted the movement's main premise—that current global economic arrangements mean more wealth for the "West" and more misery for the "rest"—as a reason why the United States should place weapons in space. The U.S. Space Command's pamphlet "Vision for 2020" argues that "the globalization of the world economy will also continue, with a widening between the 'haves' and the 'have-nots,' " and that we have a mission to "dominate the space dimension of military operations to protect U.S. interests and investments" in an increasingly dangerous and implicitly anti-American world. Unfortunately, while the eyes of military planners were firmly focused on the "control and domination" of space and "denying other countries access to space," a very different kind of space was suddenly occupied.

On the day after the September 11 attack, Democratic Senator Zell Miller of Georgia declared, "I say, bomb the hell out of them. If there's collateral damage, so be it." "Collateral damage" is another of those hateful euphemisms invented by our military to prettify its killing of the defenseless. It is the term Pentagon spokesmen use to refer to the Serb and Iraqi civilians who were killed or maimed by bombs from high-flying American warplanes in our campaigns against Slobodan Milosevic and Saddam Hussein. It is the kind of word our new ambassador to the United Nations, John Negroponte, might have used in the 1980s to explain the slaughter of peasants, Indians and church workers by American-backed right-wing death squads in El Salvador, Guatemala, Honduras and Nicaragua while he was ambassador to Honduras. These activities made the Reagan years the worst decade for Central America since the Spanish conquest.

Massive military retaliation with its inevitable "collateral damage" will, of course, create more desperate and embittered childless parents and parentless children, and so recruit more maddened people to the terrorists' cause. In fact, mindless bombing is surely one of the responses their grisly strategy hopes to elicit. Moreover, a major crisis in the Middle East will inescapably cause a rise in global oil prices, with, from the assassins' point of view, desirable destabilizing effects on all the economies of the advanced industrial nations.

What should we do? The following is a start on what, in a better world, we might modestly think about doing. But let me concede at the outset that none of this is going to happen. The people in Washington who run our government believe that they can now get all the things they wanted before the trade towers came down: more money for the military, ballistic missile defenses, more freedom for the intelligence services and removal of the last modest restrictions (no assassinations, less domestic snooping, fewer lists given to "friendly" foreign police of people we want executed) that the Vietnam era placed on our leaders. An inevitable consequence of big "blowback" events like this one is that, the causes having been largely kept from American eyes (if not Islamic or Latin American ones), people cannot make the necessary connections for an explanation. Popular support for Washington is thus, at least for a while, staggeringly high.

Nonetheless, what we *should* do is to make a serious analytical effort to determine what overseas military commitments make sense and where we should pull in our horns. Although we intend to continue supporting Israel, our new policy should be to urge the dismantling of West Bank Israeli settlements as fast as possible. In Saudi Arabia, we should withdraw our troops, since they do nothing for our oil security, which we can maintain by other means. Beyond the Middle East, in Okinawa, where we have thirty-eight U.S. military bases in the midst of 1.3 million civilians, we should start by bringing home the Third Marine Division and demobilizing it. It is understrength, has no armor and is not up to the standards of the domestically based First and Second Marine Divisions. It has no deterrent value but is, without question, an unwanted burden we force the people of this unlucky island to bear.

A particular obscenity crying out for elimination is the U.S. Army's School of the Americas, founded in Panama in 1946 and moved to Fort Benning, Georgia, in 1984 after Panamanian President Jorge Illueca called it "the biggest base for destabilization in Latin America" and evicted it. Its curriculum includes counterinsurgency, military intelligence, interrogation techniques, sniper fire, infantry and commando tactics, psychological warfare and jungle operations. Although a few members of Congress have long tried to shut it down, the Pentagon and the White House have always found ways to keep it in the budget. In May 2000 the Clinton Administration sought to provide new camouflage for the school by renaming it the "Defense Institute for Hemispheric Security Cooperation" and transferring authority over it from the Army Department to the Defense Department.

The school has trained more than 60,000 military and police officers from Latin American and Caribbean countries. Among SOA's most illustrious graduates are the dictators Manuel Noriega (now serving a forty-year sentence in an American jail for drug trafficking) and Omar Torrijos of Panama; Guillermo Rodrigues of Ecuador; Juan Velasco Alvarado of Peru; Leopoldo Galtieri, former head of Argentina's junta; and Hugo Banzer Suarez of Bolivia. More recently, Peru's Vladimiro Montesinos, SOA class of 1965, surfaced as a CIA asset and former President Alberto Fujimori's closest adviser.

More difficult than these fairly simple reforms would be to bring our rampant militarism under control. From George Washington's "farewell address" to Dwight Eisenhower's invention of the phrase "military-industrial complex," American leaders have warned about the dangers of a bloated, permanent, expensive military establishment that has lost its relationship to the country because service in it is no longer an obligation of citizenship. Our military operates the biggest arms sales operation on earth; it rapes girls, women and schoolchildren in Okinawa; it cuts ski-lift cables in Italy, killing twenty vacationers, and dismisses what its insubordinate pilots have done as a "training accident"; it allows its nuclear attack submarines to be used for joy rides for wealthy civilian supporters and then covers up the negligence that caused the sinking of a Japanese high school training ship; it propagandizes the nation with Hollywood films glorifying military service (*Pearl Harbor*); and it manipulates the political process to get more carrier task forces, antimissile missiles, nuclear weapons, stealth bombers and other expensive gadgets for which we have no conceivable use. Two of the most influential federal institutions are not in Washington but on the south side of the Potomac River—the Defense Department and the Central

Intelligence Agency. Given their influence today, one must conclude that the government outlined in the Constitution of 1787 no longer bears much relationship to the government that actually rules from Washington. Until that is corrected, we should probably stop talking about "democracy" and "human rights."

Once we have done the analysis, brought home most of our "forward deployed" troops, refurbished our diplomatic capabilities, reassured the world that we are not unilateralists who walk away from treaty commitments and reintroduced into government the kinds of idealistic policies we once pioneered (e.g., the Marshall Plan), then we might assess what we can do against "terrorism." We could reduce our transportation and information vulnerabilities by building into our systems more of what engineers call redundancy: different ways of doing the same things—airlines and railroads, wireless and optical fiber communications, automatic computer backup programs, land routes around bridges. It is absurd that our railroads do not even begin to compare with those in Western Europe or Japan, and their inadequacies have made us overly dependent on aviation in travel between U.S. cities. It may well be that some public utilities should be nationalized, just as safety aboard airliners should become a federal function. Flight decks need to be made genuinely inaccessible from the passenger compartments, as they are on El Al. In what might seem a radical change, we could even hire intelligence analysts at the CIA who can read the languages of the countries they are assigned to and have actually visited the places they write about (neither of these conditions is even slightly usual at the present time).

If we do these things, the crisis will recede. If we play into the hands of the terrorists, we will see more collateral damage among our own citizens. Ten years ago, the other so-called superpower, the former Soviet Union, disappeared almost overnight because of internal contradictions, imperial overstretch and an inability to reform. We have always been richer, so it might well take longer for similar contradictions to afflict our society. But it is nowhere written that the United States, in its guise as an empire dominating the world, must go on forever.

October 3, 2001
The Clash of Ignorance
Edward W. Said

Samuel Huntington's article "The Clash of Civilizations?" appeared in the Summer 1993 issue of *Foreign Affairs*, where it immediately attracted a surprising amount of attention and reaction. Because the article was intended to supply Americans with an original thesis about "a new phase" in world politics after the end of the cold war, Huntington's terms of argument seemed compellingly large, bold, even visionary. He very clearly had his eye on rivals in the policy-making ranks, theorists such as Francis Fukuyama and his "end of history" ideas, as well as the legions who had celebrated the onset of globalism, tribalism and the dissipation of the state. But they, he allowed, had understood only some aspects of this new period. He was about to announce the "crucial, indeed a central, aspect" of what "global politics is likely to be in the coming years." Unhesitatingly he pressed on:

"It is my hypothesis that the fundamental source of conflict in this new world will not be primarily ideological or primarily economic. The great divisions among humankind and the dominating source of conflict will be cultural. Nation states will remain the most powerful actors in world affairs, but the principal conflicts of global politics will occur between nations and groups of different civilizations. The clash of civilizations will dominate global politics. The fault lines between civilizations will be the battle lines of the future."

Most of the argument in the pages that followed relied on a vague notion of something Huntington called "civilization identity" and "the interactions among seven or eight [*sic*] major civilizations," of which the conflict between two of them, Islam and the West, gets the lion's share of his attention. In this belligerent kind of thought, he relies heavily on a 1990 article by the veteran Orientalist Bernard Lewis, whose ideological colors are manifest in its title, "The Roots of Muslim Rage." In both articles, the

personification of enormous entities called "the West" and "Islam" is reck-
lessly affirmed, as if hugely complicated matters like identity and culture
existed in a cartoonlike world where Popeye and Bluto bash each other mer-
cilessly, with one always more virtuous pugilist getting the upper hand over
his adversary. Certainly neither Huntington nor Lewis has much time to
spare for the internal dynamics and plurality of every civilization, or for the
fact that the major contest in most modern cultures concerns the definition
or interpretation of each culture, or for the unattractive possibility that a
great deal of demagogy and downright ignorance is involved in presuming
to speak for a whole religion or civilization. No, the West is the West, and
Islam Islam.

The challenge for Western policy-makers, says Huntington, is to make
sure that the West gets stronger and fends off all the others, Islam in particular. More troubling is Huntington's assumption that his perspective,
which is to survey the entire world from a perch outside all ordinary attach-
ments and hidden loyalties, is the correct one, as if everyone else were scur-
rying around looking for the answers that he has already found. In fact,
Huntington is an ideologist, someone who wants to make "civilizations"
and "identities" into what they are not: shut-down, sealed-off entities that
have been purged of the myriad currents and countercurrents that animate
human history, and that over centuries have made it possible for that history not only to contain wars of religion and imperial conquest but also to
be one of exchange, cross-fertilization and sharing. This far less visible history is ignored in the rush to highlight the ludicrously compressed and constricted warfare that "the clash of civilizations" argues is the reality. When
he published his book by the same title in 1996, Huntington tried to give
his argument a little more subtlety and many, many more footnotes; all he
did, however, was confuse himself and demonstrate what a clumsy writer
and inelegant thinker he was.

The basic paradigm of West versus the rest (the cold war opposition
reformulated) remained untouched, and this is what has persisted, often
insidiously and implicitly, in discussion since the terrible events of September 11. The carefully planned and horrendous, pathologically motivated

suicide attack and mass slaughter by a small group of deranged militants has been turned into proof of Huntington's thesis. Instead of seeing it for what it is—the capture of big ideas (I use the word loosely) by a tiny band of crazed fanatics for criminal purposes—international luminaries from former Pakistani Prime Minister Benazir Bhutto to Italian Prime Minister Silvio Berlusconi have pontificated about Islam's troubles, and in the latter's case have used Huntington's ideas to rant on about the West's superiority, how "we" have Mozart and Michelangelo and they don't. (Berlusconi has since made a halfhearted apology for his insult to "Islam.")

But why not instead see parallels, admittedly less spectacular in their destructiveness, for Osama bin Laden and his followers in cults like the Branch Davidians or the disciples of the Rev. Jim Jones at Guyana or the Japanese Aum Shinrikyo? Even the normally sober British weekly *The Economist*, in its issue of September 22–28, can't resist reaching for the vast generalization, praising Huntington extravagantly for his "cruel and sweeping, but nonetheless acute" observations about Islam. "Today," the journal says with unseemly solemnity, Huntington writes that "the world's billion or so Muslims are 'convinced of the superiority of their culture, and obsessed with the inferiority of their power.' " Did he canvas 100 Indonesians, 200 Moroccans, 500 Egyptians and fifty Bosnians? Even if he did, what sort of sample is that?

Uncountable are the editorials in every American and European newspaper and magazine of note adding to this vocabulary of gigantism and apocalypse, each use of which is plainly designed not to edify but to inflame the reader's indignant passion as a member of the "West," and what we need to do. Churchillian rhetoric is used inappropriately by self-appointed combatants in the West's, and especially America's, war against its haters, despoilers, destroyers, with scant attention to complex histories that defy such reductiveness and have seeped from one territory into another, in the process overriding the boundaries that are supposed to separate us all into divided armed camps.

This is the problem with unedifying labels like Islam and the West: They mislead and confuse the mind, which is trying to make sense of a disorderly reality that won't be pigeonholed or strapped down as easily as all that. I remember interrupting a man who, after a lecture I had given at a West Bank university in 1994, rose from the audience and started to attack my ideas as "Western," as opposed to the strict Islamic ones he espoused. "Why are you wearing a suit and tie?" was the first retort that came to mind. "They're Western too." He sat down with an embarrassed smile on his face, but I recalled the incident when information on the September 11 terrorists started to come in: how they had mastered all the technical details required to inflict their homicidal evil on the World Trade Center, the Pentagon and the aircraft they had commandeered. Where does one draw the line between "Western" technology and, as Berlusconi declared, "Islam's" inability to be a part of "modernity"?

One cannot easily do so, of course. How finally inadequate are the labels, generalizations and cultural assertions. At some level, for instance, primitive passions and sophisticated know-how converge in ways that give the lie to a fortified boundary not only between "West" and "Islam" but also between past and present, us and them, to say nothing of the very concepts of identity and nationality about which there is unending disagreement and debate. A unilateral decision made to draw lines in the sand, to undertake crusades, to oppose their evil with our good, to extirpate terrorism and, in Paul Wolfowitz's nihilistic vocabulary, to end nations entirely, doesn't make the supposed entities any easier to see; rather, it speaks to how much simpler it is to make bellicose statements for the purpose of mobilizing collective passions than to reflect, examine, sort out what it is we are dealing with in reality, the interconnectedness of innumerable lives, "ours" as well as "theirs."

In a remarkable series of three articles published between January and March 1999 in *Dawn*, Pakistan's most respected weekly, the late Eqbal Ahmad, writing for a Muslim audience, analyzed what he called the roots of the religious right, coming down very harshly on the mutilations of Islam by absolutists and fanatical tyrants whose obsession with regulating personal behavior promotes "an Islamic order reduced to a penal code, stripped of its humanism, aesthetics, intellectual quests, and spiritual devotion." And this "entails an absolute assertion of one, generally de-contextualized, aspect of religion and a total disregard of another. The phenomenon distorts religion, debases tradition, and twists the political process wherever it unfolds." As a timely instance of this debasement, Ahmad proceeds first to present the rich, complex, pluralist meaning of the word *jihad* and then goes on to show that in the word's current con-finement to indiscriminate war against presumed enemies, it is impossible "to recognize the Islamic—religion, society, culture, history or politics—as lived and experienced by Muslims through the ages." The modern Islamists, Ahmad concludes, are "concerned with power, not with the soul; with the mobilization of people for political purposes rather than with sharing and alleviating their sufferings and aspirations. Theirs is a very limited and time-bound political agenda." What has made matters worse is that similar distortions and zealotry occur in the "Jewish" and "Christian" universes of discourse.

It was Conrad, more powerfully than any of his readers at the end of the nineteenth century could have imagined, who understood that the distinctions between civilized London and "the heart of darkness" quickly collapsed in extreme situations, and that the heights of European civilization could instan-taneously fall into the most barbarous practices without preparation or tran-sition. And it was Conrad also, in *The Secret Agent* (1907), who described terrorism's affinity for abstractions like "pure science" (and by extension for "Islam" or "the West"), as well as the terrorist's ultimate moral degradation.

For there are closer ties between apparently warring civilizations than most of us would like to believe; both Freud and Nietzsche showed how the traffic across carefully maintained, even policed boundaries moves with often terrifying ease. But then such fluid ideas, full of ambiguity and skepticism about notions that we hold on to, scarcely furnish us with suit-able, practical guidelines for situations such as the one we face now. Hence the altogether more reassuring battle orders (a crusade, good versus evil, freedom against fear, etc.) drawn out of Huntington's alleged opposition between Islam and the West, from which official discourse drew its vocabulary in the first days after the September 11 attacks. There's since been a noticeable de-escalation in that discourse, but to judge from the steady amount of hate speech and actions, plus reports of law enforcement efforts directed against Arabs, Muslims and Indians all over the country, the paradigm stays on.

One further reason for its persistence is the increased presence of Muslims all over Europe and the United States. Think of the populations today of France, Italy, Germany, Spain, Britain, America, even Sweden, and you must concede that Islam is no longer on the fringes of the West but at its center. But what is so threatening about that presence? Buried in the collective culture are memories of the first great Arab-Islamic conquests, which began in the seventh century and which, as the celebrated Belgian historian Henri Pirenne wrote in his landmark book *Mohammed and Charlemagne* (1939), shattered once and for all the ancient unity of the Mediterranean, destroyed the Christian-Roman synthesis and gave rise to a new civilization dominated by northern powers (Germany and Carolingian France) whose mission, he seemed to be saying, is to resume defense of the "West" against its historical-cultural enemies. What Pirenne left out, alas, is that in the creation of this new line of defense the West drew on the humanism, science, philosophy, sociology and historiography of Islam, which had already interposed itself between Charlemagne's world and classical antiquity. Islam is inside from the start, as even Dante, great enemy of Mohammed, had to concede when he placed the Prophet at the very heart of his *Inferno*.

Then there is the persisting legacy of monotheism itself, the Abrahamic religions, as Louis Massignon aptly called them. Beginning with Judaism and Christianity, each is a successor haunted by what came before; for Muslims, Islam fulfills and ends the line of prophecy. There is still no decent history or demystification of the many-sided contest among these three followers—not one of them by any means a monolithic, unified camp—of the most jealous of all gods, even though the bloody modern convergence on Palestine furnishes a rich secular instance of what has been so tragically irreconcilable about them. Not surprisingly, then, Muslims and Christians speak readily of crusades and *jihads*, both of them eliding the Judaic presence with often sublime insouciance. Such an agenda, says Eqbal Ahmad, is "very reassuring to the men and women who are stranded in the middle of the ford, between the deep waters of tradition and modernity."

But we are all swimming in those waters, Westerners and Muslims and others alike. And since the waters are part of the ocean of history, trying to plow or divide them with barriers is futile. These are tense times, but it is better to think in terms of powerful and powerless communities, the secular politics of reason and ignorance, and universal principles of justice and injustice, than to wander off in search of vast abstractions that may give momentary satisfaction but little self-knowledge or informed analysis. "The Clash of Civilizations" thesis is a gimmick like "The War of the Worlds," better for reinforcing defensive self-pride than for critical understanding of the bewildering interdependence of our time.

October 3, 2001
Signs of the Times
Naomi Klein

As shocking as this must be to New Yorkers, in Toronto, the city where I live, lampposts and mailboxes are plastered with posters advertising a plan by antipoverty activists to "shut down" the business district on October 16. Some of the posters (those put up before September 11) even have a picture of skyscrapers outlined in red—the perimeters of the designated direct-action zone. Many have argued that O16 should be canceled, as other protests and demonstrations have been, in deference to the mood of mourning—and out of fear of stepped-up police violence.

But the shutdown is going ahead. In the end, the events of September 11 don't change the fact that the nights are getting colder and the recession is looming. They don't change the fact that in a city that used to be described as "safe" and, well, "maybe a little boring," many will die on the streets this winter, as they did last winter, and the one before that, unless more beds are found immediately.

And yet there is no disputing that the event, its militant tone and its choice of target will provoke terrible memories and associations. Many political campaigns face a similar, and sudden, shift. Post-September 11, tactics that rely on attacking—even peacefully—powerful symbols of capitalism find themselves in an utterly transformed semiotic landscape. After all, the attacks were acts of very real and horrifying terror, but they were also acts of symbolic warfare, and instantly understood as such. As Tom Brokaw and so many others put it, the towers were not just any buildings, they were "symbols of American capitalism."

As someone whose life is thoroughly entwined with what some people call "the antiglobalization movement," others call "anticapitalism" (and I tend to just sloppily call "the movement"), I find it difficult to avoid discussions about symbolism these days. About all the anticorporate signs and signifiers—the culture-jammed logos, the guerrilla-warfare stylings, the choices of brand name and political targets—that make up the movement's dominant metaphors.

Many political opponents of anticorporate activism are using the symbolism of the World Trade Center and Pentagon attacks to argue that young activists, playing at guerrilla war, have now been caught out by a real war. The obituaries are already appearing in newspapers around the world: "Anti-Globalization Is So Yesterday," reads a typical headline. It is, according to the *Boston Globe*, "in tatters." Is it true? Our activism has been declared dead before. Indeed, it is declared dead with ritualistic regularity before and after every mass demonstration: our strategies apparently discredited, our coalitions divided, our arguments misguided. And yet those demonstrations have kept growing larger, from 50,000 in Seattle to 300,000, by some estimates, in Genoa.

At the same time, it would be foolish to pretend that nothing has changed since September 11. This struck me recently, looking at a slide show I had been pulling together before the attacks. It is about how anticorporate imagery is increasingly being absorbed by corporate marketing. One slide shows a group of activists spray-painting the window of a Gap outlet during the anti-WTO protests in Seattle. The next shows The Gap's recent window displays featuring its own prefab graffiti—words like "Independence" sprayed in black. And the next is a frame from Sony PlayStation's "State of Emergency" game featuring cool-haired anarchists throwing rocks at evil riot cops protecting the fictitious American Trade Organization. When I first looked at these images beside each other, I was amazed by the speed of corporate co-optation. Now all I can see is how these snapshots from the corporate versus anticorporate image wars have been instantly overshadowed, blown away by September 11 like so many toy cars and action figures on a disaster movie set.

Despite the altered landscape—or because of it—it bears remembering why this movement chose to wage symbolic struggles in the first place. The Ontario Coalition Against Poverty's decision to "shut down" the business district came from a set of very specific and still relevant circumstances. Like so many others trying to get issues of economic inequality on the political agenda, the people the group represents felt that they had been discarded, left outside the paradigm, disappeared and reconstituted as a panhandling or squeegee problem requiring tough new legislation. They realized that what they had to confront was just not a local political enemy or even a particular trade law but an economic system—the broken promise of deregulated, trickle-down capitalism. Thus the modern activist challenge: How do you organize against an ideology so vast, it has no edges; so everywhere, it seems nowhere? Where is the site of resistance for those with no workplaces to shut down, whose communities are constantly being uprooted? What do we hold on to when so much that is powerful is virtual—currency trades, stock prices, intellectual property and arcane trade agreements?

The short answer, at least before September 11, was that you grab anything you can get your hands on: the brand image of a famous multinational, a stock exchange, a meeting of world leaders, a single trade agreement or, in the case of the Toronto group, the banks and corporate headquarters that are the engines that power this agenda. Anything that, even fleetingly, makes the intangible actual, the vastness somehow human-scale. In short, you find symbols and you hope they become metaphors for change.

For instance, when the United States launched a trade war against France for daring to ban hormone-laced beef, José Bové and the French Farmers' Confederation didn't get the world's attention by screaming about import duties on Roquefort cheese. They did it by "strategically dismantling" a McDonald's. Nike, ExxonMobil, Monsanto, Shell, Chevron, Pfizer, Sodexho Marriott, Kellogg's, Starbucks, The Gap, Rio Tinto, British Petroleum, General Electric, Wal-Mart, Home Depot, Citigroup, Taco Bell—all have found their gleaming brands used to shine light on everything from bovine growth hormone in milk to human rights in the Niger Delta; from labor abuses of Mexican tomato farmworkers in Florida to war-financing of oil pipelines in Chad and Cameroon; from global warming to sweatshops.

In the weeks since September 11, we have been reminded many times that Americans aren't particularly informed about the world outside their borders. That may be true, but many activists have learned over the past decade that this blind spot for international affairs can be overcome by linking campaigns to famous brands—an effective, if often problematic, weapon against parochialism. These corporate campaigns have, in turn, opened back doors into the arcane world of international trade and finance, to the World Trade Organization, the World Bank and, for some, to a questioning of capitalism itself.

But these tactics have also proven to be an easy target in turn. After September 11, politicians and pundits around the world instantly began spinning the terrorist attacks as part of a continuum of anti-American and anticorporate violence: first the Starbucks window, then, presumably, the WTC. *New Republic* editor Peter Beinart seized on an obscure post to an anticorporate Internet chat room that asked if the attacks were committed by "one of us." Beinart concluded that "the anti-globalization movement . . . is, in part, a movement motivated by hatred of the United States"— immoral with the United States under attack.

In a sane world, rather than fueling such a backlash the terrorist attacks would raise questions about why U.S. intelligence agencies were spending so much time spying on environmentalists and Independent Media Centers instead of on the terrorist networks plotting mass murder. Unfortunately, it seems clear that the crackdown on activism that predated September 11 will only intensify, with heightened surveillance, infiltration and police violence. It's also likely that the anonymity that has been a hallmark of anticapitalism—masks, bandannas and pseudonyms—will become more suspect in a culture searching for clandestine operatives in its midst.

But the attacks will cost us more than our civil liberties. They could well, I fear, cost us our few political victories. Funds committed to the AIDS crisis in Africa are disappearing, and commitments to expand debt cancellation will likely follow. Defending the rights of immigrants and refugees was becoming a major focus for the direct-action crowd in Australia, Europe and, slowly, the United States. This too is threatened by the rising tide of racism and xenophobia.

And free trade, long facing a public relations crisis, is fast being rebranded, like shopping and baseball, as a patriotic duty. According to U.S. Trade Representative Robert Zoellick (who is frantically trying to get fast-track negotiating power pushed through in this moment of jingoistic groupthink), trade "promotes the values at the heart of this protracted struggle." Michael Lewis makes a similar conflation between freedom fighting and free trading when he explains, in an essay in *The New York Times Magazine*, that the traders who died were targeted as "not merely symbols but also practitioners of liberty. . . . They work hard, if unintentionally, to free others from constraints. This makes them, almost by default, the spiritual antithesis of the religious fundamentalist, whose business depends on a denial of personal liberty in the name of some putatively higher power."

The battle lines leading up to next month's WTO negotiations in Qatar are: Trade equals freedom, antitrade equals fascism. Never mind that Osama bin Laden is a multimillionaire with a rather impressive global export network stretching from cash-crop agriculture to oil pipelines. And never mind that this fight will take place in Qatar, that bastion of liberty, which is refusing foreign visas for demonstrators but where bin Laden practically has his own TV show on the state-subsidized network Al-Jazeera.

Our civil liberties, our modest victories, our usual strategies—all are now in question. But this crisis also opens up new possibilities. As many have pointed out, the challenge for social justice movements is to connect economic inequality with the security concerns that now grip us all—insisting that justice and equality are the most sustainable strategies against violence and fundamentalism.

But we cannot be naïve, as if the very real and ongoing threat of more slaughtering of innocents will disappear through political reform alone. There needs to be social justice, but there also needs to be justice for the victims of these attacks and immediate, practical prevention of future ones. Terrorism is indeed an international threat, and it did not begin with the attacks in the United States. As Bush invites the world to join America's war, sidelining the United Nations and the international courts, we need to become passionate defenders of true multilateralism, rejecting once and for all the label "antiglobalization." Bush's "coalition" does not represent a genuinely global response to terrorism but the internationalization of one country's foreign policy objectives—the trademark of U.S. international relations, from the WTO negotiating table to Kyoto: You are free to play by our rules or get shut out completely. We can make these connections not as "anti-Americans" but as true internationalists.

We can also refuse to engage in a calculus of suffering. Some on the left have implied that the outpouring of compassion and grief post–September 11 is disproportionate, even vaguely racist, compared with responses to greater atrocities. Surely the job of those who claim to abhor injustice and suffering is not to stingily parcel out compassion as if it were a finite commodity. Surely the challenge is to attempt to increase the global reserves of compassion, rather than parsimoniously police them.

Besides, is the outpouring of mutual aid and support that this tragedy has elicited so different from the humanitarian goals to which this movement aspires? The street slogans—PEOPLE BEFORE PROFIT, THE WORLD IS NOT FOR SALE—have become self-evident and viscerally felt truths for many in the wake of the attacks. There is outrage in the face of profiteering. There are questions being raised about the wisdom of leaving crucial services like airport security to private companies, about why there are bailouts for airlines but not for the workers losing their jobs. There is a groundswell of appreciation for public-sector workers of all kinds. In short, "the commons"—the public sphere, the public good, the noncorporate, what we have been defending, what is on the negotiating table in Qatar—is undergoing something of a rediscovery in the United States.

Instead of assuming that Americans can care about each other only when they are getting ready to kill a common enemy, those concerned with changing minds (and not simply winning arguments) should seize this moment to connect these humane reactions to the many other arenas in which human needs must take precedence over corporate profits, from AIDS treatment to homelessness. As Paul Loeb, author of *Soul of a Citizen*, puts it, despite the warmongering and coexisting with the xenophobia, "People seem careful, vulnerable, and extraordinarily kind to each other. These events just might be able to break us away from our gated communities of the heart."

This would require a dramatic change in activist strategy, one based much more on substance than on symbols. Then again, for more than a year, the largely symbolic activism outside summits and against individual corporations has already been challenged within movement circles. There is much that is unsatisfying about fighting a war of symbols: The glass shatters in the McDonald's window, the meetings are driven to ever more remote locations—but so what? It's still only symbols, facades, representations.

Before September 11, a new mood of impatience was already taking hold, an insistence on putting forward social and economic alternatives that address the roots of injustice as well as its symptoms, from land reform to slavery reparations. Now seems like a good time to challenge the forces of both nihilism and nostalgia within our own ranks, while making more room for the voices—coming from Chiapas, Pôrto Alegre, Kerala—showing that it is indeed possible to challenge imperialism while embracing plurality, progress and deep democracy. Our task, never more pressing, is to point out that there are more than two worlds available, to expose all the invisible worlds between the economic fundamentalism of "McWorld" and the religious fundamentalism of "Jihad."

Maybe the image wars are coming to a close. A year ago, I visited the University of Oregon to do a story on antisweatshop activism at the campus that is nicknamed Nike U. There I met student activist Sarah Jacobson. Nike, she told me, was not the target of her activism, but a tool, a way to access a vast and often amorphous economic system. "It's a gateway drug," she said cheerfully.

For years, we in this movement have fed off our opponents' symbols— their brands, their office towers, their photo-opportunity summits. We have used them as rallying cries, as focal points, as popular education tools. But these symbols were never the real targets; they were the levers, the handles. They were what allowed us, as British writer Katharine Ainger recently put it, "to open a crack in history."

The symbols were only ever doorways. It's time to walk through them.

October 10, 2001
Ends and Means: Defining a Just War
Richard Falk

I have never since my childhood supported a shooting war in which the United States was involved, although in retrospect I think the NATO war in Kosovo achieved beneficial results. The war in Afghanistan against apocalyptic terrorism qualifies in my understanding as the first truly just war since World War II. But the justice of the cause and of the limited ends is in danger of being negated by the injustice of improper means and excessive ends. Unlike World War II and prior just wars, this one can be won only if tactics adhere to legal and moral constraints on the means used to conduct it, and to limited ends.

The perpetrators of the September 11 attack cannot be reliably neutralized by nonviolent or diplomatic means; a response that includes military action is essential to diminish the threat of repetition, to inflict punishment and to restore a sense of security at home and abroad. The extremist political vision held by Osama bin Laden, which can usefully be labeled "apoc-alyptic terrorism," places this persisting threat well outside any framework of potential reconciliation or even negotiation for several reasons: Its geno-cidal intent is directed generically against Americans and Jews; its pro-claimed goal is waging an unconditional civilizational war—Islam against the West—without drawing any distinction between civilian and military targets; it has demonstrated a capacity and willingness to inflict massive and traumatizing damage on our country and a tactical ingenuity and ability to carry out its missions of destruction by reliance on the suicidal devotion of its adherents.

There are three types of responses to the attack, each of which contains some merit and enjoys some support. None of them are adequate, however.

I. Antiwar/Pacifist Approach

The pacifist position opposing even limited military action overlooks the nature of the threat and is thus irrelevant to meeting the central challenge of restor-ing some sense of security among our citizenry and in the world generally.

Also, in the current setting, unlike in the civil rights movement and the interventionist conflicts of the cold war era (especially Vietnam), antiwar and pacifist stands possess little or no cultural resonance with the overwhelming majority of Americans. It may be that at later stages of the war this assess-ment will prove to have been premature, and even now Quaker, Christian, Gandhian and Buddhist forms of pacifism offer a profound critique of wars. These critiques should be seriously heeded, since they lend weight to the view that the use of force should be marginal and kept to an absolute minimum. Certainly the spiritually motivated pacifist witness can be both inspirational and instructive, and help to mitigate and interrogate militarist postures.

Another form of antiwar advocacy rests on a critique of the United States as an imperialist superpower or empire. This view also seems dan-gerously inappropriate in addressing the challenge posed by the massive crime against humanity committed on September 11. Whatever the global role of the United States—and it is certainly responsible for much global suf-fering and injustice, giving rise to widespread resentment that at its inner core fuels the terrorist impulse—it cannot be addressed so long as this movement of global terrorism is at large and prepared to carry on with its demonic work. These longer-term concerns—which include finding ways to promote Palestinian self-determination, the internationalization of Jerusalem and a more equitable distribution of the benefits of global economic growth and development—must be addressed. Of course, much of the responsibility for the failure to do so lies with the corruption and repressive policies of governments, especially in the Middle East, outside the orbit of U.S. influence. A distinction needs to be drawn as persuasively as possible between inherently desirable lines of foreign policy reform and retreating in the face of terrorism.

II. LEGALIST/UN APPROACH

International treaties that deal with terrorism on civil aircraft call for cooperation in apprehending suspects and allow for their subsequent indictment and prosecution by national courts. Such laws could in theory be invoked to capture Osama bin Laden and his leading associates and charge them with international crimes, including crimes against humanity. A tribunal could be constituted under the authority of the United Nations, and a fair trial could then be held that would avoid war and the ensuing pain, destruction and associated costs. The narrative of apocalyptic terrorism could be laid before the world as the crimes of Nazism were bared at Nuremberg.

But this course is unlikely to deal effectively with the overall threat. A public prosecution would give bin Laden and associates a platform to rally further support among a large constituency of sympathizers, and conviction and punishment would certainly be viewed as a kind of legal martyrdom. It would be impossible to persuade the United States government to empower such a tribunal unless it was authorized to impose capital punishment, and it is doubtful that several of the permanent members of the Security Council could be persuaded to allow death sentences. Beyond this, the evidence linking bin Laden to the September 11 attacks and other instances of global terrorism may well be insufficient to produce an assured conviction in an impartial legal tribunal, particularly if conspiracy was not among the criminal offenses that could be charged. European and other foreign governments are unlikely to be willing to treat conspiracy as a capital crime. And it strains the imagination to suppose that the Bush Administration would relinquish control over bin Laden to an international tribunal. On a more general level, it also seems highly improbable that the U.S. government can be persuaded to rely on the collective security mechanisms of the UN even to the unsatisfactory degree permitted during the Gulf War. To be sure, the UN Security Council has provided a vague antiterrorist mandate as well as an endorsement of a U.S. right of response, but such legitimizing gestures are no more than that. For better and worse, the United States is relying on its claimed right of self-defense, and Washington seems certain to insist on full operational control over the means and ends of the war that is now under way. Such a reliance is worrisome, given past U.S. behavior and the somewhat militaristic character of both the leadership in Washington and the broader societal orientation in America toward the use of overwhelming force against the nation's enemies.

Yet at this stage it is unreasonable to expect the U.S. government to rely on the UN to fulfill its defensive needs. The UN lacks the capability, authority and will to respond to the kind of threat to global security posed by this new form of terrorist world war. The UN was established to deal with wars among states, while a transnational actor that cannot be definitively linked to a state is behind the attacks on the United States. Al Qaeda's relationship to the Taliban regime in Afghanistan is contingent, with Al Qaeda being more the sponsor of the state rather than the other way around.

Undoubtedly, the world would be safer and more secure with a stronger UN that had the support of the leading states in the world. The United States has for years acted more to obstruct than to foster such a transformation. Surely the long-term effects of this crisis should involve a new surge of support for a reformed UN that would have independent means of financing its operations, with its own peacekeeping and enforcement capabilities backed up by an international criminal court. Such a transformed UN would generate confidence that it could and would uphold its charter in an evenhanded manner that treats people equally. But it would be foolish to pretend that the

UN today, even if it were to enjoy a far higher level of U.S. support than it does, could mount an effective response to the September 11 attacks.

III. MILITARIST APPROACH

Unlike pacifism and legalism, militarism poses a practical danger of immense proportions. Excessive reliance on the military will backfire badly, further imperiling the security of Americans and others, spreading war and destruction far afield, as well as emboldening the government to act at home in ways that weaken U.S. democracy. So far the Bush Administration has shown some understanding of these dangers, going slowly in its reliance on military action and moving relatively cautiously to bolster its powers over those it views as suspicious or dangerous, so as to avoid the perception of waging a cultural war against Islam. The White House has itself repeatedly stressed that this conflict is unlike previous wars, that nonmilitary means are also important, that victory will come in a different way and that major battlefield encounters are unlikely to occur.

Such reassurances, however, are not altogether convincing. The President's current rhetoric seems to reflect Secretary of State Colin Powell's more prudent approach, which emphasizes diplomacy and nonmilitary tactics, and restricts military action to Al Qaeda and the Taliban regime. Even here, there is room for dangerous expansion, depending on how the Al Qaeda network is defined. Some maximalists implicate twenty or more countries as supporters of terrorism. Defense Secretary Donald Rumsfeld, his deputy Paul Wolfowitz and others are definitely beating the drums for a far wider war; they seem to regard the attacks as an occasion to implement their own vision of a new world, one that proposes to rid the world of "evil" and advances its own apocalyptic vision. This vision seeks the destruction of such organizations as Hezbollah and Hamas, which have only minimal links to Al Qaeda and transnational terror, and which have agendas limited mainly to Palestinian rights of self-determination and the future of Jerusalem. These organizations, while legally responsible for terrorist operations within their sphere of concerns, but also subject to terrorist provocations, have not shown any intention of pursuing bin Laden's apocalyptic undertaking. Including such groups on the U.S. target list will surely undermine the depth and breadth of international support and engender dangerous reactions throughout the Islamic world, and possibly in the West as well.

Beyond this, there is speculation that there will be a second stage of response that will include a series of countries regarded as hostile to the United States, who are in possession of weapons of mass destruction but are not currently related to global terrorism in any significant fashion. These include Iraq, Libya and possibly even Syria, Iran and Sudan. To expand war objectives in this way would be full of risks, require massive military strikes inflicting much destruction and suffering, and would create a new wave of retaliatory violence directed against the United States and Americans throughout the world. If military goals overshoot, either by becoming part of a design to destroy Israel's enemies or to solve the problem of proliferation of weapons of mass destruction, the war against global terrorism will be lost, and badly.

Just as the pacifist fallacy involves unrealistic exclusion of military force from an acceptable response, the militarist fallacy involves an excessive reliance on military force in a manner that magnifies the threat it is trying to diminish or eliminate. It also expands the zone of violence in particularly dangerous ways that are almost certain to intensify and inflame anti-Americanism. It should be kept in mind that war occasions deep suffering, and recourse to international force should be both a last resort and on as limited a scale as possible.

But there is a fourth response, which has gained support among foreign policy analysts and probably a majority of Americans.

IV. LIMITING MEANS AND ENDS

Unlike in major wars of the past, the response to this challenge of apocalyptic terrorism can be effective only if it is also widely perceived as legitimate. And legitimacy can be attained only if the role of military force is marginal to the overall conduct of the war and the relevant frameworks of moral, legal and religious restraint are scrupulously respected.

Excessive use of force in pursuing the perpetrators of September 11 will fan the flames of Islamic militancy and give credence to calls for holy war.

What lent the WTC/Pentagon attack its quality of sinister originality was the ability of a fanatical political movement to take advantage of the complex fragility and vulnerability of advanced technology. Now that this vulnerability has been exposed to the world, it is impossible to insure that other extremists will not commit similar acts—even if Osama bin Laden is eliminated.

The only way to wage this war effectively is to make sure that force is used within relevant frameworks of restraint. Excessive force can take several forms, like the pursuit of political movements remote from the WTC attack, especially if such military action is seen as indirectly doing the dirty work of eliminating threats to Israel's occupation of Palestinian territories and Jerusalem. Excessiveness would also be attributed to efforts to destroy and restructure regimes, other than the Taliban, that are hostile to the United States but not significantly connected with either the attack or Al Qaeda.

The second, closely related problem of successfully framing a response is related to the U.S. manner of waging war: The U.S. temperament has tended to approach war as a matter of confronting evil. In such a view, victory can be achieved only by the total defeat of the other, and with it, the triumph of good.

In the current setting, goals have not been clarified, and U.S. leaders have used grandiose language about ending terrorism and destroying the global terrorist network. The idea of good against evil has been a consistent part of the process of public mobilization, with the implicit message that nothing less than a total victory is acceptable. What are realistic ends? Or put differently, what ends can be reconciled with a commitment to achieve an effective response? What is needed is extremely selective uses of force, especially in relation to the Taliban, combined with criminal law enforcement operations—cutting off sources of finance, destroying terrorist cells, using policing techniques abetted, to the extent necessary, by paramilitary capabilities.

Also troubling is the Bush Administration's ingrained disdain for multilateralism and its determination to achieve security for the United States by military means—particularly missile defense and space weaponization. This unilateralism has so far been masked by a frantic effort to forge a global coalition, but there is every indication that the U.S. government will insist on complete operational control over the war and will not be willing to accept procedures of accountability within the UN framework.

The Administration has often said that many of the actions in this war will not be made known to the public. But an excessive emphasis on secrecy in the conduct of military operations is likely to make the uses of force more difficult to justify to those who are skeptical about U.S. motives and goals, thus undercutting the legitimacy of the war.

In building a global coalition for cooperative action, especially with respect to law enforcement in countries where Al Qaeda operates, the U.S. government has struck a number of Faustian bargains. It may be necessary to enter into arrangements with governments that are themselves responsible for terrorist policies and brutal repression, such as Russia in Chechnya and India in Kashmir. But the cost of doing so is to weaken claims that a common antiterrorist front is the foundation of this alliance. For some governments the war against apocalyptic terrorism is an opportunity to proceed with their own repressive policies free from censure and interference. The U.S. government should weigh the cost of writing blank checks against the importance of distinguishing its means and ends from the megaterrorist ethos that animated the September 11 attacks. There are some difficult choices ahead, including the extent to which Afghan opposition forces, particularly the Northern Alliance, should be supported in view of their own dubious human rights record.

How, then, should legitimacy be pursued in the current context? The first set of requirements is essentially political: to disclose goals that seem reasonably connected with the attack and with the threat posed by those who planned, funded and carried it out. In this regard, the destruction of both the Taliban regime and the Al Qaeda network, including the apprehension and prosecution of Osama bin Laden and any associates connected with this and past terrorist crimes, are appropriate goals. In each instance, further specification is necessary. With respect to the Taliban, its relation to Al Qaeda is established and intimate enough to attribute primary responsibility, and the case is strengthened to the degree that its governing policies are so oppressive as to give the international community the strongest possible grounds for humanitarian intervention. We must make a distinction between those individuals and entities that have been actively engaged in the perpetration of the visionary program of international, apocalyptic terrorism uniquely Al Qaeda's and those who have used funds or training to advance more traditional goals relating to grievances associated with the governance of a particular country and have limited their targets largely to the authorities in their countries, like the ETA in Spain and the IRA in Ireland and Britain.

Legitimacy with respect to the use of force in international settings derives from the mutually reinforcing traditions of the "just war" doctrine, international law and the ideas of restraint embedded in the great religions of the world. The essential norms are rather abstract in character, and lend themselves to debate and diverse interpretation. The most important ideas are:

- the principle of discrimination: force must be directed at a military target, with damage to civilians and civilian society being incidental;
- the principle of proportionality: force must not be greater than that needed to achieve an acceptable military result and must not be greater than the provoking cause;
- the principle of humanity: force must not be directed even against enemy personnel if they are subject to capture, wounded or under control (as with prisoners of war);
- the principle of necessity: force should be used only if nonviolent means to achieve military goals are unavailable.

These abstract guidelines for the use of force do not give much operational direction. In each situation we must ask: Do the claims to use force seem reasonable in terms of the ends being pursued, including the obligation to confine civilian damage as much as possible? Such assessments depend on interpretation, but they allow for debate and justification, and clear instances of violative behavior could be quickly identified. The justice of the cause and of the limited ends will be negated by the injustice of improper means and excessive ends. Only the vigilance of an active citizenry, alert to this delicate balance, has much hope of helping this new war to end in a true victory.

November 7, 2001
Is This Really a 'Just War'?
Responses to Richard Falk's "A Just War"

SAN FRANCISCO

As a former *Nation* contributor and a longtime *Nation* reader, I congratulate you for running Richard Falk's "Ends and Means: Defining a Just War." It is a powerful antidote to some of the confused and retro thinking that has beset a certain segment of the left since September 11. Just as old generals want to fight the last war all over again, some veterans of the peace movement have a knee-jerk tendency to think this is Vietnam all over again, or even the Gulf War. But it's not. The Gulf of Tonkin attack never happened. September 11 did, with gruesome results. The world has changed.

Like Falk, for the first time in my adult life, I find myself supporting a war against a very real enemy—what Christopher Hitchens correctly calls "Islamic fascism." I appreciate the fact that Falk's endorsement of war against "apocalyptic terrorism" was nuanced, measured and admitted all the possible pitfalls.

I also agree that in retrospect the NATO bombing of Kosovo looks like not such a bad thing. Milosevic is gone, and the United States and the West helped to stop, albeit belatedly, the ethnic cleansing of Muslims—something bin Laden and the Taliban seem to have overlooked. Wars, even just wars like World War II, are inherently awful, but sometimes they are necessary, and sometimes, as in Kosovo, bombing actually works.

Steve Talbot

BOSTON

Richard Falk (a friend whom I admire and respect for his long advocacy of peace and justice) has said this is "the first truly just war since World War II." I have puzzled over this. How can a war be "truly just" that involves the daily killing of civilians; that is terrorizing the people of Afghanistan, causing hundreds of thousands to leave their homes to escape the bombs; that has little chance of finding those who planned the September 11 attacks (and even if found, no chance that this would stop terrorism); and that can only multiply the ranks of people who are angry at this country, from whose ranks terrorists are born? The stories of the effects of our bombing are beginning to come through, in bits and pieces: the wounded children arriving across the border, one barely two months old, swathed in bloody bandages; the Red Cross warehouses bombed, the use of deadly cluster bombs, a small mountain village bombed and entire families wiped out.

That is only a few weeks into the bombing. The "war against terrorism" has become a war against innocent men, women and children, who are in no way responsible for the terrorist attack on New York. I believe the supporters of the war have confused a just cause with a just war. A cause may be just—like ending terrorism. But it does not follow that going to war on behalf of that cause, with the inevitable mayhem that follows, is just.

Falk talks of "limited military action." But the momentum of war rides roughshod over limits. Atrocities are explained by the deceptive language of "accident," "military targets," "collateral damage." Killing innocent people in war is not an "accident." It is an inevitability. The moral equation in Afghanistan is clear. Civilian casualties are certain. The outcome is uncertain. Use the money allotted our huge military machine to combat starvation and disease around the world. One-third of our military budget would provide water and sanitation facilities for the billion people worldwide who have none.

Let us be a more modest nation. The modest nations of the world don't face the threat of terrorism. Let us pull back from being a military superpower and become a humanitarian superpower. We, and everyone else, will then be more secure.

Howard Zinn

NEW YORK CITY

Here is bad news indeed: Our friend Richard Falk, speaker of truth to power, guru to activists, antiestablishmentarian par excellence, has cloned himself. We now have the old Falk, on October 8 calling for "A Just Response" in his prophetic voice and on October 29 the new Falk "Defining a Just War" in tones of neorealism.

Those who took to heart the old Falk's admonition that this is "above all, a war without military solutions" are now chastised by the new Falk for being "irrelevant to meeting the central challenge of restoring some sense of security among our citizenry." The old Falk told us that "reliance on the rule of law," possibly through a due process trial under UN authority, "would be a major step in seeking to make the struggle against terrorism enjoy the genuine support of the entire organized international community." The new Falk says this is pie in the sky, since the United States would never agree to such a trial, which in any case would only offer Osama bin Laden an opportunity to have himself declared a bona fide legal martyr.

The old Falk declares "the only way to win this 'war' (if war it is) . . . is with a credible commitment to the global promotion of social justice." Correction from the new Falk: "Global suffering and injustice . . . cannot be addressed so long as this movement of global terrorism is at large." True enough, both the old and the new Falk call for limited ends and means. But, given the precedents of U.S. behavior in Central America, Serbia and Iraq, how realistic is that demand? We are bombing a country in which there was nothing left to bomb to begin with.

In dealing with this greatest of contemporary crimes against humanity, a judicious use of force cannot be ruled out altogether. But perhaps the real realist is Donald Rumsfeld, who warns that bin Laden may never be found and that the Taliban are not about to roll over and play dead. We can all hope that this prediction will turn out to be wrong. In the meantime what is needed is better security, better intelligence, better communication and that commitment to global justice, both criminal and social. Easier said than done, but absolutely necessary. Will the old Falk please stand up? We need you, Richard!

Peter Weiss, *Lawyers Committee on Nuclear Policy*
WASHINGTON, DC

Richard Falk does not bother to tell us on what evidence he bases his assertion that "a response that includes military action is essential to diminish the threat of repetition" of the terrorist acts, though this is the major premise for his conclusion that a war in Afghanistan might be just. Falk thinks that invoking the well-known "extremism" and "fanaticism" of bin Laden's brand of Islam is enough to assure us that he and his adherents will strike and strike again unless they are eliminated—liquidated, to use the apt if archaic terminology of a certain brand of Marxism—as if such a feat were either easy or sufficient. Though Falk's call for carefully limited ends and means is a welcome one, if utopian under the current circumstances, his major premise invites the very excesses he warns against.

The Bush Administration lost the "war against terrorism" the moment it began bombing Afghanistan, and the longer the bombing continues the more serious the loss. Military action in Afghanistan has already inflamed Muslims around the world. Pakistanis are reportedly crossing the border to join the Taliban, while support for the U.S. effort melts away among moderates in that country. Each new instance of "collateral damage" feeds the fires. But, more profoundly, the improbability of achieving anything like a consensual government in Kabul in the wake of the U.S. adventure insures that Afghanistan will continue to be the festering sore nurturing the pathology we are combating.

The military campaign, moreover, has only the remotest chance of capturing bin Laden and the major leaders of Al Qaeda. Even were it to do so, there is no reason to suppose that terror directed at U.S. and other targets would stop. On the contrary, the operation that succeeded in shaking the United States to its roots on September 11 was an amateur affair, guided and financed on a minor scale by Al Qaeda, if we are to believe the intelligence released so far, but scarcely dependent upon such backing. Only determined police work—of the sort being carried out now—by competent and coordinated agencies of law enforcement (something we still lack in this country) could be expected to meet this threat. Military action is irrelevant to it.

We have lost the war. Now it is up to what remains of the left and to religiously based opposition movements to try to moderate the scale of the damage by insisting that the Administration refuse the next step urged by Deputy Defense Secretary Paul Wolfowitz and others, who have openly advocated carrying the war to Iraq and beyond. And we must insist, as well, that the United States reverse course in the Middle East, starting with its unconditional support for Israel and extending to its broad tolerance for the despotic regimes that protect Israel's flanks while helping to slake our insatiable thirst for oil.

Michael W. Foley

BOULDER CREEK, CALIF.

After asserting that the war in Afghanistan is just, Richard Falk undermines his conclusion by explaining how the campaign fails to meet his requirements for a just war. He declares that legitimacy must be based on the adoption of "goals that seem reasonably connected with the attack," yet points out that "goals have not been clarified, and U.S. leaders have used grandiose language about ending terrorism and destroying the global terrorist network." He states that a just war must avoid damage to civilians, yet air campaigns almost inevitably involve serious casualties to civilians and civilian infrastructure. He states that "force must not be greater than that needed to achieve an acceptable military result," but the war in Afghanistan is not based on achieving any specific military result.

He states that the force employed "must not be greater than the provoking cause," but the force applied to Afghanistan quickly exceeded the force used by the suicide bombers. He states that "force must not be directed even against enemy personnel if they are subject to capture, wounded or under control," yet George W. Bush's "wanted dead or alive" declaration violates that requirement. And he states that "force should be used only if nonviolent means to achieve military goals are unavailable," yet the absence of military goals in this instance makes an analysis of this requirement impossible.

If the goal is to bring terrorists to justice in court, history illustrates that nonmilitary approaches work. If the goal is to counter Islamic extremism, recent developments in Iran, for example, demonstrate that nonviolent means can moderate apparently intractable regimes.

Eliminating the underlying causes that fuel terrorism would provide more security in the long run. Patience is necessary, but not passivity. Law enforcement agencies would still vigorously arrest and prosecute criminals. As Falk himself points out, "Excessive reliance on the military will backfire badly, further imperiling the security of Americans and others, spreading war and destruction far afield, as well as emboldening the government to act at home in ways that weaken U.S. democracy. . . . the militarist fallacy involves an excessive reliance on military force in a manner that magnifies the threat it is trying to diminish or eliminate." And he acknowledges that the Administration is deeply committed to unilateralism, which is characterized by a "determination to achieve security for the United States by military means." Given this recognition, how he believes the United States can wage a just war against terrorism boggles my mind.

By accepting the U.S. prerogative to "destroy and restructure regimes" like the Taliban, Falk puts himself on a slippery slope. Whatever the options may be for dealing with oppressive regimes, vesting that power in the hands of the United States is not the answer. Perhaps Bush will limit the war to trying to overthrow the Taliban, as Falk prefers. But I suspect Falk is deluding himself if he believes that the West can destroy the Al Qaeda network and similar networks that emerge. Such counterproductive reliance on force resembles the effort to stop violence in the United States by beefing up police forces, building more prisons and resorting to capital punishment.

Wade Hudson

NEW YORK CITY; PITTSBURGH

Richard Falk's endorsement of a limited war is fraught with immeasurable harm. Thousands of refugees are fleeing daily; the United Nations is predicting the death of 100,000 children; and hate for Americans is pouring into the streets of Pakistan, Indonesia and other Muslim countries. We are creating the terrorists that will visit terror upon our children. Pakistan, with its nuclear arsenal, may be destabilized. Innocents have been killed, and we may face a fractionalized and warfaring post-Taliban Afghanistan.

There was another way. Treat the attacks on September 11 as a crime against humanity (mass or systematic killing of civilians), establish a UN tribunal, extradite or, if that fails, capture the suspects with a UN force and try them. The U.S. experience with Libya demonstrates both the perils of a military response and the possibilities for international justice. U.S. officials believed that the 1986 bombing of Libya led to the downing of Pan Am 103 and that more bombing would lead to a spiraling cycle of violence. The United States turned to the UN, which applied international pressure; eventually the Libyans extradited the suspects for trial.

The objections Falk makes to such a tribunal revolve primarily around his belief that Washington would not accept such a court, in part because the court might not be authorized to give the death penalty. But since when should respected international legal experts like Falk, who generally favor peaceful resolutions of conflicts, shy away from arguing what is right simply because they believe the United States will not listen? Falk says that it is "unreasonable to expect the U.S. government to rely on the UN to fulfill its defensive needs." But Falk did not think that it was unreasonable for the Kuwaitis to rely on the UN to counteract Iraqi aggression in 1990. Is Falk bowing to U.S. exceptionalism—the UN is good for everybody else, but not for the only superpower?

It is remarkable that Falk, while recognizing that the global role of the United States has given rise to widespread resentment that fuels the terrorist impulse, claims that this role "cannot be addressed so long as this movement of global terrorism is at large." But it is now that we must examine this resentment: our tilt in the Palestinian-Israeli conflict, the use of the Persian Gulf as a U.S. base and support for corrupt, authoritarian regimes. We must do so not to "give in to terrorists" but to promote a more just and peaceful world and to enhance our long-term security. To do so only when the global terrorist movement is no longer "at large" insures that such an examination will never occur.

Developing a proper response to terrorism is incredibly difficult, and no short-term solution seems particularly attractive. Only by taking the road toward creating a more equal, democratic and just world can we create conditions of security from terrorism for our children. Bombing Afghanistan—whatever the justness of the cause—seems the wrong way to start down that path.

Michael Ratner, Jules Lobel,
Center for Constitutional Rights

MONTPELIER, VT.

Richard Falk deftly analyzes the inadequacies of the "antiwar/pacifist," "legalist/UN" and "militarist" approaches to the war on terrorism. As someone who has made a career in conflict emergency response in the UN, I don't entirely disagree with Falk's pointing out the UN's difficulties under its charter in dealing effectively with Al Qaeda, a "transnational actor that cannot be definitively linked to a state," which is "more the sponsor of the state rather than the other way around." Nevertheless, the UN has an important role in defining the *casus belli* that was the September 11 attack and certifying the armed response now under way, and Falk misses that point. Mary Robinson, the UN High Commissioner for Human Rights, has issued a statement that the attacks involved "a widespread, deliberate targeting of a civilian population" and constituted a crime against humanity. She then noted that all countries have a responsibility under international law to help bring the attackers to justice, but that in the absence of ratification of the 1998 International Criminal Court by the required number of countries, there was no appropriate venue for prosecution. This is where I had hoped that Falk's synthesis at the end of his piece was heading, arguing for appropriate "limited means and ends." For there are now dozens if not scores of venues for the prosecution of, *inter alia*, war crimes, torture, genocide, slavery and piracy: the national courts of countries that are signatories of the Geneva Conventions, the torture and genocide conventions. In fact, under the concept of universal jurisdiction, which has evolved steadily if quietly in the past few years, no less than nine European countries have brought prosecutions. (It was the 1998–99 extradition hearings in Britain of Gen. Augusto Pinochet that revealed the extent of this evolution.)

Limited means and ends. U.S. intelligence locates terrorist concentrations; aircraft attack training and administrative centers and suppress air defenses; special operations forces surgically attack the concentrations, arresting those who surrender and killing those who resist violently. Then, the terrorists are brought before national courts in Europe for prosecution in cases brought by relatives of the dead or by the governments in the countries concerned. Austria, Belgium, France and Spain have already prosecuted foreign individuals, under the aegis of universal jurisdiction, for crimes of murder, arson, assault, disappearance and crimes against humanity, all of which occurred on September 11. It is precisely the enormity of the attacks that might make the Administration and Congress more amenable to ratification of the International Criminal Court statute, and to support of the concept of universal jurisdiction.

Falk is a strong proponent of universal jurisdiction and was one of the organizers of a panel of international legal scholars in January 2001 that produced the "Princeton Principles on Universal Jurisdiction," an attempt to clarify the concept and to address the practical problems of bringing prosecutions. He apparently didn't see universal jurisdiction as an important component of a limited and appropriate U.S. response to September 11.

Stephen Green

University Park, Md.

I have admired Richard Falk's writing over the years, but his article on a "just war" misses the mark. To label the September 11 attacks "apocalyptic terrorism" is ludicrous—worthy of Bush Administration propaganda. So also is his point that Osama bin Laden's "proclaimed goal" is a genocidal war of "Islam against the West." That's nonsense right out of the odious Samuel Huntington's *Clash of Civilizations*. Isn't a war to rid the world of evil apocalyptic?

Falk should take some time to read bin Laden's proclamations rather than impose Huntington's words on him. He'll see that the number-one driving force behind bin Laden is the U.S. occupation and corruption of

Saudi Arabia. On this point bin Laden is correct, and Falk is wrong in saying that his "persisting threat [is] well outside any framework of potential
reconciliation or even negotiation." The United States has only to agree to
leave Saudi Arabia and bin Laden would give up his war on the United
States. That's a negotiable proposition, except for the fact that the United
States would never consider giving up its occupation of Saudi Arabia. It
would destroy all Islamic nations with nuclear weapons before considering
that. Who is apocalyptic?

It is well to remember that the United States is at war with Arab nationalism and has been for years. The only new thing is that a major attack
occurred on U.S. soil. If Falk and others don't like being attacked, they need
to find a way of putting an end to war, not of legitimizing it. Let's face it:
The United States has been dealing out terror on a huge scale for a century.
That is what should make us outraged.

Robert Merrill

BENNINGTON, VT.
Richard Falk wrote an edifying gift to those who make a distinction
between anti-Americanism and anti-imperialism. The former means a priori
rejection of whatever position Washington takes on a given international
issue. Anti-imperialism, on the other hand, is a normative critique of the
context, purpose and implications of particular policies. Falk is on solid
ground in characterizing the current military action "against apocalyptic
terrorism" as a just war. The point I wish to add to Falk's analysis is that
the primary victims of the Taliban have been and will be the people of
Afghanistan. Mullah Omar and company might soon conclude that the
pathological crime of September 11 was unwise, but the chances are nil that
they will come to admit their role in the destruction of Afghanistan and the
decimation of its people.

It is therefore possible that at the end of the ongoing war in Afghanistan
Osama bin Laden will be out of the picture, but the Taliban under a new
leadership will be allowed to stay on in exchange for severing its alliance

with global terrorists. What will not change, however, is the theocratic regime's cruelty toward the Afghans who disagree with it. For the *raison d'être* of the Taliban, representing a radical version of puritanical Islam, is denial of human rights and suppression of the idea of political equality. Events in the Islamic Republic of Iran illustrate the point. The militant puritans controlling the Iranian state and society are trying to normalize, in the hope of reviving the country's depressed economy, their diplomatic and trade relations with nearly all nations of the world, but they continue to brutalize their secular critics at home.

Mansour Farhang

NORTH ANDOVER, MASS.

Professor Falk has been a clear voice in opposition to many of the worst crimes of the century, and I am sad to hear him speaking out in defense of any kind of killing. The modern way of waging war renders the abstractions of just-war theory obsolete. I was most disturbed by Falk's statement, "Whatever the global role of the United States . . . it cannot be addressed so long as this movement of global terrorism is at large and prepared to carry on with its demonic work." Does this mean that paramilitaries in Colombia, killer soldiers in Israel or pilots dropping bombs on Iraq should be given free rein to terrorize people while we focus our energies on opposing global terrorism? People are suffering now in Afghanistan, in Colombia, in Palestine, in Iraq and so many other places as a result of our government's violence. Perhaps, if we can make the world more just there will be fewer people angry enough to commit the kinds of unspeakable crimes we witnessed on September 11.

Sean Donahue

NEW YORK CITY

Falk ends his excellent analysis with a call to action: It is "only the vigilance of an active citizenry" that will lead to victory. Americans must understand, however, that it is not just in America that people are terrified; and it is not just here that the potential for "apocalyptic terrorism" exists, although we are certainly the preferred target. A sense of foreboding has descended, worldwide; our collective future hangs in the balance, and at this juncture it is not at all clear that the United States will preserve it by observing the four principles of discrimination, proportionality, humanity and necessity. What does seem clear, however, along with our greatly narrowed access to information since September 11, is that no one at higher levels of government is willing to listen. Where and when and how will this "active citizenry" be heard?

Elizabeth Lara

FALK REPLIES

PRINCETON, N.J.

With each passing day, my assessment shifts to reach the conclusion that the United States is waging an unjust war in Afghanistan, and it is doing so in a manner that is likely to have severe blowback consequences. I was misled by the language of George W. Bush, Colin Powell and others, which seemed at the time to exhibit an understanding that this was a drastically different kind of war that required a core reliance on nonmilitary approaches. I accepted the claim that it was necessary to make some selective use of force so as to displace the Taliban and to disable to the extent possible the Al Qaeda network. I also proceeded from the premise that the threat posed was of an unprecedented magnitude, both because it successfully used weapons of mass destruction against U.S. civilian society in a gruesome manner that revealed its pervasive vulnerability, and because there was every likelihood of efforts to repeat the attack in even more devastating forms in the future.

Particularly in response to Howard Zinn, with whom I cannot imagine ever disagreeing on any core issue, my initial reference to the Afghanistan war as a just war was a technical matter. It qualified as a just war because the scope of the military response seemed initially to be proportional to the gravity of the attack and the continuing threat of further attacks, but as with World War II, the prospect of significant civilian casualties is consistent with such a conclusion, and an inevitable effect of any recourse to war, however justified the cause. War, even as a necessary instrument to restore security, is inherently cruel in its effects on innocent civilians, creating an urgent moral imperative that we work for nonviolent forms of global governance and conflict resolution. Tragically, we are not there yet and must adopt the least bad available alternative, which I had hoped (falsely, it turns out) would be a limited war with primary reliance on nonmilitary solutions. And, of course, I am ready to join Zinn and others in seeking to make our country "a humanitarian superpower," but in the meantime nothing is possible until the Al Qaeda sword dangling above our collective existence is removed.

To clarify, the September 11 attack was a criminal, warlike assault on this country that engaged the right of self-defense under international law and morality. How to exercise this right under such unprecedented circumstances, in which the main adversary is a nonstate actor, challenged the imagination to combine effectiveness with legitimacy. I can now say, as some of my critics perceived from the outset, that our government seems incapable of learning from its past moral and political disasters, especially the excessive reliance on bombing to achieve political goals. Any satisfactory U.S. recourse to war had to make every reasonable effort to minimize civilian casualties. The use of cluster bombs, the reliance on B-52 carpet-bombing, the failure to adapt tactics in light of targeting errors, combine to produce disastrous results from a moral, legal and political perspective. The political impact of relying on indiscriminate and cruel high-tech military tactics while shielding one's own forces from serious risk of casualty confirms the worst images of the U.S. role in the world, especially in the Islamic portions of the Third World. The predictable result is to inflame anti-Americanism around the world and to sow seeds of doubt and despair among our like-minded European allies.

But having acknowledged this much does not imply an acceptance of several lines of criticism. I can assure Peter Weiss that my values and worldview did not shift in a matter of a couple of weeks but that the nature of the challenge required a response that had some reasonable prospect of being effective. We must start with the world as it is, not as we would like it to be, although we should act to make our hopes and dreams come true. The nonstate, multistate locus of this terrorist adversary does not fit the existing structures of law and authority. In dealing with warlike attacks on major countries, the UN is not entrusted with either the capabilities or the mandate to fashion a response. International society is still based on a self-help system as far as major states are concerned, a fact acknowledged by the veto power given to the permanent members of the Security Council.

Where should we go from here? I agree very much with Mansour Farhang that the removal of the Taliban is an independently beneficial goal, especially for the Afghan people, and should have been stressed by the U.S. government. Ample justification for "humanitarian intervention" exists, but its humanitarian character is lost if the means relied upon abandon the constraints of law and morality and do not exhibit a credible commitment to the protection of the Afghan people. Such a commitment requires interveners to take casualty risks to the extent needed to avoid killing large numbers of civilians and damaging their social infrastructure. If the tactics contradict the mission, as now seems the case in Afghanistan, the case for humanitarian intervention is undermined.

Is it "ludicrous," as Robert Merrill suggests, to label the September 11 attacks as "apocalyptic terrorism"? I think not. Some have tried other labels to express their distinctiveness: Michael Ignatieff has referred to "nihilistic terrorism" and others to "megaterrorism." I think "apocalyptic" captures best the horizons of destructive violence and purifying religious salvation that animate Osama bin Laden and his followers. The point is to find language that distinguishes these attacks from prior instances of terrorism associated with ongoing conflicts over national self-determination. I have read the utterances of bin Laden, and they express an unmistakable genocidal intention, backed up by fanatical views and practices. The presence of U.S. forces near Islam's holiest sites may have pushed bin Laden over the edge, but the whole tenor of Al Qaeda, its attitude toward the totality of "Crusaders," "Jews" and "Americans," and its training programs and tactics suggests a commitment to intercivilizational warfare. To understand such operations as preparing the ground for negotiations I find implausible. Besides, it is not a breach of any fundamental code for a government, as in Saudi Arabia, to seek a foreign military presence to safeguard its security. We may not like the regime in Riyadh, but it is playing by the international rules of the game of world politics.

We find ourselves trapped between a severe continuing threat to our security and a government that is acting in such a way as to aggravate that threat. At the same time, it is not obvious what can and should be done. It is clear that the roots of terrorism are intermingled with unjust policies, and that these should be abandoned as early as possible for both pragmatic and intrinsic reasons. Pushing for a viable Palestinian state is now finally surfacing on the Western agenda in an explicit manner. Recognizing the need to address poverty, oppression and corruption in the Islamic world is clearly essential if the underlying needs of human security are to be satisfied. Even more ambitious, it should be part of the progressive discourse to propose the sort of UN—and accompanying arrangements like independent peace-keeping and enforcement capabilities, an international criminal court and police force—that is needed to overcome the deficiencies of a self-help system of world order that treats war as the ultimate arbiter. To reach these results, however, will require that the militarist political culture here at home be challenged and transformed. These undertakings are urgent, but they cannot be undertaken successfully in the midst of the atmosphere of fear and foreboding that currently grips the vast majority of Americans, a mood accentuated by the anthrax ordeal.

Finally, the disorienting character of September 11 underscores the relevance of discussion and debate. *The Nation* has been an admirable forum for the expression of diverse views, and I hope that this role will be maintained. I would also hope that all of us who take part exhibit the realization that we would benefit from listening to those with whom we disagree, and that no one has any plausible basis for certitude or condescension.

Richard Falk

October 17, 2001
The Geopolitics of War
Michael T. Klare

There are many ways to view the conflict between the United States and Osama bin Laden's terror network: as a contest between Western liberalism and Eastern fanaticism, as suggested by many pundits in the United States; as a struggle between the defenders and the enemies of authentic Islam, as suggested by many in the Muslim world; and as a predictable backlash against American villainy abroad, as suggested by some on the left. But while useful in assessing some dimensions of the conflict, these cultural and political analyses obscure a fundamental reality: that this war, like most of the wars that preceded it, is firmly rooted in geopolitical competition.

The geopolitical dimensions of the war are somewhat hard to discern because the initial fighting is taking place in Afghanistan, a place of little intrinsic interest to the United States, and because our principal adversary, bin Laden, has no apparent interest in material concerns. But this is deceptive, because the true center of the conflict is Saudi Arabia, not Afghanistan (or Palestine), and because bin Laden's ultimate objectives include the imposition of a new Saudi government, which in turn would control the single most valuable geopolitical prize on the face of the earth: Saudi Arabia's vast oil deposits, representing one-fourth of the world's known petroleum reserves.

To fully appreciate the roots of the current conflict, it is necessary to travel back in time—specifically, to the final years of World War II, when the U.S. government began to formulate plans for the world it would dominate in the postwar era. As the war drew to a close, the State Department was enjoined by President Roosevelt to devise the policies and institutions that would guarantee U.S. security and prosperity in the coming epoch. This entailed the design and formation of the United Nations, the construction of the Bretton Woods world financial institutions and, most significant in the current context, the procurement of adequate oil supplies.

American strategists considered access to oil to be especially important because it was an essential factor in the Allied victory over the Axis powers. Although the nuclear strikes on Hiroshima and Nagasaki ended the war, it was oil that fueled the armies that brought Germany and Japan to their knees. Oil powered the vast numbers of ships, tanks and aircraft that endowed Allied forces with a decisive edge over their adversaries, which lacked access to reliable sources of petroleum. It was widely assumed, therefore, that access to large supplies of oil would be critical to U.S. success in any future conflicts.

Where would this oil come from? During World Wars I and II, the United States was able to obtain sufficient oil for its own and its allies' needs from deposits in the American Southwest and from Mexico and Venezuela. But most U.S. analysts believed that these supplies would be insufficient to meet American and European requirements in the postwar era. As a result, the State Department initiated an intensive study to identify other sources of petroleum. This effort, led by the department's economic adviser, Herbert Feis, concluded that only one location could provide the needed petroleum. "In all surveys of the situation," Feis noted (in a statement quoted by Daniel Yergin in *The Prize*), "the pencil came to an awed pause at one point and place—the Middle East."

To be more specific, Feis and his associates concluded that the world's most prolific supply of untapped oil was to be found in the Kingdom of Saudi Arabia. But how to get at this oil? At first, the State Department proposed the formation of a government-owned oil firm to acquire concessions in Saudi Arabia and extract the kingdom's reserves. This plan was considered too unwieldy, however, and instead U.S. officials turned this task over to the Arabian American Oil Company (ARAMCO), an alliance of major U.S. oil corporations. But these officials were also worried about the kingdom's long-term stability, so they concluded that the United States would have to assume responsibility for the defense of Saudi Arabia. In one of the most extraordinary occurrences in modern American history, President Roosevelt met with King Abd al-Aziz Ibn Saud, the founder of the modern Saudi regime, on a U.S. warship in the Suez Canal following the February

1945 conference in Yalta. Although details of the meeting have never been made public, it is widely believed that Roosevelt gave the King a promise of U.S. protection in return for privileged American access to Saudi oil—an arrangement that remains in full effect today and constitutes the essential core of the U.S.-Saudi relationship.

This relationship has provided enormous benefits to both sides. The United States has enjoyed preferred access to Saudi petroleum reserves, obtaining about one-sixth of its crude-oil imports from the kingdom. ARAMCO and its U.S. partners have reaped immense profits from their operations in Saudi Arabia and from the distribution of Saudi oil worldwide. (Although ARAMCO's Saudi holdings were nationalized by the Saudi government in 1976, the company continues to manage Saudi oil production and to market its petroleum products abroad.) Saudi Arabia also buys about $6–10 billion worth of goods per year from U.S. companies. The Saudi royal family, for its part, has become immensely wealthy and, because of continued U.S. protection, has remained safe from external and internal attack.

But this extraordinary partnership has also produced a number of unintended consequences, and it is these effects that concern us here. To protect the Saudi regime against its external enemies, the United States has steadily expanded its military presence in the region, eventually deploying thousands of troops in the kingdom. Similarly, to protect the royal family against its internal enemies, U.S. personnel have become deeply involved in the regime's internal security apparatus. At the same time, the vast and highly conspicuous accumulation of wealth by the royal family has alienated it from the larger Saudi population and led to charges of systemic corruption. In response, the regime has outlawed all forms of political debate in the kingdom (there is no parliament, no free speech, no political party, no right of assembly) and used its U.S.-trained security forces to quash overt expressions of dissent. All these effects have generated covert opposition to the regime and occasional acts of violence—and it is from this underground milieu that Osama bin Laden has drawn his inspiration and many of his top lieutenants.

The U.S. military presence in Saudi Arabia has steadily increased over the years. Initially, from 1945 to 1972, Washington delegated the primary defense responsibility to Britain, long the dominant power in the region. When Britain withdrew its forces from "East of Suez" in 1971, the United States assumed a more direct role, deploying military advisers in the kingdom and providing Saudi Arabia with a vast arsenal of U.S. weapons. Some of these arms and advisory programs were aimed at external defense, but the Defense Department also played a central role in organizing, equipping, training and managing the Saudi Arabian National Guard (SANG), the regime's internal security force.

American military involvement in the kingdom reached a new level in 1979, when three things happened: The Soviet Union invaded Afghanistan, the Shah of Iran was overthrown by antigovernment forces and Islamic militants staged a brief rebellion in Mecca. In response, President Jimmy Carter issued a new formulation of U.S. policy: Any move by a hostile power to gain control of the Persian Gulf area would be regarded "as an assault on the vital interests of the United States of America" and would be resisted "by any means necessary, including military force." This statement, now known as the "Carter Doctrine," has governed U.S. strategy in the gulf ever since.

To implement the new doctrine, Carter established the Rapid Deployment Force, a collection of combat forces based in the United States but available for deployment to the Persian Gulf. (The RDF was later folded into the U.S. Central Command, which now conducts all U.S. military operations in the region.) Carter also deployed U.S. warships in the gulf and arranged for the periodic utilization by American forces of military bases in Bahrain, Diego Garcia (a British-controlled island in the Indian Ocean), Oman and Saudi Arabia—all of which were employed during the 1990–91 Gulf War and are again being used today. Believing, moreover, that the Soviet presence in Afghanistan represented a threat to U.S. dominance in the gulf, Carter authorized the initiation of covert operations to undermine the Soviet-backed regime there. (It is important to note that the Saudi regime was deeply involved in this effort, providing much of the funding for the anti-Soviet rebellion and allowing its citizens, including Osama bin Laden, to participate in the war effort as combatants and fundraisers.) And to protect the Saudi royal family, Carter increased U.S. involvement in the kingdom's internal security operations.

President Reagan accelerated Carter's overt military moves and greatly increased covert U.S. support for the anti-Soviet mujahedeen in Afghanistan. (Eventually, some $3 billion worth of arms were given to the mujahedeen.) Reagan also issued an important codicil to the Carter Doctrine: The United States would not allow the Saudi regime to be overthrown by internal dissidents, as occurred in Iran. "We will not permit [Saudi Arabia] to be an Iran," he told reporters in 1981.

Then came the Persian Gulf War. When Iraqi forces invaded Kuwait on August 2, 1990, President Bush the elder was principally concerned about the threat to Saudi Arabia, not Kuwait. At a meeting at Camp David on August 4, he determined that the United States must take immediate military action to defend the Saudi kingdom against possible Iraqi attack. To allow for a successful defense of the kingdom, Bush sent his Secretary of Defense, Dick Cheney, to Riyadh to persuade the royal family to allow the deployment of U.S. ground forces on Saudi soil and the use of Saudi bases for airstrikes against Iraq.

The subsequent unfolding of Operation Desert Storm does not need to be retold here. What is important to note is that the large U.S. military presence in Saudi Arabia was never fully withdrawn after the end of the fighting in Kuwait. American aircraft continue to fly from bases in Saudi Arabia as part of the enforcement mechanism of the "no-fly zone" over southern Iraq (intended to prevent the Iraqis from using this airspace to attack Shiite rebels in the Basra area or to support a new invasion of Kuwait). American aircraft also participate in the multinational effort to enforce the continuing economic sanctions on Iraq.

President Clinton further strengthened the U.S. position in the gulf, expanding American basing facilities there and enhancing the ability to rapidly move U.S.-based forces to the region. Clinton also sought to expand U.S. influence in the Caspian Sea basin, an energy-rich area just to the north of the Persian Gulf.

Many consequences have flowed from all this. The sanctions on Iraq have caused immense suffering for the Iraqi population, while the regular bombing of military facilities produces a mounting toll of Iraqi civilian deaths. Meanwhile, the United States has failed to take any action to curb Israeli violence against the Palestinians. It is these concerns that have prompted many young Muslims to join bin Laden's forces. Bin Laden himself, however, is most concerned about Saudi Arabia. Ever since the end of the Gulf War, he has focused his efforts on achieving two overarching goals: the expulsion of the American "infidels" from Saudi Arabia (the heart of the Muslim holy land) and the overthrow of the current Saudi regime and its replacement with one more attuned to his fundamentalist Islamic beliefs.

Both of these goals put bin Laden in direct conflict with the United States. It is this reality, more than any other, that explains the terrorist strikes on U.S. military personnel and facilities in the Middle East, and key symbols of American power in New York and Washington.

The current war did not begin on September 11. As far as we can tell, it began in 1993 with the first attack on the World Trade Center. This was succeeded in 1995 with an attack on the SANG headquarters in Riyadh, and in 1996 with the explosion at the Khobar Towers outside of Dhahran. Then followed the 1998 bombings of the U.S. embassies in Kenya and Tanzania, and the more recent attack on the USS *Cole*. All these events, like the World Trade Center/Pentagon assaults, are consistent with a long-term strategy to erode U.S. determination to maintain its alliance with the Saudi regime—and thus, in the final analysis, to destroy the 1945 compact forged by President Roosevelt and King Abd al-Aziz Ibn Saud.

In fighting against these efforts, the United States is acting, in the first instance, to protect itself, its citizens and its military personnel from terrorist violence. At the same time, however, Washington is also shoring up its strategic position in the Persian Gulf. With bin Laden out of the way, Iran suffering from internal political turmoil and Saddam Hussein immobilized by unrelenting American airstrikes, the dominant U.S. position in the gulf will be assured for some time to come. (Washington's one big worry is that the Saudi monarchy will face increasing internal opposition because of its close association with the United States; it is for this reason that the Bush Administration has not leaned too hard on the regime to permit U.S. forces to use Saudi bases for attacks on Afghanistan and to freeze the funds of Saudi charities linked to Osama bin Laden.)

For both sides, then, this conflict has important geopolitical dimensions. A Saudi regime controlled by Osama bin Laden could be expected to sever all ties with U.S. oil companies and to adopt new policies regarding the production of oil and the distribution of the country's oil wealth—moves that would have potentially devastating consequences for the U.S., and indeed the world, economy. The United States, of course, is fighting to prevent this from happening.

As the conflict unfolds, we are unlikely to hear any of this from the key figures involved. In seeking to mobilize public support for his campaign against the terrorists, President Bush will never acknowledge that conventional geopolitics plays a role in U.S. policy. Osama bin Laden, for his part, is equally reluctant to speak in such terms. But the fact remains that this war, like the Gulf War before it, derives from a powerful geopolitical contest.

It will be very difficult, in the current political environment, to probe too deeply into these matters. Bin Laden and his associates have caused massive injury to the United States, and the prevention of further such attacks is, understandably, the nation's top priority. When conditions permit, however, a serious review of U.S. policy in the Persian Gulf will be in order. Among the many questions that might legitimately be asked at this point is whether long-term U.S. interests would not best be served by encouraging the democratization of Saudi Arabia. Surely, if more Saudi citizens are permitted to participate in open political dialogue, fewer will be attracted to the violent, anti-American dogma of Osama bin Laden.

October 17, 2001
Wanted: Global Politics
Mary Kaldor

Four weeks on and it feels as though we are living in a black hole. The "new war on terrorism" has invaded our lives and sucked in all our usual activities. Even before the start of military action, television, newspapers, e-mail and everyday conversation had all been overwhelmed not just by grief and mourning but by the new global coalition, troop deployments, intelligence efforts, the Afghan crisis and on and on. Normal debates about issues like education and health, climate change and biodiversity, corporate responsibility and debt reduction, not to mention the Balkans or Central America, have been suspended—unless, that is, these issues can somehow be related to September 11. The crime against humanity that took place on September 11 was so horrific and so shocking that this reaction is perhaps understandable (although the world did not shut down after the genocide in Rwanda or the fall of Srebrenica). Nevertheless, it is the wrong reaction. Normal debate is exactly what is needed. If we are to confront what Michael Ignatieff has described as "apocalyptic nihilism" in a serious, sustained way, then we need politics, especially global politics. Not as a substitute for catching the perpetrators and bringing them to justice, but as a central part of the strategy for eliminating their activities.

In the past decade, since the end of the cold war, we have witnessed the emergence of something that could be called global politics. The cold war can be regarded as the last great global clash between states; it marked the end of an era when the ultimate threat of war between states determined international relations and when the idea of war disciplined and polarized domestic politics. Indeed, this may explain why we became conscious of the phenomenon known as globalization only after the end of the cold war. Nowadays, as September 11 demonstrated only too graphically, we live in an interdependent world, where we cannot maintain security merely through the protection of borders; where states no longer control what happens within their borders; and where old-fashioned war between states has become anachronistic. Today states are still important, but they function in a world shaped less by military power than by complex political processes involving international institutions, multinational corporations, citizens' groups and, indeed, fundamentalists and terrorists—in short, global politics.

The end of old-fashioned war between states does not mean the end of violence. Instead, we are witnessing the rise of new types of violence, justified in the name of fundamentalism of one variety or another and perpetrated against civilians. President Bush is perhaps right to call what happened a "new kind of war." But this is not the first "new war," although it is more spectacular and more global than ever before and, for the first time, involves large-scale loss of American lives. Wars of this type have taken place in Africa, the Middle East, the Balkans and Central Asia, especially in the past decade. And there are lessons to be learned that are relevant to the new "new war."

These new wars have to be understood in the context of globalization. They involve transnational networks, based on political claims in the name of religion or ethnicity, through which ideas, money, arms and mercenaries are organized. These networks flourish in those areas of the world where states have imploded as a consequence of the impact of globalization on formerly closed, authoritarian systems, and they involve private groups and warlords as well as remnants of the state apparatus. In the new wars, the goal is not military victory; it is political mobilization. Whereas in old-fashioned wars, people were mobilized to participate in the war effort, in the new wars, mobilizing people is *the aim* of the war effort, to expand the networks of extremism. In the new wars, battles are rare and violence is directed against civilians. The strategy is to gain political power through sowing fear and hatred, to create a climate of terror, to eliminate moderate voices and to defeat tolerance. And the goal is to obtain economic power as well. These networks flourish in states where systems of taxation have collapsed, where little new wealth is being created. They raise money through looting and plunder, through illegal trading in drugs, illegal immigrants, cigarettes and alcohol, through "taxing" humanitarian assistance, through support from sympathetic states and through remittances from members of the networks.

These wars are very difficult to contain and very difficult to end. They spread through refugees and displaced persons, through criminal networks, through the extremist viruses they germinate. We can observe growing clusters of warfare in Africa, the Middle East, Central Asia and the Caucasus. They represent a defeat for democratic politics, and each bout of warfare strengthens those with a vested political and economic interest in continued violence. The areas where conflicts have lasted longest have generated cultures of violence, as in the *jihad* culture taught in religious schools in Pakistan and Afghanistan or among the Tamils of Sri Lanka, where young children are taught to be martyrs and where killing is understood as an offering to God. In the instructions found in the car of the hijackers in Boston's Logan Airport, it is written: "If God grants any one of you a slaughter, you should perform it as an offering on behalf of your father and mother, for they are owed by you. . . . If you slaughter, you should plunder those you slaughter, for that is a sanctioned custom of the Prophet's."

What we have learned about this kind of war is that the only possible exit route is political. There has to be a strategy of winning hearts and minds to counter the strategy of fear and hate. There has to be an alternative politics based on tolerance and inclusiveness, which is capable of defeating the politics of intolerance and exclusion and capable of preserving the space for democratic politics. In the case of the current new war, what is needed is an appeal for global—not American—justice and legitimacy, aimed at establishing the rule of law in place of war and at fostering understanding between communities in place of terror. There needs to be a much stronger role for the United Nations and serious consideration paid to ways in which legitimate political authority can be re-established in Afghanistan. Thinking through how this should be done needs to be the responsibility of the new United Nations Special Representative to Afghanistan, Lakhdar Brahimi, in consultation with neighboring states and a range of relevant political and civic actors. There also needs to be a clear demonstration of evenhandedness in places like the Middle East, and real support for democratic and moderate political groupings—in other words, an alternative network involving international institutions as well as civil society groups committed to similar goals. What this entails in concrete terms has to be discussed and debated. In this crisis, there has been much handwringing about the need for better human intelligence. An excellent source of human intelligence and guide to evenhanded policymaking are pro-democracy, human rights and liberal Islamic groups in the Middle East and among exile communities.

Political action has to be combined with serious attention to overcoming social injustice. Of particular importance is the creation of legitimate methods of making a living. In many of the areas where war takes place and where extreme networks pick up new recruits, becoming a criminal or joining a paramilitary group is literally the only available opportunity for unemployed young men lacking formal education. Where some progress has been made, as in Northern Ireland and the Balkans (and it is always slow and tortuous, since these wars are so much harder to end than to begin), what has made a difference has been the provision of security, including the capture of criminals, support for civil society and for democrats, and efforts at economic reconstruction.

Such a political strategy is not an alternative to military action. Indeed, military action may be needed in support of alternative politics. But in these wars there is no such thing as military victory; the task of military action is to create conditions for an alternative politics. Thus military action is needed to catch war criminals and protect civilians—to establish areas where individuals and families feel safe and do not depend on extremist networks for protection and livelihood. Devices like safe havens or humanitarian corridors, effectively defended, help protect and support civilians and establish an international presence on the ground.

Tolerant politics cannot survive in conditions of violence—this is the point of the new wars. Military action may be needed to provide not national security but individual security. In old-fashioned wars, the aim of military action was to take territory and to destroy the enemy, defined not as individuals or networks but as entire states and military machines. Thus military action typically maximized enemy casualties and minimized its own casualties. This new type of military action is more like policing; it must involve minimizing casualties on all sides even at the risk of its own casualties. Moreover, to be legitimate, such action must take place within the framework of international law. Both *jus ad bellum*, the goal of war, and *jus in bello*, the methods of war, need scrupulously to respect both the laws of war and human rights law.

It's this new kind of war that characterizes the twenty-first-century globalized world; indeed, some aspects of these wars have already been experienced in the United States itself—for example, in the Oklahoma City bombing. But until now, America has assumed that it is more or less immune and that wars happen elsewhere. In effect, the United States has acted as though it were the last nation-state, in which the priorities are domestic politics and what happens elsewhere doesn't matter. It has been able to maintain the myth, so important to the American psyche, that there are still wars on the model of World War II, in which virtuous states triumph over evil states, and the United States can act as leader of the virtuous states at a distance. National missile defense is part of this myth; it would allow the United States to bomb evil states at a distance, safe in the knowledge that its territory is protected.

The events of September 11 exposed the vulnerability of the United States and, to that extent, may have prevented the immediate knee-jerk reaction of misdirected airstrikes, which Clinton undertook after the embassy bombings in Kenya and Tanzania. This time, the situation was much more serious, and the U.S. administration apparently needed time to think through its response. The emphasis, we are told, is on targeted strikes, and the aim is to capture Osama bin Laden and restore legitimate political authority in Afghanistan. Great stress has been placed on America's multilateral approach and the forging of a global coalition, as well as on the fact that this is a war against terrorism and not Islam. So does this imply a conversion to a global political approach?

As yet, it is difficult to judge. The diplomacy and the military action have not so far been undertaken within an international institutional framework. It is not yet clear whether the airstrikes will be followed up with sufficient ground troops to provide security through such means as safe havens. Although the politicians insist that the strikes are not directed against civilians, the problem is not just "collateral damage" but the psychological trauma of daily bombing; whatever the rhetoric, it is hard for ordinary Afghans to believe that airstrikes are not directed against them. The first strikes against Afghanistan seem to have handed bin Laden a propaganda victory. His picture appears beside Bush's on the backdrop to news broadcasts. He is becoming America's enemy and the hero of all those who believe, mainly as a result of their leaders' propaganda, that America is responsible for their desperate plight. There is talk of extending the strikes to Iraq, Syria and elsewhere. Moreover, Bush's polarizing language, demanding that everyone is either "with us or with the terrorists," leaves no room for antiterrorist critics of the United States. Is there a serious plan, consistent with international law, to contain the terrorist network? Or have the military strikes been undertaken in response to American public opinion, a desperate attempt to show that something is being done? Did the four weeks' respite occur because of restraint and reflection, or rather because time was needed to assemble military forces and identify targets? If what is happening is a classic cold war-type approach, devised in order to respond to domestic political imperatives, then there is a real risk of a dangerous global "new war."

The danger is not just the escalation of violence. The campaign is going to be long and sustained, we are told, more like the cold war than World War II. And therein lies a grim prospect. The United States still seems to be thinking in terms of a world of states led by America, not a genuine new form of multilateralism. In the new war against terrorism, America is still putting the emphasis on military action and on alliances with states. It is becoming a new hot and cold war of America and its allies against fundamentalist Islam. The new global coalition is in some ways reminiscent of American support for military dictatorships in Latin America in the 1970s, under the guise of hunting down Communists and Marxists. States that are ready to support the

United States are part of the alliance, no matter what their domestic behavior. Russia is in, despite its war crimes against Chechens; Pakistan, so recently an outcast because of its military coup and development of nuclear weapons, is a good guy again. And then there are Saudi Arabia, Israel and Uzbekistan, to name the most notorious. I am told by human rights groups in the Caucasus that Russia is threatening Georgia for harboring terrorists (among the Chechen refugees) and that human rights activists in Azerbaijan are being dubbed terrorists. There has to be a global coalition, of course, but it should be linked to the UN and be responsive to the concerns of democrats and civic activists in the countries involved.

So-called antiglobalization protests were just beginning to be taken seriously before September 11, but now we are at risk of shutting down the global conversation that began after the end of the cold war. We do live in a globalized world, and the frustrations in repressive societies cannot any longer be confined to particular territories. Those frustrations will not always be expressed as democratic demands, as was the case in Latin America. They will be expressed in the language of extremes and in the acts of nihilism that characterize the new wars. The current approach might work for a few years by pouring money into repressive states and by killing known terrorists. But if the United States continues to act as a nation-state, wielding its military might to satisfy public demands for quick responses to acts of nihilism, the danger is that we will see a "new war" on a global scale—a sort of global Israel/Palestine conflict with no equivalent to the international community to put pressure on the warring parties.

In his Labour Party conference speech, British Prime Minister Tony Blair talked about the need for global justice, for creating peace in the new wars and social justice. If this is more than rhetoric, then it requires discussion about how these goals are to be achieved. Such an effort must engage all levels of society all over the world. Global politics is not just desirable in itself; it is the only way we can even begin to tackle the new "new war."

October 31, 2001
Which America Will We Be Now?
Bill Moyers

For the past several years I've been taking every possible opportunity to talk about the soul of democracy. "Something is deeply wrong with politics today," I told anyone who would listen. And I wasn't referring to the partisan mudslinging, the negative TV ads, the excessive polling or the empty campaigns. I was talking about something fundamental, something troubling at the core of politics. The soul of democracy—the essence of the word itself—is government of, by and for the people. And the soul of democracy has been dying, drowning in a rising tide of big money contributed by a narrow, unrepresentative elite that has betrayed the faith of citizens in self-government.

But what's happened since the September 11 attacks would seem to put the lie to my fears. Americans have rallied together in a way that I cannot remember since World War II. This catastrophe has reminded us of a basic truth at the heart of our democracy: No matter our wealth or status or faith, we are all equal before the law, in the voting booth and when death rains down from the sky.

We have also been reminded that despite years of scandals and political corruption, despite the stream of stories of personal greed and pirates in Gucci scamming the Treasury, despite the retreat from the public sphere and the turn toward private privilege, despite squalor for the poor and gated communities for the rich, the great mass of Americans have not yet given up on the idea of "We, the People." And they have refused to accept the notion, promoted so diligently by our friends at the Heritage Foundation, that government should be shrunk to a size where, as Grover Norquist has put it, they can drown it in a bathtub.

These ideologues at Heritage and elsewhere, by the way, earlier this year teamed up with deep-pocket bankers—many from Texas, with ties to the Bush White House—to stop America from cracking down on terrorist money havens. How about that for patriotism? Better that terrorists get their dirty money than tax cheaters be prevented from hiding theirs. And these people wrap themselves in the flag and sing "The Star-Spangled Banner" with gusto.

Contrary to right-wing denigration of government, however, today's heroes are public servants. The 20-year-old dot-com instant millionaires and the preening, pugnacious pundits of tabloid television and the crafty celebrity stock-pickers on the cable channels have all been exposed for what they are—barnacles on the hull of the great ship of state. In their stead we have those brave firefighters and policemen and Port Authority workers and emergency rescue personnel—public employees all, most of them drawing a modest middle-class income for extremely dangerous work. They have caught our imaginations not only for their heroic deeds but because we know so many people like them, people we took for granted. For once, our TV screens have been filled with the modest declarations of average Americans coming to each other's aid. I find this good and thrilling and sobering. It could offer a new beginning, a renewal of civic values that could leave our society stronger and more together than ever, working on common goals for the public good.

Already, in the wake of September 11, there's been a heartening change in how Americans view their government. For the first time in more than thirty years a majority of people say they trust the federal government to do the right thing at least "most of the time." It's as if the clock has been rolled back to the early 1960s, before Vietnam and Watergate took such a toll on the gross national psychology. This newfound respect for public service—this faith in public collaboration—is based in part on how people view what the government has done in response to the attacks. To most Americans, government right now doesn't mean a faceless bureaucrat or a politician auctioning access to the highest bidder. It means a courageous rescuer or brave soldier. Instead of our representatives spending their evenings clinking glasses with fat cats, they are out walking among the wounded.

There are, alas, less heartening signs to report. It didn't take long for the wartime opportunists—the mercenaries of Washington, the lobbyists, lawyers and political fundraisers—to crawl out of their offices on K Street determined to grab what they can for their clients. While in New York we are still attending memorial services for firemen and police, while every-where Americans' cheeks are still stained with tears, while the President calls for patriotism, prayers and piety, the predators of Washington are up to their old tricks in the pursuit of private plunder at public expense. In the wake of this awful tragedy wrought by terrorism, they are cashing in. Would you like to know the memorial they would offer the thousands of people who died in the attacks? Or the legacy they would leave the children who lost a parent in the horror? How do they propose to fight the long and costly war on terrorism America must now undertake? Why, restore the three-martini lunch—that will surely strike fear in the heart of Osama bin Laden. You think I'm kidding, but bringing back the deductible lunch is one of the proposals on the table in Washington right now. And cut capital gains for the wealthy, naturally—that's America's patriotic duty, too. And while we're at it, don't forget to eliminate the corporate alternative minimum tax, enacted fifteen years ago to prevent corporations from taking so many cred-its and deductions that they owed little if any taxes. But don't just repeal their minimum tax; refund to those corporations all the minimum tax they have ever been assessed.

What else can America do to strike at the terrorists? Why, slip in a spe-cial tax break for poor General Electric, and slip inside the EPA while every-one's distracted and torpedo the recent order to clean the Hudson River of PCBs. Don't worry about NBC, CNBC or MSNBC reporting it; they're all in the GE family. It's time for Churchillian courage, we're told. So how would this crowd assure that future generations will look back and say "This was their finest hour"? That's easy. Give those coal producers free-dom to pollute. And shovel generous tax breaks to those giant energy com-panies. And open the Alaska wilderness to drilling—that's something to remember the 11th of September for. And while the red, white and blue waves at half-mast over the land of the free and the home of the brave—why, give the President the power to discard democratic debate and the rule of law concerning controversial trade agreements, and set up secret tribunals to run roughshod over local communities trying to protect their environment and their health. If I sound a little bitter about this, I am; the President rightly appeals every day for sacrifice. But to these mercenaries sacrifice is for suckers. So I am bitter, yes, and sad. Our business and political class owes us better than this. After all, it was they who declared class war twenty years ago, and it was they who won. They're on top. If ever they were going to put patriotism over profits, if ever they were going to practice the magnanimity of winners, this was the moment. To hide now behind the flag while ripping off a country in crisis fatally separates them from the common course of American life.

Some things just don't change. When I read that Dick Armey, the Republican majority leader in the House, said "it wouldn't be commensurate with the American spirit" to provide unemployment and other benefits to laid-off airline workers, I thought that once again the Republican Party has lived down to Harry Truman's description of the GOP as Guardians of Privilege. And as for Truman's Democratic Party—the party of the New Deal and the Fair Deal—well, it breaks my heart to report that the Democratic National Committee has used the terrorist attacks to call for widening the soft-money loophole in our election laws. How about that for a patriotic response to terrorism? Mencken got it right when he said, "Whenever you hear a man speak of his love for his country, it is a sign that he expects to be paid for it."

Let's face it: These realities present citizens with no options but to climb back in the ring. We are in what educators call "a teachable moment." And we'll lose it if we roll over and shut up. What's at stake is democracy. Democracy wasn't canceled on September 11, but democracy won't survive if citizens turn into lemmings. Yes, the President is our Commander in Chief, but we are not the President's minions. While firemen and police were racing into the fires of hell in downtown New York, and now, while our soldiers and airmen and Marines are putting their lives on the line in Afghanistan, the Administration and its Congressional allies are allowing multinational companies to make their most concerted effort in twenty years to roll back clean-air measures, exploit public lands and stuff the pockets of their executives and shareholders with undeserved cash. Against such crass exploitation, unequaled since the Teapot Dome scandal, it is every patriot's duty to join the loyal opposition. Even in war, politics is about who gets what and who doesn't. If the mercenaries and the politicians-for-rent in Washington try to exploit the emergency and America's good faith to grab what they wouldn't get through open debate in peacetime, the disloyalty will not be in our dissent but in our subservience. The greatest sedition would be our silence. Yes, there's a fight going on—against terrorists around the globe, but just as certainly there's a fight going on here at home, to decide the kind of country this will be during and after the war on terrorism.

What should our strategy be? Here are a couple of suggestions, beginning with how we elect our officials. As Congress debates new security measures, military spending, energy policies, economic stimulus packages and various bailout requests, wouldn't it be better if we knew that elected officials had to answer to the people who vote instead of the wealthy individual and corporate donors whose profit or failure may depend on how those new initiatives are carried out?

That's not a utopian notion. Thanks to the efforts of many hardworking pro-democracy activists who have been organizing at the grassroots for the past ten years, we already have four states—Maine, Arizona, Vermont and Massachusetts—where state representatives from governor on down have the option of rejecting all private campaign contributions and qualifying for full public financing of their campaigns. About a third of Maine's legislature and a quarter of Arizona's got elected last year running clean— that is, under their states' pioneering Clean Elections systems, they collected a set number of $5 contributions and then pledged to raise no other money and to abide by strict spending limits.

These unsung heroes of democracy, the first class of elected officials to owe their elections solely to their voters and not to any deep-pocketed backers, report a greater sense of independence from special interests and more freedom to speak their minds. "The business lobbyists left me alone," says State Representative Glenn Cummings, a freshman from Maine who was the first candidate in the country to qualify for Clean Elections funding. "I think they assumed I was unapproachable. It sure made it easier to get through the hallways on the way to a vote!" His colleague in the Statehouse, Senator Ed Youngblood, recalls that running clean changed the whole process of campaigning. "When people would say that it didn't matter how they voted, because legislators would just vote the way the money wants," he tells us, "it was great to be able to say, 'I don't have to vote the way some lobbyist wants just to insure that I'll get funded by him in two years for re-election.'"

It's too soon to say that money no longer talks in either state capital, but it clearly doesn't swagger as much. In Maine, the legislature passed a bill creating a Health Security Board tasked with devising a detailed plan to implement a single-payer healthcare system for the state. The bill wasn't everything its sponsor, Representative Paul Volenik, wanted, but he saw real progress toward a universal healthcare system in its passage. Two years ago, he noted, only fifty-five members of the House of Representatives (out of 151) voted for the bill. This time eighty-seven did, including almost all the Democrats and a few Republicans. The bill moved dramatically further, and a portion of that is because of the Clean Elections system they have there, Volenik said.

But the problem is larger than that of money in politics. Democracy needs a broader housecleaning. Consider, for example, what a different country we would be if we had a Citizens Channel with a mandate to cover real social problems, not shark attacks or Gary Condit's love life, while covering up Rupert Murdoch's manipulations of the FCC and CBS's ploy to filch tax breaks for its post-terrorist losses. Such a channel could have spurred serious attention to the weakness of airport security, for starters, pointing out long ago how the industry, through its contributions, had wrung from government the right to contract that security to the lowest bidder. It might have pushed the issue of offshore-banking havens to page one, or turned up the astonishing deceit of the NAFTA provision that enables secret tribunals to protect the interests of investors while subverting the well-being of workers and the health of communities. Such a channel—committed to news for the sake of democracy—might also have told how corporations and their alumni in the Bush Administration have thwarted the development of clean, home-grown energy that would slow global warming and the degradation of our soil, air and water, while reducing our dependence on oligarchs, dictators and theocrats abroad.

Even now the media elite, with occasional exceptions, remain indifferent to the hypocrisy of Washington's mercenary class as it goes about the dirty work of its paymasters. What a contrast to those citizens who during these weeks of loss and mourning have reminded us that the kingdom of the human heart is large, containing not only hatred but courage. Much has been made of the comparison to December 7, 1941. I find it apt. In response to the sneak attack on Pearl Harbor, Americans waged and won a great war, then came home to make this country more prosperous and just. It is not beyond this generation to live up to that example. To do so, we must define ourselves not by the lives we led until September 11 but by the lives we will lead from now on. If we seize the opportunity to build a stronger country, we too will ultimately prevail in the challenges ahead, at home and abroad. But we cannot win this new struggle by military might alone. We will prevail only if we lead by example, as a democracy committed to the rule of law and the spirit of fairness, whose corporate and political elites recognize that it isn't only firefighters, police and families grieving their missing kin who are called upon to sacrifice.

October 31, 2001
A War We Cannot Win
John le Carré

OCTOBER 8

"The bombing begins," screams today's headline of the normally restrained *Guardian*. "Battle Joined" echoes the equally cautious *Herald Tribune*, quoting George W. Bush. But with whom is it joined? And how will it end? How about with Osama bin Laden in chains, looking more serene and Christ-like than ever, arranged before a tribune of his vanquishers with Johnnie Cochran to defend him? The fees won't be a problem, that's for sure.

Or how about with a bin Laden blown to smithereens by one of those clever bombs we keep reading about that kill terrorists in caves but don't break the crockery? Or is there a solution I haven't thought of that will prevent us from turning our arch-enemy into an arch-martyr in the eyes of those for whom he is already semi-divine?

Yet we must punish him. We must bring him to justice. Like any sane person, I see no other way. Send in the food and medicines, provide the aid, sweep up the starving refugees, maimed orphans and body parts—sorry, "collateral damage"—but bin Laden and his awful men, we have no choice, must be hunted down.

But unfortunately what America longs for at this moment, even above retribution, is more friends and fewer enemies. And what America is storing up for herself, and so are we Brits, is yet more enemies; because after all the bribes, threats and promises that have patched together the rickety coalition, we cannot prevent another suicide bomber being born each time a misdirected missile wipes out an innocent village, and nobody can tell us how to dodge this devil's cycle of despair, hatred and—yet again—revenge.

The stylized television footage and photographs of bin Laden suggest a man of homoerotic narcissism, and maybe we can draw a grain of hope from that. Posing with a Kalashnikov, attending a wedding or consulting a sacred text, he radiates with every self-adoring gesture an actor's awareness of the lens. He has height, beauty, grace, intelligence and magnetism, all great attributes unless you're the world's hottest fugitive and on the run, in which case they're liabilities hard to disguise. But greater than all of them, to my jaded eye, is his barely containable male vanity, his appetite for self-drama and his closet passion for the limelight. And just possibly this trait will be his downfall, seducing him into a final dramatic act of self-destruction, produced, directed, scripted and acted to death by Osama bin Laden himself.

By the accepted rules of terrorist engagement, of course, the war is long lost. By us. What victory can we possibly achieve that matches the defeats we have already suffered, let alone the defeats that lie ahead? Terror is the-ater, a soft-spoken Palestinian firebrand told me in Beirut in 1982. He was talking about the murder of Israeli athletes at the Munich Olympics, but he might as well have been talking about the twin towers and the Pentagon. The late Bakunin, evangelist of anarchism, liked to speak of the propaganda of the Act. It's hard to imagine more theatrical, more potent acts of propa-ganda than these.

Now Bakunin in his grave and bin Laden in his cave must be rubbing their hands in glee as we embark on the very process that terrorists of their stamp so relish: as we hastily double up our police and intelligence forces and award them greater powers, as we put basic civil rights on hold and curtail press freedom, impose news blackpoints and secret censorship, spy on ourselves and, at our worst, violate mosques and hound luckless citizens in our streets because we are afraid of the color of their skin.

All the fears that we share—"Dare I fly?" "Ought I to tell the police about the weird couple upstairs?" "Would it be safer not to drive down Whitehall this morning?" "Is my child safely back from school?" "Have my life's sav-ings plummeted?"—are precisely the fears our attackers want us to have.

Until September 11, the United States was only too happy to plug away at Vladimir Putin about his butchery in Chechnya. Russia's abuse of human rights in the North Caucasus, he was told—we are speaking of wholesale torture, and murder amounting to genocide, it was generally agreed—was an obstruction to closer relations with NATO and the United States. There were even voices—mine was one—that suggested Putin join Milosevic in The Hague; let's do them both together. Well, goodbye to all that. In the making of the great new coalition, Putin will look a saint by comparison with some of his bedfellows.

Does anyone remember anymore the outcry against the perceived economic colonialism of the G8? Against the plundering of the Third World by uncon-trollable multinational companies? Prague, Seattle and Genoa presented us with disturbing scenes of broken heads, broken glass, mob violence and police brutality. Tony Blair was deeply shocked. Yet the debate was a valid one, until it was drowned in a wave of patriotic sentiment, deftly exploited by corporate America.

Drag up Kyoto these days and you risk the charge of being anti-American. It's as if we have entered a new, Orwellian world where our personal reliability as comrades in the struggle is measured by the degree to which we invoke the past to explain the present. Suggesting there is a historical context for the recent atrocities is by implication to make excuses for them. Anyone who is with us doesn't do that. Anyone who does, is against us.

Ten years ago, I was making an idealistic bore of myself by telling anyone who would listen that, with the cold war behind us, we were missing a never-to-be-repeated chance to transform the global community. Where was the new Marshall Plan? I pleaded. Why weren't young men and women from the American Peace Corps, Voluntary Service Overseas and their Continental European equivalents pouring into the former Soviet Union in their thousands? Where was the world-class statesman and man of the hour with the voice and vision to define for us the real, if unglamorous, enemies of mankind: poverty, famine, slavery, tyranny, drugs, bush-fire wars, racial and religious intolerance, greed?

Now, overnight, thanks to bin Laden and his lieutenants, all our leaders are world-class statesmen, proclaiming their voices and visions in distant airports while they feather their electoral nests.

There has been unfortunate talk, and not only from Signor Berlusconi, of a crusade. Crusade, of course, implies a delicious ignorance of history. Was Berlusconi really proposing to set free the holy places of Christendom and smite the heathen? Was Bush? And am I out of order in recalling that we actually lost the Crusades? But all is well: Signor Berlusconi was misquoted and the presidential reference is no longer operative.

Meanwhile, Blair's new role as America's fearless spokesman continues apace. Blair speaks well because Bush speaks badly. Seen from abroad, Blair in this partnership is the inspired elder statesman with an unassailable domestic power base, whereas Bush—dare one say it these days?—was barely elected at all.

But what exactly does Blair, the elder statesman, represent? Both men at this moment are riding high in their respective approval ratings, but both are aware, if they know their history books, that riding high on Day One of a perilous overseas military operation doesn't guarantee you victory on Election Day. How many American body bags can Bush sustain without losing popular support? After the horrors of the twin towers and the Pentagon, the American people may want revenge, but they're on a very short fuse about shedding more American blood.

Blair—with the whole Western world to tell him so, except for a few sour voices back home—is America's eloquent White Knight, the fearless, trusty champion of that ever-delicate child of the mid-Atlantic, the Special Relationship. Whether that will win Blair favor with his electorate is another matter, because he was elected to save the country from decay, and not from Osama bin Laden. The Britain he is leading to war is a monument to sixty years of administrative incompetence. Our health, education and transport systems are on the rocks. The fashionable phrase these days describes them as "Third World," but there are places in the Third World that are far better off than Britain.

The Britain Blair governs is blighted by institutionalized racism, white male dominance, chaotically administered police forces, a constipated judicial system, obscene private wealth and shameful and unnecessary public poverty. At the time of his re-election, which was characterized by a dismal turnout, Blair acknowledged these ills and humbly admitted that he was on notice to put them right. So when you catch the noble throb in his voice as he leads us reluctantly to war, and your heart lifts to his undoubted flourishes of rhetoric, it's worth remembering that he may also be warning you, sotto voce, that his mission to mankind is so important that you will have to wait another year for your urgent medical operation and a lot longer before you can ride in a safe and punctual train. I am not sure that this is the stuff of electoral victory three years from now. Watching Blair, and listening to him, I can't resist the impression that he is in a bit of a dream, walking his own dangerous plank.

Did I say war? Has either Blair or Bush, I wonder, ever seen a child blown to bits, or witnessed the effect of a single cluster bomb dropped on an unprotected refugee camp? It isn't necessarily a qualification for generalship to have seen such dreadful things, and I don't wish either of them the experience. But it scares me all the same when I watch uncut, political faces shining with the light of combat, and hear preppy political voices steeling my heart for battle.

And please, Mr. Bush—on my knees, Mr. Blair—keep God out of this. To imagine that God fights wars is to credit Him with the worst follies of mankind. God, if we know anything about Him, which I don't profess to, prefers effective food drops, dedicated medical teams, comfort and good tents for the homeless and bereaved, and, without strings, a decent acceptance of our past sins and a readiness to put them right. He prefers us less greedy, less arrogant, less evangelical and less dismissive of life's losers.

It's not a new world order, not yet, and it's not God's war. It's a horrible, necessary, humiliating police action to redress the failure of our intelligence services and our blind political stupidity in arming and exploiting Islamic fanatics to fight the Soviet invader, then abandoning them to a devastated, leaderless country. As a result, it's our miserable duty to seek out and punish a bunch of modern-medieval religious zealots who will gain mythic stature from the very death we propose to dish out to them.

And when it's over, it won't be over. The shadowy armies of bin Laden, in the emotional aftermath of his destruction, will gather numbers rather than wither away. So will the hinterland of silent sympathizers who provide them with logistical support. Cautiously, between the lines, we are being invited to believe that the conscience of the West has been reawakened to the dilemma of the poor and homeless of the earth. And possibly, out of fear, necessity and rhetoric, a new sort of political morality has indeed been born. But when the shooting dies and a seeming peace is achieved, will the United States and its allies stay at their posts or, as happened at the end of the cold war, hang up their boots and go home to their own backyards? Even if those backyards will never again be the safe havens they once were.

(Copyright ©2001 by David Cornwell)

November 14, 2001
The Foreign Policy Therapist
Wallace Shawn

To: The Foreign Policy Therapist
From: The United States of America
Date: November 12, 2001

Dear Foreign Policy Therapist,

I don't know what to do. I want to be safe. I want safety. But I have a terrible problem: It all began several weeks ago when I lost several thousand loved ones to a horrible terrorist crime. I feel an overwhelming need to apprehend and punish those who committed this unbearably cruel act, but they designed their crime in such a diabolical fashion that I cannot do so, because they arranged to be killed themselves while committing the crime, and they are now all dead. I feel in my heart that none of these men, however, could possibly have planned this crime themselves and that another man, who is living in a cave in Afghanistan, must surely have done so. At any rate I know that some people he knows knew some of the people who committed the crime and possibly gave them some money. I feel an overwhelming need to kill this man in the cave, but the location of the cave is unknown to me, and so it's impossible to find him. He's been allowed to stay in the cave, however, by the fanatical rulers of the country where the cave is, Afghanistan, so I feel an overwhelming need to kill those rulers. As they've moved from place to place, though, I haven't found them, but I've succeeded in finding and killing many young soldiers who guarded them and shepherds who lived near them. Nonetheless, I do not feel any of the expected "closure," and in fact I'm becoming increasingly depressed and am obsessed with nameless fears. Can you help me?

* * *

To: The United States of America
From: The Foreign Policy Therapist

Dear United States,

In psychological circles, we call your problem "denial." You cannot face your real problem, so you deny that it exists and create instead a different problem that you try to solve. Meanwhile, the real problem, denied and ignored, becomes more and more serious. In your case, your real problem is simply the way that millions and millions of people around the world feel about you.

Who are these people? They share the world with you—one single world, which works as a unified mechanism. These people are the ones for whom the mechanism's current way of working—call it the status quo—offers a life of anguish and servitude. They're well aware that this status quo, which for them is a prison, is for you (or for the privileged among you), on the contrary, so close to a paradise that you will never allow their life to change. These millions of people are in many cases uneducated—to you they seem unsophisticated—and yet they still somehow know that you have played an enormous role in keeping this status quo in place. And so they know you as the enemy. They feel they have to fight you. Some of them hate you. And some will gladly die in order to hurt you—in order to stop you.

They know where the fruits of the planet, the oil and the spices, are going. And when your actions cause grief in some new corner of the world, they know about it. And when you kill people who are poor and desperate, no matter what explanation you give for what you've done, their anger against you grows. You can't kill all these millions of people, but almost any one of them, in some way, some place, or some degree, can cause damage to you.

But here's a strange fact about these people whom you consider unsophisticated: Most of the situations in the world in which they perceive "injustice" are actually ones in which you yourself would see injustice if you yourself weren't deeply involved. Even though they may dress differently and live differently, their standards of justice seem oddly similar to yours.

Your problem, ultimately, can only be solved over decades, through a radical readjustment of the way you think and behave. If the denial persists, you are sure to continue killing more poor and desperate people, causing the hatred against you to grow, until at a certain point there will be no hope for you. But it's not too late. Yes, there are some among your current enemies who can no longer be reached by reason. Yes, there are some who are crazy. But most are not. Most people are not insane. If you do change, it is inevitable that over time people will know that you have changed, and their feeling about you will also change, and the safety you seek will become a possibility.

To the Oracle at Delphi
Lawrence Ferlinghetti

Great Oracle, why are you staring at me,
do I baffle you, do I make you despair?
I, Americus, the American,
wrought from the dark in my mother long ago,
from the dark of ancient Europa—
Why are you staring at me now
in the dusk of our civilization—
Why are you staring at me
as if I were America itself
the new Empire
far greater than any in ancient days
with its electronic highways
carrying its corporate monoculture
around the world
And English the Latin of our day—
Great Oracle, sleeping through the centuries,
Awaken now at last

And tell us how to save us from ourselves
and how to survive our own rulers
who would make a plutocracy of our democracy
in the Great Divide
between the rich and the poor
in whom Walt Whitman heard America singing
O long-silent Sybil,
You of the winged dreams,
Speak out from your temple of light
as the serious constellations
with Greek names
still stare down on us
as a lighthouse moves its megaphone
over the sea
Speak out and shine upon us
the sea-light of Greece
the diamond light of Greece
Far-seeing Sybil, forever hidden,
Come out of your cave at last
And speak to us in the poet's voice
the voice of the fourth person singular
the voice of the inscrutable future
the voice of the people mixed
with a wild soft laughter—
And give us new dreams to dream,
Give us new myths to live by!

*(Spoken to the Oracle by the author at UNESCO's World Poetry Day,
March 21, at Delphi)*

November 25, 2001, *Los Angeles Times*
What's Left? A New Life for Progressivism
Joel Rogers and Katrina vanden Heuvel

In the aftermath of September 11, pundits were quick to proclaim the American left a victim of the war on terrorism, for two reasons.

The first is that progressives, since Vietnam, have stood solidly in opposition to the use of U.S. military force. This stance could be honorably maintained then and during a host of sordid U.S. military ventures since, but leaves them unbalanced or marginal in today's case, where force seems justified.

The second is that this war is about securing the "open society" that terrorism threatens—a society in which individual and corporate freedoms, resting on secure property rights, can be exercised worldwide without restraint. But the left—in its World Trade Organization protests in Seattle and Genoa, in its opposition to fast track—has been most visible for opposing the corporate domination that naturally follows from such rules. And so, the pundits reason, any left support now for the war against terrorism is at odds with its recent actions. But this reasoning strikes us as wrong. Only the pacifist left has ever opposed all use of U.S. military force; other progressives simply have strong views on when it is appropriate and believe that blank, ubiquitous endorsement of military action does not serve the country. And there is no reason to equate opposition to terrorism, a crime against humanity, with support for a particular program on how humanity should be organized, a matter that remains a subject of legitimate debate.

If anything, the war on terrorism creates an opening for progressives, not closure—indeed, it presents the opportunity of a lifetime.

It is a truism of modern politics that war generally mobilizes and helps the democratic left. It does so, despite the repression of dissent that wartime also often brings, because war raises the stakes in politics and invites consideration of wider goals, including justice. War's mobilization of the populace against a shared threat also heightens social solidarity, while underscoring the need for government and other social institutions that transcend or replace the market. And war's horrors daily press the question of how military action can be avoided in the future without abandoning core principles of domestic order.

All this shifts the playing field of political debate away from those who counsel "let's leave it to the market or the military" as the answer to all human concerns. Far from seeming hard-nosed and realistic, they suddenly appear beside the point, if not immoral. Those who believe in social justice and shared democratic effort in problem solving, by contrast, seem onto something important and even admirable.

Consider the birth of "new normal" America. On September 11 the public saw terrorists flying into buildings to kill innocents—most of them ordinary workers, many of them foreign-born. It saw public servants running in to save them, freely sacrificing their own lives in doing so. It was not private corporations that lined up afterward to find the dead and comfort the families, but volunteer workers, more public servants, and nonprofits of all kinds.

From this, the public drew some natural conclusions. Government regulation—of airport safety, offshore banks, weapons dealers, etc.—is sometimes a bargain despite the costs. "Big government" is no longer automatically a "big evil." Public-sector workers, precisely because they are not profit-seeking, are essential in emergencies—when what's required is "whatever it takes," not bare satisfaction of the terms of some previously negotiated private contract. Moreover, as America's response to 9/11 began, the public was reminded that taking on a stateless enemy requires the cooperation of other states—and that unilateralism and isolationism have their limits. Americans also got a crash course in the unsavory aspects of U.S. foreign policy.

And so, along with the odd spectacle of Congressional Republicans voting blank checks to federal relief and reconstruction efforts, and now even authorizing the federalization of airport security, "new normal" America gives us opinion polls showing the strongest support for and trust in the federal government in a generation and the greatest support for international peace institutions like the United Nations in forty years. Meanwhile, in communities and families, each new act of hostility toward the foreign-born has been swamped by countless personal efforts of understanding and engagement. And the hot Christmas dolls this year are firefighters, emergency medical personnel and municipal police.

In brief, September 11 has made the idea of a public sector, and the society that it serves, attractive again. It enlarged the public's view that unilateral military action is a bad recipe for international peace. This doesn't describe a political space from which the left is forever excluded, but one in which it is virtually invited to reenter mainstream politics.

The real question today is whether progressives have the wit and collective will to accept that invitation. Doing so will require us to affirm our values in ways understood and respected by ordinary Americans, to present a concise and clear agenda for advancing those values and to enter and compete for support in electoral arenas. At these things, American progressives have not been particularly effective over the past generation, whatever their other achievements—most notably, in helping make this society a more tolerant one. We have largely hidden from our values, missing opportunities to state them in publicly understood terms of opportunity, fair dealing and responsibility. Our organizational divisions have obscured our fundamental shared agenda—to build a high-road economy of shared prosperity, to protect and repair the environment, to fix our broken system of campaign finance and voting, to seek peace through sustainable development, not just military threat, and to provide universal access to quality health care, education and housing. And, until recently, we have avoided the hard, grimy work of fighting in electoral arenas, which the right has increasingly occupied by default.

Now is the time to change this. Far from losing faith or withdrawing from politics, American progressives should assert their public presence more forcibly than they have in a generation, rededicating themselves to practically advancing America's democratic promise and acting with renewed confidence that the American people, given half a chance, are prepared to help in that good work.

BACKGROUND

Articles on the roots of Islamic fundamentalism,
a talk with Osama bin Laden, asymmetrical warfare,
and no-win wars

October 2001
How To Lose a War
Walden Bello

After over two weeks of Anglo-American bombardment of Afghanistan, once one gets beyond the sound and fury of American bombs and the smokescreen of CNN propaganda, it appears that in the war between the United States and Osama bin Laden, the latter is coming out ahead.

"Making the Rubble Bounce"
It is doubtful if Washington has achieved anything of tactical or strategic value except to make the "rubble bounce"—as the consequences of multiple nuclear explosions in one area were cynically described during the cold war. Indeed, the bombing, which has taken the lives of many civilians, has worsened the U.S.'s strategic position in Southwest and South Asia by eroding the stability of the pro-U.S. regimes in the Muslim world. A radical fundamentalist regime is now a real possibility in Islamabad, while Washington faces the unpleasant prospect of having to serve ultimately as a police force between an increasingly isolated Saudi elite and a restive youthful population that regards bin Laden as a hero.

Meanwhile in the rest of the developing world, the shock over the September 11 assault is giving way to disapproval of the U.S. bombing and, even more worrisome to Washington, to bin Laden's emergence in the public consciousness as a feisty underdog skillfully running circles around a big bully who only knows one response: massive retaliation. A telling sign of the times in Bangkok and many other cities in Southeast Asia is the way young people are snapping up bin Laden T-shirts, and not only for reasons of novelty.

Anglo-Saxon Brotherhood
CNN images of U.S. President George Bush, Prime Minister Tony Blair, and U.S. Secretary of State Colin Powell ticking off the latest statement of sup-

port for the U.S. mask the reality that Washington and London are losing the propaganda war. Their effort to paint the military campaign as a conflict between civilization and terrorists has instead come across as a crusade of the Anglo-Saxon brotherhood against the Islamic world. So jarring has British Prime Minister Tony Blair's public relations drive to make Britain an equal partner in the war effort that the foreign minister of Belgium, which currently holds the presidency of the European Union, has felt compelled to criticize Blair for compromising the interests of the EU.

In the aftermath of the September 11 assault, a number of writers wrote about the possibility that that move could have been a bait to get the U.S. bogged down in a war of intervention in the Middle East that would inflame the Muslim world against it. Whether or not that was indeed bin Laden's strategic objective, the U.S. bombing of Afghanistan has created precisely such a situation. Moderate leaders of Thailand's normally sedate Muslim community now openly express support for bin Laden. In Indonesia, once regarded as a model of tolerant Islam, a recent survey revealed that half of the respondents regard bin Laden as a fighter for justice and less than 35% regard him as a terrorist.

The global support that U.S. President George Bush has flaunted is deceptive. Of course, a lot of governments would express their support for the UN Security Council's call for a global campaign against terrorism. Far fewer countries, however, are actually actively cooperating in intelligence and police surveillance activities. Even fewer have endorsed the military campaign and opened up their territory to transit by U.S. planes on the way to Southwest Asia. And when one gets down to the decisive test of offering troops and weapons to fight alongside the British and the Americans in the harsh plains and icy mountains of Afghanistan, one is down to the hardcore of the Western cold war alliance.

Translating Guerrilla War To a Global Setting

Bin Laden's terrorist methods are despicable, but one must grant the devil his due. Whether through study or practice, he has absorbed the lessons of guerrilla warfare in a national, Afghan setting and translated it to a global setting. Serving as the international correlate of the national popular base is the youth of the global Muslim community, among whom feelings of resentment against Western domination were a volatile mix that was simply waiting to be ignited.

The September 11 attacks were horrific and heinous, but from one angle, what were they except a variant of Che Guevara's "foco" theory? According to Guevara, the aim of a bold guerrilla action is twofold: to demoralize the enemy and to empower your popular base by getting them to participate in an action that shows that the all-powerful government is indeed vulnerable. The enemy is then provoked into a military response that further saps his credibility in what is basically a political and ideological battle. For bin Laden, terrorism is not the end, but a means to an end. And that end is something that none of Bush's rhetoric about defending civilization through revenge bombing can compete with: a vision of Muslim Asia rid of American economic and military power, Israel, and corrupt surrogate elites, and returned to justice and Islamic sanctity.

LOST OPPORTUNITY

Yet Washington was not exactly without weapons in this ideological war. In the aftermath of September 11, it could have responded in a way that could have blunted bin Laden's political and ideological appeal and opened up a new era in U.S.-Arab relations.

First, it could have foresworn unilateral military action and announced to the world that it would go the legal route in pursuing justice, no matter how long this took. It could have announced its pursuit of a process combining patient multinational investigation, diplomacy, and the employment of accepted international mechanisms—like the International Court of Justice.

These methods may take time but they work, and they ensure that justice and fairness are served. For instance, patient diplomacy secured the extradition from Libya of suspects in the 1988 bombing of a Pan Am jumbo jet over Lockerbie, Scotland, and their successful prosecution under an especially constituted court in the Hague. Likewise, the International Criminal Tribunal for former Yugoslavia, set up under the auspices of the ICJ, has successfully prosecuted some wartime Croat and Serbian terrorists and is currently prosecuting former Serbian strongman Slobodan Milosevic, though of course much remains to be done.

The second prong of a progressive U.S. response could have been Washington's announcing a fundamental change in its policies in the Middle East, the main points of which would be the withdrawal of troops from Saudi Arabia, the ending of sanctions and military action against Iraq, decisive support for the immediate establishment of a Palestinian state, and ordering Israel to immediately refrain from attacks on Palestinian communities.

Foreign policy realists will say that this strategy is impossible to sell to the American people, but they have been wrong before. Had the U.S. taken this route, instead of taking the law—as usual—in its own hands, it could have emerged as an example of a great power showing restraint and paved the way to a new era of relations among people and nations. The instincts of a unilateral, imperial past, however, have prevailed, and they have now run rampage to such an extent that, even on the home front, the rights of dissent and democratic diversity that have been one of the powerful ideological attractions of U.S. society are fundamentally threatened by the draconian legislation being pushed by law-and-order types like Secretary of Justice John Ashcroft, who are taking advantage of the current crisis to push through their pre-September 11 authoritarian agendas.

No Win Situation

As things now stand, Washington has painted itself into a no-win situation. If it kills bin Laden, he becomes a martyr, a source of never-ending inspiration, especially to young Muslims. If it captures him alive, freeing him will become a massive focus of resistance that will prevent the imposition of capital punishment without triggering massive revolts throughout the Islamic world. If it fails to kill or capture him, he will secure an aura of invincibility, as somebody favored by God, and whose cause is therefore just.

As Tom Spencer, a policy analyst of Britain's Conservative Party, has observed, bin Laden has been turned into a "Robin Hood."

September 11 was an unspeakable crime against humanity, but the U.S.

response has converted the equation in many people's minds into a war between vision and power, righteousness and might, and, perverse as this may sound, spirit versus matter. You won't get this from CNN and *The New York Times*, but Washington has stumbled into bin Laden's preferred terrain of battle.

(Originally published in *Foreign Policy in Focus*.)

December 2001
Post-Industrial Warfare:
The Changing Character of Contemporary Conflict
Michael T. Klare

The September 11 terrorist assault on New York and Washington, no less than the 1941 Japanese attack on Pearl Harbor and the 1945 nuclear strikes on Hiroshima and Nagasaki, has fundamentally altered the landscape of global conflict. Before September 11, most analysts assumed that the next major American war would entail all-out combat with the well-equipped armies of a modern state; instead, U.S. forces are now engaged in a global struggle against a secretive, multinational terrorist organization backed by a clique of religious fanatics. What we are seeing, in fact, is an entirely new *system* of warfare. The industrial-style fighting methods that prevailed in most of the wars of the 20th century have been replaced by a different mode of combat: post-industrial warfare.

Post-industrial warfare is distinguishable from earlier systems of combat in a number of ways. Most important, it relies on irregular forces (often of a non-state character) plus unconventional methods of fighting to inflict disproportionate damage on more powerful, conventional forces. In place of traditional, "heavy metal" weapons—tanks, combat planes, warships, and so on—it employs cheap, low-tech weapons and commercially-available technologies (including biotechnology) to inflict damage on an opponent.

And, while the practitioners of such combat often espouse backward-looking ideologies, they seek to exploit every innovation of modern technology to their advantage.

All of these characteristics were evident in the September 11 terror attack. The perpetrators of the assault were self-made warriors, not professional soldiers in an established state's armed forces. In place of firearms, they carried penknives and box-cutters; instead of combat planes, they used civilian airliners to strike their targets. And while motivated by an extremely reactionary form of Islam, they employed e-mail, computers, and other modern systems to expedite their operations.

It is true, of course, that guerrillas, outlaws, and revolutionaries have always relied on unconventional means of warfare to defeat more powerful foes. In this sense, the September 11 attack was but a modern variant of a familiar form of combat. But there is much about this event, and the larger terror campaign of which it is a part, that sets it off from similar episodes in the past. This is not a localized insurgency against a particular ruler or authority; it is a global assault on the very structure of modern, Western society. And yet, for all of its anti-Western ideology, it is a campaign that is thoroughly grounded in the high-tech, transnational processes of globalization.

Nor is Al Qaeda, the terror organization behind the September 11 attack, the only violent group to exhibit these characteristics. Around the world, one can find many insurgent and outlaw entities that employ a similar mix of post-industrial tactics. In Sri Lanka, for example, the rebel Tamil Tigers have utilized a sophisticated, world-spanning procurement network to obtain advanced explosives for a relentless campaign of suicide bombings at important sites in Colombo, the nation's capital. In Sierra Leone, rebel forces use machetes to maim and mutilate any civilians caught in their path while using globalized trade channels to sell their diamonds on the international market. And the drug cartels and their guerrilla partners in Colombia have established an international banking system every bit as sophisticated as that employed by the large multinational corporations.

The U.S. Department of Defense uses the term "asymmetrical operations" to describe tactics of this sort. Such operations, it is said, represent an attempt by America's adversaries "to circumvent or undermine U.S. strengths while exploiting its weaknesses, using methods that differ significantly from the usual mode of U.S. operations." (Department of Defense *Annual Report* for 1999, p. 2.) President Bush and Secretary of Defense Donald Rumsfeld have made frequent use of this term to describe the September 11 assault and other terrorist attacks by the Al Qaeda organization. But "asymmetry" only describes one aspect of these attacks, the use of unconventional methods by a weaker party against the strong; it fails to capture other aspects of the emerging combat milieu, including the anti-modern, anti-Western ideology of many outlaw forces combined with the use of "off-the-shelf" commercial technologies to foil the industrial-style weaponry of the major powers.

The United States military is now engaged in a global "war against terrorism"—a campaign that by definition entails a clash between industrial and post-industrial modes of combat. Other wars of the future are also likely to exhibit this sort of confrontation. As a result, future battles will look very different from those of the past, with surprising and possibly disturbing outcomes. It would be very useful, then, to identify and describe the defining characteristics of the new combat environment.

Non-State Actors

For most of the 20th century, the practice of warfare—as it was commonly understood—entailed a clash between the regular armed forces of established states. To prevail in such contests, all nations large and small sought to assemble modern military forces and to provide those forces with as many guns, tanks, aircraft, and ships as it could afford. This, in turn, required the mobilization of the nation's scientific and industrial capabilities for the design, development, and production of ever more potent military systems—a process that culminated in the introduction of the nuclear bomb. Following the 1945 strikes on Hiroshima and Nagasaki, every major power sought to acquire nuclear weapons of their own, or to align themselves with a nuclear-armed superpower. Under these circumstances, it was widely assumed that any major war of the future—a World War III—would produce human casualties on an unprecedented scale.

The end of the Cold War greatly diminished the risk of a global nuclear exchange, but did not erase the common association between the concept of "war" and the mobilization of industrial resources for the development and production of modern weapons. Since 1990, however, the emphasis has been on the development of high-tech conventional munitions rather than nuclear weapons and ballistic missiles. America's concentrated use of air-power and "smart" munitions during the Gulf war of 1991 and the Kosovo campaign of 1999 has become the new standard of combat that all other major powers seek to emulate. And despite its stated emphasis on asymmetrical warfare, the Department of Defense recently announced a $200 billion program to develop a new family of advanced jet aircraft.

All of these state-based efforts to develop increasingly capable professional armies have had a paradoxical effect: as the costs and risks of a major military encounter between the regular forces of established states have risen, the inclination of most governments to engage in such action has greatly diminished. As a result, the outbreak of interstate warfare has become a relatively rare occurrence. Of the 50 armed conflicts that broke out in the 1990s, only four entailed combat between two or more states, and only one—the 1991 Persian Gulf conflict—involved all-out fighting between large numbers of air, ground, and sea forces. "As the 20th century approached its end," Martin van Crevald of the Hebrew University in Jerusalem observed recently, "major interstate wars appeared to be on the retreat."

But while interstate combat has become rare, internal conflict involving non-state actors—insurgents, terrorists, brigands, warlords, ethnic militias, and so on—has become quite common. Such conflict can take several forms: revolutionary (or fundamentalist) struggles to replace existing authorities with more ideologically (or religiously) "correct" regimes; nationalistic campaigns by repressed minorities in multi-ethnic states to break off a piece of territory and create an ethnically-pure state of their own; and efforts by local warlords to gain control of valuable resources—gold mines, diamond fields, rare timber stands, and the like—for their personal benefit. Almost all of the wars now under way around the world fit into one or another of these three categories.

Conflicts of this sort may arise from distinctive local conditions, but most exhibit certain characteristics in common. Typically, the forces involved are composed of non-professional soldiers who are recruited from the local population on the basis of ideological or religious fervor, unabashed greed, or a lust for combat (or some combination of all three). Most of these combatants are young men (in many cases, teen-aged boys) who are attracted by the camaraderie and sense of purpose of such forces, and/or the opportunity to earn a regular income (in what are often economically depressed areas). Combatants of this type rarely possess the learning or skills to operate high-tech weapons, but are perfectly capable of wielding a club or firing an AK-47 assault rifle at a crowd of unprotected civilians.

Forces of this type usually operate in a remote and inaccessible part of the country, or in urban slums and shantytowns. Given their outlaw status, they cannot draw on the financial and industrial resources of the state, and so must arm themselves with the limited weaponry at hand—hunting guns, stolen pistols and rifles, black-market firearms, common explosives, and so on. Armies equipped in this manner are no match for the professional forces of an established state, and so normally avoid combat with them. Instead, they seek to undermine government authority by attacking isolated police and army outposts, by disrupting economic activity, and by conducting terrorist strikes on symbolically important urban facilities (train stations, banks, and so on). Because the state, in most of these conflicts, is viewed as an agent of modernization, every manifestation of the modern—especially industrial facilities of one sort or another—are considered a legitimate target of attack. As a result, wars in such places as Bosnia, Chechnya, the Congo, Kosovo, Liberia, and Sierra Leone have become, in effect, wars of de-industrialization.

These conflicts often share another distinguishing characteristic: the marriage of political/religious objectives with criminal forms of resource acquisition. Because non-state actors of the sort described above are normally barred from participation in the open, legal economy, they must rely on illegal forms of activity to obtain the funds they need to buy their arms and pay their soldiers. This can mean engagement in the illegal drug trade, as is said to be the case of the Taliban and the warlords associated with the Northern Alliance of Afghanistan. Other forces, such as the Revolutionary United Forces (RUF) of Sierra Leone and the Union for the Total Independence of Angola (UNITA) rely on illicit sales of diamonds to cover their operating expenses. Still other groups have engaged in kidnapping, extortion, or the sale of protected timber and animal products.

To conduct their illicit endeavors, non-state actors of this type have been forced to insert themselves, one way or another, in the global underground economy. And because the underground economy operates as a hidden branch of the legal, aboveground economy, insurgent forces have had to learn to mimic the operating techniques of multinational corporations—opening offshore banking accounts, moving money around the world by wire transfers, establishing foreign offices, using satellite phones and fax machines to transmit instructions, and so forth. No matter how opposed to the effects of globalization, therefore, these forces have become dependent on the continuing operation of its financial and communications infrastructure. This is true as much of Osama bin Laden and his terrorist network as it is of the guerrillas in Colombia and the warlords of the Congo.

LOW-TECH WEAPONS/UNCONVENTIONAL TACTICS

Non-state actors possess neither the means nor the capacity to operate modern, high-tech weapons of the types found in the arsenals of established nation-states. In any head-on battle with a state's regular forces, therefore, non-state actors are likely to come out on the losing side. But belligerents of this sort rarely engage in such combat, preferring instead to slip away in the night whenever the state marshals its forces for attack. To achieve their objectives—or just to stay alive—rebel and insurgent forces must rely on low-tech weapons and unconventional tactics to overcome the advantages of their more powerful opponents.

In any firefight between a rifle and a tank, the rifle-carrier is likely to perish. This has led most modern strategists to denigrate the importance in combat of basic infantry weaponry. But in an internecine struggle over the control of isolated towns and villages, modern assault rifles and rocket-propelled grenades (RPG) can be employed with devastating effect. According to some estimates, 80 to 90 percent of all casualties inflicted in recent wars have been caused by small arms and light weapons—a category that includes rifles, RPGs, machine guns, lightweight mortars, and man-portable anti-tank weapons. Light weapons of these types can also be used to assassinate government officials, protect illegal drug facilities, and expedite the "ethnic cleansing" of targeted neighborhoods. (See Michael Klare, "The New Arms Race: Light Weapons and International Security," *Current History*, April 1997.)

Insurgent forces have also made effective use of common explosives to destroy military installations and terrorize civilian populations. Terror bombings in crowded urban settings have, in fact, become an all-too-common feature of contemporary conflict. The Irish Republican Army (IRA), for example, conducted a wave of bombings in major English cities in the late 1990s, one of which, the massive 1996 blast at Canary Wharf in London, killed or injured scores of people. Terror attacks of this sort have also become a standard technique of the Tamil in Sri Lanka. Typically, the Tigers use teen-aged boys and girls who are persuaded (through promises of a heavenly reward) to slip into public areas and detonate the explosive charges hidden beneath their clothes—killing themselves in the process.

Suicide bombings are just one of the unconventional tactics employed by insurgent and terrorist groups to inflict pain and damage on their more powerful opponents. The systematic assassination of government officials—police officers, tax collectors, school teachers, or anyone else who presents the public face of governmental authority in slums or rural areas—is another common tactic. By eradicating government authority in this manner, the insurgents seek to undermine ordinary people's faith in the ability of the government to provide day-to-day protection, and thus force them to submit to the guerrilla's demands (for food, cash, recruits, and so on). This has long been the practice in Colombia's guerrilla-dominated areas, and was a noted feature of the recent fighting in Sierra Leone. A number of rebel forces, such as the Armed Islamic Group (GIA, by its initials in French) in Algeria, have taken to slaughtering the entire population of isolated rural villages, so as to demonstrate the impotence of the national government.

Economic warfare is another tactic employed by rebel groups seeking to undermine the power and authority of the established government. In Egypt, for example, militant fundamentalists have attacked foreign visitors at famous archaeological sites—thus producing a sharp drop in tourist income (a major factor in the Egyptian economy). One such raid, at the Temple of Hatshepsut in Luxor in 1997, resulted in the death of 58 foreigners. (This attack has been attributed to Egyptian Islamic Jihad, one of the groups associated with Al Qaeda.) In Colombia, the guerrillas of the National Liberation Army (ELN, by its initials in Spanish) bombed the 480-mile Limón-to-Covenas pipeline 79 times in 1999, causing millions of dollars in damage and lost oil revenues. And while there is no proven case of an insurgent/terrorist group spreading computer viruses to paralyze the information and financial systems of the advanced industrial nations, it is widely believed that such attacks will be a common feature of unconventional warfare in the future.

Most of these techniques, and others like them, have been employed by Al Qaeda in its campaign to undermine pro-Western governments in the Middle East and to eject U.S. forces from the region. Terrorist bombings were conducted on U.S. facilities in Saudi Arabia (1995 and 1996), U.S. embassies in Kenya and Tanzania (1998), and the USS *Cole* in Yemen (2000). Al Qaeda has also been linked to guerrilla and terrorist activities in several other locations, including Egypt, Indonesia, Kashmir, the Philippines, and Uzbekistan. To finance its operations, Al Qaeda has engaged in various forms of licit and illicit commerce, including the sale of illegal narcotics. But it was the September 11 assault on the Pentagon and the World Trade Center that most dramatically revealed the organization's capacity for daring and improvisation, entailing the use of fuel-laden civilian airliners as flying super-bombs.

The September 11 attacks are also revealing in terms of the terrorists' approach to technology. While supposedly disdaining everything Western, the soldiers in Osama bin Laden's multinational army (and others like it) are fully prepared to make use of modern, Information Age technologies—cell phones, computers, e-mail, the Internet, international banking networks, mass communications, and so on—whenever it suits their purpose. "The new wars make use of new technology," Mary Kaldor of the London School of Economics wrote in 1997. "In particular, modern communications are crucial in coordinating horizontally organized military [and terrorist] units, for propaganda, and for connecting transnational networks."

Insurgent and terrorist organizations have also sought to employ modern pharmaceutical technologies to manufacture biological warfare (BW) agents. Although, as of this writing, no firm link had been established between the terrorists responsible for the September 11 hijack attacks and the anthrax outbreaks now plaguing parts of the United States, it is believed that Al Qaeda and other extremist groups have considered the use of BW agents in attacks on civilian populations. The technologies used to produce such weapons are closely related to those used in non-military pharmaceutical research efforts; because these technologies have been widely disseminated in recent years, it is now possible for underground organizations like Al Qaeda to obtain BW-related equipment and materials from scores of locations around the world.

GLOBALIZATION AND ITS DISCONTENTS

The utilization of modern technology by insurgent and terrorist organizations is part and parcel of another distinctive aspect of post-industrial warfare: the close relationship between economic globalization and the emergence of new forms and foci of revolt.

Globalization has influenced the outbreak and character of conflict in a number of ways. To begin with, the creation of a global market has resulted in a growing divide between rich and poor, with new pockets of affluence arising in areas of widespread poverty and stagnation. Rapidly changing class dynamics of this sort are often a source of friction, but become especially explosive when new class disparities correspond to long-standing ethnic and religious divisions. Thus, while globalization has improved living conditions in certain countries, it has also increased the risk of conflict in some areas. As noted by the Pentagon-funded Institute for National Security Studies (INSS), "forces associated with economic globalization have threatened near-term stability in several key countries, aggravated social and economic tensions, and increased the potential for backlash against globalization."

This tendency is especially prevalent in parts of Africa, the Middle East, and Southeast Asia, where economic growth has lagged behind other regions or has left some populations in a stagnant or declining position. When the Asian economic crisis spread to Indonesia, for example, many native Indonesians turned against the resident Chinese community, which was viewed (not always accurately) as having benefited disproportionately from the "crony capitalism" of the Suharto era. More recently, continuing economic decline appears to have exacerbated the long-standing hostility between Muslims and Christians in the Moluccas, and between the Acehenese and other inhabitants of Sumatra. Economic grievances have also contributed to the antagonism between Israelis and Palestinians, and between the Tamils and the Sinhalese in Sri Lanka. Similarly, Islamic fundamentalist groups in Egypt and Saudi Arabia have aroused significant grass-roots support by denouncing the lavish lifestyles of the ruling elites.

Economic discontent of this sort can also lead to the demonization of globalization itself. "Many nongovernment groups see globalization as serving large corporate interests at the expense of the poor," the INSS reported in 1999. Such perceptions have been voiced, for example, at the anti-globalization protests at World Bank meetings in Seattle and Washington, D.C. The same outlook can be seen in the statements of many insurgent organizations, such as the Zapatistas of Mexico and the Revolutionary Armed Forces of Colombia (FARC, by its initials in Spanish). Opposition to globalization is also seen in terrorist attacks on and vandalism of international banks and the outlets of such prominent multinational firms as McDonalds and Nike.

Globalization is also associated with the intrusion of Western values and behavior patterns into traditional societies, producing anxiety and resentment among those who feel alienated from (or threatened by) the emerging, consumer-based world culture. For some, this has led to nostalgia for an earlier, supposedly more just and puritanical epoch. Many followers of Islamic fundamentalism, for example, seek to recreate the (seemingly) utopian world of the early Muslim era. Some of these believers, including the leaders of the Taliban, are prepared to use armed violence to achieve this purpose. The use of force to purge society of Western influences is also advocated by proponents of other fundamentalist denominations.

In some cases, anti-globalization campaigns have taken on a decidedly anti-American character. "Although economic globalization is not the same as Americanization, it is largely driven by Americans," the INSS reported in its 1999 strategic assessment. "U.S. companies are at the forefront of global trade, investment, finance, and information technology." Inevitably, this leads to anti-American sentiments on the part of those who remain immured in poverty. "Washington has often been blamed for other people's grievances, and it will continue to be a target. . . . The social and economic strains associated with globalization give rise to the charge that the United States is advancing its own commercial interests under a global banner at the expense of the poor."

Globalization is thus a contributing factor in the outbreak of conflict, and often determines its particular targets. But, however strongly they may oppose the effects of globalization, many insurgent and terrorist groups rely on its various manifestations to further their revolutionary or reactionary purposes. As noted, this entails the use of modern information and communications technologies—computers, e-mail, the Internet, and so on—as well as advanced biotechnology. Indeed, it is striking to note just how closely transnational terror groups like Al Qaeda and the Tamil Tigers have come to resemble large multinational corporations, with their far-flung communications, information-processing, and financial networks. It is this, more than anything, that sets off the new insurgencies from those of the past.

IMPLICATIONS

The distinctive characteristics of post-industrial warfare pose a significant challenge to the international community and to status-quo powers like the United States. Transnational terrorist organizations like Al Qaeda, and the transnational criminal organizations with which they are often associated, have successfully breached long-standing defense mechanisms and produced great harm to Western societies. Given their proven capacity for stealth and improvisation, moreover, it is likely that these groups will continue to evade and circumvent the determined efforts that are being made to incapacitate them. Political violence and organized criminality will thus remain significant features of the international landscape.

Clearly, it will not be possible to successfully address this challenge without a better understanding of post-industrial warfare and the development of strategies capable of counteracting its effects. This, in turn, will require a deeper investigation into the various phenomena described above, along with their respective causes and consequences. Ultimately, it will also require a more rigorous effort to chart the many complex links between economic globalization and violent conflict.

Much has been said in artistic and literary circles about post-modernism and the post-industrial landscape. Now we are seeing the impact of these phenomena on the global battlespace. But while many belligerents have begun to appreciate—and take advantage of—the distinctive characteristics of the emerging military environment, strategic theory and practice in the United States (and other advanced industrial nations) has not kept pace with developments on the ground. Only by understanding and adapting to the exigencies of post-industrial warfare can we successfully face the challenges that surely lie ahead.

(Originally published in *Current History*, December 2001.)

October 2001
An Enemy With No Forwarding Address
Marwan Bishara

September 11 was the end of the era in which the United States perfected its zero-dead approach to conflict, with minimum casualties to the U.S. and maximum damage to the enemy. President George W. Bush had to declare the

U.S. at war before nominating an enemy. The new enemy is mobile, transnational, or sub-national. So now begins the era of asymmetric conflicts.

For decades the U.S. spent trillions of dollars to ensure minimum casualties in any confrontation. In the Vietnam War, it spent hundreds of thousands of dollars for each dead Vietnamese fighter. In the Gulf War, it kept U.S. casualties low. With rapid, massive bombardment from afar (the Colin Powell doctrine), the U.S. hoped for zero casualties in future symmetrical wars. Its missiles and superior fighters, supported with the most sophisticated airborne intelligence, could guarantee such a result by inflicting unbearable destruction on the enemy.

But now we have the asymmetric war scenario some American strategists have warned against in the last few years: one that hit where it hurt most, hit the pride of America's might, the Pentagon and Wall Street. Washington, trying to adapt to an evolving, globalising world, had been introducing a revolution in military affairs (RMA).

There were two distinct concepts. The first was fourth generation warfare, stateless or asymmetric, to be fought by an opponent who might have a non-nation-state base, such as an ideology or religion. In February 2001, before a Senate committee on world threats, CIA director George Tenet said what struck him most forcefully was the accelerating pace of change in so many arenas that affect our nations interests. To the U.S., asymmetry means Osama bin Laden and other international terrorists, mafiosi and drug dealers. But the idea also covers non-state actors like those the U.S. has already encountered in Somalia, Kosovo, and Lebanon in 1983, when a bomb killed 239 U.S. Marines. Those analysts who think the future will be asymmetrical propose a rethink of the usefulness of billion-dollar fighter planes and advanced frigates if two men and a boat could kill 17 men and damage the USS *Cole* (12 October 2000 in Aden).

The second concept has been the anti-missile defence shield Star Wars to protect America from incoming ballistic missiles carrying chemical, biological or nuclear weapons. The Bush administration, with vice-president Dick Cheney and defence secretary Donald Rumsfeld, has concentrated its efforts on this, which has the merit of subsidising the military-industrial complex.

There was international condemnation of this return to policies of proliferation, so Bush explained that his shield was not against other nuclear powers, but against rogue states or, worse, groups capable of launching missiles against American soil or interests abroad.

Both of these ideas and their believers seemed to converge into a coherent strategy to fight a new war against an asymmetric enemy. But who, aside from bin Laden, is the enemy? Not mafias and drug-dealers: hostilities are bad for business. Unless Washington intends to bomb one of the rogue states, why would their leaders launch a missile against the U.S. when they would be punished like Libya, or Iraq over the last decade? To what extent has America created new enemies, and just how dangerous, beyond the 11 September outrage, are they? How is this terrorism different from that which Arab nations or certain European countries have faced over 20 years? Is it a qualitative difference or just (if one can say just) quantitative?

Asymmetry must be distinguished from di-symmetry, meaning a quantitative difference in firepower and force, a strong state against a weak one (the U.S. against Iraq). Asymmetry is about the qualitative difference in the means, values and style of the new enemies. Once a power like the U.S. insists on exclusive superiority in world affairs as well as in conventional warfare, its disadvantaged enemies resort to unconventional asymmetrical means to fight it, avoiding its strengths and concentrating on its vulnerabilities.

NOT FIGHTING FAIR

The Pentagon says the new enemies don't fight fair; their strategy, based in a globalised world, uses all possible sophisticated modern means: communication, transportation, information, psychological terror, international media and the internet. In their arsenal are also such low-tech weapons as penknives, fishing boats, homemade explosives and civilian planes. As we have seen, these work. Even though these enemies must be based somewhere, no permanent location can be assigned to them, because they have no permanent home, their network is dispersed. The world is both their address and area of operation.

Asymmetric enemies have a common interest: weakening state sovereignties and boosting international market forces. In this they are like

McDonalds, CNN and AOL. All use the grey areas in a globalised world, the gaps in the legal structure, to ensure maximum profits and escape the accountability that results from constitutional or democratic legitimacy. In this sense, asymmetric enemies are creatures of the neo-liberal version of globalisation. They have more room for manoeuvre than states. That is why the American media describe bin Laden not just as a political Islamist, rooted in a particular society, but as the representative of a new cosmopolitan Islam that is a global threat, like the Islamist movement of Hassan al-Turabi (now in prison in Sudan). This movement is thought to be confronting the U.S., to weaken or destroy its power.

If you put together all the characteristics that the American strategists attribute to the new model asymmetric enemy, they add up to a profile of Osama bin Laden. If he didn't exist, it would be necessary to invent him. As we all now know, he was groomed by the CIA in the 1980s, only to turn against his creator after the Gulf War. Should an asymmetric enemy be distinguished from a state and that state's intelligence network? Is it possible to organise a movement of international violence without some state support? It is not clear how a new enemy could reduce its operations to being only virtual. And even enemies whose heartland is an ideology need physical space somewhere for their logistics and tools. Their bank accounts have to be kept somewhere, too.

What about the rogue or failed states? The intervention in Somalia taught the U.S. a hard lesson. When, in October 1993, Hussein Aydid humiliated the U.S., killing 17 American soldiers, the Clinton administration became convinced that it could not manage, let alone win, a war against militias not accountable to the conventions of a state.

Operation Just Cause in Panama in December 1989 was also an asymmetric war, even though it was the largest American operation since Vietnam. It was meant to recapture Manuel Antonio Noriega and it succeeded. The U.S. went on to target Saddam Hussein, Slobodan Milosevic and Radovan Karadzic, all of whom it considered to be more like bandits than heads of state. Such operations were no different from U.S.

operations during the cold war targeting South American or the Middle Eastern leaders. What is new?

Perhaps what is new is the possibility of deploying many new non-orthodox methods of prevention and dissuasion that were impossible, or illegitimate, before 11 September. Less than a week after, Congress lifted the ban on assassinating foreign leaders. An upgraded level of American violence is now possible.

LEARNING FROM ISRAEL

Strategies against a new enemy have centred on the need for new precise weaponry of maximum deadliness. Intelligence services must be reinforced with software reconnaissance and satellite spies, and also human spies. Police work, including racial profiling, is recommended. The strategists want to spy on potential sources of support for the new enemy, including NGOs and charities, expatriate communities and internet sites. A U.S. senator complained recently that the CIA was replacing the State Department in diplomacy.

The missile defence shield is now possible too, since who knows what an asymmetric devil is planning for the next attack? Congress has given the president new powers: the Senate voted unanimously and the House of Representatives approved the authorization by a 420-1. The one dissident, Democrat Barbara Lee, insisted that military action would not prevent further acts of international terrorism against the U.S. Most of the material about asymmetry focuses on the U.S. and, since the second intifada, on Israel. The U.S. has been working with Israel for a long time on projects including the Arrow anti-missile missile. Israel's fighting style, especially in the West Bank and Gaza are of special interest to U.S. experts, who detect asymmetry in Israel's wars.

Under the headline How to Fight an Asymmetric War, General Wesley Clark, commander of Nato forces in Kosovo, explained that the Palestinians inside Israel (somebody remind Clark that West Bank and Gaza are not in Israel) learned how to resist using non-lethal force. It was a tactic aimed at exploiting world sensitivities, forcing Israeli security forces to overreact. Occasionally non-lethal force was supplemented with armed men among the rock throwers or terror bombings. Responding with fighter planes, tanks and artillery was impossible; responding with troops on the ground risked casualties. No society is more reluctant than Israel to accept losses, so the country developed new equipment, forces and tactics. To secure its borders, Israel deployed more heavily armoured tanks and troop-carrying vehicles and procured Apache helicopters, unmanned aerial vehicles and very long-range optics. To protect itself internally, Israel issued its infantrymen plastic bullets and riot-control gear. Special security forces were organised to help relieve the conventional Israeli units of responsibility for keeping order.

Clark's admiration for Israel's skills is deeply worrying: this policy has led to nearly 700 Palestinian dead, and thousands injured. And in the absence of an Israeli political or diplomatic option, force has not improved security. Anthony Cordesman, defence analyst at the Centre for Strategic and International Studies, suggested that Israel was forcing the Palestinian Authority to suppress Palestinians and curb democratic freedoms to attain stability. When the intifada continued, he said the Palestinians had two options: peace with violence or war. Cordesman described a situation in which Israel would do the dirty work for the PA and against it: that is also asymmetric warfare. It means more social control, more assassinations and crippling of the economy.

Listening to Bush, it is clear that U.S. strategy is heading towards Israeli-style asymmetric warfare, even though it failed in Palestine. This choice would be a catastrophe. The world's grey areas created by war, globalisa-tion and impoverishment are danger zones. Public institutions and develop-ment are more necessary in grey areas than are military interventions. The events of 11 September reflect a transformation of the world that we must try to understand. The response that has been made to them is in service of a strategy that aims to impose an international security order in the inter-ests of the U.S. Will we see the same behaviour that followed the victory over Iraq, which favoured the advance of radical Islamist groups? The new asymmetric enemy cannot be beaten by force, even less by technology without a political project.

(Originally published in *Le Monde Diplomatique*, NYT Syndicate.)

March 6, 1999
Roots of the Religious Right
Eqbal Ahmad

They belong to differing, often contrasting religious systems—Hinduism, Judaism, Christianity and Islam. Yet their ideas and behaviour patterns bear remarkable similarities. In India they have burned down churches and destroyed a historic mosque. In Palestine they describe themselves as "pioneers," desecrate mosques and churches, and with state support dispossess the Muslim and Christian inhabitants of the ancient land. In Algeria they are engaged in savage warfare with a praetorian government. In Serbia, they attempted genocide and ran rape camps. In Pakistan, they have hit Christians, Ahmedis and Shi'a Muslims and also each other. They wage holy wars, and commit atrocities sanctimoniously, yet nothing is truly sacred to them. They spill blood in bazaars, in homes and in courts, mosques and churches. They believe themselves to be God's warriors, above man-made laws and the judgment of mankind.

They are the so-called "fundamentalists," an epithet reserved by the western media for the Muslim variety who are invariably referred to as "Islamic fundamentalists." Others of the ilk are assigned more neutral nouns. The Jewish zealots in Palestine are called "settlers" and, occasionally, "extremists." The Hindu militant is described as "nationalist," and the Christian is labelled "right-wing" or "messianic." The bias in the use of language obscures an important reality: They are reflections of a common problem, with shared roots and similar patterns of expression. Here we briefly review first the environment which gives birth to these political-religious movements, then the commonality of their style and outlook.

The mistakenly called "fundamentalists" are a modern phenomenon, a response to the crises of modernity and identity. Modernity is a historical process. It refers to the development of societies from one mode of production to another, in our age from an agrarian/pastoral mode to the capitalist/industrial mode of production. The shift from one to another mode of production invariably brings revolutionary changes in society. It compels a new logic of social and economic life, threatens inherited styles of life, and forces transformations in the relationship of land, labour and capital. As such, it requires adaptations to new ways of being and doing, and demands drastic changes in human values and in the relations of sexes, classes, individuals, families and communities. It transforms the co-relation and arrangement of living spaces, requires change in how the workplace is organized, how new skills are gathered and distributed, and how people are governed.

When this process of change sets in, older values and ways of life become outdated and dysfunctional much faster than newer, more appropriate values and ways of life strike roots. The resulting social and cultural mutations are experienced by people both as threat and loss. For millennia, humanity had experienced this unsettling process, for example, when it moved from the stone age to the age of iron, or when it discovered fire and shifted from hunting and gathering to agriculture. But never had this process been more intense and more revolutionary than it became with the rise of capitalism and the industrial mode of production. This latter development has been more revolutionary in its impact on societies than any other event in history.

The industrial mode threatened nearly all values and institutions by which people had lived in the agrarian order. It induced large-scale migrations from villages to cities, shifted the locus of labour from farm to factory and the unit of production from the family/community to the individual, forced increasing numbers of women into the labour market, shifted the focus of social regulation from customs to laws, re-ordered the structure of governance from the empire to the nation, obliterated distances to permit the penetration of markets, and transformed the focus of economic life from subsistence toward production en masse and consumerism.

A transformation so systemic was bound to threaten old ways of life. It destroyed the autonomy of rural life lived for millennia, shrank the distances that had separated communities from each other, forced diverse peoples and individuals to live in urban proximity and compete with each other, undermined the structures and values of patriarchy as it had prevailed for centuries, and threw millions of people into the uncertain world of transition between tradition and modernity. In brief, the phenomenon puts into question, and increasingly renders dysfunctional, traditional values and ways of life. Yet, cultures tend to change more slowly than economic and political realities. All societies caught in this process undergo a period of painful passage. How peacefully and democratically a society makes this journey depends on its historical circumstances, the engagement of its intelligentsia, the outlook of its leaders and governments, and the ideological choices they make.

The capitalist and industrial revolution started from Europe. European responses to its dislocating effects offer meaningful variations which scholars have not yet examined with sufficient rigour. The western and non-western experiences are, nevertheless, comparable in that they reveal that when faced with a crisis so systemic, people have tended to respond in four ways. We might call these restorationist, reformist, existential, and revolutionary responses.

The restorationist wants to return somehow to an old way of life, re-impose the laws or customs that were, recapture lost virtues, rehabilitate old certainties, and restore what he believes to have been the golden past—Hindutva and Ramraj, Eretz Israel, Nizam-e-Mustafa. Restorationism invariably entails rejection of the Other—e.g. Muslim, Arab, Hindu, Christian, Ahmadi—and what are construed to be the Other's ways which can range from woman's dress and man's beard to song, dance and such symbols of modern life as the television and radio.

The restorationist ideology and programme can range from relatively moderate to totally extremist. Mr. Atal Behari Vajpayee offers a "moderate" example of Hindu restorationism, Mr. Bal Thackeray is an extremist, and Lal Krishna Advani falls somewhere in between. Similarly, the Jamaat-I-Islami's Amir Qazi Hussain Ahmed may be viewed as a moderate Islamist while Mulla Omar, the Taliban leader, occupies the extreme end.

The reformists are of modernist disposition, men and women who care deeply about preserving the best and most meaningful in their religious tradition while adapting them to the requirements of modern life. The obverse is also true: they seek to integrate modern forms and values into inherited cultures and beliefs. An early reformist in India was Raja Ram Mohan Roy, founder of the Brahmo Samaj movement. The first great Indian Muslim reformist was Sir Syed Ahmed Khan, and the last to be so regarded is Mohammed Iqbal whose "Reconstruction of Religious Thought in Islam" is a quintessential example of reformism in modern Islam. In the Arab world, the al-Manar group led by Mufti Mohammed Abduh, and in the Maghreb Shaykh Ben Badis, Tahir al-Haddad and Abdel Aziz Taalbi were influential reformists. Like the restorationist, the reformist trend emerged as a response to the perceived decline of Muslim power and encounter with the colonizing western powers. From the second half of the 19th century it gained hegemony in the Muslim world, but stagnated in the post-colonial period.

Reformism suffered an initial setback in the Ottoman empire where successive attempts at reform failed, mainly because they were feebly attempted. The Turks' revolutionary turn was premised on the failure of Ottoman reforms. Mustapha Kemal's was the first revolutionary response in the Muslim world. He abolished the Caliphate, established an uncompromisingly secular republic, suppressed many religious institutions, proscribed the veil, prohibited polygamy, and enacted secular laws regulating property rights and women's rights on the basis of equality. No other Muslim country has so far equalled Ataturk's radical break from tradition and from the association of Islam with state power. Yet, in the 1980s and 1990s Turkey did not escape the resurgence of Islamism.

In Iran, the ulema legitimized the constitution of 1906 of which the promise and premises were secular. Shaykh Mohammed Husayn Naini

(1860–1936) delineated the doctrinal justification for the ulema's support for constitutional government, a position later affirmed by the Ayatullah-e-Uzma Husayn Burudjirdi (1875–1962) who was the sole marja of his time and remains a figure of great authority among contemporary Shi'a clerics. But the coup d'etat led first by Reza Shah Pahlevi and another engineered by the American CIA in 1953 put an end to what might have been the most successful experiment in democratic reformism in the Muslim world. Under partial reformist influence, the nationalist regimes in a number of states—Tunisia, Algeria, Egypt, Syria, Iraq, Indonesia, and Malaysia among others—instituted secular constitutions without effecting a radical break from the tradition of associating religion and power. Many of these secular authoritarian regimes are now being challenged by Islamist movements.

With Pakistan's exception, the secular alternative has been favoured in post-colonial South Asia. Under Jawaharlal Nehru's leadership India adopted a secular constitution so that lawmaking in India is not required to conform to religious beliefs. However, as the official restoration of the Somnath temple indicated soon after independence, India's Congress Party governments evinced a special sensitivity toward the feelings of the majority population, a fact widely criticized by left-leaning Indians. In recent years, the rise of the Hindu nationalists to power in several provinces and recently in the federation has greatly undermined the secular character of the Indian republic, a problem to which I shall return later. In Pakistan, on the other hand, the issue of the relationship between religion and the state has remained a source of confusion, instability and misuse of Islam in politics, a phenomenon which contributed greatly to the violent separation of East Pakistan in 1971.

The dominant feature of the post-colonial period has been the existential style of deploying religion whenever it suits the political convenience of those in power, and of ignoring the challenge of defining the relationship of religion and politics when governments and the ruling elites feel secure and contented. This posture came under assault with the rise of Islamic militancy in the eighties and nineties, a period that witnessed accelerated globalization of the world economy. The Islamists were further propelled by the Iranian revolution (February 1979), and more importantly by the Afghan jihad which, thanks to the generosity of the United States, became a transnational project. Ironically, the pro-U.S. governments of Egypt and Algeria later became the prime targets of the Afghanistan trained Mujahideen.

The resurgence of right-wing religious movements in the eighties and nineties was world-wide. They have a particularly violent role in Israel where the state-armed Zionist zealots became specially oppressive toward the Arabs of Palestine. In India, the Hindu movement launched a campaign against the Babri mosque as part of its effort at mobilizing mass support. It ended in the destruction of the 16th century mosque, widespread communal violence, and the rise of the BJP to national power. After the Russians withdrew, the victorious and faction-ridden Mujahideen of Afghanistan tore the country apart. In Sudan, an Islamic government imposed a reign of terror, and mismanagement which has yielded a horrific famine. Christian "fundamentalism" linked with Serb nationalism and Milosevic's diabolic opportunism has aided a reign of terror and ethnic cleansing in Bosnia-Herzegovina, and now it battles on in Kosovo.

PROFILE OF THE RELIGIOUS RIGHT

In two earlier essays I had argued one, that all religio-political movements are products of the shift from the agrarian\pastoral to the capitalist\industrial mode of production and the many forms of dislocations that it entails and two, that the religious tradition they invoke is more imagined than real, an outcome of political opportunism and contemporary compulsions rather than of a return to sources and fundamentals. Given their shared roots, the so-called "fundamentalist" movements bear remarkable similarities which are outlined in the following paragraphs:

The Jew as well as the Christian, the Hindu no less the Muslim "fundamentalist" plies an ideology of superior difference. Each confronts an inferior and threatening Other. Each engages in the politics of exclusion. Hence each poses a menace to the minority communities within its boundary. The Jewish ones regard the Arab, especially the Palestinian Arab whose land they covet and colonize, as the Other—violent, wily, dirty, uncivilized, oversexed, and dangerous. Notably, the Jewish zealots enjoy the full support of their state in dispossessing the Arabs, and they alone are officially armed amidst the unarmed natives. For long, the Hindu militants' sole Other was the Muslim; Christians have now been added to their enemies' list. The Christian bigot had long regarded the Jew as the conspiratorial, grasping Other. In the decades after World War II and the Holocaust, antisemitism became a widely decried prejudice and receded into the interstices of Christian societies. Gradually, Muslims and colored immigrants are taking the place of Jews in the western world. For the Muslim militants the Other are the Jews, occasionally Christians and, in South Asia, the Hindus, Christians, and Ahmedis. I know of no religio-political formation today which does not have a demonized, therefore threatened, Other.

The Other is always an active negation. All such movements mobilize hatred, and often harness unusual organizational effort to do so. The Ram Janam Bhoomi campaign lasted nearly two years during which the BJP leaders and their partners reached out to thousands of villages and towns throughout India, with their mobilizing rituals of preparing bricks to build a temple where then stood the 16th century Babri mosque. The campaign ended in December 1992 in a national march to Ayodhya where the mosque was violently demolished by a frenzied mob. Riots and massacres inevitably followed.

Hate pays, however temporarily. The mobilization contributed to the dramatic transformation of the BJP from a marginal political grouping to one of two largest parliamentary parties in India. In Israel, the right wing Likud and its extremist allies began their rise to national power as they mobilized a campaign of hate and colonization of Palestinians under occupation. In Bosnia, the Serbs' campaign of ethnic cleansing preceded and accompanied a mobilization of Christian hatred of Muslims. In Kashmir, where despite the Maharaja's harsh and discriminatory rule Hindus and Muslims had coexisted peacefully, the Hindu Mahasabha and the RSS played an important role in alienating the Muslim population. In recent years "Islamic" militants have assaulted Hindu homes and villages in Kashmir and committed atrocities that are strictly forbidden in Islamic laws of war.

The cult of violence and proliferation of enemies are inherent in ideologies of difference. All express their hate for the Other by organized violence. All legitimize their violence with references to religion and history. In nearly all instances the enemy multiplies. At first, the Indian Parivar had the Muslim Other as its target. It has now turned on Christians. The Dalit, Sikh, and tribal communities will most likely be its future targets. The Jewish militants are increasingly turning on the liberal and secular Jews of Israel. They have already assassinated one prime minister and caused growing internal strife. In Pakistan, Christians have been hit, and Ahmedis. At the same time intra-militant violence has proliferated in Pakistan, and wanton killings occur even inside mosques and imambarahs. In Algeria, brutalities have become so complex that it is nearly impossible to identify the perpetrators and, occasionally, even the victims.

Since all religio-political formations bear but little relationship to lived religious traditions and histories, they tend to invent and, in the process, distort their own history and tradition. "I see but only shadows of Judaism and Jewish history in their writings and statements," Moshe Menuhin, a great Jewish scholar and father of the famous violinist Yehuda Menuhin, said of Zionist ideologues during a meeting I had with him in 1972. In recent decades, an eminent group of Israeli historians have been documenting the ahistorical character of Zionist historiography. When I pointed out to M.R. Malkani, a well-known theoretician of the RSS and currently a member of the Lok Sabha, that India's most respected historians had questioned the validity of their historical claims, he responded with an exclusionary declaration: "Aisay ittihaasiyon ke liye Hindustan mein koii asthan naheen hai. [For such historians there is no place in India.]" In Pakistan, as Dr. K.K. Aziz has amply documented, in the heyday of the "Islamization" process, even the school and college history texts were contaminated with historical inaccuracies and sectarian claims. They still await a cleaning up which is an essential requirement of the educational enterprise.

All such movements share a patriarchal outlook, and to varying degrees discriminate against women. Amrita Basu, a political scientist at Amherst College, has shown that hostile attitude toward minorities parallels in the 'parivar's' literature a patriarchal outlook and discriminatory practices toward women. One may add that the religious right's misogynic outlook parallels an unusual degree of obsession with sex, a deep seated fear of seduction and a tendency to regulate sexual behavior. In these regards, the Islamists outdo their Hindu, Jewish and Christian counterparts for they alone aim at full segregation and veiling of women, and insist on laws which perpetuate gender inequalities in nearly all walks of life.

The cadres and constituents of all religio-political movements present comparable profiles. They appeal to urban more than rural people, to the lumpen proletariat and lower middle class more than the working or upper classes, technical more than the liberal professionals, and to the expatriate bourgeoisie more than the national one. The pattern suggests that they attract especially those persons and classes which are caught in the "middle of the ford" between tradition and modernity and who, in differing ways, feel marginal, socially uprooted, and insecure about their place in their social environment.

Given their transitional social standing leaders and cadres of the contemporary religio-political parties evince ambivalence toward products and symbols of modernity. They love the products of technology and put it to political and personal uses. But they evince a negative attitude toward science with its emphasis on rationality and causation. Nearly all have a proclivity to find, post hoc, the evidence of scientific discovery in religious texts, and proclaim the existence of an Islamic, Hindu, Jewish and Christian science that predates the modern discovery of it. Invariably, they find a scientific discovery in their religious texts or tradition only after it has been discovered by modern science.

All tend to be grim and humorless. All, to varying degrees, frown on joy and pleasurable pastimes. They have few positive links to culture and knowledge, and regard these as dangerous sources of corruption. Hence the control of educational institutions and regulation of society's cultural life becomes the primary objective of these movements. This tendency has climaxed with the Taliban who have prohibited chess, football, the homing pigeon, kite flying, singing, dancing, and leather jackets as un-Islamic.

All religio-political parties are inherently undemocratic even when they operate in a democratic framework. In theory and practice they reject basic democratic values—acceptance of pluralism, emphasis on reason as the organizing principle of social and political life, commitment to the resolution of differences by dialogue, and secular legislation. Nearly all favor a centralist and absolutist structure of governance.

As movements and political parties, they are nevertheless quite normal in hankering after power. For power's sake, they make compromises and, when necessary, strike Faustian deals. The BJP leaders had no problem coalescing with the Janata Party even when it was led by the very secular Prime Minister V.P. Singh. Ironically it was Mr. Singh who risked the dissolution of his government rather than compromise with the BJP's campaign to demolish the Babri mosque. The Jamaat-I-Islami, currently a champion of democracy, happily embraced Mohammed Ziaul Haq, a military dictator. Similarly in 1948, when Pakistan's foundations were shaky, Maulana Abul Aula Maudoodi, the Jamaat's founder and theoretician, declared that combat in Kashmir can not qualify as Jihad. Yet in 1999, its Amir Qazi Hussein Ahmed claims that it is Jihad fi sabi-lillah and must be carried on till total victory. In Sudan, the National Islamic Front was part of the coalition against Jaafer Nimeiri's dictatorship. When opportunity occurred it became an ally of the dictator, and later ousted the ally that had catapulted it to power. Morals have not been an encumbrance in any religio-political pursuit of power.

What then is the future of these "fundamentalist" movements and parties? I think it is limited and quite dim. The reasons for it are multiple: Their links to the past are twisted. Their vision of the future is unworkable. And their connections to contemporary forces and ideals are largely negative or opportunistic. Yet, in their limit lies the reason for us to fear. Between their beginnings and end, right wing movements are known to have inflicted great damage upon countries and peoples. So help us God!

(Originally published in *Dawn*, Karachi, Pakistan.)

September 21, 1998
A Talk with Osama bin Laden
Robert Fisk

The last time I saw Osama bin Laden was in a tent on a mountaintop camp in Afghanistan last year. A few meters away was a twenty-five-foot-high air raid shelter cut into the rock, a relic of bin Laden's days fighting the Soviet Army, but bombproof against even a cruise missile. bin Laden had entered the tent in his white Saudi robes, shaken hands with me and sat cross-legged on the rug, when he noticed that I had the latest Beirut daily newspapers in my bag. He seized upon them and pored over their pages for almost half an hour, one of his Arab mujahedeen in Afghan clothes holding a sputtering gas lamp over the papers. Carefully, bin Laden read the news from Iran, from his own country, from the Israel-occupied West Bank. Was it true, he asked me, that Iran was making a diplomatic démarche to Saudi Arabia?

As I sat there watching the man who had declared a "holy war" against the United States a year earlier—the man who was supposedly the "mastermind of world terrorism"—I reflected that he didn't seem to know much about the world he was supposedly terrorizing. A Saudi who regards the leadership of his country with contempt, he had told me at a previous meeting in 1996, "If liberating my land is called terrorism, this is a great honor for me."

But not as great as the honor bestowed on him by President Clinton in the aftermath of the American missile attacks on Sudan and Afghanistan last month. "America's Public Enemy Number One"—Clinton's infantile description of bin Laden—must have appealed to a man whose simple view of the world is as politically naïve as it is dangerous. Last year, upon that remote mountaintop amid the snow—so cold that there was ice in my hair when I awoke in the tent before dawn—bin Laden had seemed an isolated, almost lonely figure, largely ignored by a United States that was still obsessed with the "evil" Saddam Hussein.

Clinton has changed all that. By endowing bin Laden with his new title, he has given the Saudi dissident what he sought: recognition as the greatest enemy of Western "corruption," the leader of all resistance against U.S. policy in the Middle East.

It would be funny if it weren't so tragic, the way America now treats its opponents as if they were Hollywood bandits. It was Oliver North who branded Palestinian killer Abu Nidal America's Public Enemy Number One. Saddam was compared to Hitler, even though Saddam hero-worships the memory of Stalin. Before that, when Saddam was one of our guys, busy invading Iran, we had demonized the Ayatollah Khomeini. Libya's Muammar el-Qaddafi was described by Ronald Regan as "that mad dog of the Middle East." Even Yasir Arafat was a super-terrorist until his support for Saddam Hussein after the invasion of Kuwait rendered him weak enough to make peace with Israel—at which point we turned him in to a super-statesman.

I doubt if Osama bin Laden understands the hierarchy of U.S. hate figures—or whether he would care if he did. The Afghan conflict against the Soviets molded him, taught him the meaning of his religion, made him think. "What I lived in two years there," he told me, "I could not have lived in a hundred years elsewhere." When he brought his 9,000 Arab fighters to support the Afghans in their conflict against the Soviet occupation army, hacking out the mountain trails with his construction equipment, building hospitals and arms dumps, he became a war hero. Some of his current Afghan fellow fighters had been trained earlier by the CIA in the very camps that were the target of the recent U.S. missiles—but whereas they had been called camps for "freedom fighters" when U.S. agents set them up in the early eighties, now they had become camps for "terrorists." He and his comrades never saw "evidence of American help" in Afghanistan, he told me, but he must have been aware of the CIA's presence.

When I first met bin Laden, in the desert north of Khartoum in 1993 where he was building roads for isolated villages—and, so the Egyptians were claiming, training Egyptian President Hosni Mubarak's Islamist enemies in the same Sudanese desert—I persuaded him to talk about the effect of the Russian war. "Once I was only thirty meters away from the Russians and they were trying to capture me," he said. "I was under bombardment, but I was so peaceful in my heart that I fell asleep. This experience has been written about in our earliest books. I saw a 120-millimeter mortar shell land in front of me, but it did not blow up. Four more bombs were dropped from a Russian plane on our headquarters, but they did not explode. We beat the Soviet Union. The Russians fled. No, I was never afraid of death. As Muslims, we believe that when we die, we go to heaven. Before a battle, God sends us *sequina*—tranquillity." Here was a man, then, who felt God protected him. "My fellow Muslims did much more than I. Many of them died but I am still alive."

I was myself in Afghanistan in 1980, when bin Laden arrived there. I still have my reporting notes from those days. They record Afghan mujahedeen fighters burning down schools and cutting the throats of Afghan Communist schoolteachers because the government had ordered boys and girls to sit together in mixed classes. In those days, *The London Times* was calling them "freedom fighters." Later, when Afghan mujahedeen shot down an Afghan civilian airliner carrying forty-nine passengers and five crew members (with a British-made Blowpipe missile), the same paper called them "rebels." Oddly enough, the word "terrorists" was never used—except by the Russians.

In 1996 Sudan expelled bin Laden, partly because of American pressure—for which the United States has now rewarded Khartoum with a missile attack—and, stripped of his passport, he returned to the land where he fought the Russians. Already, Arabs dressed in Afghan clothes were fighting the government of Algeria after Islamists were prevented from winning a general election. bin Laden regards the Saudi regime as traitors who sold their birthright when Abdul Aziz Al Saud failed to apply full Islamic law. "The country was set up for his family. Then, after the discovery of petroleum, the Saudi regime found another support—the money to make people rich and give them the services and life they wanted and to make them satisfied." But this was nothing compared with what happened in 1990.

"When the American troops entered Saudia Arabia [after Iraq's invasion of Kuwait], the land of the two holy places [Mecca and Medina], there was strong protest from the ulema [religious authorities] and from students of the Shariah law all over the country against the interference of American troops," bin Laden said to me in a meeting in Afghanistan in 1996. "This big mistake by the Saudi regime of inviting the American troops revealed their deception. They had given their support to nations that were fighting against Muslims. They [the Saudis] helped Yemen Communists against the southern Yemeni Muslims and helped Arafat's regime fight against Hamas. After it had insulted and jailed the ulema . . . the Saudi regime lost its legitimacy."

His own country still keeps contact directly with bin Laden, via the Saudi Embassy in Islamabad, Pakistan, because he has supporters among important figures in the kingdom—a fact the United States prefers to ignore. He told me that an emissary from the Saudi royal family had offered his family 2 billion Saudi riyals (about $535 million) if he abandoned his "holy war." He rejected the offer.

Somewhere in the Sudanese desert, bin Laden decided that if he could drive the Russians out of Afghanistan, he could drive the Americans out of the Middle East. He denied to me any involvement in the 1996 bombing of U.S. service personnel at the Khobar Towers in Saudi Arabia, in which nineteen Americans died, although he said he knew two of the three young men later beheaded by the Saudis for the explosion. "The explosion at Khobar did not come as a direct result of American occupation but as a result of American behavior against Muslims," he said. "When sixty Jews are killed inside Palestine, all the world gathers . . . to criticize the action, while the deaths of 600,000 Iraqi children [because of the U.S. sanctions] did not receive the same reaction. Killing those Iraqi schoolchildren is a crusade against Islam. . . . Resistance against America will spread in many, many places in Muslim countries. Our trusted leaders, our ulema, have given us a fatwa that we must drive out the Americans." Because of America's refusal to acknowledge any reason for the U.S. Embassy bombings in Kenya and Tanzania—hatred of America, per se, is the usual explanation—few chose to point out that they occurred on the eighth anniversary, to the very day, of the arrival of the first U.S. troops in Saudi Arabia in 1990.

When I last saw bin Laden, he was still obsessed with the Israeli massacre of 107 Lebanese refugees sheltering at the UN camp at Qana in April 1996. Israel claimed it was a "mistake," the UN conceded otherwise and

President Clinton called it only a "tragedy"—as if it was a natural disaster. It was, said bin Laden, an act of "international terrorism." There must be justice, he said, and trials for the Israeli perpetrators.

Clinton used almost exactly the same words about bin Laden and his supporters in August. But the deaf, as usual, were talking to the deaf.

November 3, 2001
September 11th and the Aftermath: Where is the World Heading?
Noam Chomsky

The new millennium has begun with two monstrous crimes: the terrorist attacks of September 11, and the reaction to them, surely taking a far greater toll of innocent lives.

The atrocities of September 11 are widely regarded as a historic event, and that is most definitely true. But we should be clear about exactly why it is true. These crimes had perhaps the most devastating instant human toll on record, outside of war. The word "instant" should not be overlooked; it is unfortunate, but true, that the crimes are far from unusual in the annals of violence that falls short of war. The aftermath is only one of innumerable illustrations. The reason why "the world will never be the same" after September 11, to borrow the phrase now commonly used, lies elsewhere.

The scale of the catastrophe that has already taken place in Afghanistan, and what may follow, can only be guessed. But we do know the projections on which policy decisions are based, and from these we can gain some insight into the question of where the world is heading. The answer is that it is heading along paths that are well-traveled.

Even before September 11, millions of Afghans were being sustained— barely—by international food aid. On September 16, *The New York Times* reported that Washington had "demanded [from Pakistan] the elimination of truck convoys that provide much of the food and other supplies to

Afghanistan's civilian population." There was no detectable reaction in the U.S. or Europe to the demand that enormous numbers of destitute people be subjected to starvation and slow death. In subsequent weeks, the world's leading newspaper reported that "The threat of military strikes forced the removal of international aid workers, crippling assistance programs"; refugees reaching Pakistan "after arduous journeys from Afghanistan are describing scenes of desperation and fear at home as the threat of American-led military attacks turns their long-running misery into a potential catastrophe." "The country was on a lifeline," one evacuated aid worker reported, "and we just cut the line."

The UN World Food Program and others were able to resume some food shipments in early October, but were forced to suspend deliveries and distribution after the bombing, resuming them later at a much lower pace, while aid agencies leveled "scathing" condemnations of U.S. air drops that are barely concealed "propaganda tools."

The New York Times reported, without comment, that the number of Afghans needing food aid was expected to increase by 50 percent as a result of the bombing, to 7.5 million. In other words, Western civilization is basing its plans on the assumption that they may lead to the slaughter of several million innocent civilians—not Taliban, but their victims. On the same day, the leader of Western civilization once again dismissed with contempt Taliban offers of negotiation and their request for some credible evidence to substantiate the demands for capitulation. His stand was regarded as right and just, perhaps even heroic. The UN Special Rapporteur on the Right to Food pleaded with the U.S. to end the bombing that was putting "the lives of millions of civilians at risk," renewing the appeal of UN High Commissioner of Human Rights Mary Robinson, who warned of a Rwanda-style catastrophe. Both appeals were rejected, as were those of the major aid and relief agencies. And virtually unreported.

The Food and Agricultural Organization (FAO) had warned in late September that over 7 million people might face starvation unless aid were immediately resumed and the threat of military action terminated. After bombing began, the FAO issued even more grave warnings of a humanitarian catastrophe, and advised that the bombing had disrupted planting that provides 80 percent of the country's grain supplies, so that the effects next year will be even more severe. All unreported.

These unreported appeals happened to coincide with World Food Day, which was also ignored, along with the charge by the UN Special Rapporteur that the rich and powerful easily have the means, though not the will, to overcome this "silent genocide."

The airstrikes have turned cities into "ghost towns," the press reported, with electrical power and water supplies destroyed, a form of biological warfare. Seventy percent of the population were reported to have fled Kandahar and Herat, mostly to the countryside, where in ordinary times 10–20 people are killed or crippled every day by land mines. Those conditions are now much worse. UN mine-clearing operations were halted, and unexploded U.S. ordnance adds to the torture, particularly the lethal bomblets scattered by cluster bombs, which are much harder to clear.

The fate of these miserable people will never be known, or even investigated, if past precedents are a guide. Careful inquiry into consequences is reserved for crimes that can be attributed to official enemies. In such cases, inquiry properly considers not only those immediately killed but the far vaster numbers who die as a result of the policies that are condemned. For our own crimes, if there is any inquiry at all, standards are entirely different. The effects of criminal acts are disregarded. In the case of Afghanistan, whatever happens, if investigated at all, will be blamed on something else— the drought, the Taliban—but crucially not those who have consciously and purposefully implemented crimes that they expect will cause mass slaughter of innocents.

Only those entirely ignorant of modern history will find any of this surprising. The victims, after all, are only "uncivilized tribes"—Winston Churchill's contemptuous reference to Afghans and Kurds when he insisted upon the use of poisoned gas to inspire a "lively terror" among them 80 years ago. But in this case too, we will learn little about the aftermath. Ten years ago Britain instituted an "open government" initiative. Its first act was to remove from the public records office all files concerning the use of poison gas against the uncivilized tribes. If it is necessary to "exterminate the indigenous population," so be it, as the French Minister of War declared while announcing that the process was underway in Algeria in the mid-nineteenth century, not for the last time. It is all too easy to proceed. What is happening to Afghans now is conventional, a central theme of modern history. It is therefore natural that it should arouse little interest or concern, even report.

The crimes of September 11 are indeed a historic turning point, but not because of their scale; rather, because of the choice of target. For the U.S., this is the first time since the British burned down Washington in 1814 that the national territory has been under attack, or even threatened. There should be no need to review what has happened to those who were in the way or disobedient in the centuries since. The number of victims is huge. For the first time, the guns have been pointed in the opposite direction. That is a historic change.

The same is true, even more dramatically, of Europe. Europe has suffered murderous destruction, but from internal wars. Meanwhile European powers conquered much of the world, not very politely. With rare and limited exceptions, they were not under attack by their foreign victims. The Congo did not attack and devastate Belgium, nor the East Indies the Netherlands, nor Algeria France. The list is long and the crimes horrendous. It is not surprising, therefore, that Europe should be shocked by the terrorist atrocities of September 11. But while these do signal a dramatic change in world affairs, the aftermath represents no change at all.

It has been rightly emphasized by U.S. and other world leaders that confronting the terrorist monster is not a short-term task, but a lasting one. We should therefore consider carefully the measures that can be taken to mitigate what has been called, in high places, "the evil scourge of terrorism," a plague spread by "depraved opponents of civilization itself" in "a return to barbarism in the modern age."

We should begin, surely, by identifying the plague and the depraved elements that have been returning the world to barbarism. The curse is not new. The phrases I just quoted are from President Ronald Reagan and his Secretary of State George Shultz. The Reagan administration came to office twenty years ago proclaiming that the struggle against international terrorism will be the core of U.S. foreign policy. They responded to the plague by organizing campaigns of international terrorism of unprecedented scale and violence, even leading to a World Court condemnation of the U.S. for "unlawful use of force" in Nicaragua and a Security Council resolution calling on all states to observe international law, which the U.S. vetoed, also voting alone with Israel (and in one case El Salvador) against similar General Assembly Resolutions. The World Court order to terminate the crime of international terrorism and pay substantial reparations was dismissed with contempt across the spectrum; the UN votes were scarcely even reported. Washington reacted at once by escalating the economic and terrorist wars. It also issued official orders to the mercenary army to attack "soft targets"—undefended civilian targets—and to avoid combat, as it could do, thanks to U.S. control of the skies and the sophisticated communication equipment provided to the terrorist forces attacking from neighboring countries.

Those orders were considered legitimate as long as pragmatic criteria were satisfied. One prominent commentator, Michael Kinsley, regarded as the spokesperson of the left in mainstream discussion, argued that we should not simply dismiss State Department justifications for terrorist attacks on "soft targets": a "sensible policy" must "meet the test of cost-benefit analysis," he wrote, an analysis of "the amount of blood and misery that will be poured in, and the likelihood that democracy will emerge at the other end"—"democracy" as Western elites understand the term, an interpretation illustrated quite clearly in the region. It is taken for granted that they have the right to conduct the analysis and pursue the project if it passes their tests.

And it did pass the tests. When Nicaragua finally succumbed to superpower assault, commentators across the spectrum of respectable opinion lauded the success of the methods adopted to "wreck the economy and prosecute a long and deadly proxy war until the exhausted natives overthrow the unwanted government themselves," with a cost to us that is "minimal," leaving the victims "with wrecked bridges, sabotaged power stations, and ruined farms," and thus providing the U.S. candidate with "a winning issue": ending the "impoverishment of the people of Nicaragua" (*Time* magazine). We are "United in Joy" at this outcome, *The New York Times* proclaimed, proud of this "Victory for U.S. Fair Play," a *Times* headline read.

The civilized world was "United in Joy" again a few weeks ago as the U.S. candidate won the Nicaraguan election after stern warnings from Washington of the consequences if he did not. The *Washington Post* explained that the victor had "focused his campaign on reminding people of the economic and military difficulties of the Sandinista era"—that is, the U.S. terrorist war and economic strangulation that devastated the country. Meanwhile the President instructed us about the "one universal law": all varieties of terror and murder "are evil"—unless, of course, we are the agents.

Prevailing Western attitudes towards terrorism are revealed with great clarity by the reaction to the appointment of John Negroponte as UN Ambassador to lead the "war against terrorism." Negroponte's record includes his service as "proconsul" in Honduras in the 1980s, where he was the local supervisor of the international terrorist campaign for which his government was condemned by the World Court and Security Council. There is no detectable reaction. Even Jonathan Swift would be speechless.

I mention the case of Nicaragua only because it is uncontroversial, given the judgments of the highest international authorities; uncontroversial, that is, among those who have a minimal commitment to human rights and international law. One can estimate the size of that category by determining how often these elementary matters are even mentioned. And from that exercise alone one can draw some grim conclusions about what lies ahead, if existing centers of power and ideology have their way.

The Nicaraguan case is far from the most extreme example. In the Reagan years alone, U.S.-sponsored state terrorists in Central America left hundreds of thousands of tortured and mutilated corpses, millions of maimed and orphaned, and four countries in ruins in Central America. In the same years, Western-backed South African depredations killed a million and a half people and caused $60 billion of damage. I need not speak of West and Southeast Asia, South America, or much else. And that decade was not unusual.

It is a serious analytic error to describe terrorism as a "weapon of the weak," as is often done. In practice, terrorism is the violence that THEY commit against US—whoever WE happen to be. It would be hard to find a historical exception. And since the powerful determine what counts as History, what passes through the filters is the terrorism of the weak against the strong and their clients.

(Excerpt from the Lakdawala Memorial Lecture under the sponsorship of the Institute of Social Sciences, New Delhi, November 3, 2001.)

DEADLINE POET

Calvin Trillin

Day-O, an Afghan Calypso
(With apologies to Harry Belafonte, among others)

Bombed all night by dat Yankee bunch
Daylight come and de bombers go home
Now dey'll drop some cashew crunch
Daylight come and de bombers go home

Day-o, day-o
Bad guys hide in dere catacomb
Day-o, day-o,
'Til dose bombers have said shalom.

Hey, Mr. Taliban, shoutin' your hosannas
Daylight come and de bombers go home
You're de Kool-Aid makin' dese Guyanas
Daylight come and de bombers go home

Day-o, day-o,
Daylight come and de bombers go home
Day-o, day-o,
Daylight come and de bombers go home.